The Political Economy of Macroeconomic Policy Reform in Latin America

In memoriam of Francisco Wiesner Rozo

The Political Economy of Macroeconomic Policy Reform in Latin America

The Distributive and Institutional Context

Eduardo Wiesner

Wiesner and Associates, former Minister of Finance, Colombia

Edward Elgar

Cheltenham, UK • Northampton, MA, USA

Published by
Edward Elgar Publishing Limited
Glensanda House
Montpellier Parade
Cheltenham
Glos GL50 1UA
UK

Edward Elgar Publishing, Inc.
William Pratt House
9 Dewey Court
Northampton
Massachusetts 01060
USA

A catalogue record for this book
is available from the British Library

Library of Congress Cataloging in Publication Data

Wiesner Durán, Eduardo.
    The political economy of macroeconomic policy reform in Latin America: the distributive and institutional context/by Eduardo Wiesner.
        p.   cm.
    Includes bibliographical references and index.
    1. Latin America—Economic conditions—21st century. 2. Economic development—Latin America. 3. Economics—Latin America. 4. Latin America—Economic policy. I. Title.
HC125.W485   2007
339.5098—dc22

                                                                                    2007038476

ISBN 978 1 84720 579 7 (cased)

Printed and bound in Great Britain by MPG Books Ltd, Bodmin, Cornwall

Contents

Figures

Tables

Acknowledgments

I wish to recognize my deep appreciation to the Inter-American Development Bank at Washington, DC and to its Office of Evaluation and Oversight (OVE), where its Director, Stephen Quick, its Deputy Director, Sixto Aquino and its Senior Economist, Inder Jit Ruprah, provided most valuable initial support and advice. I should also like to express my particular gratitude to Professors Alberto Alesina, Dean of the Economics Department of Harvard University, Avinash Dixit, from Princeton University; Ricardo Hausmann, Director of the Center for International Development (CID) at the Kennedy School of Government of Harvard University; Daron Acemoglu from the Massachusetts Institute of Technology, MIT; Martin Feldstein, President of the National Bureau of Economic Research, NBER; Albert Hirschman, from the Institute for Advanced Study, Princeton; Donald Kohn, Vice-Chairman of the Federal Reserve System; Edwin M. Truman and John Williamson, Senior Fellows at the Peterson Institute for International Economics at Washington, DC; and John B. Taylor from Stanford University. They all gave me their time, advice and comments generously which helped enormously in the process of research and of writing this book. I am also grateful to anonymous reviewers who helped me see areas where there was room for improvement. Needless to say, I am solely responsible for the text and for any errors and flaws it may contain.

Below I have listed the names of other colleagues and policy makers in different countries and institutions whom I visited in 2006 and 2007 and who provided me with immensely valuable comments and suggestions. I acknowledge my debt and gratitude for their generosity and hospitality. In Bogotá, Minister of Finance of Colombia, Alberto Carrasquilla, and Maria Inés Agudelo, Vice-Minister of Finance, as well as José Dario Uribe, Governor of the Central Bank, Hernando Vargas, Technical Manager, and Gerardo Hernández Correa, Executive Manager, were all very generous with their time and comments and facilitated my task by providing data and relevant research results. Lucia Feney Pérez, Library Director at the Fundación para la Educación Superior y el Desarrollo, FEDESARROLLO, provided me with impeccable help and assistance, as did Maria Emma García de Anzola from the Governor's office of the Banco de la República de Colombia.

Argentina

Martin Redrado, President of the Central Bank; Roberto Lavagna, Former Minister of Finance; Mariano Tommasi, Professor of Economics, Universidad de San Andres; Mario Teijeiro, President of the Centro de Estudios Públicos; Pablo Guidotti, Dean of the School of Government, Universidad Torcuato Di Tella; Ricardo López-Murphy, Senior Economist, Fundación de Investigaciones Económicas Latinoamericana, FIEL; Roque Fernández, Former Minister of Finance, Professor, Universidad del CEMA.

Brazil

Afonso Bevilaqua, Central Bank Executive Board Member; Ilan Goldfajn, Former Central Bank Executive Board Members; José Roberto Rodriguez Afonso, Independent Consultant; Fabio Giambiagi, Senior Economist, IPEA.

Chile

Vittorio Corbo, President, Central Bank of Chile; Alejandro Foxley, Minister of Foreign Affairs; Luis Felipe Cespedes, Deputy Minister of Finance; Mario Marcel, Former National Budget Director; Rodrigo Valdéz, Director of Economic Studies, Central Bank; Carlos Massad, Former Governor of Central Bank; Edgardo Boeninger, Former Senator; Eduardo Aninat, Former Minister of Finance; Ernesto Fontaine, Professor, Universidad Católica; Felipe Larrain, Professor, Universidad Católica; Fernando Ossa, Professor, Universidad Católica; Jaime Crispi Lago, Senior Economist, Budget Office; Juan Eduardo Coeymans, Professor, Universidad Católica; Luis Felipe Lagos, Professor, Universidad Católica; Rolf Luders, Former Minister of Finance and Professor, Universidad Católica; Leticia Celador, Capital Markets Advisor, Ministry of Finance.

Colombia

Carlos Gustavo Cano, Member of the Central Bank's Executive Board; Fernando Tenjo, Member of the Central Bank's Executive Board; Juan José Echabarria, Member of the Central Bank's Executive Board; Juan Mario Laserna, Member of the Central Bank's Executive Board; Leonardo Villar, Member of the Central Bank's Executive Board; Sergio Clavijo, Director, Asociación Nacional Instituciones Financieras, ANIF; Salomón Kalmanovitz, Former Member of the Central Bank's Executive Board; Santiago Montenegro, Former Director, National Planning Department;

Mauricio Santamaría, Deputy Director, National Planning Department; José Leibovich, Former Deputy Director, National Planning Department; Gabriel Piraquive, Director of Economic Studies DNP; Hugo López, Director of Poverty Studies, DNP; Juan Camilo Restrepo, Former Minister of Finance; Juan Carlos Echeverri, Former National Planning Department and Dean of the School of Economics, Universidad de los Andes; Alejandro Gaviria, Dean of Economics Department, Universidad de los Andes; Juan Pablo Zarate, Director, Macroeconomic Studies, Ministry of Finance; Mauricio Cárdenas, Director, FEDESARROLLO.

Costa Rica

Laura Chinchilla M., First Vice-President of Costa Rica; Guillermo Zuñiga, Minister of Finance; Kevin Casas, Minister of Planning; José Adrian Vargas B., Viceministro de Hacienda; Francisco de Paula Gutiérrez, President of Central Bank; Eduardo Lizano, Former President of Central Bank; Leonardo Garnier, Minister of Education; Oscar Rodríguez Ulloa; Superintendente General de Entidades Financieras; Roy Gonzalez Rojas, Gerente Banco Central de Costa Rica; William Calvo Villegas, Chief Economist; Rocio Aguilar, Controller General; Miguel Loria, Economist.

Economic Commission for Latin America and the Caribbean United Nations, CEPAL, Santiago, Chile

José Luis Machinea, Executive Secretary.

Harvard University and John F. Kennedy School of Government

Dani Rodrik, Professor, Economics Department and Kennedy School of Government.

Independent Consultants

Osvaldo Feinstein, Independent Consultant, Former Manager, Independent Evaluation Group (IEG), World Bank.

Inter-American Development Bank

Eduardo Lora, Principal Advisor; Rodrigo Parot, Director IDB Office Bogotá; Agustín García-López, Director Ejecutivo México y la República Dominicana; Alberto Franco-Mejía, Consejero para Centroamerica y Belice; Carlos Scartascini, Senior Evaluation Office, OVE; Eduardo

C. Cobas, Modernization of State Principal Specialist, OVE; Luis Guillermo Echeverry, Executive Director for Colombia; Iván Duque, Deputy Executive Director for Colombia, IDB; Fernando Straface, Country Coordinator for Costa Rica; German Quintana, Executive Director for Chile; Hector E. Luisi, Senior Advisor; Jorge Requena, Director, IDB Office at Costa Rica; Juan José Neyra, Counselor to the Executive Director for Chile and Peru; Luis Consenza, Executive Director for Honduras; Vito Tanzi, Senior Advisor; Luis Estanislao Echavarria, Director, IDB Office, Santiago Chile; Roberto Iunes, Senior Advisor, OVE; Christof Kuechemann, IDB's Representative, Peru.

International Monetary Fund

Agustin Carstens, Managing Director; Anoop Singh, Director, Western Hemisphere Department; Radhuram Rajan, Director of the Research Department; Roberto Steiner, Deputy Executive Director for Colombia; Charles V. Collyns, Senior Economist, WHD; Jose Fajgenbaum, Deputy Director, Western Hemisphere Department; Jacques Polak, Former IMF's Chief Economist.

Latin American Institute for Planning, ILPES

Juan Carlos Ramírez; Director.

Peru

Pedro-Pablo Kuczynski G., Former Prime Minister; Fernando Zabala, Minister of Finance; Renzo Rossini Miñan, General Manager Central Bank; Waldo Mendoza Bellido, Vice-Ministro de Hacienda; Adrian Armas Rivas, Director of Economic Studies Central Bank; Carlos Oliva, Independent Consultant; Diether W. Beuermann, Independent Consultant; Fritz Du Bois Freund, Gerente, Instituto Peruano de Economía, IPE; Hugo Santa María, Socio-Gerente de Estudios Económicos, Economista Principal; Jakke Valakivi Alvarez, Asesor Alta Dirección, Superintendencia de Banca, Seguros y AFP; José Valderrama, Latin Source, Senior Consultant; Juan José Marthans León, Superintendente de Banca, Seguros y Administradoras Privadas de Fondos de Pensiones.

Stanford University

Barry Weingast, Professor Political Science, Senior Fellow Hoover Institution; Avner Greif, Professor, Economics Department.

United Nations

José Antonio Ocampo, Under-Secretary-General, Department of Economic and Social Affairs.

University of Maryland

Allan Drazen, William Hiber Professor of Economics at the Hebrew University of Jerusalem and Professor of Economics and Co-director of the Center for International Economics at the University of Maryland, Economics Department.

World Bank

Vinod Thomas, Vice-President, Independent Evaluation Group (IDG); Patrick Grasso, Senior Advisor (IDG); Jose Guilherme Reis, Senior Economist.

Center for Global Department

Nancy Birdsall, President.

New York University

Professor Nouriel Roubini at the Stern School of Business.

PART I

Conceptual Framework

Introduction

As soon as a social phenomenon has been fully explained by a variety of converging approaches and is therefore understood in its majestic inevitability and
perhaps even permanence, it vanishes . . .[1]

Albert O. Hirschman (1981, p. 134)

I. OBJECTIVES OF THE BOOK

Something quite extraordinary took place in the last twenty or thirty years,
a rather short period of time in the evolution of economic thought and
ideas.[2] The 'received view' of the 1960s and 1970s about the sources of
economic development changed to what amounted to a new conceptual paradigm, that is that incentives and institutions are the key explanatory variables of long term development across countries and even cultures. The
theory of incentives appears to be the most important development in economics in the last 40 years (Arrow, 2002) and there is broad consensus that
the quality of institutions, more than anything else, determines economic
performance over time. According to Douglass C. North 'We cannot understand today's choices without tracing the incremental evolution of institutions' (1990, p. 100). In brief, the new paradigm in the political economy of
development and in the economics of politics[3] is that the 'right' or the
'wrong' institutions emerge from endogenous[4] and history[5] determined
processes where information asymmetries,[6] political regimes,[7] opportunism[8]
and self interested rational[9] choices[10] play the most important roles.[11]

Notwithstanding the empirical problems related to measuring the links
between the 'right' and the 'wrong' institutions and development, the 'institutions hypothesis' has come to be regarded as the key explanatory variable
for overall long term[12] economic, social and political results across developed and developing countries. Within this context the research agenda of
the political economy of institutions and development is not so much to
further the notion that institutions matter, or that they influence – and result
from – policies,[13] but to 'unbundle' this finding into its causal effects and
into the identification of which institutions – and why – matter the most
(Acemoglu, 2005b, p. 1045).[14] The broad aim of this book is to advance this
research agenda by focusing on a particular set of institutions and their

characteristics and on how the demand for their reform and effectiveness determines – and is determined by – long term economic growth and distributive justice over time.

Within institutions as a whole the macroeconomic institutional arrangements[15] regulating the interaction and 'coordination'[16] between Central Banks, Ministries of Finance and financial sector supervision are considered the most critical ones,[17] because they determine macroeconomic volatility, affect private and public revenues and expenditures and, hence, provide the overall[18] incentive environment.[19] But more importantly, they determine macroeconomic performance and growth and hence poverty levels and distributive justice[20] in general.[21] An expansive literature perceives poverty, equity[22] and income inequality as strong impediments to pro-growth and even to some modalities of pro-poor reforms. The policy implication is that pro-poor and pro-growth poverty reduction need[23] to be mutually reinforcing.[24] In fact, they appear indispensable to each other.

The limited effectiveness of Latin American macroeconomic governance structure has been the most important factor in explaining its long term growth and equity evolution.[25] On both fronts, on growth and on equity, the record for the region is a dismal one compared to other regions of the world. Although it may have had some fast growth periods,[26] with the exception of Chile[27] since the 1990s, Latin America's relative growth record is amazingly slow and volatile. From 1960 to 2000, Latin America's average annual real per capita rate of growth was 1.4 per cent, while Asia's was over 200 per cent faster, at 4.6 per cent. From 1960 to 2002, Latin America had 31 years in which GDP growth was negative or below 1 per cent. The comparable figure for Asia was 15 years. From 1950 to 2001, Latin America's per capita income, as a percentage of that of the United States, came down from 0.28 per cent to 0.22 per cent. In the same period Asia's ratio more than tripled from 0.16 per cent to 0.55 per cent. Between 1900 and 2001, Brazil and Venezuela were the only two countries in the region which saw a rise in their GDP per capita ratio relative to that of the US. More recently, between 1998 and 2003 Latin America's real per capita average annual rate of growth was −0.1 per cent. In 2006, Latin America's Purchasing Power Parity share of the world's GDP was below 7 per cent (about the size of Japan's).

Since the mid-1990s up to 2006 some Latin American countries grew below their potential, faced exchange rate crisis and suffered deep recessions, while others were able to manage their domestic and external macroeconomic challenges better. In spite of some important advances – like giving greater independence to Central Banks and much lower inflation rates – there is the overall question of why the region, with the relative exception of Chile,[28] experienced considerable macroeconomic instability and may still be quite vulnerable to domestic or external adverse developments. What explains these different macroeconomic performances? What common domestic or international patterns may there be? Can different macroeconomic institutional characteristics and arrangements explain these differences? What determines the effectiveness of macroeconomic policy 'coordination'[29] in assuring policy consistency? More importantly, there is the need to ascertain the extent to which some of the better specific country economic performances were the result of well anchored political demand for reforms or the results of favorable external[30] and cyclical factors.[31]

Poverty and inequality have long been a salient feature of Latin America. This region is 'an unfortunate example of historic high concentration of land and the concentration of income associated with exploiting mineral wealth which have left a legacy of limited educational opportunities, a small and state-dependent middle class and a large majority of poor and near-poor households' (Birdsall, 2005a, p. 1). 'Between 1950 and 1970 Latin America was the only region in the world where the share of income going to the poorest 20 per cent of the population consistently declined' (Edwards, 1995, p. 252). 'Inequality in Latin America is higher than in Asia, Eastern Europe and the developed countries' (Ferranti et al., 2004, p. 54).[32] 'At least since the end of the second world war inequality in Latin America has been much higher than in most parts of the world' (Ferranti et al., 2004, p. 56). Rajan and Zingales (2006, p. 5) aver that the initial distribution of education may well be the most important determinant of inequality. Even after 'controlling' for the level of development, Latin America is a region that suffers from 'excess inequality'[33] when compared to other regions of the world. Fortunately this is changing for the better and in several countries of the region there has been significant decline in poverty levels. However, Gini income coefficients have proven to be much more difficult to reduce.

Macroeconomic volatility[34] continues to be a major if not the major equity[35] and development issue and challenge in Latin America (Hausmann and Gavin, 1996, p. 1). Although the recent gains in lower rates of inflation are a very positive development, much more needs to be understood about the underlying factors[36] and macroeconomic trade-offs before it can be concluded that those gains are sustainable and solidly anchored in fiscal rules. After all, the sustainability of disinflation[37] depends, to a large extent, on the initial conditions and causes that brought about the lower inflation levels[38] and on which specific policy responses were adopted by the authorities. It also depends in a fundamental way on the collective learning of what may have brought about the crisis in the first place. This learning experience is the transmission mechanism for information[39] to illuminate what really matters in social and political processes.

The macroeconomic volatility problems faced by Latin America which go back well over a century (Singh, 2006, p. 3)[40] are seldom the result of a lack of technical understanding of the problems faced. As Hausmann and Gavin (1996, p. 1) have so aptly observed:

> Latin America is not volatile because it labors under some ancient and ineradicable curse. It is volatile because its institutions and policy regimes have been ill-equipped to cope with the large shocks that hit the region. This means that policymakers can do much to reduce macroeconomic volatility and its costs, if they focus on building appropriate institutional structures.

The challenge is to find the right 'positive' strategy to nurture a modicum of trust in the 'right' institution and in the market system (Feldstein, 2002, p. 36).[41]

These growth and equity developments are intimately interdependent and influence each other. The slow rates of economic growth are largely explained by macroeconomic volatility which, itself, comes mainly from the existence of growth retarding policies.[42] These, in their turn, come basically from high poverty levels and inequality, which find a large portion of their origin in macroeconomic volatility and attendant low rates of economic growth. In brief, there are strong distributional implications from macroeconomic performance,[43] on the one hand, and macroeconomic implications from equity dynamics, trade-offs[44] and reforms,[45] on the other. 'Macroeconomic volatility is part of the explanation for the high income concentration' (Williamson, 2003, p. 29). According to Velasco (2006, p. xiv) 'poor growth performance is one reason why populism is once again raising its ugly head in the region.'

It has become well known over the decades that Latin American countries, on the whole, do not save enough, have high fiscal deficits, incur excessive internal and external debt, have the 'wrong' and persistent incentives underpinning the relative ineffectiveness of public (particularly social) expenditures, that total factor productivity (TPF) is low and is growing slowly, and that the region tends to favor protectionism over competition and market forces. In other words, what should change is largely known. What has remained elusive is why those changes and reforms are not fully adopted or end up being insufficient. The key message this book conveys is that a large component of the answer is that reforms are not adopted because there is not sufficient political demand for particular reforms while there is plenty of political support for short term policies that can hardly deliver long term prosperity in terms of faster growth and more distributive justice. Why is this so? Cole et al. (2004, p. 31), blame 'the idiosyncratic and long standing Latin American choices'. But the question still remains: what explains those idiosyncratic choices?

It is difficult not to conclude that this amounts to a major historical failure, one that should continue to prompt a thorough revision of what this region has been doing and why for the last 50 years. As it will be appreciated, most of the explanation for this abysmal record has to do with the 'initial historical conditions' and the different institutional[46] and equity[47] paths followed by these two regions (Sokoloff and Engerman, 2000, p. 218; Acemoglu et al., 2001, p. 1369). This is the key macroeconomic perspective afflicting and challenging Latin America's policy makers, governments and multilateral institutions working in this region of the world.

This overall picture motivates the basic question of why Latin America has not been able or willing to catch up with or not to lose relative weight in comparison to most Western and East Asian countries. This is a major and portentous issue with regional and worldwide economic and political implications. There are two broad tracks in the search for answers to this question. One is to blame external forces, avatars and flaws in the international economic and financial public or private arrangements, and to insist that these problems ought to be changed. The other is to recognize that, although a better international architecture and multilateral environment would help, the most important share of responsibility for the results observed rests with the political and economic policy choices made by politicians and policy makers in the region for well over 50 years.

On these two broad tracks there have been advances. The capacity to blame the external avatars as a way to avoid political accountability is being restricted by a better informed and more discerning public in Brazil, Chile, Colombia, Argentina, Mexico and the region in general. Ideology is losing ground to learning from experience and to the empirics of development. Each country is learning from its own experience, and the endogenous process of institutional transformation is gradually providing better collective rules and incentives. On the other hand, there is worldwide concern and interest in better understanding and managing global capital mobility and international macroeconomic volatility.[48] There is a growing political interest in the welfare of all citizens of the world. The incentives for this are now more discernible.

Within this global context, the two broad key questions that the book addresses throughout are, first, why are the 'right' combination of pro-poor and pro-growth reforms often not adopted, delayed[49] or ultimately ineffective? (Alesina and Drazen, 1991, p. 1171). And, secondly, what are the restrictions that need to be overcome to strengthen the political demand for those policy reforms and for the attendant institutional transformation in developing countries in general and in Latin America in particular? From the start, the key analytical premise is that the answer has more to do with the political demand and tolerance for those reforms than with their

particular supply-side technical characteristics. The book concludes with –
and shares – the view that the specific answers to these questions often differ
from country to country, from sector to sector, and ultimately depend on
the particular idiosyncratic political economy restrictions affecting distinct
development situations in different ways. To deal with such heterogeneity
an explicit diagnostic approach is necessary. The crucible of reform 'is
getting the diagnosis right and addressing the most binding constraints'
(Hausmann et al., 2006, p. 13). 'These constraints differ from setting to
setting' (Rodrik, 2006, p. 973).[50]

The perspective is always the demand side of the origin of the most critical reforms and institutions and the emergence of social and political preferences for policy reform.[51] The book suggests that to unbundle further the
institutional hypothesis, there is a need to understand better the causalities
between initial conditions of inequality and poverty, on the one hand, and
the political demand for the reforms to reduce macroeconomic volatility,
on the other. The central theme is the political economy of the demand for
policy reform and for institutional transformation. The central premise is
'that the connection between economics and politics is a fundamental part
of the development process' (North et al., 2006, p. 4). Needless to say, no
originality is claimed at all with this approach. The literature on the political explanation of development is vast, solid and goes back many years.
What may be a contribution is to apply it largely to the macroeconomic
governance structures, to specific crisis events and to the way in which
different recent findings from research strands (like transaction costs) are
capitalized to adumbrate how countries can mitigate the effects of political
economy factors restricting welfare gains.

Within the context of the broad questions posed above, the more
specific objectives of the book are the following: (i) to identify the institutional characteristics which may explain the different macroeconomic
performances across countries in Latin America during the last ten years;
(ii) through the examination of recent macroeconomic crisis as stress tests
in Latin America to discern the real determinants of the demand for the
institutions with the potential to deliver macroeconomic performance
and distributive justice; and (iii) from the findings for the region as a
whole and for each country in particular to draw policy implications and
recommendations for policy makers in each country and for multilateral
institutions.

Different macroeconomic results such as rates of growth, inflation rates
and variability, real exchange rate movements and volatility in general are
explained by different institutional characteristics[52] such as the degree of
Central Bank credibility and independence,[53] the existence of inflation targeting, of effective 'fiscal rules', the information agents have, the depth of

the financial sector and the strength of its regulatory body, and policy[54] credibility in general. A key institutional characteristic with enormous implications for the effectiveness of macroeconomic policy coordination is the degree to which the relevant 'principals' share a given conceptual paradigm to guide their specific policy postures.[55] Very high transactions costs can be traced back to differences in those conceptual paradigms. To a large extent the effectiveness of any institutional arrangements is determined by how accurately they can link particular results with specific characteristics. 'In fact, evaluation effectiveness can be judged in terms of its efficiency in identifying public sector institutional obstacles and in contributing to the productive mediation between the demand for and supply of the "right" institutional arrangements' (Wiesner, 1998, p. xiii).

The organizing objective is to discern what the broad political economy strategy could be for Latin America and for some countries to exit from the 'precarious equilibrium' in which they currently seem to find themselves. In effect, Latin America has adopted some key reforms (Lora, 2007, p. 51)[56] as inflation targeting, it has dramatically reduced inflation, it has increased tax revenues and it has expanded enormously its social spending in the hope of reducing poverty and inequality. And yet, there is not much political demand and support for some pending critical fiscal, financial and social security reforms. At the same time, the political pressures for even higher – and at times regressive – social spending levels are not abating. The 'tax and spend' policies in some countries have led to high real rates of interest, excessive external financing and exchange rate appreciation. The concern is whether the overall policy framework is really resilient enough to withstand a sudden change in the so far favorable external cycle.

Since an expansive literature has concluded that 'inequality is conducive to the adoption of growth retarding policies'[57] (Alesina and Rodrik, 1994, p. 465) and that it is 'harmful to growth' (Persson and Tabellini, 1994, p. 600), and we know that economic growth largely explains poverty conditions, the book blends together the following four interdependent components of any development process: (i) macroeconomic performance and volatility; (ii) equity, poverty, social mobility and distributive justice; (iii) fiscal deficits and the redistributive effectiveness of social public expenditures; and (iv) the demand for the 'right' institutions and for policy reform in Latin America. The book builds on findings from different strands of economic research[58] with the aim of supporting a specific strategy to move forward the process of institutional and policy reform in Latin America.

In a truly seminal work Albert Hirschman (1973, p. 561) warned that political tolerance for inequality depended on poverty levels and expectations (the famous 'tunnel effect') and that political support for reforms was conditioned on people's perception of actually benefiting from those reforms. Later on, Alesina and Rodrik (1994, p. 465) asserted that 'inequality is conducive to the adoption of growth retarding policies'. This may be happening in Latin America. Although there have been substantial economic reforms[59] and progress in the last five years, the region as a whole may have unintentionally cornered itself into a dysfunctional 'bad' equilibrium. Brazil, for instance, has been able to maintain inflation under control, has increased its public expenditures and has made progress in equity issues, but it has not been able to grow fast or to achieve its potential.

Although Latin America may have prevented extreme 'fiscal dominance' and in general has adopted well conceived inflation targeting regimes, it has done so largely through a higher level of taxation, indebtedness and 'a tax and spend damage control' strategy. In this way it has managed to respond to immense political pressures for redistributive social expenditures without incurring major macroeconomic volatility. But this has meant high real rates of interest, and growth rates not fully anchored in long term economic or social infrastructure investment or productivity gains. It has also meant that the fundamental issue of the requirements for social expenditures to actually be redistributive has not been fully addressed. The region, with the possible exception of Chile, is still very vulnerable to external capital market conditions. It is also still vulnerable to political populism.

The current case of Argentina (mid-2007) is somewhat different from that of the region as a whole as this country is still largely in the relatively 'easy stage of recovery' in which fast GDP growth recuperation can mask persistent underlying problems (Teijeiro, 2006). This would be a case of 'dysfunctional convalescence'. For Argentina the key question is whether the post-crisis emerging policy framework has been enriched by the lessons of such calamity (Feldstein, 2002, p. 14).[60] Most of the collective errors incurred in the developments leading to the crisis, and during the attempts to manage it, may well be redeemed by history if the emerging policy framework incorporates those lessons.

The daunting question for the region is how these modalities of 'dysfunctional' equilibrium will unravel since (i) the pressures for more social expenditure are not abating; (ii) in several countries a portion of those expenditures is actually regressive; (iii) the external favorable economic cycle will recede; and (iv) there is political intolerance for the policy reforms that would untangle the current policy predicament. The aspiration of this book is to add understanding to these challenges by putting together a 'political economy information based strategy' to unlock the current political and policy jinx.

II. THE ORGANIZATION AND STRUCTURE OF THE BOOK

The book is organized around two main parts. Part I contains the Introduction and Chapters 1 and 2. The Introduction summarizes the specific objectives of the book and the conceptual framework on which it is developed. The idea is to underscore early on the relevance of the thematic questions that the book addresses as well as the distinct conceptual premises on which its analysis is built. As will be seen, the specific conceptual premises have been gleaned out of findings from the research agenda of, for example, institutional economics, the politics of policies, incentive theory, transaction costs economics, public choice theory and, in general, from the political economy of pro-growth and pro-poor literature. The Introduction is followed by Chapter 1, which offers an overview summarizing the most relevant and recent macroeconomic developments in Latin America. The idea is to encapsulate the main features of what has happened in the last few years, what has prompted the reforms now in place and what the remaining policy challenges are. These stylized facts have been extracted from the empirical research conducted on the recent experiences of Argentina, Brazil, Chile, Colombia, Costa Rica and Peru.

These six countries were chosen because they were perceived as a 'satisficing sample' where the basic objectives of the research could be pursued better. They combine requirements representing different (i) economic sizes; (ii) macroeconomic policy frameworks; (iii) equity conditions; and (iv) policy responses to sudden stops and to volatility in general. On the whole, the comparative analysis confirms the view that although each country's macroeconomic arrangement is strongly influenced by its own political history, at the bottom of it all compliance with some fundamental core macroeconomic and microeconomic principles are the final determinants of economic performance.

Chapter 2, entitled 'The political economy of macroeconomic policy making in Latin America', provides the broad regional context and possible political economy explanations for the actual policies that end up being adopted. It frames the analysis around the evolution and origins of institutions in general and on how they are mainly the result of endogenous political and equity conditions and perceptions on how public and private markets serve, or not, the public interest. After the core of generally accepted macroeconomic principles is summarized, a perspective on Latin America's macroeconomic and equity performance is presented and placed in the context of the strength or weakness of the political demand for macroeconomic stability and for attendant fiscal and financial reforms. The general conclusion is that short term political interests tend to have a stronger capacity to influence public policies than longer term considerations of policy consistency or of the general welfare. This chapter ends offering information and transaction costs based strategy for policy reform and for institutional transformation.

The second part of the book is comprised of six chapters containing the specific country narratives. These country narratives are intended more as political economy perspectives on the reform processes in these countries than as mainstream economic country reports. They should be read within the conceptual context detailed in the Introduction. Each one contains the following:

(i)   A political economy diagnostic and entry-point into the recent and current macroeconomic and equity developments;

(ii) an analysis of how the institutional framework responded to a 'stress test' in which macroeconomic stability was challenged by internal or external turbulence. The underlying principle here is that to understand geology one must study earthquakes (Arrow, 1985, p. 321). In other words, to identify the real determinants of the effectiveness of a given macroeconomic policy arrangement, the analysis should focus on a specific macroeconomic crisis because it is then and there that the real characteristics and the predominant incentives of that framework come to the surface;

(iii) A summary of the recent equity developments as there is a growing body of literature linking in dynamic causalities distributive justice with macroeconomic volatility and with the political support for policy reforms.

There are separate notes for each major chapter and for each country narrative. They are integral parts of the text of the book and could be read *pari passu* as part of the unfolding of its contents. The idea is to provide background to facilitate further reading, and to point out the direction in which the particular research agenda seems to be evolving. The analysis in each country narrative as well as that of the book in general enjoys the benefit of hindsight and nearly full knowledge of *ex post* developments. It is not intended a criticism of what policy makers or any institution may have done, right or wrong. It is a heuristic exercise from which to learn and to inform emerging policy.

III.   CONCEPTUAL FRAMEWORK

The following conceptual premises have been selected from the 'received view'[61] and from the literature to configure the particular political economy approaches applied throughout the book: (i) rules are incentives; (ii) macro-economic stability is part of property rights; (iii) equity is tantamount to equality of opportunity; (iv) macroeconomic volatility is a distributional issue; (v) macroeconomic policy making is a Principal Agent Problem; and (vi) the limits of income induced welfare.

Rules and Incentives as the Path Towards Evaluable History

Rules are incentives.[62] They matter because they frame the process through which accountability and the relevant information can be estab-lished. But formal or nominal rules[63] or ad hoc accountability, by itself, matters less than the learning process of discerning the real incentives that influence – reward or sanction – a given individual or collective behav-iour.[64] Accountability requires rules to govern the processes through which attribution, causality or possible association can be established. Just as there are rules governing the separation of powers, which assumes a modality of hierarchical political governance structure and an incentive compatibility framework, there is a need for attendant rules to link *ex post* results with the *ex ante* decisions that led to those results. This is the way to build accountability; through 'evaluable history', verifiable (see Laffont and Martimort, 2002, p. 264) baseline and end results scenarios as well as by a 'paper-trail' to inform the process in between. Rules also reduce random or deliberate ambiguity between the intervening factors and actors. In this interaction, accountability and rules spawn the institutional and political incentive structures determining decision-making behavior. That incentive structure is the main determinant of effectiveness. In brief, accountability, rules and incentives need to be understood not as three separate concepts or factors but comprehensively in their mutual interac-tions and effects.

Macroeconomic Stability as a Property Rights Preserving Institution

Macroeconomic and price stability are an integral part of 'market-preserving institutions'. After all, they protect the citizens of a given country from the stealthy – intended or unintended – dissipation of their income and assets. Without the protection of macroeconomic stability, markets can hardly function as money cannot serve as a store of value. It may function as a means of payment, at least in the short run, but not as a credible trustee for savings and investment. At the bottom of it all, in several Latin American countries citizens do not fully trust their local cur-rencies. This is the result of a long history of macroeconomic volatility. In spite of some recent important advances, Latin America's reform agenda still has ample room for improvement, especially in the fiscal and financial sector components of macroeconomic policy making in general and of inflation targeting in particular.

Equity and Distributive Justice as Equality of Opportunity

The concept of equity includes the ideas of fairness perception and distributive justice as processes leading to specific outcomes such as income and wealth. The emphasis is more on the initial conditions and on the processes than on the outcomes or income.

> A society with relatively high income inequality might be an equitable society if the observed inequality were the outcome of an entirely fair process – in which some worked harder[65] or took more economic risks with resultant greater economic gains than others. Equity is sensibly thought of as equality of opportunity and is a more satisfactory concept from a normative point of view; but it is harder to measure. (Birdsall, 2005b, p. 3)

In many developing countries income inequality is the product of inequitable processes. Those results will not be considered politically 'fair' and will lead to meager political support for policy reform and for the development of the 'right' institutions.[66]

Macroeconomic Volatility as a Distributional Issue

To reduce macroeconomic volatility the political economy of the bidirectional[67] causal relationships between macroeconomics and inequity need to be unbundled.[68] After all, macroeconomic volatility is largely a political and distributional issue (Tanzi, 2000, p. 93). Without a strong political demand for macroeconomic stability there will hardly be sufficient political support for the monetary and fiscal policies that deliver such stability.[69] There will not be sufficient political incentives for the reforms to be really adopted by those who, as rational political actors, will wonder about the viability or wisdom of trying to sell reforms that are not fully shared by the public at large.[70] And those who think the system is 'unfair' will hardly be willing to wait for growth to lower poverty. 'Inequality is conducive to the adoption of growth retarding polices.' (Alesina and Rodrik, 1994, p. 465). And it could be added that inequality is often also conducive to the 'wrong' pro-poor policies. In brief, political economy restrictions make it very difficult for an 'efficient institutions' solution (Acemoglu, 2005a, p. 4).

To the question of why there is not a Coasean political solution analogous to the economic theorem,[71] Daron Acemoglu (2003a, p. 2) answers that an extension of the Coasean theorem to politics would suggest the answer is no. There are strong empirical and theoretical grounds for believing that inefficient policies and institutions are prevalent. We conclude that these inefficient institutions and policies are chosen because they serve the interests of politicians or social groups that hold political power at the expense of the rest. The theoretical case depends on commitment problems inherent in politics; parties holding political power cannot make commitments to bind their future actions because there is no outside agency with the coercive capacity to enforce such arrangements.

Macroeconomic Policy Making as a Principal–Agent Problem

If macroeconomic volatility is largely a political economy problem and if politics impacts policies, the question that emerges is which economic model should be applied to understand those political economy[72] factors[73] and to be able to influence macroeconomic outcomes? Should it be the neoclassical competitive model? Or should it be one that responds to the characteristics that distinguish macroeconomic policy making? To answer these questions it should be remembered that macroeconomic policy making is a delegated task.[74] It is not one that markets will autonomously clear or manage.[75] It implies specialization and division of labor. As such, it involves many of the elements developed by the 'Principal–Agent' framework to deal with delegation and contractarian arrangements in which information asymmetries, ambiguous incentives (Laffont and Martimort, 2002, p. 30) and verifiability problems are so pervasive. It can be said then that macroeconomic policy making is predominantly a 'Principal–Agent' problem, one in which incentives, political and economic, play a major and interdependent role.

As will be seen, for the particular case of Latin America, the challenge that arises is that we are dealing with what could be called an 'absentee principal' who does not seem to be sufficiently politically motivated to demand from its macroeconomic 'agents' macroeconomic stability and low transaction costs to achieve it. This is an asymmetric information problem that unravels into multiple principals, multiple agents and diffused political intertemporal accountability. In brief, macroeconomic policy making in Latin America could be characterized as a 'multiple principal–agent problem' under an ambiguous political accountability context and limited repeated game learning process (Laffont and Martimort, 2002, p. 29). The key policy implication of this characterization is that the strategy to reform macroeconomic arrangements and most institutional frameworks needs to be built on information and incentives in their many modalities of attire.

History, for instance, is information. Beyond the events and causalities involved, history is a major source of information, just as its interpretation is a source of information. When it is said that history matters, perhaps the most critical dimension of that importance is the one derived from the information it offers to those who live it, interpret it, or try to learn from it. When we say that history may explain Chile's fiscal conservatism or appreciation for macroeconomic stability, and when it is said that in Brazil the markets are influencing political economy factors and preventing populist inclinations from prevailing, we are saying that in these countries history has informed the public at large about the costs of inflation and about the benefits of macroeconomic stability. History has been the source of information and has engendered a political posture propitious to reform and to macroeconomic stability.

The Limits of Income Induced Welfare

The basic purpose of the search for the 'right' combination of pro-growth and pro-poor policies is to raise the level of welfare over time of a given country or society in terms of its own particular (bounded) perception of its individual (utility) and collective social welfare function.[76] This monumental challenge[77] needs to be parsed out into more specific and, hopefully, more measurable concepts such as income, consumption and other quality of life indexes. This is the task of applied research as well as the goal of public policies. But in the process of interaction between these two fronts the abstract vision of welfare and its metric can get confused. This interplay is now the subject of renewed intense research[78] to better ascertain under what conditions 'growth without significant greater happiness' should enter a personal or even a collective welfare function (Di Tella and MacCulloch, 2006, p. 26). This is not an irrelevant issue for the search of the 'right' combination of pro-growth and pro-poor policies, or of macroeconomic stability, since at the bottom of both of these themes (growth and equity) lies the fundamental purpose of enhancing individual and collective welfare, as the two appear to be inseparable in any social contract.[79] Given Latin America's equity imbalance it may well be that gains in social justice[80] could be a major source of additional welfare (or 'happiness') even without requiring large increases in income. To Rafael Di Tella and Robert MacCulloch (2006, p. 39), 'the potential uses of happiness data in political economy are vast'. It appears to be a major quarry from which to inform public policies.[81] Within the context of this book and of its main recommendation on the critical role of information in engendering the political demand for the 'right' pro-growth and pro-poor policies, this line of research is highly welcomed. It should be extended further[82] into Latin America.

NOTES

1. Albert O. Hirschman (1981, p. 134), commenting on the ephemeral nature of analytical or empirical 'discovery', developed the following theorem: 'As soon as a social phenomenon has been fully explained by a variety of converging approaches and is therefore understood in its majestic inevitability and perhaps even permanence, it vanishes'. . . 'Why things should work this way is left to readers to figure out; just in case they find the proof of my theorem troublesome, they can take heart from the fact that Hegel expressed the same thought less paradoxically and more beautifully when he wrote 'the owl of Minerva spreads its wings only with the falling of dusk'. See his 'The turn to authoritarianism in Latin America and the search for its economic determinants' (Hirschman, 1981).
2. For a review of the development of modern economic thought, see Heilbroner and Milberg (1995).
3. During the last two decades political economics has become one of the most active research areas in the pursuit of better answers for the causes of long term development. Political economics builds on earlier work on public choice theory, game theory, rational choices by economic and political agents, rational expectations, macroeconomics, political cycles, incentive theory and the political economy of asymmetric information.
4. An endogenous process is one in which its results are determined by the interaction of variables within the system in which the process itself takes place. Those variables can, simultaneously or with lagged effects, act as causes and consequences of the observed results. The direction of causality can have stochastic dynamics depending on particular interactions between the factors at play. If institutions result from endogenous social preferences it is difficult to frame the problem in terms of dependent and independent variables and in terms of only explained and explicatory variables. On approaches to deal with this identification problem see Acemoglu et al. (2006).
5. Historian Niall Ferguson finds that the 'nexus between economics and politics is the key to understanding the modern world. But the idea that there is a simple causal link from one to the other – in particular, from capitalism to democracy – is mistaken. One version of the relationship does indeed produce the happy outcome of the capitalist democracy: the double helix of Western development. But like DNA, the cash nexus is capable of mutation. Sometimes democracy can stifle economic growth. Sometimes an economic crisis can undermine a dictatorship. Sometimes democracy can prosper even as the economy flounders. Sometimes growth can strengthen an authoritarian ruler.' (Ferguson, 2001, p. 19).
6. Joseph Stiglitz (2002a, p. 487) posits that 'information affects political process as well as economic ones'.
7. The literature on the relationships between political regimes (democratic or authoritarian) and economic performance is vast, complex and inconclusive. To Daron Acemoglu, democracy may be a critical ingredient for economic growth but 'there is no robust statistical relationship to back it up'. On the other hand, there are different kinds of democracy. Some of them are dysfunctional. Others are quite successful, particularly in protecting rights and in assuring 'creative destruction', which is indispensable for sustained growth (Acemoglu, 2007).
8. Oliver E. Williamson (1996b, p. 378) defines 'opportunism' as follows: 'Self-interest seeking with guile, to include calculated efforts to mislead, deceive, obfuscate, and otherwise confuse. Opportunism should be distinguished from simple self-interest seeking, accordance to which individuals play a game with fixed rules that they reliably obey.'
9. On rational opportunistic models see Alesina et al. (1997). See also Rogoff and Sibert (1988), and Persson and Tabellini (1999).
10. According to Daniel Kahneman and Amos Tversky (1986, p. 68), 'The logic of choice does not provide an adequate foundation for a descriptive theory of decision making'.
11. According to Alesina and Perotti (1994, p. 351), 'Economic policy is the result of a political struggle within an institutional framework'.

12. Following Baumol, the proximate causes of growth in a given country are basically its capital and investment, labor supply and productivity as well as its capacity for techno-logical change. In 1987, Professor Solow received the Nobel prize for his contribution to growth theory by underscoring the importance of technological change as the factor that can contribute significantly to economic growth even if capital and labor are not increased. The issue, of course, is where does technological innovation come from if it is not from institutions propitious to research and to technological change? The long term causes of growth and equity are the institutions that determine how a society adopts the policies that lead to a given supply of capital and labor productivity.

13. Adam Przeworski (1994, p. 227) warns that 'even if we knew the impact of institutions on policies, we should remain skeptical about institutional prescriptions. What we sorely need is empirical knowledge about what works and what does not: crude facts.'

14. On the challenge of 'unbundling institution' Daron Acemoglu (2005b, p. 1043) insight-fully observes that there is a need to go beyond the notion that institutions matter. The real challenge is to ascertain 'which specific dimensions of institutions matter for which outcomes. It is only the latter type of knowledge that will enable better theories of insti-tutions to be developed and practical policy recommendations to emerge from this new area. Consequently, the issue of "unbundling institutions", that is, understanding the role of specific components of the broad bundle, is of first order importance.'

15. According to Oliver Williamson (1996, p. 378), an institutional arrangement refers to 'The contractual relation or governance structure between economic entities that defines the way in which they cooperate and/or compete.'

16. The concept 'coordination' is meant here to denote policy making in general as well as deliberate or non-deliberate interaction between Central Banks and Ministries of Finance. On the whole it can be said that in most countries there is a deliberate process of intended or unintended coordination at some point in the budgetary process or in the establishment of inflation targets and monetary rules or policy. To Allan H. Meltzer (2005, p. 145) the word 'coordination' runs the risk of being interpreted within a Keynesian 'model with the implication that monetary and fiscal policy should be coordinated'.

17. According to Kemal Dervis (2006, p. 197), 'for development to work an effective macro strategy is needed. Serious mistakes in macro strategy can be dramatic and create a tremendous amount of damage, as evidenced in the past decades. If the macro strategy is wrong, despite the little bit of help that can be rendered at the project or sector levels, most of the financing is going to go to waste. And worse, unless the financing is in the form of pure grants, it is going to create larger debt for the country.'

18. On the question of which institutions may matter the most see Daron Acemoglu (2005c, p. 1045), 'The question is which economic institutions matter more. Entry barriers? Labor market regulations? Property rights enforcement? Limits on government corrup-tion? These are important, but also very difficult questions. It seems that these questions will be almost impossible to answer with cross-country data alone, and micro data inves-tigations, for example, exploiting differences in regulations across markets and regions appear to be the most promising avenue.'

19. Acemoglu and Robinson (2006a, p. 325) call these 'a cluster of economic institutions' to denote the spread of the extent of some institution 'across a broad section of society'.

20. According to Andrés Solimano (2000, p. 32), 'The modern theory of distributive justice distinguishes between "outside" (or morally arbitrary) factors (gender, race, initial assets, talent) and "personal responsibility" elements (effort, risk-taking attitudes) in shaping the level of income, wealth, and welfare of the individual in society. Social inequality is a reflection of individual differences in these two sets of wealth-creating factors.'

21. Javier Santiso (2006, p. 56) observes that 'macroeconomic volatility has its counterpart in the political and institutional realms, since both reinforce each other'.

22. Following Nancy Birdsall (2005b, p. 3), 'A society with relatively high income inequality might be an equitable society if the observed inequality were the outcome of an entirely fair process – in which some worked harder or took more economic risks with resultant

greater economic gains than others. Equity is sensibly thought of as equality of opportunity and is a more satisfactory concept from a normative point of view; but it is harder to measure. I argue that in developing countries high money inequality is likely to be a sign of processes that are not equitable.'

23. Although it is difficult to define pro-growth and pro-poor policies precisely, the former can be associated more with capital investment than with, say, employment. The latter can be associated more with 'progressive' public expenditures (for example education, health and other public goods) in the sense that they benefit the poor more than the rich. But these differences are static in nature and dim when a long term view is taken and the respective externalities are subsumed in a general equilibrium process.

24. 'The bidirectional relationship between growth and poverty reduction suggests that ideally consideration of policies should take into account their direct and indirect effects on growth and poverty reduction. This awareness introduces new but necessary levels of complexity in the evaluation of policy options on both agendas.' See p. 11, Chapter 1, 'From vicious to virtuous circles', in Perry et al. (2006).

25. The importance of the effectiveness of macroeconomic management in developed countries is also immense, both in terms of macroeconomic performance as well as a policy framework. In 1933 the US GDP was 31 per cent below its 1929 level. For a history of the evolution of macroeconomic theory and practice see Gregory N. Mankiw (2006, p. 30) and V.V. Chari and Patrick J. Kehoe (2006).

26. Cárdenas Enrique et al. (2000, p. 16) have found that 'Latin American economic performance during the three decades that followed the Second World War was remarkable, inducing a widespread transformation of society. On the one hand, continental GDP grew at 5.6 per cent per year in 1945–1974, or 2.7 per cent per capita.' This pace was not sustained from the 1980s onwards. In their view, and after certain specific policy flaws are considered, the global explanation for Latin America's lackadaisical performance during the last two decades 'has to do with politics and political economy' (p. 30).

27. Chile's case seems consistent with Olson's (1996, p. 20) observation that 'The fastest-growing countries are never the countries with the highest per capita incomes but always a subset of the lower-income countries.'

28. Even Chile experienced a negative rate of growth (−0.8 per cent) in 1999.

29. According to Richard Cooper (1988, p. 229), 'Coordination can be rule-based or process oriented. Under rule-based coordination, parties agree on certain basic rules concerning the issue at hand and are free to act independently within those rules. Process-oriented coordination, in contrast, involves close consultation on actions to be taken shortly before they are taken'. In practice these two approaches tend to mix but when trying to discern how a given policy decision was taken, the rules or the process approach help establish respective accountabilities. And accountabilities matter.

30. Mauricio Cárdenas and Eduardo Lora (2006, p. 3) 'consider that recent better fiscal results in Latin America are not only the outcome of a propitious business cycle, there is also a genuine effort to manage well the fiscal and debt accounts.'

31. This is a relevant question not only to Latin American countries but also to developed ones. Ben S. Bernanke and Michael Woodford ask 'To what extent are the improvements in performance observed in countries that have adopted inflation targeting the direct result of the change in policy regime, as opposed to other causes? For example, many countries that did not adopt inflation targeting, or adopted only parts of the approach, also experienced substantial improvements in macroeconomic performance in the 1990s. Would these countries have done better if they had adopted full-fledged inflation targeting? Would the inflation-targeting countries have done as well if they had not gone the inflation-targeting route? Are there certain preconditions for inflation targeting to be helpful? Are there institutional or economic circumstances under which adopting inflation targeting can be counterproductive?' (Bernanke and Woodford, 2006, p. 2).

32. Inequality can also afflict developed countries: 'In the United States between 1979 and 1997 the average income of the richest fifth of the population jumped from nine times the income of the poorest fifth to around 15 times. In 1999 Britain income inequality reached its widest level in 40 years'. See *The Economist* (2001, p. 9).

33. 'It is sometimes argued that inequality is related to the state of development in a country and comparisons should therefore be made that control for this factor. Londoño and Székely (2000) use regression analysis to compute the difference between actual inequality and expected inequality given the level of development of many countries in the world. The difference for Latin American countries is positive; that is, the region suffers from "excess inequality", which Londoño and Székely (2000) find has fluctuated around 13 Gini points over time.' See Ferranti et al. (2004, p. 54).

34. 'The volatility of Latin America is striking' posit Gavin et al. (1996, p. 4).

35. According to Nancy Birdsall (2005a, p. 2), 'Global markets are inherently disequalizing, making rising inequality in developing countries more rather than less likely.'

36. Guillermo Calvo and Carlos Végh (1999, p. 1605) consider that 'much work remains to be done on the empirical regularities of disinflation'.

37. If disinflations occur because of a possible overshooting of the interest rates and because of a resulting banking and financial crisis, and the underlying fiscal problems have not been fully addressed, then the resurgence of inflation is a highly likely development, although not while the economy is in recession or stagnant.

38. On the question of what makes disinflation sustainable see Marc Hofstetter (2005).

39. The Nobel prizes for the year 2001 were awarded to three eminent scholars who for decades had worked in the field of 'information economics'. All of them felt that information flaws and limitations had not been given adequate relevance in 'completing' the competitive paradigm that 'had dominated economic thinking for two centuries' (Stiglitz, 2002a, p. 486). While it would be difficult to summarize their main policy tenets, four key messages are particularly relevant: (i) information imperfections and asymmetries are pervasive in all economies (Stiglitz, 2002a, p. 469; Akerlof, 2002, p. 413; Spence, 2002, p. 434); (ii) most economic markets are lacking information and political markets tend to be even more informationally deprived; (iii) one of the key roles of the state is to generate information and to support an environment conducive to a growing demand for information; and (iv) information affects political processes as well as economic ones (Stiglitz, 2002a, p. 487).

40. According to Singh (2006, p. 3), 'Over the past century, countries in the Latin American region have demonstrated a marked predisposition toward macroeconomic instability. The region has been unusually prone to bouts of hyperinflation, exchange rate devaluations, failed currency reforms, banking sector collapses, and debt default.'

41. Referring to the political frustration that countries and the IMF often experience when dealing with macroeconomic crisis, Professor Martin Feldstein insightfully observes that the long term country distrust in the market system 'may be the most serious and lasting effects of the crisis' (Feldstein, 2003).

42. Joan Esteban and Ray Debraj (2006, p. 275) aver that 'high inequality will induce voters to support higher degrees of redistribution, thereby inducing heavier distortions on intertemporal resource allocation, specifically dampening investment.'

43. According to Agustin Carstens (2004, p. 4), 'The costs of inflation are borne most heavily by the poor, who lack the wealth needed to diversify into inflation-proof assets.'

44. 'If there were a trade-off between growth and distribution, governments would face tough choices: the welfare-enhancing gains of greater equity could be eliminated by the losses associated with lower growth. In fact, the evidence suggests that the trade-offs work in the other direction. Extreme inequality is not just bad for poverty reduction – it is also bad for growth. Long-run efficiency and greater equity can be complementary. Poor people remain poor partly because they cannot borrow against future earnings to invest in production, the education of their children and assets to reduce their vulnerability. Insecure land rights and limited access to justice can create further barriers to investment.' See UNDP (2005, p. 53).

45. For the social impact of reforms in Latin America during the 1990s see Eduardo Lora (2004, p. 105).

46. According to Mancur Olson (1996, p. 19), 'the large differences in per capita income across countries cannot be explained by differences in access to the world's stock of productive knowledge or to its capital markets, by differences in the ratio of population to

land or natural resources, or by differences in the quality of marketable human capital or personal culture. Albeit at a high level of aggregation, this eliminates each of the factors of production as possible explanations of most of the international differences in per capita income. The only remaining plausible explanation is that the great differences in the wealth of nations are mainly due to differences in the quality of their institutions and economic policies.'

47. For the developing world as a whole, José Antonio Ocampo (2005b, pp. 1, 6) cautions that 'ignoring inequality in the pursuit of development is perilous. Focusing exclusively on economic growth and income generation as a development strategy is ineffective, as it leads to the accumulation of wealth by a few and deepens the poverty of many.' 'Addressing inequality requires efforts to achieve a balance between many complex, countervailing socio-economic forces. Although economic growth is necessary, it is not a sufficient condition to reduce poverty.'

48. For a serious and well thought out reform proposal for the international monetary system see Stephany Griffith-Jones and José Antonio Ocampo (1998).

49. Alesina and Drazen (1991, p. 1171) argued, in one of the seminal papers on the reasons why reforms are delayed or not adopted, that: 'the timing of stabilizations and, in particular, their postponement cannot be easily understood in terms of models in which the policymaker is viewed as a social planner maximizing the welfare of a representative individual. On the contrary, heterogeneity in the population is crucial in explaining these delays. In many cases, the process leading to a stabilization can be described as a war of attrition between different socioeconomic groups with conflicting distributional objectives. Delays in stabilization arise due to a political stalemate over distribution; stabilizations occur when a political consolidation leads to a resolution of the distributional conflict.'

50. To Dani Rodrik (2006, p. 973), the World Bank's 'Economic growth in the 1990s: Learning from a decade of reform' is 'an extraordinary document demonstrating the extent to which the thinking of the development policy community has been transformed over the years. But there are other competing perspectives as well. One (trumpeted elsewhere in Washington) puts faith on extensive institutional reform, and another (exemplified by the UN Millennium Report) puts faith on foreign aid. Sorting intelligently among these diverse perspectives requires an explicitly diagnostic approach that recognizes that the binding constraints on growth differ from setting to setting.'

51. This approach is different from the 'declining electoral turn out' in many countries which Robert Putnam (2000, p. 404) so aptly examined. The issue here has more to do with the intrinsic policy content of what a political constituency and well organized interest groups will support, than with how many people are going to the polls. The two processes are not totally independent. Over time, the nature of the policy content may influence the turnout, and vice versa, but, at the end of the day, what matters more is what policies become actual legislation. The tenet in this book is that the protection of macroeconomic stability often ends up with scant political demand and electoral support for the policy frameworks that would deliver it.

52. Certain characteristics or key features of public policies are the main determinants of the effectiveness of such policies. Those characteristics include: stability, adaptability, coherence, quality of implementation and enforcement, public support and efficiency. See Ernesto Stein et al. (2005, p. 17).

53. According to Marcela Eslava (2006, p. 49), 'Central Bank independence is a popular recipe to free monetary policy from both inflation bias and the influence of the political cycle. In practice, however, political, philosophical, and economic considerations have moved societies to maintain institutional links between the government and the Central Bank. This gives rise to the question of whether the institutional design of the Central Bank can be adapted to bring out the desired benefits of independence, in an environment in which such independence is, de facto, only partial.

54. Ernesto Stein et al. (2005, p. 16) point out that 'one important characteristic of policies that has been widely recognized in recent work on macroeconomics, trade policy, regulation, and other areas of economics is policy credibility'.

55. Differences over macroeconomic paradigms are not an exclusive possibility in developing countries. For the differences between two Nobel winners, Robert Solow and George Lucas, on whether 'markets clear' in developed countries, see Gregory N. Mankiw (2006, p. 38).

56. According to Eduardo Lora (2007, p. 51), the 'unbundling of reforms seems to have been the result of governments trying to exploit political spaces, however small, to push change in the desired direction, with the hope perhaps of later generating interest to continue the process.'

57. According to Alberto Alesina and Dani Rodrik (1994, p. 465), 'Inequality is conducive to the adoption of growth retarding policies.'

58. These interdependent strands deal with: (i) the politics of economics, institutions, information and incentives; (ii) transaction costs economics and the endogenous origin of the demand for institutions; (iii) fiscal dominance and the fiscal determination of the price level and volatility; (iv) inflation targeting as an integrated monetary, financial and fiscal policy regime; (v) macroeconomics as a political, information and behavioral problem (Akerlof, 2002, p. 427); (vi) poverty, distributional justice and the perception of social fairness; and (vii) 'Prospect theory' and the determinants of collective decision making processes (Kahneman and Tversky, 1979).

59. For an examination of results of the reforms adopted, see Jeromin Zettelmeyer (2006, p. 18). His overall finding is that the reforms of the 1990s have been good for long-term growth. But much remains to be done.

60. In terms of lessons Martin Feldstein (2002, p. 14) avers that 'a fixed exchange-rate system, even one based on a currency board or other "hard" fix, is a bad idea that is likely to lead to an overvalued exchange rate, a currency crisis, and widespread defaults. A market-determined floating exchange rate is the only way to avoid these problems. Second, substantial foreign borrowing in dollars is a very risky strategy. This is particularly true of short-term debt but is also a problem with longer-term borrowing. It is a problem regardless of whether the borrower is the government or the private sector.'

61. On the evolution of the 'received view' in science and in economics and on how empirical work informs old and emerging paradigms, see D. Wade Hands (2001, p. 95) and his review of the Duhem-Quine 'underdetermination thesis'. According to Hands (2001, p. 96), 'In a nutshell, the Duhem-Quine underdetermination thesis asserts that any scientific theory can be immunized against refuting empirical evidence, that is, that no test is truly definitive. The problem is that no theory is ever tested in isolation.'

62. According to Kenneth J. Arrow (quoted in Laffont and Martimort, 2002), 'The most important development in economics in the last forty years has been the study of incentives to achieve potential mutual gains when the parties have different degrees of knowledge.'

63. Scholars (Buchanan, 1991; Persson and Tabellini, 2004a, p. 94; Rodrik, 2003, p. 10; Acemoglu and Robinson, 2000) use the concept of 'rules' as well as that of institutions as restrictions which can have a formal expression in constitutions and laws as well as in informally accepted norms regulating societal organizations and exchanges. Another line of research relates rules to cooperative and uncooperative 'games'. This approach has spawned the field of game theory and of economic development as a learning 'cooperative game' in which some societies prosper by designing for themselves 'the right' rules (North, 1990; Weingast, 1995; Bardhan, 2001, p. 276) and restrictions.

64. For a discussion of why incentives are not purposely more intensively used see Eduardo Wiesner (2003a).

65. An *NBER Working Paper No. 11895* by Peter Kuhn and Fernando Lozano (2006) explains why high wage and income earners work harder. In their conclusion, many salaried men work longer because of an increase in 'marginal incentives'.

66. The issue here is whether inequality is exogenous or not. The premise in this book is that there is a large portion of inequality that is not exogenous and that it depends on some 'controllable' initial factor endowments such as education, health and asset ownership. See Robert Margo (2006, p. 534).

67. Under bidirectional or reverse causality a dependant variable can cause changes in one or more explanatory variables. See Rodney Ramcharan (2006, p. 36).

68. The political economy of microeconomics (particularly in the labor markets) can also have a substantial adverse impact by retarding recovery and by adding downward inflexibility to the cycle. See Caballero et al. (2004, p. 12).
69. Alejandro Gaviria (2006, p. 20) has pointed out that in Latin America the challenges of growth and equity cannot be tackled in sequence but simultaneously.
70. To deal with these situations 'Clever and determined leadership is needed to overcome such obstacles by creating short-term wins and displaying the courage to take and explain the long-term benefit of reform.' See Ajay Chhibber (2006a, p. xv).
71. Coase's economic theorem holds that 'efficiency will be achieved as long as property rights are fully allocated and that completely free trade of all property rights is possible. The importance of the theorem is in demonstrating that it does not matter who owns what initially, but only that everything should be owned by someone. Trade will place resources in their highest-value occupation eventually.' See Bannock et al. (1989, p. 62).
72. The term 'political economy' seems to have originated in France in the seventeenth century. Sir James Steurt (1761) was the first English economist to put the term in the title of a book on economics, *An Inquiry into the Principles of Political Economy*. See Drazen (2002, p. 3).
73. In political economy analysis the focus is on the effects of different policy choices on economic outcomes. This contrasts with political science, which tends to concentrate more on the political mechanisms for decision making processes and their respective political outcomes. Under a public choice approach, choice mechanisms are studied using tools of economic analysis. According to Drazen (2000, p. 60), 'public choice theory considers not simply the positive and normative aspects of different ways of making collective choices, but also the question of how a society can choose over the set of possible choice mechanism.'
74. See Drazen (2002, p. 22), 'The delegation of decisions to policymakers with different preferences is pervasive in the making of collective choices. In fact, one may argue it is inherent to collective decision making. In any society with a large number of interests, decision making will necessarily be representative, in that individuals will choose representatives to make policy who do not have exactly the same preferences as they do over policies. Not every position can be directly represented, so that delegation in the above sense follows almost automatically from heterogeneity of interests in the population as a whole. The relation between the policies that are chosen and the policies individuals desire will depend on the preferences of the representatives and on the incentives that the voters give them. Hence, from a theoretical perspective, representative politics is an example of a principal–agent problem.'
75. For some of the different equilibrium implications between macroeconomics and microeconomics see Jorge Iván González (2004, p. 75).
76. 'The theory of social choice is preoccupied with the links between individual values and collective choice. The fundamental question is whether – and, if so, in what way – preferences for society as a whole can consistently be derived from the preferences of its members. The answer is crucial for the feasibility of ranking, or otherwise evaluating, different social states and thereby constructing meaningful measures of social welfare or helping public decision making' (Wallace, 2004, p. 6).
77. This is the 'impossibility theorem' idea ascribed to Kenneth Arrow (1951). In essence, the first welfare theorem reads as follows: (i) if there are enough markets, (ii) if all consumers and producers behave competitively and (iii) if an equilibrium exists, then that equilibrium is Pareto optimal. Arrow (1951) and Debreu (1959) concluded that these conditions cannot be met and market failure is the result.
78. Richard Easterlin (1974) was the first economist to pose and to reflect on the question of whether increases in personal income over time actually increased the level of happiness of individuals and of a given society. A related question is which public policies have positive effects on social welfare and actually increase 'happiness'.
79. Perhaps the most influential work in the last 30 years is that of John Rawls, *A Theory of Justice* (1971), in which he is concerned with the distributive aspects of the basic structure of society. To Rawls the principles of justice are those 'that free and rational persons

concerned to further their own personal interests would accept in an initial position of equality' (p. 11). The 'original position' is a hypothetical situation in which individuals are behind a 'veil of ignorance' about their places in society, that is their assets, attributes, weaknesses, and so on. Since personal differences are unknown and so the future of each one, the 'veil of ignorance' makes possible a collective choice of a particular conception of justice. Rawls posits that two justice principles would be chosen in the original position. 'The first emphasizes equality, including equal rights, liberties, and opportunities. The second principle (later called the difference principle) has been the subject of greater commentary. Rawls himself states this second principle as the general conception of his theory: "All social primary goods – liberty and opportunity, income and wealth and the bases of self-respect – are to be distributed equally unless an unequal distribution of any or all of these goods is to the advantage of the least favored" (p. 303). The difference principle, then, is a maximum rule for the distribution of the goods, material and other, that Rawls regards as primary. The difference principle is the part of Rawls's theory that has generated the greatest volume of hostile reaction and on which, he is generally considered most vulnerable.' See James Konow (2003, p. 1195).

80.   The concept of 'social justice' is a complex one. It poses enormous challenges when attempts are made to explicitly translate it into public policies. 'Despite the consensus over the relevance of fairness or of justice, no agreement yet exists among economists or for that matter among psychologists, political scientists, sociologists or philosophers about the proper theory of justice' (Konow, 2003, p. 1189).

81.   'Results based on happiness surveys should be treated critically and cautiously. But the two main alternatives for determining social welfare – either trying to back social welfare out of observed behavior or simply giving up and leaving it to the politicians – surely need to be treated critically and cautiously, too. The patterns observed in the empirical measures of welfare and happiness deserve to play at least some role in the evaluation of what social goals to emphasize, what macroeconomic tradeoffs are acceptable and what public policies are pursued.' See Di Tella and MacCulloch (2006, p. 43).

82.   Most of the applied research has been in comparisons between the United States and Europe. See Alesina et al. (2005).

1. Overview: the current status and prospects of the reform process

> Deductive reasoning no longer suffices for predicting economic behavior without constant assistance from empirical observation.
>
> Herbert A. Simon (1957)

This overview offers a summary of the current status of the process of macroeconomic policy reform in Latin America. The focus is on the main reforms emerging out of the macroeconomic crisis that several countries experienced since the mid-1990s. The central objective is to extract the underlying political economy factors (that is, the real interests and incentives) that may explain the nature and rationale of the policies adopted and of the results observed. The idea is not only to look at the immediate past or even at the present but also to try to extract the political economy and policy implications that are particularly relevant for a forward-looking perspective. In general terms Latin America has done well since about 2002–03; the question is, to what extent have the reforms adopted actually given the region enough macroeconomic resiliency and political tolerance to assimilate the upcoming unfolding of international adjustment processes and of each country's own particular circumstances? The answer seems to vary across countries and appears to be largely a function of the pace at which distributive justice and equity challenges are perceived and are actually addressed and corrected.

The overview ends with the key policy implication that one of the most important sources and origins of the political demand for reforms and for institutional transformation, on the one hand, and for the eventual supply of the 'right' institutions and policies, on the other, is the public's awareness of high transaction costs as well as of potentially lower ones. This is the incentive. The awareness of this potential reward is a function of the information that all political actors have – a function of the interpretation those actors make of the information they have. In conclusion, information is the most binding political economy restriction. The strategy for policy reform and for the development of the 'right' institutions has to focus on mitigating this restriction.

I. THE POLITICAL DEMAND FOR POLICY REFORM

The conceptual essence of political economy is that economics impacts politics as much as politics impacts economics. This circular causation is the crucible of contemporary developmental policy. The implication is that public policies towards redistribution can make societies more equal. The key premise for policy making is that inequality tends to be inimical to the adoption of pro-growth and even to pro-poor policies.[1] As early as 1973, Albert O. Hirschman (1973, p. 545) was warning about the degrees of tolerance or intolerance that a society may have with respect to inequality.[2] In contrast, reductions in poverty levels and effective additional access by the poor[3] to more equal initial conditions to education, health and markets have enormous potential to engender political support for both pro-growth and pro-poor policies. 'Greater equity is thus doubly good for poverty reduction: through potential beneficial effects on aggregate long-run development and through greater opportunities for poorer groups within any society' (World Bank, 2006b, p. 2).

Macroeconomic stability ultimately depends more on the existence of a political demand for that stability than on formal or informal rules or institutional characteristics of the macroeconomic and even the political governance structures. This is the initial 'falseable hypothesis'[4] on the question of what may explain the differences in macroeconomic performance across countries in Latin America. Although this hypothesis is vulnerable to the observation that it involves a tautology, with better retrospective than predictive explicatory power, it is the most 'satisficing' one to guide further empirical research.[5] The political demand for macroeconomic stability appears to be the least imperfect independent variable. The dependent variables are those that express the absence of macroeconomic stability such as high inflation, exchange rate crisis, unsustainable fiscal deficits, volatile growth rates and equity conditions.

This is so because without a strong political demand for macroeconomic stability there will hardly be sufficient political support for the monetary and fiscal policies that deliver such stability. There will not be sufficient political incentives for the reforms to be really supported and adopted by those who, as rational political actors, will wonder about the viability or wisdom of trying to sell reforms that are not fully shared by the general public. And those who think the system is 'unfair' and wanting in distributive justice will hardly be willing to wait for growth to lower poverty. The political economy challenge is to nurture and strengthen the political demand for the determinants of macroeconomic stability.

The political demand for reforms and for macroeconomic stability and for an effective coordination of fiscal and monetary policies comes from the realization that transaction costs in terms of, for example, inflation, stability, growth, employment and interest rate variability, are too high. The simple theorem or tautology would be that: 'The lower (higher) the real political demand for macroeconomic stability the higher (lower) will be the transactions costs of coordination between fiscal and monetary policy and the less (more) macroeconomic stability will result.' This approach is susceptible to the criticism that it is a tautological or excessively self-referenced argumentation. After all, to prove that there is or that there was political demand for reform can only be demonstrated, if at all, *ex post*. There is retrospective explicative power but limited predictive capacity. Perhaps there are other more independent variables to explain more neatly the direct and indirect causalities involved. The relevance of the demand approach should be contrasted with the alternative supply approach in which the risk is that the 'supplied institutions' may not respond to a real political demand. The literature offers numerous examples of these 'institutional failures' which originated in 'supply strategies' that were not sustainable through a real political demand for those institutions.

There is a strong relationship between macroeconomic stability and growth, on the one hand, and poverty reduction, on the other. But poverty reduction requires much more than additional levels of public expenditure. This route has already being tried in most Latin American countries and the results, in terms of real equity gains, do not warrant an unqualified insistence on this approach. What is needed is a transformation of the microinstitutional characteristics and incentive structures under which most social expenditures[6] take place in the region. This transformation should include, as its centerpiece, moving away from supply-driven systems to more demand-driven ones. But this encounters strong political resistance from well-organized public sector rent-seekers.[7] This is one of the major reasons why social development and macroeconomic stability are a political-intensive problem, a very serious problem for which each country will have to develop its own endogenous path. 'No unique "recipe" for economic development will work for every country. The essence of democracy and institutional development is diversity and learning' (Ocampo, 2004b, p. 107).

Few, if any, factors can explain Latin America's macroeconomic volatility better than the very limited capacity of its fiscal institutions to play a countercyclical fiscal role and to smooth out sudden stops in business cycles.[8] On the contrary, fiscal policy and, at times, even monetary policy, have played a pro-cyclical role accentuating the severity of external shocks. Changing this homegrown vulnerability will involve, *inter alia*, transforming the fiscal institutions[9] in a similar way to that in which independent

Central Banks reformed monetary policy making. In other words, there is a major need to nurture fiscal reforms to play a countercyclical role. Probably there is no other more pressing reform priority in the region.

In all countries' cases of a macroeconomic crisis the trigger largely came from external capital markets. Domestic initial conditions and financial weaknesses worsened the effects, severity and duration of the crisis. The most important of those weaknesses were informal dollarizations, unsustainable exchange rate appreciation, current account deficits, limited fiscal countercyclical capacity, downward inflexibility in labor and other markets, 'fear of floating and pass through inflations' and asset bubbles. With the benefit of hindsight it can be said that institutional credibility and unresolved issues of rules versus discretions may have led in some cases to unintended interest rate overshooting and to high 'sacrifice ratios' in the disinflation process. The capacity of interest rates to induce growth, restrain inflation and induce fiscal corrections is determined largely by the theoretical model[10] underpinning a particular policy but also, to some extent, by the risk-taking (that is, the incentives to protect the interests and the interests that become the incentives) that each macroeconomic 'principal' is willing to take. This risk-taking approach to macroeconomic policy making is derived, in the first place, from the formal and legal political accountabilities assigned to each 'principal'.

Under this hypothetical characterization the Central Bank will tend to raise interest rates to avoid the accusation of not being independent enough or to build its credibility. Indeed, a very legitimate posture. The fiscal authorities will find it difficult not to continue spending to avoid the blame of being indifferent to growth, equity and employment. The financial sector will tend to go to the limit of external exposure if it can blame the external avatars for being caught 'unbalanced', and hope for a government or Central Bank bail out. The blaming game can go on as long as independent and credible information is not provided to the public and to those who will want to seek office on the grounds of reforms. In brief, there is a huge role for information creation and dissemination.

In most countries there were three interdependent policy innovations emerging as lessons from the crisis: (i) inflation targeting and more intertemporal policy making; (ii) stronger formal and informal Central Bank independence; (iii) softer and more discretionary interest and exchange rate policy. On the whole, the emerging policy has been more discretion and flexibility in the use of the interest rate and exchange rate as shock absorbers. This latter innovation had been recommended by John Williamson as early as 1965 (2000, p. 5). However, the key need for a more effective fiscal countercyclical capacity still has much room for improvement.

Even within the difficult current political climate in Latin America, political economy restrictions (the traditional welfare costly ones) may no longer be driving policy making as predominantly as before. In some countries like Brazil, markets may be gaining a stronger foothold where there is a growing political demand and appreciation for macroeconomic stability. This political demand is forcing politicians (in the use of their rational choice politics of economics) to seek stability or to refrain from tinkering with it. This is a positive development. However, markets are not infallible; when they happen to fail, those who combated them will have their day and countries may shun orthodox remedies and fall back again on ineffective recipes. There will be a failure to distinguish between market failures and policy failures.

II. INFLATION TARGETING AS THE MACROECONOMIC COORDINATION TEMPLATE

Inflation targeting is now the formal framework under which monetary policy is conducted in several Latin American countries. Since the mid-1990s Chile, Brazil, Colombia, Peru and Mexico, with different degrees of intensity, have adopted inflation targeting as the main macroeconomic coordination template. Judged by its broad results, this policy has been a success, as inflation rates have not only come down but have remained low by historical standards. Furthermore, most countries have adopted a well structured analytical and institutional framework integrating fiscal[11] interest and exchange rate policies with a flexible and 'constrained discretion' management approach to deal with short term volatility without losing medium term perspective (Truman, 2003, p. 5). However, three qualifications need to temper these results.

First, it should be remembered that lower inflation rates were more the result of autonomous disinflation processes and large unintended 'sacrifice ratios' than of structural fiscal corrections. Actually, the severe financial and macroeconomic crisis of the 1990s led to disinflation 'overshooting' which can hardly be considered a success (Fischer, 2000, p. 3). Secondly, with the exception of Chile, 'fiscal dominance' is still prevalent in the region and efforts to deepen fiscal and budgetary reforms have not found sufficient political support. Thirdly, the better fiscal results and lower inflation rates of the last five years have been aided by a very favorable external business cycle. The question that emerges is whether, in fact, the lower rates of inflation fully reflect a structural, political and institutional transformation, particularly on the fiscal front. Has the region finally and permanently corrected the root causes of high inflation? The concern is that, although there is currently an appreciation for the benefits of low inflation levels, there is still not enough political demand for macroeconomic stability and for all the policy requirements and reforms that are needed to make it sustainable even under adverse conditions (Aninat, 2000b, p. 5).

In brief, how can one feel confident that a fiscally prudent Latin Americas era has finally come about, or is firmly evolving, when it is so difficult, or practically impossible, to get political support for the pending reforms to control unsustainable rates of public spending and commitments? Is Latin America's democracy so precarious that it often needs to run the risk of macroeconomic crisis to navigate or absorb immense political pressures to constantly incur fiscal imbalances? Is that democracy in a 'double bind', as even if it spends more on social needs it finds it so difficult to do it in a cost effective way and thus fails to nurture a more equitable society?

With all its importance, the adoption of inflation targeting by several Latin American countries and the lower inflation rates observed in parallel since the late 1990s should not be confused or necessarily identified with the final triumph over the underlying political and institutional factors which were determining in the first place the persistence of inflation as a long term historical trait in this region. After all, the effectiveness of inflation targeting is conditioned by the absence or presence of 'fiscal dominance'. To a large extent inflation targeting assumes 'monetary dominance' in contrast to 'a fiscal dominance', one in which the 'government budget plays a central role' (Woodford, 1995, p. 41).

However, the literature, from Sargent and Wallace (1981) and the 'unpleasant monetarist arithmetic', as well as the 'fiscal theory of the price level' (Woodford, 1995, p. 5) suggests that an unsustainable fiscal balance can restrict the smoothing out role of interest rates and have perverse effects on inflation in general and on inflation targeting in particular.[12] It can lead to costly inflation overshooting or undershooting. Inflation targeting has as its main requirement that an integrated policy regime controls for 'fiscal dominance'[13] and that it is credible even under the pressures of external shocks. If 'fiscal dominance' is the predominant condition (Eichengreen and Taylor, 2003) and other factors obscure such a situation, like when external financing is abundant or when the terms of trade have risen well above sustainable levels, countries may fall into a bad fiscal and monetary 'equilibrium'.

This may have been the case for Brazil in 2002 (Favero and Giavazzi, 2004) or the current situation in Colombia, Peru and Costa Rica. In all these countries, during the last few years, there have been some significant fiscal improvements for a number of reasons. But the main one has not been because of adequate and sustainable primary surpluses or because of long-term fiscal rules and attendant institutional transformation, and is certainly not of the same level as the transformation that has taken place at the monetary policy front with the creation of more independent Central Banks.

Such 'bad equilibrium' can go on for a while. Countries may even get used to it. But the 'transaction costs' of such equilibrium may be enormous both in terms of forgone income and missed opportunities to lower poverty rates and to improve long term distributive justice. What lies at the bottom of it all is the political economy restriction of immense pressures, that is political incentives, to expand public sector expenditures and commitments for as long as there is financing to do it. What is worrisome is that this is done under the pretense or the disingenuousness that such social expenditure is needed to reduce inequality and to get political support for policy reforms.

Currently the most critical policy question for Brazil is why it is not growing at a faster and more stable rate. Although there is no simple answer to this vast question it would be difficult to exclude in the explanations for the recent low growth rates the high real rates of interest, the high level of taxation and social security contributions and the uncertainty regarding external financing and default risk. These are all the immediate determinants. But the point that cannot be stressed enough is that these macroeconomic realities are not the primary causes. They are the 'damage control' manifestations or external symptoms of the underlying, largely still unresolved, political problem of 'fiscal dominance'.

III.   FISCAL DOMINANCE IN LATIN AMERICA

Although 'fiscal dominance' is the most important restriction affecting monetary policy and macroeconomic management in general, microeconomic rigidities and inflexibilities can – and have – played a major adverse role. In fact, they have raised the costs of disinflations and prolonged recovery periods. Rigid labor markets and other underlying institutional weaknesses, such as access to credit, work against smoothing out crisis and negative shocks. The policy implication of all this is that more specific strategic evaluations should be conducted to examine key specific micro-institutional arrangements in areas like labor markets, basic education and health, as well as regulatory frameworks. These evaluations would discern the 'right' and the 'wrong' incentives in 'public goods markets' and provide much-needed information to obtain political support for reform proposals of those micro-environments.

The second, and probably even costlier, consequence of fiscal dominance is that, by jeopardizing compliance with inflation targets, they diminish the public's credibility on the government's announced policies. This nurtures a 'rational expectation' that those policies are not fully credible and, more importantly, should not be 'discounted', that is, they should not be endogenized into private markets' own policies and behavior. This loss of credibility is a social loss. It reduces social welfare. It reduces the size of the 'pie' by stealth and makes distribution of what remains more difficult and conflictive.

The importance of 'fiscal dominance' is not so much that it restricts meeting inflation targets – by pushing demand beyond supply capacity – but that it creates the wrong incentives. Unanticipated fiscal deficits means that some agents can operate without a budget restriction and need not seek to be cost-effective to maintain access to public resources. The end result is that inflation targets are jeopardized and, in the case of social expenditures, distributional gains may be lost. Nothing can be more inequitable than inefficient social spending. This at its turn will make it more difficult for political support to be forthcoming for fiscal rules and macroeconomic stability in general. The key concept here is that of unanticipated fiscal deficits, that is, those that were not built in *ex ante* at the time of the overall macroeconomic programming exercise as part of the 'permissible' use of monetary space in the economy as a whole. They are the source of the wrong incentives. Not all fiscal deficits are necessarily destabilizing. There can be room for discretionary fiscal policy (Taylor, 2000, p. 22).[14] But unintended fiscal deficits can be very welfare costly.

The loss of credibility means a loss in the effectiveness of a powerful instrument of public policy making, namely, the capacity of the markets to adopt self correcting measures by those who are relatively better informed to make them. This may mean, for instance, 'softer landings', more sustainable recoveries, better countercyclical[15] management and in general a flatter 'Taylor curve'. In terms of institutional economics, credibility is a collective public good in which there is 'incentive compatibility' in the sense that the public at large and the government find it in their interest to cooperate.

IV. ENHANCED CENTRAL BANK INDEPENDENCE

One distinct consequence of the crisis of the late 1990s is that most countries in the region strengthened their Central Bank independence and adopted inflation targeting as the anchor for their macroeconomic policy regimes. These are analytical frameworks comprising (i) interest rates; (ii) exchange rate management; (iii) fiscal restrictions; and (iv) financial oversight components. The key policy implication is that 'no financial sector reform can be successful in an environment characterized by macro-economic instability' (Galindo et al., 2007, p. 292). One major element that deserves particular underscoring is the nascent institutional use of infor-mation and transparency to assure that the markets and the public know what the authorities intend to do in a given circumstance. The best example is the 'Open Letter' option that Brazil's Central Bank can send to the Minister of Finance when the inflation targeting may be in jeopardy. This instrument saved the day for Brazil in the management of the 2003 crisis.

In the pre-crisis years most countries were afraid to float their exchange rates, basically to avoid endangering their inflation aspirations and to induce fiscal prudence. After the crisis, countries seem to feel more confident about how to manage the trilogy of interest rates, exchange rates and fiscal outcomes. Up to mid-2006 the fear was more of floating 'down-wards' as some exchange rates were appreciating and thus providing some-what unsustainable gains in inflation targeting. After the crisis most countries adopted a more prudent fiscal policy, at least in relative terms, in the sense that fiscal deficits, although still prevalent, did not get much worse because the additional expenditures were financed by more tax revenues. This is the case for Brazil in particular. However, the favorable economic cycle has provided additional resources masking real lingering fiscal weak-nesses in some countries.

V. THE LESSONS FROM THE MACROECONOMIC CRISIS

Although the lessons learned and attendant policy reforms emerging out of the macroeconomic crisis of the late 1990s are not identical across coun-tries, there are some discernable common patterns or similar orientations in the direction in which policy moved. Within this broad context the main lessons can be grouped around the following interdependent themes: (i) the importance of information; (ii) pre-existing decision-making algorithms; (iii) prospect theory and political accountability; (iv) enhanced Central Bank Independence; (v) less fear of floating; (vi) tax and spend fiscal damage control; (vii) the role of the International Monetary Fund; and (viii) the political role of markets.

In most cases if policy makers had had better information about the vul-nerabilities of their financial sectors and particularly better 'real-time' information about what was going on during the actual development of the crisis, the costs would have been much lower. If they had known more about the impending and fast evolving real market developments (this means knowing which unintended incentives were having which unanticipated effects in policy areas hitherto not considered relevant) they probably would have modified some of the measures they actually took. The Hippocrates principle of 'first do no harm' may be easier to apply in medicine than when exchange rates are under pressure or when inflation targeting is compromised and Central Bank credibility is at stake. In brief, there were unexpected information vulnerabilities which made everything more hectic and costly.

Once a crisis starts and events begin to unravel fast there is not much that policy makers can do. Even 'market mechanisms will likely break down' (Truman, 2006b, p. 99). And although all crises may have some common features, they almost always start or are triggered by an unanticipated event. For this reason having in place previously agreed decision making rules and procedures with clear accountability enhancing incentives, is of critical importance. These rules would have to be politically and institutionally binding (within also pre-established boundaries) for given sets of probabilistic scenarios. They would have to be rules adopted 'away from the immediate interests' as J. Rawls (1971 and 1993) would advise. In any case they should be evaluable rules based on Popperian 'falsifiability' hypotheses. No country can always avoid crises. This is not the point. What matters are the learning game and the minimization of welfare losses particularly for the 'unprotected' groups.

According to prospect theory,[16] a decision making process and the choices finally made depend on the framing of the problem (Kahneman and Tversky, 1979). Applying prospect theory to the political economy analysis of macroeconomic crisis it could be said that if there are intended or unintended occult incentives in the way a crisis is discounted, or politically discussed, this framing of the problem will influence the policy choices made. The way the problem is framed may then contain the incentives to act before a crisis sets, during it, or afterwards. According to Professor Avinash Dixit this could be called the 'political framing of counterfactuals' in which different actors try to influence the political decision process by 'opportunistic' framing of the problem. Wage flexibility is one area where this can happen.

The lesson and the policy implication would be that in the past the forecasting of a crisis may have been politically biased to favor waiting for the crisis to happen. To minimize the costs of crisis the political framing of counterfactuals and of 'hindsight bias'[17] need to be changed so that the decision making process has the 'right' incentives to minimize costs and to enhance political accountability. This is already beginning to happen. Central Banks, for instance, seem more proactive in stating warnings which in fact build on counterfactuals and illuminate potential political accountabilities.

VI. THE REFORM PROCESS OF MULTILATERAL INSTITUTIONS

The role and effectiveness[18] of multilateral institutions[19] and of the International Monetary Fund[20] can be critical in several respects.[21] First, because they perform under a 'collective action' environment (Wiesner, 2007) and may provide financing[22] without being able to obtain full conditionality[23] compliance.[24] That is, they may be unwittingly inducing postponement[25] of reforms as countries receiving emergency and *de facto* Balance of Payments financing may[26] end up confusing financing with adjustment.[27] They may also find themselves in a difficult political economy position[28] trying to argue fiscal austerity in the face of available external financing.[29] Second, multilaterals have a major role because they can act as 'coordination templates' and induce solutions to international[30] or domestic coordination failures[31] by providing consistent analytical policy frameworks. Thirdly, they count because they can support research on critical policy areas and offer informed technical advice[32] and cross-country best practices.[33]

The 'emerging' process of policy reform[34] is largely focused on the role of the International Monetary Fund. This seems appropriate. After all, as Fred Bergsten opines, 'The IMF is the principal multilateral institution responsible for global economic prosperity and financial stability' (Bergsten, 2006b, p. ix). And, 'stripped of all its technicalities, the IMF remains the equity-funded financial institution that has been since its inception in 1944' (Lachman, 2006, p. 472).[35] The central issues continue to revolve around (i) surveillance;[36] (ii) the management of country-specific or systemic financial crisis;[37] and (iii) the interaction and coordination between the Fund, member countries[38] and the global capital markets.[39] Morris Goldstein (2006, p. 153) emphasizes the role of the Fund as an arbiter who has to make difficult 'calls' to regulate the international financial 'game'.

From a political economy perspective the point that needs to be underscored is that, notwithstanding the high level of technical competence that characterizes this institution, at the end of the day, its decisions are political decisions. Truman (2006b, p. 31) puts it well: 'The Fund is a political organization . . . its members are governments.' And this is as it should be. The political nature of the Fund is not a major issue in question. What is a major issue is the political[40] accountability of a political and multilateral institution (Bergsten, 2006a, p. 280). Within this context what matters the most is its effectiveness in terms of long term macroeconomic systemic stability.[41] And to enhance that effectiveness, what seems to be needed is more political accountability and better evaluation of results mechanisms (Wiesner, 2003c, p. 137; 2004 and 2007).

The reform process at the multilateral level is much influenced by the World Bank and the International Monetary Fund. The 2007 Malan Committee Report underlined the need for these two institutions to better coordinate their respective roles so that they could then be more efficient in providing support to member countries. The Report also called for a new 'Understanding on Collaboration' to replace the 1989 'Concordat'. These calls are understandable but, by themselves, may be insufficient to modify significantly the inescapable underlying complexities in a systemic macro institutional arrangement. This is an arrangement which tries operationally to separate macroeconomic and Balance of Payments problems, on the one hand, with policy-specific and more broad, equity and political development problems, on the other. The reality is that these issues are largely inseparable, and assigning distinct roles to different institutions to deal with them places those institutions in a technical and political predicament. When there are two 'principals' it is very difficult to have a 'contract' that does not end up short of delivering on its remit. This situation probably reflects unresolved political economy problems at the domestic levels of the developed and developing countries. These unresolved issues have much to do with the political economy challenge of combining and balancing pro-growth and pro-poor policies.

VII.   REMAINING POLICY AND POLITICAL ECONOMY CHALLENGES

Although there have been evident improvements in macroeconomic management in most counties in the region in the last few years, there are still some pending reforms and challenges. On the whole most countries have not been able to cope with the immense political pressures for public expenditures, particularly for social expenditures with little regard for whether those expenditures are effectively redistributive (Clements et al., 2007, p. 22). Currently the region seems to be in a state of 'dysfunctional equilibrium' in which fiscal dominance restricts monetary policy, and high real rates of interest adversely affect the rates of growth. It would seem that democracy needs very high levels of public expenditure but competition in the political markets is constrained by what could be called a re-election syndrome in which constitutional rules end up accommodating political opportunism. The major concern, as was said before, is that the region is still highly vulnerable to sudden stops in external financing.

Dysfunctional Equilibria

Countries can get used to high inflation levels and to dysfunctional disequilibrium as well as to non-performing macroeconomic arrangements.[42]
They may see them as the 'natural' state of affairs or as one that largely and
legitimately reflects a political social function preference. Costa Rica and
Brazil, for some time in the past, may fit this characterization. The hidden
costs of 'intermediate' inflation or of recurrent macroeconomic volatility
can morph in varied forms. In 1979 Feldstein

> warned against too easy an acceptance of the view that the costs of sustained
> inflation are small relative to the costs of unemployment. If a temporary reduc-
> tion in unemployment causes a permanent increase in inflation, the present value
> of the resulting future welfare costs may well exceed the temporary short-run
> gain. In the important case in which the growth of aggregate income exceeds the
> social discount rate, no reduction in unemployment can justify any permanent
> increase in the rate of inflation (Feldstein, 1979, p. 675).

Countries can also end up with 'bad' equilibria even under a low and
'controlled' inflation. Brazil's situation since the crisis of 1998–1999 may
fit these characteristics. For the period 2003–05, this country's average
annual rate of growth (2.23 per cent) was lower than Latin America's
(4.06 per cent) and of the world in general (4.46 per cent). At the same
time, Brazil has had in place a serious and credible macroeconomic
regime anchored on inflation targeting. The unintended 'bad' equilibrium
comes from the combination of very high real rates of interest, high levels
and expanding public sector expenditures and the uncertainty of global
capital volatility. But, on the whole, Brazil seems well poised to continue
to build strong political and economic institutions (*The Economist*,
2006b, p. 31).[43]

The Inequality of Regressive 'Redistributive' Policies

One of the most striking situations in several countries is not so much the
existence but the apparent extent of public policies and of public expenditures which are actually regressive and adversely affect income redistribution and poverty reduction efforts. It would be naïve to assume that the fast
pace of growth of public expenditure and of social expenditures in particular, which has taken place in Latin America in the last 10 years, would not
be vulnerable to 'capture' by some public and private sector rent-seekers.
What is surprising is that significant amounts of resources are actually
openly allocated to benefit not the poorest segments of the population, but
low and middle income class groups. This is not done in hiding but under

the guise of allegedly being redistributive and pro-poor. Apparently the real poor have little political clout.

In Brazil and Colombia and to a lesser extent in Costa Rica a significant portion of transfers to finance pensions and to subsidize the allegedly low income groups actually end up in the hands of middle and even upper income groups. This can happen under two interdependent conditions. One, very asymmetric information permitting the surreptitious capture of transfers taking place behind the back of an uninformed public. The other, a permissive or soft budget constraint that lacks the right incentives for potential users of public funds to really exercise vigilance over who benefits from public expenditures.

The important policy implication is that you could reduce poverty levels and improve equity conditions without increasing the total level of public expenditure. But often it is less difficult to raise tax revenue further (like in Brazil or Colombia) than to confront the well organized political constituencies of those who are close to the decision making mechanisms and who can profit from regressive public expenditures. This reality underscores the fact that the provision of information on who benefits from public expenditures should be an integral part of a poverty reduction and equity improving strategy.

The 'Blame the External Avatars' Syndrome

From a political economy perspective and its inherent 'rational choice' foundation the decision making process[44] in a given country at some point in time may mean that what could be called the 'blame the external avatars' syndrome becomes politically attractive and acts as an incentive to delay reforms. As long as sudden stops or cycle reversals can be blamed on a third party or external mischief there will be an incentive to do so. It may become the preferred option in many cases. This is the essence of political rational choice, that is to be able to elude political accountability and to survive with the minimum political cost. This can be done if information is asymmetrically distributed between the public and the political leadership, and if the former can be manipulated within much 'bounded rationality'. Avoiding political accountability is part of the blaming game. Unfortunately it is also the way for a society to miss the learning game.

External shocks,[45] often in the form of 'sudden stops',[46] have been a major source of macroeconomic volatility in several Latin American countries in the last two decades. Sudden stops put to test the coordination capacity of macroeconomic arrangements. However, external shocks are not the source of macroeconomic volatility. Initial conditions are. Sudden stops just reveal the fragility of the domestic fiscal and financial systems.

External shocks, in the form of sudden stops, offer a good example of how a political economy explanation is at the bottom of the apparent permissiveness or imprudence with which some countries deal with their external financial vulnerability. Why, the question is often asked, do some Latin American countries fail to learn from history and often repeat the same mistake of excessively exposing themselves to external volatility?

Well, from a political economy perspective, in which rational choices respond to the real incentives, the answer is, why go through the hassle of preventive policies if, at the end of the day, the political consequences of the sudden stop can largely be blamed on external factors? Under this perspective, risk cannot play a stabilizing role and some countries will let things evolve to the limit (Wiesner, 1985, p. 193).[47] External vulnerability will be less a function of inherent financial underdevelopment and more a function of risk-taking under a perspective in which the costs of running excessive risks can be diluted in a vacuum of political accountability. In brief, vulnerability to external shocks becomes more a function of who can be blamed for the consequences of the shocks than a function of inherent and unavoidable domestic or external volatility.[48] 'Confidence is often the mirror image of moral hazard' (Tirole, 2002, p. 30).

The major policy implication is that it is very difficult to induce prudent and pre-emptive corrections on the basis of a theoretical counterfactual or actual history if the political incentives will not reward that posture. In trying to predict what will become actual policy making in some countries, more than a theoretical model guide, what would be needed would be to ascertain how well informed the public is and how effectively it can judge relative causalities and accountabilities.[49] Information becomes the incentive for the development of political accountability. Information is the shock absorber to assimilate sudden stops which are, to some extent, unavoidable in global capital markets.

Fiscal Deficits are not the Ultimate Culprit

Fiscal deficits explain much of Latin America's macroeconomic volatility over time. Notwithstanding this finding, the remedy to reduce this volatility will lie not so much in not having fiscal deficits, nor even in financing them, but in assuring the effectiveness of public expenditures and the existence of real and performing public assets backing the liabilities and public debt that those fiscal deficits gave rise to. Those public assets would be represented by, for example, lower poverty levels, improved distributive justice, market-enhancing public infrastructure and international competitiveness. The critical policy implication is that more than trying to lower fiscal deficits or even financing them, policy makers and multilateral institutions need to focus more on the complex political economy micro-institutional frameworks where the effectiveness of public expenditures is determined.

Rigorous empirical evaluations and better diagnostics of specific interventions will reveal the most binding constraints and who the real culprits may be (Hausmann et al., 2006, p. 13). This information will pave the way for more political tolerance for reforms and for institutional transformation. Fiscal deficits tend to be deleterious to the financial health of almost any country. However, the real essence of the political development challenge in most countries in Latin America lies in incurring fiscal deficits and not having, on aggregate, the corresponding public assets and not understanding why those assets are not performing or why the public expenditures those fiscal deficits financed were ineffective.

Fiscal deficits and the quality or effectiveness of public expenditure can be linked in complex direct and reverse causalities. You can have fiscal deficits that do not lead to loss of effectiveness and you can have very ineffective public expenditures precisely because you incur fiscal deficits. In the first case you may be having a deliberate fiscal deficit for expansionary and transitory reasons, while keeping in place the budget institutions and other ancillary instruments to preserve a level of effectiveness in your public expenditures. In the second case, you may be having a situation in which the expansion of unanticipated fiscal deficits results from weak budget institutions and induces further deterioration in the quality control of public expenditures. The underlying explanation for both developments is the quality of the institutional fiscal and budgetary infrastructure. The fiscal deficits, in principle and by themselves, are not the culprits. They are the manifestations or expressions of deeper problems.

First and Second Political Economy Fiscal Insights

Most scholars[50] rightly relate political and institutional factors (such as cycles, public choices, common pool problems, party systems, interest groups, opportunism, information asymmetries, 'wrong' incentives and collective action problems in general) to the size and sign of fiscal outcomes. This is all fine.[51] This is what could be called 'the first institutional insight'. It was a major finding linking fiscal institutional arrangements to fiscal results. But it may be incomplete in the sense of what matters the most, namely, in relating those political and institutional factors not so much to the size of public spending, nor even to fiscal deficits, but to the effectiveness and quality of public spending. This is what has real distributional implications for long term institutional transformation and development. A proposed 'second institutional insight' would be that the micro-institutional arrangements – where the money is actually spent – are the ones that really determine overall resource allocation effectiveness and distributional results (Wiesner, 1998, p. 115; 2003a, p. 20). The policy implications of this 'second institutional insight' are momentous. It means that countries, in principle, should not just spend more on social sectors in the hope that they will reduce poverty. They have first or simultaneously to change the micro-institutional incentive structures within which social spending takes place. This is a more formidable political challenge than raising taxes to finance more social spending. Perhaps they need to do both.

These latter implications are the key ones from a long term developing countries perspective. These aspects have been underestimated. Almost every political party, any multilateral institution and many well intentioned social scientists insist that developing countries should spend more on social needs such as education, health, social security and pro-poor infra-structure. But seldom is enough consideration given to the meeting of the micro-institutional and incentive requirements for such expenditure to be really redistributive, pro-poor and pro-growth. Further, fiscal deficits and national debt are not 'bad' in themselves. What is 'bad' is not having 'cor-responding' performing assets on the other side of the equation or balance sheet. The existence of such assets largely depends on the quality of public spending. And this quality is what matters from a poverty and income dis-tribution perspective. This, in its turn, is what determines the political via-bility of reforms. This is what may be taking place in Chile.

A further policy implication is that a 'tax and spend policy', even under a primary surplus fiscal framework, can lead to a 'bad' macroeconomic equilibrium in which you may not have destabilizing fiscal deficits but you stifle economic growth through high taxes and high real rates of interest. This may well be the current case of Brazil. Perhaps the most deleterious consequence is that since the real problem of the effectiveness of public expenditure has not been mitigated, social spending will not contribute to lower poverty and to the equalization of initial conditions. It may even be that some of that social public expenditure causes equity conditions to worsen, as is happening in Colombia and Brazil where some transfers and fiscal expenditures accrue to middle and even upper income groups.

The developmental and policy implications of the complex causalities between fiscal deficits, the effectiveness of public expenditures, equity and poverty dynamics, and political economy restrictions, cannot be exagger-ated. After all, this encapsulates the 'bad' macroeconomic and equity 'equilibrium' in which Latin America has cornered itself. With the excep-tion of Chile, during the last 10 years Latin America has substantially expanded its social public expenditures in real terms, but it has not been able to correspondingly or significantly improve poverty and equity con-ditions nor to elevate its rates of growth beyond the business cycle effects.

As a consequence, there is a loss of credibility in past reforms[52] and little political support for the pending ones. The growing fiscal deficits have not helped but the ultimate answer lies not so much in not having them but in assuring that there are public assets on the other column of the public balance sheet, in terms of, for instance, public goods infrastructure, improved distributive justice and international competitiveness.

The 'more social spending or more poverty' may well be a false dichotomy. It may even be that more social spending is hardly pro-poor. After all, in several countries social spending has been increased by more than 50 per cent in real terms in the last ten years and actual and corresponding gains by the poor and in social welfare in general have been difficult to confirm (Singh, 2006, p. 12).[53] This is an empirical question that needs to be answered in each country, *in situ*, in accordance with the specific micro-institutional incentive characteristics predominant in each particular case.[54] In the case of Colombia (Montenegro and Rivas, 2006, p. 20), 'most of the social expenditure, particularly for pensions, favors those with the higher incomes.'[55]

In Latin America what is particularly deleterious may not be the fiscal deficits just by themselves. What really matters is their not being sustainable. Such sustainability depends largely on the quality of public (particularly social) spending, and such quality depends enormously on political factors. This is the main reason why politics matter. Not only because politics can be linked to fiscal outcomes or even to deficits; the root causes of under-development are the previous historical, cultural and political conditions leading not so much to fiscal deficits but to wasteful public expenditures conducted under the 'wrong' micro-institutional arrangements.[56] This point was not missed by Vito Tanzi (2000, p. 93). Comparing income distribution dynamics between Southeast Asia and Latin America, he observed that: 'the main differences between the two countries' groups seem to lie in the incidence of benefits from public expenditure'. To enhance distributional effects he recommends 'improving institutional incentive structures, introducing rules rather than discretion, strengthening transparency and accountability, and strengthening budgetary procedures.'

Breaking the Constitutional Rules and the Re-election Syndrome in Latin America

A common thread across most Latin American countries that faced severe macroeconomic crisis in the last 10–15 years is the changing of the Constitutional rules to accommodate the re-election of an incumbent president. This could be called the 're-election syndrome'. In essence, it comprises the changes that can take place in the whole incentive structure of a given public sector and the effects those changes can have on the quality of economic policies, particularly in the management of the inherent risks in any policy choice. Since the mid-1990s the Constitutional rules restricting the re-election of the incumbent president in Brazil, Colombia, Argentina, Venezuela and Peru have been changed to facilitate and make possible the continuation of a given president.

The hypothesis is that when an incumbent president and his party seek re-election they will have intended and unintended incentives to vie for and 'buy' political support for their campaign through, *inter alia*, higher public spending and particular concessions to politically powerful groups. If needed, innovative fiscal accounting arguments will be found by well qualified economists who may feel, in good faith, that different judgments can be made to evaluate, for instance, a liquidity risk vis-à-vis a solvency one. However, larger fiscal deficits will not always be the result of higher spending, as often a 'tax and spend' strategy is the damage control response, and (as may be the case in Brazil) the net result can be a 'bad' or dysfunctional equilibrium in which growth is adversely affected by high tax rates and by high interest rates. What may be more arresting is that the additional social public spending does not necessarily improve distributive justice and may even worsen income distribution. This, in its turn, reinforces the political pressures for higher social public spending.

The point is not that re-election per se is questionable. After all, many developed and developing countries have it, but 'changing the rules within the game'[57] tends to engender the 'wrong' incentives (Buchanan, 1991, p. 39). Nor is the point that such changes are blatantly and necessarily out of the legal or political order. After all, constitutional frameworks need to have a constitutional procedure for amendments. The point is that if constitutional rules shape economic policy (Persson and Tabellini, 2004a, p. 94), 'bending' those rules under different ad hoc procedures does not augur well for the future preservation of self imposed restrictions. Changing the rules of the game within the game seldom leads to a higher welfare-inducing political 'game'. Institutional credibility is part and parcel of 'property rights' and this is one of the key requirements for development on which there is close to unanimity.

The fiscal data for these countries suggests that this has been largely the case. In all of them and for the relevant periods, public expenditures have grown much faster than GDP, public debt has risen as a percentage of GDP, and has done so over the relative size of the 'above the line' fiscal deficits. On the other hand, exchange rates have tended to appreciate, and downward price and wage flexibility has become more difficult. Although it is very difficult to isolate the effects of these particular developments and assign direct causalities for their emergence and consequences it would also be naïve to assume that the Constitutional rules can be broken or re-interpreted, through different semblances of legality, without this not compromising the quality of economic policy making. In the end, the 're-election syndrome' may well be what tips the policy balance and the decision making process in some critical choices in favor of risks that otherwise would not be assumed. A former Minister of Finance of Argentina put it well when he stated that 'it will be very difficult to maintain fiscal expenditures under control when the economy is growing at the rate of 6% on an annual basis; it will be even more difficult if the president is seeking reelection' (Machinea, 2002, p. 17). The possible political vigilance of those political forces that may oppose the expenditure policies over the re-election itself can be neutralized by short term interests. The surveillance of multilateral institutions is also weakened by the cooperative nature of those institutions vis-à-vis a member country.

Perhaps the maintenance of a minimum of democratic order in some Latin American countries demands a precarious balance between growing social expenditures, some updated form of 'caudillismo' and a tortuous learning process which, at the time, took many more years to evolve in today's developed democracies. Przeworski and Limongi (1993, p. 64) aver that 'we do not know whether democracy fosters or hinders economic growth'. What this book suggests is that democracy and development in Latin America are currently impaired by enormous information gaps that conspire against the 'right' distributive and growth policies.

The Political Economy of Learning from History

All across Latin America a constant theme around the macroeconomic crisis of the last 10 years is the importance of lesson-taking and of improving economic policies with the learning from those experiences.[58] Prescribing that countries should learn is understandable. After all, it seems obvious that mistakes should not be repeated. Also, crises are often the only opportunity to really learn, as they put to test the existing nominal arrangements and reveal how and why they perform in a given way. But this normative posture assumes that lesson-taking is a politically neutral exercise. It also assumes that it is a technically neutral undertaking. Furthermore, it assumes that mainstream evaluation requirements have been met and that, therefore, even under less than politically pure circumstances, the evaluation of processes and of results appears credible and robust. Reality is quite different. It is so because the incentives driving different evaluation exercises and the attendant lesson-taking are quite different for each individual actor and for each institutional[59] and conceptual realm.[60] This reality will not change and is part of the ongoing interchange and 'game' between different interests and visions.[61] There are varied incentives between the blaming game and the learning game.

To deal with this situation and to actually enhance the credibility of different lesson-taking exercises, the first requirement is to have *ex ante* evaluable history.[62] Other evaluability requirements will include (i) traceable decision making processes; (ii) initial falseable hypotheses; (iii) quantified base and end line scenarios; (iv) specific verifiability mechanisms and rules for accountability. Without evaluable history, technical, institutional and political accountability is nearly impossible. The 'right' incentives for accountability will not be there. Actually, in most cases, what will evolve will be the 'wrong' incentives in the form of ambiguous arrangements and even 'contracts'. Even accepting that evaluable history itself is not a perfectly neutral exercise, transparent evaluation frameworks can be constructed 'behind the veil of ignorance'[63] and to which most interested parties can agree and commit. The policy implication is that applied research by independent domestic and international research centers, by 'think-tanks' and by evaluation offices in multilateral institutions, has a major role to play in the generation of better diagnostics and new information, and in the dissemination of results for the public at large and for the political process. The key point is that what matters is the plurality of information sources and the role of the information markets in and informing the political process.

VIII. CONCLUSIONS AND POLICY IMPLICATIONS

Although the formal institutional characteristics of Latin American macroeconomic frameworks do not differ substantially, inter-country macroeconomic performance varies significantly. The explanation lies in the different degrees of political demand for macroeconomic stability. Political demand appears to be the main and ultimate independent explanatory variable and the key source of the effectiveness of the real institutional characteristics. Any country can nominally adopt inflation targeting. The real test is to have enough 'fear of inflation' to then provide political support for the 'right' interest rate, fiscal and exchange rate policies. The policy implication is that to enhance macroeconomic performance, the strategy would be to focus more on the underlying determinants of the political demand for macroeconomic stability than on nominal compliance with 'stylized' institutional characteristics. Information and a well informed society are the critical underlying determinants of the demand for macroeconomic stability and performance. Information is the critical algorithm that links together the demand for macroeconomic stability, macroeconomic performance and, ultimately, distributive justice.

With all its mighty capacity to create serious problems, fiscal deficits in Latin America are not the main explanation for this region's economic, political and social woes. Underdevelopment is not the result of fiscal deficits. It is the result of the political economy difficulties these countries have in assuring a minimum effectiveness out of their public expenditures in general and of their pro-equity ones in particular. The policy implication is that reform and research priorities should focus more on making the 'right' diagnostics, identifying the 'wrong' incentives and understanding the micro-institutional and political economy restrictions that afflict and restrict the effectiveness of public expenditures than on financing the fiscal deficits. After all, Latin America has been able to finance its fiscal deficits and its expanding levels of public expenditure for decades and does not have much to show for this in terms of growth, macroeconomic stability or equity gains. The real priority is overcoming those restrictions. Once that is largely done, the financing, even the deficit financing, does not necessarily pose insurmountable macroeconomic challenges. The fiscal deficits will have the backing of some public and social assets and of the credibility of the public sector.

The key political economy implication is that further gains in reducing poverty and 'unfairness perception' are indispensable to obtain political support for pending fiscal and financial structural reforms. This means pro-growth and pro-poor policies will need to work in tandem, complement each other and be seen and perceived as deliberate political efforts to bring about distributive justice and a more 'fair' collective environment.[64] Since asymmetrical information between the 'losers and winners' of reforms is a major political economy restriction, the strategy to gain more political support for those reforms needs to be anchored in strategic and independent research agendas to generate new information to the general public. These evaluations will focus on the key micro-institutional arrangements where public policies and markets need to complement each other, such as education, health, social security and information generation.

The Transaction Costs Origins of Policy Reform and Institutions

To many politicians in Latin America the political transaction costs of supporting policy reform and institutional transformation appear to exceed the potential lower economic transaction costs resulting from those reforms. Under these circumstances there will be insufficient political incentives for them to take the initiative to defend a given reform proposal. The status quo will tend to prevail with its existing incentive framework until a demand-induced approach emerges, pressing for reform and for institutional change. But where will that demand for change come from? How will it be known, and to whom, that lower transaction costs are possible? In brief, where will the political incentives to accept reform and to propose change come from? The short answer is from information. But where will information come from? Why will it emerge?

Information is a function of many possible factors such as history, experience, the learning patterns of societies, research, comparisons across countries and the results of evaluations of the effectiveness of interventions. Information appears as the ultimate independent variable. Governments and multilateral institutions can take the initiative to promote the creation and dissemination of information or can remain passive. In the end, the inescapable tautological answer is that they will adopt one or the other posture, depending on the perceived incentives to do either one.

In Chile the current political incentives reward macroeconomic stability. In Peru the political incentives are in a fluid state, but in mid-2006 they did not reward the macroeconomic performance of the last five years. In Costa Rica the political incentives seem to reward political and economic policy ambiguity. In Colombia there may be some incipient political incentives to reward or protect macroeconomic stability but there is political confusion as to how precisely to do so. In Brazil there is a dual situation, in which political incentives protect macroeconomic stability but a very high level of public expenditure for well over ten years seems also to be necessary to preserve that support.

Few, if any, factors can explain Latin America's macroeconomic volatility better than the very limited capacity of its fiscal institutions to play a countercyclical role and to smooth out business cycles.[65] On the contrary, fiscal policy and, at times, even monetary policy, have played a pro-cyclical role accentuating the severity of external shocks (Birdsall and Dervis, 2006, p. 8).[66] Changing this homegrown vulnerability will involve, *inter alia*, transforming the fiscal institutions in a similar way to that in which independent Central Banks reformed monetary policy making. In other words, there is a major need to nurture fiscal reforms to play a countercyclical role. Probably there is no other more pressing reform priority in the region.

If the political demand for macroeconomic stability and for the reforms that tend to deliver it, is the main explanatory variable of macroeconomic stability and performance, what then is the source or origin of such political demand? How then can such political demand be created or nurtured? The short answer is that new information[67] revealing the high transaction costs (Williamson and Masten, 1999, p. xi) that a given country may be paying, for example, 'acceptable' inflation, for volatility,[68] for unsustainable fiscal deficits or for inequitable social expenditures,[69] will be the basis for the political demand for that country's particular institutional transformation.[70] This political demand contains the political incentives to respond to it. Under this context the central recommendation for multilaterals is to further support, through strategic evaluations and 'research partnerships', the generation of new performance information and empirical work (Alcorn and Solarz, 2006, p. 46) in the areas comprising the interface between pro-growth and pro-poor policies.

Selected strategic research-based evaluations in partnerships with established Latin American and international research centers can and need to be robustly expanded to provide new empirical findings to inform policy and to get the diagnosis right (Hausmann et al., 2006, p. 13).[71] There is a major need to give further empirical support to the alleged failure of some of the so-called Washington Consensus[72] policy reforms. There is the grave risk that a Gresham law in reverse (Guidotti and Rodríguez, 1992, p. 518) will take hold and inadequate pro-poor reforms prevail over more proven and 'satisficing'[73] pro-poor and pro-growth 'right' reforms. This is not an ideological problem. It is an information and political problem. The clue is to inform political markets about the potential incentives and rewards that can be harvested from much-needed reforms and institutional transformations.

A more specific recommendation related to the key area of fiscal policy is for Latin American policy makers to consider nurturing and developing a 'Fiscal and Budget Authority' analogous, but *mutatis mutandis* in some institutional characteristics, to the 'autonomous central banks' created since the mid-1990s. This would be the way to complete the necessary dual and complementary institution needed to enhance the consistency of monetary policy, fiscal and budget policy. A 'similar' institutional development is also needed for the financial sector supervision. Much of this latter evolution is already well in process in several countries in the region.

If inequality is conducive to growth-retarding policies, then lowering poverty levels and improving access by the poor to public and private goods should engender political support for the 'right' pro-growth and pro-poor policies. But this is largely comparative static analysis between high and low poverty levels. The challenge is, how do you actually move from one stage to the other? How do you nurture the political demand for those 'right' policies? The answer is with information on the existing transaction costs of inefficient interventions. Information is the crux of it all. It should be remembered that the explanation for institutional transformation and for the demand for (the 'right') institutions is the awareness of existing high transaction costs and the potential for gains from lower transaction costs under a different institutional arrangement. In other words, by and large, the political demand for policy reform and for institutional transformation originates in the incentives to economize on transaction costs.

This was the seminal Coasean insight.[74] At the private sector level the information on transaction costs flows autonomously from the incentives of competition. But in the public sector and in the provision of public goods, this information does not emerge spontaneously. It needs the explicit support of governments (and of multilaterals) in the discharge of their responsibilities in assuring competition in public and private markets. In brief, the essence of the strategy to nurture the political demand for policy reform and for the 'right' macroeconomic and micro-institutional arrangements is to develop new information to reveal the transaction costs environment of the relevant intervention level.

One possible example could be Brazil. This country was twice rescued from the 1998 and 2002 crises by the adept use of information from the authorities to the public on how it was going to confront the crisis. Institutional credibility saved the day. Now, again, it would seem that to overcome the 'bad' macroeconomic equilibrium in which it finds itself, information could be the deux ex machina. The authorities could 'inform' the public what they intend to do to grow at a faster rate and to assure that public expenditures have full redistributive effects.

This may sound like naïve[75] recommendations which assume that the government is a benevolent guardian of the public welfare and seldom 'captured' by special interests.[76] However, in some countries in Latin America and in other regions, it has been possible for some politicians to find political 'positive' incentives to take political positions to actually enhance the effectiveness of public interventions in general and expenditures in particular. This is not so much out of altruism[77] or social enlightenment but because the political incentives and potential rewards for self-interested[78] reasons have become attractive enough.[79] It is important to realize that this recommendation in favor of more information is targeted not so much at what Latin American countries should do in terms of policy reform or of institutional transformation. That is pretty much already known. Take the case of the prevention of currency crisis: to reduce this risk, Feldstein (2003, p. 10) summarizes five primary ways in which a country can reduce its exposure. They are:

i.   Avoiding an overvalued currency by allowing the currency's value to float;
ii.   maintaining a substantial level of foreign exchange reserves;
iii. keeping short-term foreign exchange liabilities low relative to reserves;
iv.   maintaining a sound banking system; and
v.   avoiding large amounts of dollar-denominated debt, especially the debt of the private sector.

Most policy makers and economists from different political perspectives will tend to agree with these policies. The challenge is to unbundle and characterize the specifics needed in each country for each particular historical context and circumstance. The challenge is to identify and endogenize the particular country-specific political economy restrictions that impede the adoption of these policies. To do this, rigorous *in situ* applied research is indispensable. Furthermore, as Feldstein (2003, p. 10) wisely warns, 'all that countries can do to protect themselves is to avoid the policies that caused crisis in the past'. To anticipate new conditions that may create new causes of crisis, even more rigorous applied 'local' research is needed.

In conclusion, the source of the political demand for institutional transformation, on the one hand, and for the eventual supply response of (the 'right') institutions, and policies, on the other, is the awareness of high transaction costs as well as of potentially lower ones. This has been the experience at the industry and firm levels in public and private markets in developed and some developing countries. The concluding recommendation of this book on the informational origins of demand driven institutional change and policy reform is not a naïve one. It aims at nothing more than meeting what North (1990, p. 108) calls the 'institutional rationality postulate of neoclassical theory' in the sense that all interventions have the information and institutional framework necessary for achieving the 'desired ends'.[80]

Another distinguished Nobel prize winner put it in these terms: 'One of the most important determinants of the pace of growth is the acquisition of knowledge' (Stiglitz, 2002a, p. 483). Finally, Rodrik (2006, p. 986), makes the perceptive point that to understand the economics of reform one should 'be skeptical of top-down, comprehensive, universal solutions – no matter how well intentioned they may be. And it reminds us that the requisite economic analysis – hard as it is, in the absence of specific blueprints – has to be done case by case.'[81]

The Policy Implications of Inter-country Comparisons

Besides a consideration for economic size and for some degree of geographical representation, the country cases were selected largely on the basis of their relative capacity to inform general policy and broad principles through the consequences of their different approaches to macroeconomic management in general and to sudden stops in particular. The idea was to seek policy guidelines with general validity and relatively unencumbered by particular country economic and political histories. What mattered was to try to extract policy conclusions that were relatively independent of specific political histories or particular economic situations. In other words, to control for particular political factors and to focus on generally valid principles.

On the whole, the comparative analysis across the selected countries revealed that, although there are institutional differences in the macroeconomic arrangements and reform processes at the end of the day, the ultimate explanation for the differences in their economic performance has more to do with the degree of compliance with some hard core macroeconomic and microeconomic principles than with their own particular economic and political histories The policy implication is enormous. Countries have some degrees of freedom. They have the option of some choices. Although the applicability or replicability of 'universal' reform approaches is limited by particular 'local' and endogenous conditions, the access to fundamental principles is relatively unimpeded. All countries may claim to want macroeconomic stability, low inflation and distributive justice, but to actually achieve it a modicum of compliance with those hard core principles has to prevail over some critical 'local' political economy restrictions. This is the challenge.

Chile's relative success is probably explained more by the long-standing quality of its public institutions and by its fiscal rules and aversion to inflation than by any other local or history-specific factors. Brazil has also become a country that is afraid of inflation and this may explain its 'tax and spend' policies to at least protect its fiscal balance. Argentina was not able to overcome the weaknesses of its political framework and paid a huge price for it. It is not yet clear that its political institutions are finally aligned with its long term welfare interests. Peru seems to have been able to learn from past mistakes but is still vulnerable to external volatility. Colombia is now also a country afraid of inflation, and has known the severity of a deep recession. But it has not been able to adopt a strong fiscal institutional framework largely because there is political confusion about how precisely to avoid fiscal deficits, to control the growth of social public expenditures and to assure that such expenditures are actually redistributive. Finally, Costa Rica is facing very difficult long term issues as its traditional compromising approach may no longer suffice to meet rapidly changing external and internal circumstances. In brief, countries do not need to have similar 'local' conditions or political histories to enhance their economic performance. In fact, they seldom do. But they need to overcome their own political restrictions to capitalize on well established macroeconomic and political competition core principles with great potential to deliver better standards of living.

A first general conclusion with ample empirical support is that the region as a whole seems unable or unwilling to resist political pressures for growing social expenditures even if they hardly favor the poor, and in spite of the macroeconomic risks such fiscal policies involve. The policy implication is momentous. It would mean that real political power in Latin

America is more in the hands of those who benefit from social public expenditures than in the hands of an unidentified 'elite'. It would question the often held view in some academic and political quarters (Acemoglu, 2003a, p. 44)[82] that development in Latin America does not take firm hold because some 'elites' oppose change and are only interested in preserving their power.

The first question before any characterization of the role or intent of any 'elite', is to ask 'what is the most binding restriction on development?' Whoever holds the control of that restriction is the truly relevant enabling political power. The culprit cannot be an 'elite' in general terms, but one *ex ante*, defined by its capacity to control the most critical obstacle to development. In forensic terms, the indictment cannot come before the definition of the transgression. Under the assumption that such restriction is the demand for macroeconomic stability and that such demand, in its turn, depends on equity conditions and fairness perception, then, whoever restricts the contribution of social expenditure to improve distributive justice, that person or group, is the opposing 'elite'. In Latin America those groups are, on the whole, the public sector rent-seekers who control the micro-institutional arrangements in which most social public expenditures take place. Those groups may not be the oligarchies to which Acemoglu and Robinson (2006b, p. 329) were referring. This is the analytical sequence required to move the reform process forward: to first identify and define, as Rodrik and Hausmann put it, the most binding constraint and then to unbundle the incentives driving public policies. The specific solution or mitigation of that constraint will come from applied and empirical research for each particular sector, policy or country.

A second general conclusion with regional applicability is that although there is political demand for low inflation, this does not necessarily mean that there is attendant political demand for the ingredients or inputs of a fully integrated and consistent macroeconomic framework; one comprising fiscal, financial, exchange and interest rate management. This is largely an asymmetric information problem. People can easily perceive inflation, but fiscal deficits or high rates of interest or excessive indebtedness can go on undetected for a while. After all, it should be remembered that the process that brought about the current low levels of inflation in most countries was more an unintended severe disinflation and collapse of growth than a deliberate and intended political commitment to tame inflation, even if that meant fiscal constraint. In brief, it may be too soon to claim that Latin America has finally arrived at a fully fiscally backed aversion to inflation or to a full comprehension of the requirements integral to macroeconomic policy making. This will be better ascertained once the current favorable external financial and commodity cycle comes to an end.[83]

Fiscal Trends and Social Spending

Although primary fiscal balances have increased in the region since 2002, this has been more the result of surging revenues from higher commodity prices than from expenditure constraint (Clements et al., 2007, p. 5). When primary balances are rising because revenues grow fast they do not have the same policy implication as when they take place within a long term 'structural' revenue perspective. They do not have, in particular, the same political implications. After all, political pressures for growing expenditures are being met independently of all the difficult work needed to make such expenditures sustainable and really effective. In other words, there are no political costs in having transitory primary surpluses. It simply may mean that the surge in revenues was so fast or unanticipated that even a historical proclivity towards higher levels of spending was not able to arrange for those expenditures to take place right away. Primary expenditures have trended upwards and continue to follow a procyclical pattern, and public debt ratios at the end of 2006 remain at about 50 per cent of GDP, a ratio similar to the one prevailing in the mid-1990s. In brief, debt burden remains a challenge and a serious risk to macroeconomic stability. Procyclical fiscal policy has prevented a significant decline of public debt and the attendant reduction in macroeconomic vulnerability.

Social spending has been growing as a share of GDP since the mid-1990s through 2004. Although in more recent years it may have fallen slightly, real total outlays have continued to rise. If social spending were to actually favor the poor this would be a welcomed process contributing to acclimatize proposals for policy reform. However, while social spending absorbs a large share of total government outlays (about 13 per cent of GDP), inefficiencies in public spending restrict the redistributive impact on the poor. As Clements et al. (2007, p. 22) observe, 'poverty rates remain high and are the region's most glaring development lag. At an estimated 41 per cent of the population in 2005, poverty exceeds the level predicted by the region's level of development'.

There are two key policy implications from this broad picture. First, the equity versus the political demand for policy reform remains largely a valid restriction. In spite of social spending attempts to improve poverty conditions through growing social expenditures, at the end of the day, the 'wrong' incentive public sector environment conspires against significant gains in poverty reduction and in equity in general. In brief, more social spending appears to have been an incomplete response to the equity challenge. The second and quite worrisome policy implication is that the current rate of growth of public revenues does not seem sustainable. If the international current high price commodity and financial liquidity cycles were to moderate, not an unlikely event, this would probably force a reduction in the rate of growth of total expenditures and (although not necessarily) of social spending as well. If this happens before the coalescing of current reform processes to improve the incentive structures of social expenditures, the poor would be the major losers and political pressures for their protection will intensify. The risk is that much-needed reforms will then face even stronger political resistance than up to now. The region, on the whole, could be back to the vicious cycle of insufficient political demand for policy reform because equity conditions and inadequate pro-poor public expenditure are not delivering the 'right' political incentives. As Calvo (2006) has summarized it,

> Inequality causes political tension, which causes politicians to pursue policies that cater to the poor by taxing capital, which induces capital flight, which lowers growth. Eventually, the situation gets so bad that even left-of-center governments change policies and adopt a more market oriented approach. This works for a while. You get increased growth but income distribution deteriorates again. That is the story and seems to fit the facts. It is a real trap. It is not clear how you get out of it.

IX.   THE DEMAND APPROACH FOR A POLICY REFORM STRATEGY

A strategy for policy reform and for institutional transformation can be developed from the following interdependent sequenced questions: (i) is there a political demand for reforms and for institutional change? (ii) is there political support for the measures to actually make the change? and (iii) is there an appropriate supply response? These questions are, on the whole, the pillars of the demand approach to economic reform and to institutional change with its focus on the recognition that transaction costs can be lower and that there are political incentives and rewards for those who achieve institutional change.

The first question deals with the political and economic demand for policy and institutional transformation. Usually the markets will be the first to adumbrate that something is amiss. They will manifest themselves through market signals such as inflation, exchange rate pressures and unemployment. The public's response against inflation will most likely be to demand a restoration of price stability. This will largely satisfy the first condition . . . Then, the second one is triggered in the sense that the public may demand price stability but eschew political support for the policies conducive to sustainable price stability. Maybe it has different views and fragmented interests as to how to go about it. Maybe it hopes to have it several ways, to have price stability but continued fiscal deficits or an appreciated exchange rate. The third condition then enters through the door of the 'right' supply response in the sense that the whole policy approach is consistent and sustainable. This will mean that there is potentially a different institutional arrangement (like a decentralized Central Bank) that will deliver price stability with much lower overall transaction costs than the previous arrangement.

Depending on the economic and political history of each country as well as on the balance of who loses and who wins (the distributive conflict) there will be more of one specific supply response than another. Each sector or political constituency will press for the protection of its interests through the discussion of 'how' to implement the attendant changes. Notwithstanding the specifics of this political struggle, the design of a strategy for reform and for institutional transformation can be planned through a combination of the following three tracks: (i) a macro-constitutional rules-based framework; (ii) a micro-institutional 'contractarian' incentive-intensive process; and (iii) a politically 'opportunistic' approach.

The first line of development is built on the empirical finding that 'Constitutional rules shape economic policy' (Persson and Tabellini, 2004a, p. 94) as well as on the Rawlsian 'behind the veil' and 'away from the immediate interests' principle. The idea is that although few political processes can remain hidden or in secret, it is possible to design some Constitutional rules that will elicit some political support if the constituencies do not see themselves threatened – but rather protected – by some principles which theory and experience suggest can deliver a more efficient social framework. The division of powers is the key Constitutional rule to induce *inter alia* political competition and a major role for checks and balances in all markets. In principle there is relatively less political opposition to this approach than to, say, more taxes or less public expenditure.

The second line of development will imply an intensive use of principal–agent contracts and incentives to resolve policy problems where market competition is not the predominant environment. This is the characteristic of most public markets where many activities are delegated ones and competition has to be deliberately inserted through 'contractual' incentives. The third line to approach the reform strategy is to 'opportunistically' seize on the particular political demand for transformation that may exist, vis-à-vis a given social problem, and to build around it a politically viable 'second best' policy reform process. This alternative is, of course, not risk-free, but policy makers can seldom choose the optimum or wait for the 'right' political demand for the most strategic long term problem.

These three lines of strategy development are not mutually exclusive and they can complement each other in several policy areas. On the whole the broad strategy is to work on information creation and dissemination of information. The assumption is that people respond to incentives, and although acting from a 'bounded rationality' they will tend to vote and favor their interests. Information is the key public good to assure that such pursuit of individual interests takes place in political and economic markets where there is growing competition. Competition is the ultimate 'right' institution. There are two final components of a reform strategy. First, to unmask the 'wrong' institutions, because that will reveal who opposes the reform process and why. Secondly, a good reform strategy never assumes that normative approaches will work.

NOTES

1. Glaeser (2005).
2. 'In the early stages of rapid economic development, when inequalities in the distribution of income among different classes, sectors, and regions are apt to increase sharply, it can happen that society's tolerance for such disparities will be substantial. To the extent that such tolerance comes into being, it accommodates, as it were, the increasing inequalities in an almost providential fashion. But this tolerance is like a credit that falls due at a certain date. It is extended in the expectation that eventually the disparities will narrow again. If this does not occur, there is bound to be trouble and, perhaps, disaster.' See Hirschman (1973, p. 545).
3. On 'access' by the poor and by the middle class to micro-institutional finance, see Raghuram Rajan (2006, p. 57). He points out the critical importance of infrastructure and technology in bringing down transaction cost in all financial processes.
4. Following Popper (1965), one cannot really prove a hypothesis. One can only fail to disprove it. This is the way science and knowledge advances, by successfully replacing transitory paradigms (Khun, 1970). The key condition is that the hypothesis be falsifiable. According to Friedman (1953, pp. 8, 9), 'Viewed as a body of substantive hypotheses, theory is to be judged by its predictive power for the class of phenomena which it is intended to "explain".'
5. According to Riccardo Viale (1997, p. 19) the importance of the initial hypothesis lies 'in the way it directs and shapes the research'.
6. Roberto Perotti (2005, p. 273) distinguishes between 'social services (for example education and health), social insurance (for example old age and invalidity pensions and unemployment insurance), social assistance (cash transfers to the poor, family assistance benefits, maternity benefits, in-kind transfers) and employment generating programs.'
7. Generally speaking, policies and 'economic institutions are decided by groups or individuals that possess more political power. Political power, in turn, consists of de jure power regulated by formal political institutions and de facto political power, which comes from the ability of various different social groups to solve their collective action problems, lobby or bribe politicians, capture and control political parties, or use para-militaries or other means of repression.' See Acemoglu and Robinson (2006b, p. 56).
8. Eduardo Sarmiento (2005, p. 10) argues that 'Latin America's macroeconomic instability results from the fiscal proclivity of the Balance of Payments and from external indebtedness at "rates of interest which are higher than the rate of growth."'
9. Discussing fiscal sustainability, Richard Bird (2006, p. 92) advises that 'indicators of a government's relative degree of fiscal sustainability need to extend beyond outcomes to take into account both initial conditions and processes and structures'.
10. Optimal 'monetary policy should be conducted so as to keep nominal interest rates close to zero'. See Chari and Kehoe (1999, p. 1673). Zero nominal interest rates, however,

would create serious challenges for monetary policy. After all, the real rate of interest must be positive in the long run.

11. On whether fiscal policy should be part of the 'flexibility' or of the 'discretion', Stanley Fischer (2000, p. 6) observes that 'A purist, a constitutionalist, will say that monetary policy deals with inflation, while fiscal policy deals with the current account; so, if the fiscal authorities are not doing their job, that is not the concern of the central banker. And if the economy goes into a crisis, then we will all blame fiscal policy. That is a nice a priori approach, but it does not resolve the issue.'

12. 'A lack of correlation between deficits and inflation might be naively interpreted as indicating that inflation is somewhat driven by something other than the government's fiscal policy and that it has a life of its own' (see Burnside, 2005, p. 18).

13. Edwin M. Truman (2003, p. 50) avers that 'if the government cannot finance its operations in the market and requires uncertain but substantial amounts of direct central bank financing, including revenues from seigniorage, to meet its domestic obligations, then it is risky for the country to adopt inflation targeting as its monetary policy framework. The reason is that in such an environment – often referred to as fiscal dominance – a country's fiscal requirements rather than other objectives are likely to determine and dominate the central bank's monetary operations. If those needs force too expansionary a monetary policy on the central bank, because the central bank is constrained to finance an excessively large fiscal deficit, the inflation target will be more difficult to achieve.'

14. John B. Taylor (2000, p. 22) suggests that to consider discretionary fiscal policy 'one has to have a model that describes how the instruments of monetary and fiscal policy affect the economy'.

15. Alesina and Tabellini (2005, p. 23) find that credit constraints and the 'malfunctioning' of credit markets 'makes it hard or impossible for developing countries to borrow exactly when they need it more, in bad times. But this argument fails to explain why welfare maximizing governments don't take this into account, building up reserves in good times, so as to avoid being credit constrained in bad times. Moreover, our evidence suggests that procyclicality is more often driven by a distorted policy reaction to booms, rather than to recessions. And whatever procyclical policy response there is to recessions, does not seem to be explained by available measures of credit constraints.'

16. Prospect theory is a 'positive' theory of decision making under uncertainty 'but it does not tell us how people will spontaneously create their own frameworks' (Thaler, 2000, p. 137).

17. 'Under a "hindsight bias", events that happened are thought to have been predictable', see Thaler (2000, p. 138).

18. Multilateral institutions are afflicted by restrictions emerging from the collective action environment in which they perform, see Wiesner (2007).

19. According to Dani Rodrik (1996, p. 189), 'multilateral lending has no independent economic rationale. It is needed only insofar as policy monitoring and conditionality cannot be performed adequately unless backed by credits from multilaterals sources. In other words, lending plays a subsidiary role to the informational functions.' The information role appears to be the critical one.

20. See Edwin Truman (2006b, p. 31) for an in-depth analysis of the role of the IMF.

21. On the role of multilaterals see Taylor (2003, p. 41). In his view these institutions should focus on raising productivity. Governance improvement is part of that process.

22. Daniel Titelman (2004, p. 341) thinks that multilateral banks can play a major role as conduits or catalyzes for the provision of private resources.

23. According to Chhibber (2006b, p. xxiii), 'Conditionality as we know it does not work. If the policymakers are persuaded, conditionality is not needed, and if they are not persuaded, conditionality does not work; therefore, it is important to try to shift more to outcome-based support rather than to old style ex ante conditionality. There are instances where even within a reforming government a full consensus may not exist on all aspects of reform, its timing, or sequencing. In such cases, the more reform-minded parts of the government may find conditionality an expedient mechanism to carry their colleagues in government along – there are several instances where this has worked – but it must be used carefully.'

24. Eduardo Wiesner (1984, p. 241) avers that 'conditionality has its origins in the scarcity of resources and nowhere else. It is its inevitable by-product. It is a positive and not a normative product.'
25. For the particular case of Colombia, R. Javier Fernández (2006, p. 2) observes that financing from the IMF has allowed the government to overspend and has weakened the fiscal structure of the country. See also Mauricio Cabrera (2006, p. 30), who posits that the fiscal deficit in Colombia has remained at a 6 per cent of GDP level for seven years.
26. Miguel Urrutia (2006, p. 67) underscores the importance of the 'relationships between macroeconomics and Bank program'.
27. See Salomón Kalmanovitz (2005, pp. 1, 2). He posits that in the case of Colombia the IMF's 'seal of approval' meant that the country could go on borrowing without sufficient real adjustment.
28. See Jean Tirole (2002, p. 123) for an excellent discussion of the collective action problems between multilaterals and countries.
29. Francisco Sagasti and Fernando Prada (2004, p. 269) point out that the World Bank has 'negative flows' with Latin America in this situation. They think multilateral banks have played a positive role in the development of Latin America.
30. In discussing ways through which countries can get back into international capital markets José Luis Machinea (2004, p. 192) underscores the importance of the 'coordination problem' arising from the existence of conflicting interests and incentives in the part of numerous bank creditors.
31. José Antonio Ocampo (2005c, p. 19) thinks that the 'first role of international financial institutions, from the point of view of developing countries, is to counteract the pro-cyclical effects of financial markets'.
32. In the case of Colombia, for instance, the IMF helped 'resolve' the issue of who within the government is responsible for fiscal measurements.
33. Joaquín Levy (2006, p. 102) considers that 'conditionality has to strengthen the domestic institutional capacity of countries'.
34. On reforming the IMF see Truman (2006c, p. 124). Truman's recommendations are as follows: '(i) In the crucial area of governance, the membership of the IMF should promptly address the reallocation of IMF shares (voting power) and the reallocation of chairs (representation on the IMF executive board), and it is time to discard the old conventions and to adopt a merit-based approach to the choice of the IMF's leadership, (ii) mechanisms should be put in place to increase the IMF's leverage over systemically important members, and the IMF must act more forcefully in discharging its responsibility to exercise firm surveillance over members' exchange rate policies; (iii) the Fund's central role in external financial crises should be reaffirmed; (iv) the IMF should narrow and refocus its involvement with its low-income members; (v) the IMF's activities should be updated with respect to members' capital account policies and financial sectors; and (vi) the IMF should put in place procedures for borrowing from the market to guard against the possibility that it will not receive timely increases in its quota resources.' See also Truman (2006a).
35. Desmond Lachman (2006, p. 472) relevantly points out the special character of the Fund as a 'lending cooperative'.
36. According to Ocampo (2005d, p. xvii), 'multilateral surveillance should focus not only on crisis-prone countries, but increasingly on the system as a whole; this implies a more central role for IMF in the management of the world economy.'
37. To Nouriel Roubini and Brad Setser (2004), a key element in dealing with financial crisis is to distinguish promptly between a liquidity and a solvency situation.
38. The Governor of the Central Bank of Argentina, Martin Redrado (2006, p. 277), opines that the 'the role of the IMF as a global provider of liquidity has proven to be problematic'.
39. On the differences between 'lender of final resort and lender of last resort', see Mussa (2006, p. 413).
40. In discussing the role of the G-7, Fred Bergsten (2006a, p. 280) underscores the importance of political factors influencing the global governance structure and global performance.

41. According to Jacques De Larosiere (2004, p. 29), 'a Managing Director should be able to say no to the G7, or to any other strong shareholder or grouping. This is a matter of authority and credibility for the international institutions'.
42. See Jean Tirole (2002, p. 30) for an excellent discussion of the trade-offs between *ex ante* (pre-crisis) incentives and *ex post* efficiency (satisfactory crisis resolution). 'Orderly workouts may conflict with the incentives of countries and investors to avoid crises. In other words, confidence is often the mirror image of moral hazard.'
43. According to *The Economist* (30 September, 6 October, 2006b, p. 31), 'Some Brazilians are not altogether downhearted, though. Their country may be growing more slowly than the other BRIC countries, but its institutions are sturdier, asserts Antonio Delfim Netto, a congressman from the centrist Party of the Brazil Democratic Movement.'
44. 'Policies depend not only on theories and evidence but also on the structure of policy-making bodies and the procedures by which policies are made, implemented, and changed' (Meltzer and Plosser, 1993, p. i).
45. See Bergsten and Williamson (2003) for volatility emerging from dollar overvaluation.
46. Calvo et al. (2006, p. 405) offer the following conceptual definition of a sudden stop episode. Under a sudden stop 'the economy faces a sharp increase in international interest rates or outright exclusion from capital markets. Thus, the economy may be pushed to eliminate its current account deficit (CAD) or even generate a current account surplus. A current account surplus implies that the country would be paying back outstanding debt, whereas CAD is an indicator of the adjustment that the country may not be able to circumvent, even if it defaults on its outstanding debt. This is so, because CAD > 0 implies that the country is acquiring new debt, something that can occur only with the approval of creditors. This is not a decision that can be taken unilaterally like debt default. Thus, bringing CAD to zero is, in a way, the minimum adjustment that an economy must make if subject to a Sudden Stop.'
47. In the crisis of the 1980s risk perception played an important role in leading to volatility and restoring confidence. See Wiesner (1985, p. 193).
48. On the factors behind global capital flows volatility see Larrain (2000, p. 3).
49. An interesting question would be why some Asian countries do not seem to be so inclined to recur to the external avatars syndrome as a political excuse. Two answers are possible. Latin America may have a stronger relative tradition of 'imperialism' and populism. And, more importantly, Asian countries have less shallow financial sectors and thus better information on the 'states of nature'. This 'evaluable history' restricts the political exploitation of what actually are domestic and home grown external vulnerabilities.
50. See Alesina and Perotti (1995, 1999, p. 13); Alesina et al. (1997); Alesina et al. (1996); Acemoglu et al. (2006); Dixit (1996, p. 45); Drazen and Easterly (1999); Jones et al. (1999, p. 148); Persson and Tabellini (1999, 2004b); Perotti (1993); Poterba and von Hagen (1999, p. 5); Stein et al. (1999, p. 132); Velasco (1999, p. 39); Weingast (1995).
51. For an examination of the determinants of fiscal balances, that is, opportunistic behavior by policy makers, heterogenous fiscal preferences of voters or policy makers, and budget institutions, in developing countries, see Eslava (2006, p. 29).
52. For a review of the results of the reforms of the 1990s, see Zagha et al. (2006, p. 11).
53. Singh (2006, p. 12) observes that 'in many countries, too much spending continues to be directed to inefficient programs and too little is being directed toward the public infrastructure that will support growth and stability, or toward well-targeted social programs that can ensure that the benefits of growth are well distributed.'
54. This may be the sort of exogeneity problem which Professor Daron Acemoglu warns about (2005c, p. 1026) in the sense that causality relations amongst institutional arrangements pose daunting identification problems. Policy should not proceed just on the basis of association but only after the 'right' institutional characteristics have been unbundled from the diverse number of possibilities.
55. 'In Colombia 50% of social expenditures is received by the richest 40% of the population. The biggest challenge to make public expenditure more redistributive is the pension problem.' See Montenegro and Rivas (2006, p. 20).
56. For the case of Colombia see Eduardo Wiesner (2004b).

57.   'Central to the analysis of constitutional choice is a distinction between the "constitu-
      tional" and "in-period" level of decision making. The latter is choice within rules; the
      former is choice of the rules. Or, as James Buchanan sometimes puts it, constitutional
      choice is the choice among constraints in contrast to choice under constraints, which
      is the central preoccupation of ordinary economics.' See Brennan and Hamlin (2001,
      p. 117).
58.   See, for instance Cardoso, 2004, p. 13; Calvo et al., 2003, p. 38; Galiani et al., 2002, p. 20.
59.   For the requirements of evaluating partnerships see Feinstein et al. (2003, p. 121).
60.   See Picciotto (2000, p. 358) on the implications that institutional economics can have on
      evaluation.
61.   For the requirements for Country Program Evaluations see Peters (2006, p. 45).
62.   On the concept of 'evaluable history' see Wiesner (2004a, p. 5).
63.   This is the Rawlsian approach to uncertain future social choice preferences and out-
      comes. John Rawls (1971), in *A Theory of Justice*, develops the concept of the 'veil of
      ignorance' behind which welfare-enhancing results are the more likely policy outcome.
64.   Albert Berry (1998, p. 9) has observed that 'there is accumulating evidence that the
      market friendly policy shift since the 80's has been systematically associated with an
      abrupt and important deterioration of income distribution'.
65.   Referring to developing countries in general, Montiel and Servén (2006, p. 165)
      observe that 'fiscal procyclicality in developing countries peaked in the 1980s and
      declined somewhat over the 1990s – but still remains much higher than in industrial
      countries. Indeed, procyclical fiscal policy played a key role in some of the major crises
      of recent years, Argentina being a prime example (Mussa, 2002; Montiel and Servén,
      2006).
66.   Birdsall and Dervis (2006, p. 8) posit that 'the capital market shocks of the past 25 years
      in high-debt countries have undermined the capacity of their governments to develop
      and sustain the institution and programs they need to protect their own poor. With
      global market players doubting debt sustainability in many of the emerging-market
      economies at the time of any shock, countries are forced, as noted above, to resort to
      procyclical fiscal policy to reestablish market confidence. The procyclical austerity poli-
      cies that the global capital market demands are the opposite of what industrial
      economies implement when there is lack of growth – including not only reduced inter-
      est rates and increased public spending in general but also unemployment insurance,
      increased availability of food stamps, emergency public works employment, and other
      ingredients of a sound and permanent social safety net.'
67.   There is a link between asymmetric or limited information and market and macroeco-
      nomic volatility. To Akerlof (2002, p. 428), 'macroeconomics must be based on behav-
      ioral considerations' and as considerable theory and empirical research suggest,
      information plays a major role in behavior.
68.   Ricardo Ffrench-Davis (2005, p. 209) opines that better information and more rigorous
      financial regulation are 'public goods'.
69.   See Sebastian Mallaby (2005, p. A-21), 'Class matters', on the inequality of fiscal and
      social programs in the United States. He reports that 'In the United States in 1980 the
      top fifth of families earned 7.7 times as much as the bottom fifth; by 2001, that ratio had
      risen to 11.4. So even though the bottom fifth of households made modest gains, the
      inequality ratio jumped by almost 50 percent. If you measure inequality by wealth rather
      than earnings, the results are even more preposterous. Inequality in the United States is
      now more pronounced than in any other advanced country.'
70.   John Williamson (2004, p. 17) observes that 'exactly what form of institutions will best
      serve a country is not pinned down by economic analysis'.
71.   Reform strategies can have occult drawbacks, as Hausmann et al. (2006, p. 13) point out.
      To them, reform priorities should be 'based on the size of their direct effects. The idea
      behind this strategy is that, since the full list of requisite reforms is unknowable or
      impractical, and figuring out the second-best interactions across markets is a nearly
      impossible task, it is best to focus on the reforms whose direct effects are expected to be
      significant.'

72.   Moises Naim (2000, p. 100) observes that even after all the tribulations ascribed to the reforms of the 1990s, 'market reforms have exhibited a surprising resiliency in most countries'.
73.   Herbert Simon (1982), in his *Models of Bounded Rationality*, advises that in economics optimal conceptual and operational solutions are seldom possible, nor necessary, and that progress is achieved gradually by marginal 'satisficing' improvements.
74.   In the *Nature of the Firm* (1937), Ronald Coase argued that the 'existence of transaction costs leads to the emergence of the firm'. See Coase (1994, p. 9).
75.   Albert O. Hirschman (1981, p. 134), commenting on the ephemeral nature of analytical or empirical 'discovery', developed the following theorem: 'As soon as a social phenomenon has been fully explained by a variety of converging approaches and is therefore understood in its majestic inevitability and perhaps even permanence, it vanishes' . . . 'Why things should work this way is left to readers to figure out; just in case they find the proof of my theorem troublesome, they can take heart from the fact that Hegel expressed the same thought less paradoxically and more beautifully when he wrote "the owl of Minerva spreads its wings only with the falling of dusk" '.
76.   'Interests' may well be balancing factors in the complex process of social interaction. Hirschman (1997, p. xxii) quotes Montesquieu's sentence in *L'esprit des lois*. 'It is fortunate for men to be in a situation where, though their passions may prompt them to be wicked (*méchants*), they have nevertheless an interest in not being so.'
77.   The literature distinguishes 'warm-glow' from altruism. 'When individuals get utility from the act of giving, independent of the benefit to the recipient, it is termed warm-glow giving. Altruism is defined as giving to the public account with the intent of increasing the earnings of others in the group.' See Anderson (2001, p. 501). On altruism and selfless individual behavior, see also Rose-Ackerman (1996, p. 715).
78.   The literature on narrow self-interests as a potential social regulator found in Albert Hirschman's (1997, p. 119) its most brilliant rendition.
79.   According to Bénabou and Tirole (2006, p. 1674), 'People's actions indeed reflect a variable mix of altruistic motivation, material self-interest and social or self-image concerns. Moreover, this mix varies across individuals and situations, presenting observers seeking to infer a person's true values from his behavior (or an individual judging himself in retrospect) with a signal-extraction problem.'
80.   According to Douglass C. North (1990, p. 108), 'the instrumental rationality postulate of neoclassical theory assumes that the actors possess information necessary to evaluate correctly the alternatives and in consequence make choices that will achieve the desired ends.
81.   The World Bank's 'Economic growth in the 1990s: Learning from a decade of reform' (2005) is, according to Dani Rodrik (2006, p. 973), 'an extraordinary document demonstrating the extent to which the thinking of the development policy community has been transformed over the years. But there are other competing perspectives as well. One (trumpeted elsewhere in Washington) puts faith on extensive institutional reform, and another (exemplified by the UN Millennium Report) puts faith on foreign aid. Sorting intelligently among these diverse perspectives requires an explicitly diagnostic approach that recognizes that the binding constraints on growth differ from setting to setting.'
82.   Acemoglu (2003a, p. 43), 'Do collective choices maximize the welfare of society as a whole or do they select policies and institutions that benefit certain politically powerful groups at the expense of other segments of society? If societies choose inefficient policies, strong political and social forces will push them back towards efficient policies. Alternatively, societies may choose inefficient policies, not due to failures in the political process, but because the beliefs of politicians and citizens are mistaken.' Later on, Acemoglu and Robinson (2006a, p. 329) refine the argument in the sense that what matters is not so much the 'elites' 'but the persistence of incentives of whoever is in power to distort the system for their own benefit.' This is the right analytical conclusion. Unfortunately, they go on on the same page with a diatribe against 'an oligarchic structure in which a group of agents monopolize political power and are difficult to displace'.

The final answer as to who is the real anti-reform elite will have to come from rigorous country-specific empirical research.

83. Calvo et al. (1996, p. 138) examined capital inflows into emerging markets and observed that they 'provide ambiguous signals to market participants. Inflows may reflect confidence about long term investment prospects. Alternatively, capital may pour in for purely speculative reasons.' In brief, having financing available is an insufficient proof that the policies are right.

2. The political economy of macroeconomic policy making in Latin America

> Rational self-interested individuals will not act to achieve their common interest . . . unless some separate incentive is offered.
>
> Mancur Olson (1965, p. 2)

This chapter reviews the institutional and political economy context of macroeconomic policy making in Latin America. Its objective is to identify and examine the political economy explanations that may be behind actual macroeconomic policies. It frames the analysis around the evolution and origins of the 'right' institutions and on how they are mainly the result of endogenous political and equity conditions and perceptions of how public and private markets serve, or not, the general interest and welfare. After the core of generally accepted macroeconomic principles is summarized, a perspective on Latin America's macroeconomic and equity performance is presented and placed in the context of the strength or weakness of the political demand for macroeconomic stability and for attendant fiscal and financial reforms. The general conclusion is that short term political interests and incentives, under asymmetric information restrictions, often have a stronger capacity to influence public policies than long term considerations of policy consistency. To mitigate these 'collective actions problems' there seems to be a need for externally enforced rules (Ostrom, 2000, p. 137). It ends offering an information based strategy for policy reform and for institutional transformation.

I. THE PRIMACY OF INSTITUTIONS AND INCENTIVES

The emerging paradigm in the political economy of development and in the economics of politics is that institutions as constraints and rules, and the incentives they contain, are the main determinants of long term country prosperity. This political economy context builds on public choice theory,[1] game theory,[2] rational expectations macroeconomics,[3] political cycles,[4] incentive theory,[5] transaction-costs politics,[6] and the political economy of asymmetric information. Notwithstanding the empirical problems related to measuring the links between the 'right' and the 'wrong' institutions and development, the 'institutions hypothesis' has come to be regarded as the key explanatory variable for overall long term[7] economic, social and political results across developed and developing countries.

But ascribing 'differences in development to differences in institutions raises the challenge of explaining where the differences in institutions come from' (Sokoloff and Engerman, 2000, p. 218). If it is not geography or capital or surplus labor or a calculated 'Rostowing' (Rostow, 1960) strategic take-off, what then explains development? The short answer is that human influences have much more explicatory capacity than any other factors. This vision signals the full arrival of the primacy of institutions and of economic history and cliometrics[8] to better explain the sources of development. As Professor Jeffrey Williamson has put it (1991), 'Economic history is far better equipped to educate contemporary debate in the less developed world than it was back in the 1950s and 1960s.'

But not all institutions lead to development. What are then the characteristics of the institutions that engender long term development? According to Acemoglu (2003b, p. 27), the 'right' institutions have three key characteristics: (i) 'enforcement of property rights for a broad cross section of society, so that a variety of individuals have incentives to invest and take part in economic life', (ii) 'constraints on the actions of elites, politicians, and other powerful groups, so that these people cannot expropriate the incomes and investments of others or create a highly uneven playing field', and (iii) 'some degree of equal opportunity for broad segments of society, so that individuals can make investments, especially in human capital, and participate in productive economic activities.' But then, again, where does the institution of property rights come from? This key question was addressed by David Hume who suggested that property rights, in its most primeval concept, came from intuitive 'human action' and 'spontaneous order' self interest. This may be what 2005 Nobel prize winner Professor Robert Aumann calls 'the folk theorem'.[9] But again, this is an endogenous preference revelation that could be challenged in its pretense of acting as an independent variable.[10]

The search for the right conditions to nurture the right institutions has focused on those that are 'market-creating institutions', such as those that protect property rights and reduce information asymmetries in economic and political markets. Rodrik and Subramanian (2003, p. 32) classify these institutions as follows: (i) market regulating – namely, those that deal with externalities, economies of scale, and imperfect information. Examples include regulatory agencies in telecommunications, transport and financial services; (ii) market stabilizing – namely, those that ensure low inflation, minimize macroeconomic volatility, and avert financial crises. Examples include central banks, exchange rate regimes, and budgetary and fiscal rules; and (iii) market legitimizing – namely, those that provide social protection and insurance, involve redistribution and manage conflict. Examples include pension systems, unemployment insurance schemes and other social funds.

But if the 'right' characteristics of institutions are known, how come all countries do not have them? The short answer is that practically all institutional factors and all institutions are highly endogenous. 'For each of the functions performed by institutions there is an array of choices which are context and country specific' (Rodrik and Subramanian, 2003, p. 33). These arise from different historical experiences, geography, political economy and various initial conditions. This is the reason why successful developing countries often combine unorthodox elements with orthodox policies. Getting the mix 'right' is not easy. As Hoff and Stiglitz (2001, p. 389) have put it: 'Although the institutions that arise in response to incomplete markets and contracts may have as their intention an improvement in economic outcomes, there is no assurance that improvement will actually result. Institutions may be part of an equilibrium and yet be dysfunctional.'

Another related answer to the question of why some societies apparently choose or end up with the 'wrong' institutions, focuses on the distributional origins and consequences of some types of institutions. In other words, what are the real incentives for a society to have the 'right' institutions? According to Acemoglu (2003b, p. 29):

> There are no compelling reasons to think that societies will naturally gravitate toward good institutions. Institutions not only affect the economic prospects of nations but are also central to the distribution of income among individuals and groups in society. In other words, institutions not only affect the size of the social pie, but also how it is distributed.

How the social pie was distributed 'originally' strongly influences what types of institutions are adopted and what prosperity-enhancing or hindering consequences they may produce. Economies 'with a more equal distribution of wealth will accumulate more human capital and grow faster than those marked by a more inegalitarian distribution. High inequality will also make it easier to adopt distortionary policies that will negatively affect individuals' investment decisions, stifle growth, and conceivably generate political instability' (Bruno et al., 2000, p. 53).

The importance of the distributional origins and consequences of initial conditions is rapidly becoming the key explanatory factor to understand historical developments in some parts of the world as well as the current difficulties of many countries to develop the 'right' institutions. What could perhaps be called 'historical geography' has a lot to do in explaining the sources of the 'right' and the 'wrong' institutions across countries and history. 'Historical geography' would refer to the poverty and income distribution conditions prevailing at some point in time in history or in current developing countries (Sachs, 2003).

The question that emerges is what links there may be between fast gains in distributive justice and political support for the policies that make possible good macroeconomic performance. This is an area where empirical research, probably more on a country by country and sector by sector basis, still has a lot of causalities to narrow down. However, it seems that

> More unequal societies are much less likely to have democracies or governments that respect property rights. Unequal societies have less redistribution, and we have little idea whether this relationship is caused by redistribution reducing inequality or inequality reducing redistribution. Inequality and ethnic heterogeneity are highly correlated, either because of differences in educational heritages across ethnicities or because ethnic heterogeneity reduces redistribution. Finally, there is much more inequality and less redistribution in the US than in most other developed nations (Glaeser, 2005, p. 1).

II. THE DEMAND FOR INSTITUTIONS AND THE ROLE OF TRANSACTION COSTS

Few, if any, research areas have been more investigated by contemporary economics than the explanation of how the 'right' and the 'wrong'[11] institutions are formed and how they function.[12] In general terms, the market for institutions has two main components: a demand side and a supply side. The key to understanding the origins of the demand side of institutional change is to focus on the transaction costs[13] of the existing institutional arrangement. To understand the origin and evolution of the supply side, the focus would have to be on 'collective action'. Real and effective institutional transformation would come more from changes led by a demand-driven process than by those led by a supply side process.

The demand-induced approach to institutional change comes from the recognition that existing arrangements leave margin for potential gains (Feeny, 1993, p. 176), that transaction costs may be too high, and that a Coasen solution may be worked out by the actors to lower transaction costs. Analogous to the theory about the demand for technological change (Hicks, 1963), the demand-induced theory of institutional change is based on the search for lower transactions costs (Coase, 1960). This search, in principle, will induce successive autonomous new institutional arrangements on the supply and demand side of the process.[14]

Within the particular scope of an evaluation of the effectiveness of macroeconomic frameworks or of a given policy, the application of the demand-induced approach for the 'right' institutional arrangement would mean the recognition that existing transaction costs are too high and that an alternative modality of institutional arrangement is possible. More specifically, it would mean that under the existing institutional arrangement, for example, inflation rates are too high, or that unemployment is also high or that long term real rates of interest are excessively high. If these are the conditions generally prevailing, it is likely that there may be a political demand, for example, for a more independent Central Bank or for fiscal correction under a special modality of corrective institutional arrangement.[15] This would be to supply a response to the demand for institutional change and for potentially lower transaction costs. In principle, a tentative theorem linking the political demand origin of institutions with the transactions costs of the extant institutional arrangement could be framed as follows: 'The lower (higher) the real political demand for macroeconomic stability the higher (lower) will be the transactions costs of coordination between fiscal and monetary policy and the less (more) macroeconomic stability will result.'

Although the key requirement for reform and for economic transformation is the emergence of the political demand for change, the emergence of the 'right' institutions is not automatically assured. For any given institutional change proposal, even if there is a Pareto potential gain, the potential losers may not engage in a successful cooperative collective action. On the contrary, if they end up being politically or economically stronger, institutional change will not occur and a country may find itself with the 'wrong' institutions and without an effective political demand for policy reform. To a large extent this is what has happened and continues to happen in several Latin American countries.

III. THE SUPPLY OF INSTITUTIONS AND COLLECTIVE ACTION PROBLEMS

The difficulty in completing an 'efficient market solution' for the macroeconomic institutional arrangement comes not only from the uncertainties related to the *ex nihilo* birth of the demand for institutional change but also from the attendant collective action problems on the supply side.[16] The demand for reforms and for institutional change may evolve, but the 'institutional supply' may be 'captured' by a collective action response in which some rent-seekers[17] will attempt to free-ride the resources coming from the demand[18] side. This would mean that potential losers from the institutional change will attempt to build into the macroeconomic institutional arrangement hidden rules and wrong incentives to protect their perceived interests (Wiesner, 2004b, p. 33).[19] One form of dealing with collective action problems is to find a way in which the gains from the institutional change are given as 'a cooperation dividend' to those who support the change (Ostrom and Walker, 1997, p. 35). While these considerations may appear remote to the examination of the effectiveness of macroeconomic frameworks, they are not. They are applicable – *mutatis mutandi* – to what may have happened in Chile where the reduction in poverty levels seems to have induced political support for policies to correct fiscal imbalances and to preserve macroeconomic stability.

Given the endogenous origin of the demand and supply of institutions and the complex causal relationships with underlying historical and political processes, it is not surprising to find that prominent economists[20] such as Joseph Schumpeter (1954), Nelson and Winter (1982) and before them, Alfred Marshall (1930), have proposed an evolutionary[21] theory of institutional development. The idea is that evolution is akin to the complex process of development in its selection, differentiation and competition by firms and individuals for resources and thus to 'natural selection' (Mokyr, 2006, p. 1005). However, many issues remain unresolved, particularly how to make evolutionary economics operational. After all, 'there is nothing like a market place in natural history' (Mokyr, 2006, p. 1010).

IV.   INSTITUTIONS AND INCENTIVES AS DEUS EX MACHINA

Is the incentives paradigm truly a new revelation? Something that classical economics (Smith et al.) or neoclassical economics (Marshall et al.) did not anticipate or overlooked? How can it be that Schumpeter in his monumental history of economic thought (1954) does not mention the world 'incentives'? The answer to these questions has more to do with classical and neoclassical thought underestimating the immense role of information than in overlooking the role of incentives. After all,

> Neoclassical economics postulates rational individual behavior in the market. In a perfectly competitive market, this assumption translates into profit maximization for firms' owners, which implies cost minimization. In other words, the pressure of competitive markets solves the problem of incentives for cost minimization. Similarly, consumers faced with exogenous prices have the proper incentives for maximizing their utility levels. The major project of understanding

how prices are formed in competitive markets can proceed without worrying about incentives (Laffont and Martimort, 2002, p. 1).

Although Adam Smith was aware of the incentive problems, particularly in sharecropping contracts (Smith, 1776, Book 3, Chapter 2), neoclassical economics may have underestimated them because it assumed that individual rational behavior in the markets would suffice. Maybe it does in competitive private markets. But this is much less the case in public and non-competitive markets or in principal–agent environments where incentives will need to be nurtured or explicitly inserted within firms,[22] markets, management realms and in all collective processes, be they economic or political. It is not that economic analysis was flawed or wrong but that it assumed that the role of incentives and institutions would spontaneously flow out of the neoclassical model of perfectly competitive markets. In other words, it assumed the role of incentives and institutions as a combined process emerging out of markets. Now we know that there are serious problems with the assumption of perfect markets delivering – by themselves – the 'right' incentives and institutions. Since the 1970s it has gradually become evident that the neoclassical model was incomplete.

Stiglitz (1996) and others showed that perfect information in markets is more the exception than the norm and that adverse selection, moral hazard,[23] and non-verifiability strongly influenced actual market and agents' behavior. Not all agents have the same information, and therefore conduct or transact in the market place under different conditions. If information is not equally shared by all economic agents the behavior of some is influenced not so much by competition but by their own private interests. In fact, as long as they have an information advantage they can, even within a somewhat competitive market, pursue their own private interests. If there are information asymmetries for some actors, for them the real incentives are their own private interests. The markets cannot automatically align incentives with interests. But 'better' informed agents can configure institutional, personal or firm incentives to actually deliver their own private interests.

V.   THE MEASUREMENT OF INSTITUTIONAL EFFECTIVENESS

Within endogenous frameworks it is very difficult to quantify and establish causal links – beyond association or correlation – between measurements of variables which can simultaneously perform as causes and as consequences and can even result from a third or more overarching independent instrumental variable.[24] This is the case for institutions which can be seen as resulting from development and also giving rise to it. Professor Charles F. Manski (2003, p. 242) summarized the identification problem as follows:

> Identification problems pervade every aspect of empirical research and every attempt by ordinary people to learn about the world in which they live. Overall, I view myself as presenting a mixed message. My pessimistic side would argue that it is rarely possible to credibly 'solve' identification problems. The optimist in me would argue that the more we understand these problems, the better we will be able to cope with them.

If institutional evolution is mostly a historical and endogenous process, the road to solve or to mitigate the 'identification problem' would be to find 'exogenous' differences in institutions. However, in practice truly exogenous variations do not exist. According to Acemoglu (2005a, p. 34), 'we have to find the source of variation that is plausible orthogonal to other determinants of current economic performance'. A very promising line of empirical and econometric research is the one pioneered by Daron Acemoglu, Simon Johnson and James Robinson (2001) in which they include an instrumental[25] variable for institutions using historically determined components of institutions. According to Dani Rodrik (2003, p. 9) this work has 'provided convincing evidence that institutional quality is truly causal'.

In 2003 a research program at the IMF[26] sought to advance the debate on the links between institutions and economic performance by relating country macroeconomic outcomes to: (i) a measurement of its institutions; (ii) measures of macroeconomic policy; and (iii) a set of exogenous variables. The measures were not objective but, rather, the subjective perspectives of country experts or the results of surveys carried out by international organizations and non-governmental organizations. The idea was to consider competing explanations of development, notably the role of institutions, policies and geography. The conclusion of the study was that institutional quality does have a significant effect, not only on the level of income, but on growth and on the volatility of growth.[27]

VI.   THE CORE OF MACROECONOMIC PRINCIPLES

Since the early 70s with the work of Milton Friedman (1969), Edmund Phelps (1968) and the Lucas 'critique' (Lucas, 1976), macroeconomics has been transformed largely by advances in microeconomics principles and applied macroeconomic research.[28] Arguing from microeconomics principles[29] Friedman and Phelps predicted that inflation could rise without a permanent reduction in unemployment. This was the breakdown of the

Phillips curve. Then came Robert Lucas's 'critique' (1976). Just as the Phillips curve was flawed in overlooking the basic microeconomics of the labor market and of firms, the empirical relations that made up large scale investment and consumption models really depended 'crucially on expectations of the future course of the economy' (Mankiw, 1990, p. 1647). Until Lucas, macroeconometric models treated expectations in a cavalier way. He pointed out that most policy interventions change the way individuals form expectations about the future. 'Therefore, these models should not be used to evaluate the impact of alternative policies' (Mankiw, 1990, p. 1647). Lucas's 'critique' transformed macroeconomic policy making. After him the issues of rational expectations and of credibility of policy postures became key vectors for macroeconomic policy formulation. This is fully consistent with the institutional premise that history matters and that 'path dependency' can work to retard development or to enhance it.

Since the 1990s macroeconomic policy formulation, particularly monetary policy, has been guided largely[30] by the following five core – Taylor – principles: (i) the focus should be on long-term economic growth and the supply side of the economy; (ii) there is no long-term trade-off between the rate of inflation and the rate of unemployment; (iii) there is a short-run trade-off between inflation and unemployment; (iv) people's expectations are highly responsive to policy, and thus, expectations matter for assessing the impact of monetary and fiscal policy;[31] and (v) 'when evaluating monetary and fiscal policy one should not think in terms of a one-time isolated change in the instruments of policy, but rather as a series of changes linked by a systematic process or a policy rule'.[32]

The implication of the first principle is that policy should aim at the long term determinants of the supply side of the economy, that is labor productivity, investment, savings and, in general, on how to raise potential GDP growth. The policy implication of the second principle is that Central Banks should establish a long-run target range for inflation and stick to it. The policy implication of the third principle is for monetary policy to keep the growth of aggregate demand stable. The fourth principle informs policy that rational expectations should be built into macroeconomic models and formats. The fifth principle implies that policy evaluation should be done in terms of policy rules. These can take different forms.

> Should the interest rate or the money supply be the instruments in the rule? Should the instrument react to the exchange rate or solely to inflation and real output? How large should the reaction of policy be to inflation? Is the rule a guideline or should it be legislated and used to add accountability to policy-making?[33]

In brief, the key is the credibility of institutions in the policies they announce. If they are credible, a disinflation target will have a lower short-run cost. 'Similarly, a plan to reduce the budget deficit will have a smaller short-run contractionary effect if it is credible' (Taylor, 1997, p. 234).

VII. LATIN AMERICA'S MACROECONOMIC AND EQUITY PERFORMANCE IN PERSPECTIVE, 1960–2006

Latin America's growth performance over the last 40 years is remarkable for its relative precariousness compared to other regions of the world. With the exception of Chile in the 1990s, Latin America's growth record is amazingly slow and volatile. Table 2.1 shows that from 1960 to 2000 Latin America's average annual rate of GDP growth was 1.4 per cent, East Asia's was 4.6 per cent, that is, three times as fast, and Chile's was 70.0 per cent faster. Although several qualifications can be made to this data, for example, that Chile's fast growth is concentrated in the 1990s, that the region on the whole did better in the 1960s and 1970s, and that the calculations themselves may vary depending on the specific methodologies and time periods, in the end the overall thrust of the numbers is persuasive – in other words, a very disappointing performance over a long period of time. Long enough to absorb particular episodes or 'outlier' developments.

More recently, between 1998 and 2003 the average per capita rate of GDP growth for Latin America was −0.1 per cent. Table 2.2 shows that in

Table 2.1   Latin America's GDP per capita in regional perspective

Countries	1960s	1970s	1980s	1990s	1960–2000
Chile	2.2	1.2	1.3	4.8	2.4
Latin America*	2.2	2.5	−0.9	1.8	1.4
East Asia**	4.7	5.4	4.5	4.0	4.6
Japan	9.3	3.1	3.5	1.1	4.2
USA	2.9	2.7	2.2	2.3	2.5

Notes:
* The 15 countries with largest GDP: Argentina, Bolivia, Brazil, Chile, Colombia, Costa Rica, Dominican Republic, Ecuador, El Salvador, Guatemala, Mexico, Paraguay, Peru, Uruguay, Venezuela.
** China, Hong Kong, Indonesia, Korea, Malaysia, Philippines, Singapore, Taiwan and Thailand.

Source: De Gregorio (2004, p. 6, Table 3).

Table 2.2   Selected Latin American countries: real per capita GDP, 1998–2003 (average annual percentage change)

Latin America	*−0.1*
Argentina	−2.6
Bolivia	0.1
Brazil	0.0
Chile	1.1
Colombia	−0.9
Ecuador	−0.3
Mexico	1.3
Peru	0.3
Uruguay	−2.7
Venezuela	−4.9

Source: IMF, World Economic Outlook database. See Singh et al. (2005, p. xiv).

Table 2.3   Regional GDP per capita relative to the US (regional averages for selected countries)

Year	Europe	Asia	Latin America
1950	0.40	0.16	0.28
1980	0.70	0.46	0.30
2001	0.67	0.55	0.22

Source: Cole et al. (2004, p. 40).

this period Brazil's per capita GDP remained stagnant. Practically all countries had a negative rate of growth. Chile was the exception.

Table 2.3 shows the relative loss of Latin America in terms of per capita income when compared to Europe and Asia in terms of US per capita income for the period 1950–2001. While Europe and Asia grew, Latin America's ratio declined from 0.28 per cent to 0.22 per cent, Asia's more than tripling from 0.16 per cent to 0.55 per cent. An intriguing question is why from 1950 to 1980 Latin America's relative decline is small, from 0.28 per cent to 0.30 per cent, but accelerates after the 1980s, reaching 0.22 per cent in 2001.

Table 2.4 shows the disaggregated data for several Latin American countries at four points in time from 1900 to 2001. Although, again, this data may vary depending on methodological factors and other considerations, it is probably 'satisficing' for the purpose of the exercise. That is, the direction of

Conceptual framework

Table 2.4   GDP per capita relative to the US

Year	1900	1950	1980	2001
Argentina	0.67	0.52	0.44	0.29
Bolivia	–	0.20	0.14	0.09
Brazil	0.17	0.17	0.28	0.20
Chile	0.48	0.40	0.31	0.36
Colombia	0.24	0.23	0.23	0.18
Costa Rica	–	0.21	0.26	0.22
Ecuador	–	0.19	0.22	0.14
Mexico	0.33	0.25	0.34	0.25
Paraguay	0.25	0.18	0.18	0.11
Peru	0.20	0.24	0.23	0.13
Uruguay	0.54	0.49	0.35	0.27
Venezuela	0.20	0.78	0.55	0.30
Average	0.29	0.28	0.31	0.22

Source: Cole et al. (2004, p. 40).

the trend is probably right. Some particular evolutions deserve special attention: first, the decline of Argentina and the rise of Costa Rica, Brazil and Venezuela; the deep decline of Bolivia; the recovery of Chile from 1980 to 2001.

Table 2.5 is a very important one because it points out not only the differences in real GDP per capita between East Asia and Latin American but also the differences in specific macroeconomic results. The significance of this is enormous as it suggests possible explanations for the differences in per capita GDP growth. To begin with, inflation is much higher in Latin America. So are fiscal deficits. Savings are lower in Latin America, as are exports. Broad money tends to be higher in Latin America. These numbers reflect quite clearly different policy choices and approaches to development. These tables summarize a most telling story for a whole subcontinent. Close to a major historical debacle. One that should prompt a major revision of what this region has been doing for over 50 years.[34] Part of the explanation for this abysmal record can be associated with the different 'initial conditions' and different equity paths followed by these regions.

But the overall picture for Latin America may obscure substantial inter-country differences in macroeconomic performance over time. Table 2.6 shows that from 1950 until 2000 there were large differences in the rates of growth of each country. The decade of the 1980s was a very difficult one for all countries. From 1990 onwards, Chile's rate of growth has surpassed that of the rest, and Brazil and Mexico have been growing at a much slower

Table 2.5   Growing divergence: performance differences between East Asia (EA) and Latin America and the Caribbean (LAC)

Indicators	1971–1980		1981–1990		1991–2000		2000–2005	
	EA	LAC	EA	LAC	EA	LAC	EA	LAC
	(percentage change)							
Real GDP per capita	4.8	3.6	6.1	−0.6	7.0	1.8	7.0	1.0
Consumer prices	10.3	30.9	6.3	337.7	5.9	45.4	2.6	8.6
	(percent of GDP)							
Private capital flows (standard deviation in GDP)	...	...	4.3	5.2	4.9	5.8	2.5	3.9
Gross domestic investment	28.8	23.4	31.4	21.3	34.2	21.1	32.7	19.8
Gross national savings	30.1	20.0	30.9	19.5	35.6	18.2	36.8	19.6
Broad money	29.5	17.7	58.6	27.6	100.4	36.1	139.4	35.9
Overall government deficit	−0.3	−2.2	−1.5	−3.7	−1.5	−1.6	−1.8	−2.4
Exports and imports (G&S)[1]	41.2	28.3	51.8	30.2	65.9	33.2	77.6	45.9
Trade balance	1.0	−2.2	1.1	2.2	1.8	−1.5	4.0	0.9
Foreign direct investment	0.8	0.2	1.9	0.7	3.3	3.2	2.5	3.7

Notes:
Data are averages for each region based on purchasing power parity country weights, except those for consumer price inflation, terms of trade, private capital, flows, and foreign direct investment, which are based on equal country weights.
. . . denotes data not available.
[1]   G&S = goods and services.

Source: IMF, World Economic Outlook database. See Elson (2006, p. 38, Table 2).

Table 2.6   Economic growth in eight major Latin American countries (percentage on an annual basis)

Time span	Argentina	Brazil	Chile	Colombia	Mexico	Peru	Uruguay	Venezuela, R.B. de
1950–1960	1.1	3.7	1.5	1.6	2.3	2.9	0.6	3.4
1960–1970	3.9	3.1	1.9	2.2	3.4	2.3	0.8	2.4
1970–1980	2.1	5.8	0.9	2.9	2.5	1.7	2.1	0.1
1980–1990	−2.4	−0.2	1.2	1.1	−0.1	−3.3	−0.2	−1.9
1990–1997	5.0	1.5	6.1	1.3	1.0	3.0	3.2	1.1
1980–2000	0.4	0.4	2.9	1.1	0.2	−0.5	0.7	−1.0
1997–2000	−1.2	0.0	0.9	0.6	−0.5	0.8	−2.0	−3.2

Source: Prados de la Escosura (2005). See Perry et al. (2006, p. 47).

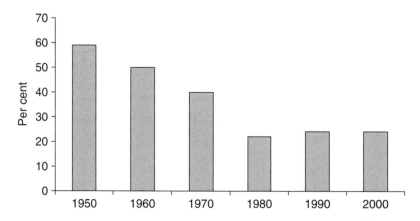

Note: We used a poverty line of US$2 a day; poverty rates for 1950–1980 are estimated using a lognormal approximation.

Source: Perry et al. (2006, p. 2).

Figure 2.1   Poverty rates in Latin America, 1950–2000

rate than in the first 30 years of the second half of last century. The recent slow growth of these two important countries is a major puzzle.

Figure 2.1 shows that the extreme levels of poverty in 1950 (close to 60 per cent) have been reduced by more than half by the year 2000. The question of course is why is there such a slow rate of reduction, and, even more telling, what about the Gini coefficient? Figure 2.2 shows how difficult it is to make gains in income distribution as measured by the Gini coefficient. The effects of the crisis of the 1980s seem to have increased it for the 1990s.

Figure 2.3 shows that the effects of the crisis in Latin America at the end of 1990s seem to have reversed the reduction in poverty achieved in the mid-1990s.

Table 2.7 shows the relationships between growth and equity for a number of countries.

What can explain the wide differences in macroeconomic performance[35] between Latin American countries and other developed and selected developing countries? Can it be lack of technical knowledge? Or of political vision? Or a limited capacity to learn from experience? Most likely little of all these. More likely a limited political capacity to adopt the 'right' institutions and reforms. Most likely that limited political capacity originates in the initial equity conditions and the little relative progress that has been observed in the last 50 years. In brief, initial inequity may have engendered growth-retarding policies, scant political demand for macroeconomic stability and

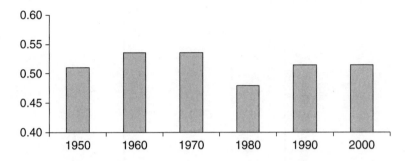

Note: Based on data for Brazil, Chile, México and Republica Bolivariana de Venezuela.

Source: Perry et al. (2006, p. 2).

Figure 2.2 Gini coefficient for Latin America, 1950–2000

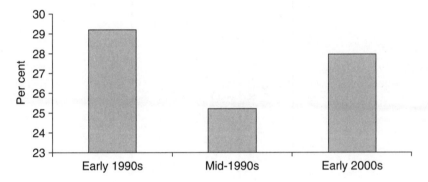

Note: The data refer to unweighted poverty rates.

Source: Perry et al. (2006, p. 24).

Figure 2.3 The evolution of Latin American poverty during the 1990s

elusive political support for the fiscal and monetary policies that tend to deliver macroeconomic stability as well as micro-institutional effectiveness in the provision of public goods.

Engerman and Sokoloff (1997, 2000, 2002) and Acemoglu et al. (2001, 2002):

Argue that the contemporary situation cannot be understood without recognizing that extreme inequality emerged soon after the Europeans began to colonize the Americas half a millennium ago, and has been reflected in the institutions they put in place. Both this initial inequality and institutions were shaped largely

Table 2.7 Change in the poverty rate and decomposition of the change into growth and redistribution effects

	Period	Poverty line	Initial Poverty Rate	Final Poverty Rate	Total Change	Percentage of the change due to:		
						Growth	Redistribution	Residual
Brazil	1985–95	Extreme	10	11.1	10.2	−40	145	−5
		Moderate	30.4	28	−7.9	−40	−70	10
Bolivia	1990–95	Moderate	52.4	47.1	−10.1	−147	44	3
Chile	1987–96	Moderate	45.1	23.2	−48.6	−85	−7	−8
Colombia	1991–95	Moderate	58.5	58.5	−0.1	−103	6	−3
Costa Rica	1986–95	Moderate	29.4	25.6	−12.9	−117	17	0
Peru	1985–96	Moderate	43.1	50.5	17.2	99	−27	28

Source: Attanasio and Székely (2005, p. 46, Table 6).

by the factor endowments that the Europeans found in Central and South America, rather than the nature of the colonial powers themselves. Although these colonies ultimately gained independence and the development of technology and the world economy brought about important changes, extreme inequality persisted into the 19th and 20th centuries because the evolution of political and economic institutions tended to reproduce and reinforce highly unequal distributions of wealth, human capital, and political influence.[36]

Two main policy conclusions can be drawn. First, initial high poverty rates seem to affect the final poverty ones. Secondly, although redistribution matters, it is growth that seems indispensable. Chile was able to reduce its poverty rate from 45.1 per cent in 1987 to 23.2 per cent in 1996, a remarkable achievement obtained largely as a result of high growth rates. By 2003, Chile had reduced its poverty rate to 18.8 per cent.

VIII. THE MACROECONOMIC IMPLICATIONS OF POVERTY AND INEQUALITY

Poverty and inequality may well not only be the consequence of the lack of development but its root cause as well. This complex endogeneity can be appreciated through the enormous difficulty which growth and welfare-enhancing policies face to be politically accepted and binding. A growing body of literature is finding that inequality is conducive to the adoption of growth-retarding policies. 'Inequality is bad for the poor' (Ravallion, 2005) but also deleterious to macroeconomic stability and to welfare-enhancing reforms in general. Equity and long term prosperity are often complementary because: 'High levels of economic and political inequality tend to lead to economic institutions and social arrangements that systematically favor the interests of those with more influence. Such inequitable institutions can generate economic costs.'[37] That said, it should be added that the precise identification of who or which political groups have the decisive influence is still not a well defined concept. It is widely used perhaps because it seems obvious that *ex post* the policies failed, and can be blamed on an *ex post* identified source of influence. A perfect tautology proving itself. But the issue is much more complex and it is still in need of further empirical case by case research.

Under these conditions the poor and even the middle income groups are finding it difficult to perceive that macroeconomic stability and the fiscal measures to support it are in their interest. They may feel that the system is unfair, that some people do not get what they deserve while others get what they do not deserve. The views a society has on fairness have implications, on the way it votes,[38] allocates resources and regulates private and public goods. Just as when high levels of poverty have a negative effect on reform processes and on the political viability of, for example, 'fiscal rules', the consequences of macroeconomic volatility are a worsening of poverty and income distribution conditions. If macroeconomic policy coordination fails to deliver macroeconomic stability and sustainable employment, the poor and the low income groups are the ones who suffer the most. They have little protection against inflation or exchange rate depreciation.[39] In the words of Ocampo (2004b, p. 84), 'macroeconomic stability needs to be expanded to include not only low inflation rates and budget deficits, but also high and stable growth rates and employment.'[40] In the case of Colombia, a study by Nuñez et al. (2005, p. 31) found that the biggest explanation for increases in poverty levels between 1996–2000 was the loss of employment.[41]

The issue that emerges is a circular one. Namely, that to perform well at the macro-institutional level a country would need to have political support for the fiscal measures that sustain macroeconomic stability. But that political support may not be forthcoming unless the public at large sees, in the short term, the poverty reduction effects of orthodox fiscal policies and of efficient institutional frameworks. In other words, macroeconomic stability would be a more likely outcome when a large percentage of the low income population become stakeholders in that macroeconomic stability. In brief, macroeconomic stability and support for the policies to sustain it are more likely when there is a real political demand for such collective public good.

This 'transaction-cost politics' (Dixit, 1996) hypothesis would need to be tested when looking at possible links between country macroeconomic performance and evolution of their distributional situation. A political economics approach would suggest that the 'right' macroeconomic institutional frameworks are exogenously determined by the political demand for macroeconomic stability (Persson and Tabellini, 2002). That political demand would be real and effective in the sense that it would express itself in political support for the fiscal and monetary reforms that sustain it. In this case, the overall social welfare function would be reflected in the political support for macroeconomic stability.[42]

IX.   CENTRAL BANK INDEPENDENCE AND COMPLEMENTARY 'FISCAL RULES'

Since the 1990s, developed and developing countries came to the view that more independent central banks was the 'right' institutional arrangement to deal more effectively with inflationary pressures. Many countries in the world and in Latin America proceeded to give their central banks substantial independence. The results have been extraordinary. According to Professor Kenneth Rogoff, from 1990 to 1994 annual inflation averaged 230 per cent in Latin America and is now in single digits.[43] Although other factors contributed to the lowering of price levels it is clear that central bank independence is the main explanatory variable for what has been achieved. The emerging question is 'why is it that a similar independence-based institutional development has not taken place in the other pillar of macroeconomic policy formulation, namely, the fiscal and budgetary frameworks?' After all, the critical policy goal is not only lower inflation but one anchored on fiscal sustainability.[44] Furthermore, the overarching policy objective is to achieve macroeconomic stability and its attendant key outcomes in terms of growth, employment, interest rate levels and countercyclical capacity. These have not been the results in many countries in Latin America during the last 10 years.

One of the most challenging problems for Central Banks and for monetary policy in particular is its relation to the fiscal side of the macroeconomic realm. In principle, monetary policy has 'instrumental independence' to follow its inflation targets but these objectives can be severely restricted by what is called 'fiscal dominance'. It is not so much that it restricts meeting inflation targets – by pushing demand beyond supply capacity – but that it creates the wrong incentives. Unanticipated fiscal deficits means that some agents can operate without a budget restriction and need not seek to be efficient to maintain access to public resources. The end result is that inflation targets are jeopardized and, in the case of social expenditures, distributional gains may be lost. Nothing can be more inequitable than inefficient social spending. This in its turn will make it more difficult for political support to be forthcoming for fiscal rules and macroeconomic stability in general. The key concept here is that of unanticipated fiscal deficits, those that were not built in *ex ante* at the time of the overall macroeconomic programming exercise as part of the 'permissible' use of monetary space in the economy as a whole. They are the source of the wrong incentives. Not all fiscal deficits are necessarily destabilizing. But unintended fiscal deficits can be very welfare costly.

X.   FINANCIAL DEPTH AND INFORMAL DOLLARIZATION

The economic literature has long recognized the links between financial development and economic growth. Latin American financial markets have grown considerably, but stock market capitalization, bond markets and the banking sector are still modest in comparison to East Asian Countries. 'A close look at Latin American capital markets reveals a disheartening picture. Local financial markets continue to be dominated by banks and are characterized by high rates of dollarization, short-terms and illiquidity' (De la Torre and Schmukler, 2004, p. 41).[45] Deep financial markets are 'shock absorbers' while shallow and vulnerable financial systems are the transmission mechanisms through which external shocks are potentiated in their consequences at the domestic level. The ensuing crisis brings about a collapse of GDP and a lowering of the average rates of growth for over long periods of time. Macroeconomic volatility is very costly in terms of average growth. During the period 1998–2003, Latin America's average annual per capita rate of growth was −0.1.[46] Macroeconomic volatility since the 1980s may well explain a large part of the much lower rates of growth in Latin America compared to Asia for the last 40 years.

Vulnerability is a function of exposure, and exposure is a function of 'dollarization'. However, dollarization is not the cause of financial crisis (Berg and Borensztein, 2000, p. 41). It is the symptom that reveals financial fragility and the risk of a potential banking crisis (Mishkin, 1996). Dollarization is not necessarily a curse. It 'has provided a means through which countries with low macroeconomic policy credibility are able to resist capital flight and hold savings within the domestic financial system. Highly dollarized countries are, however, subject to heightened liquidity and credit risks' (see Singh et al., 2005, p. xviii). In principle, a country that is highly dollarized should not be able to obtain much credit in its own currency. In fact it is dollarized to the extent that it cannot borrow abroad in its own currency.

XI. SUDDEN STOPS AND THE EFFECTIVENESS OF MACROECONOMIC POLICY COORDINATION

External shocks in the form of 'sudden stops' have been the major source of macroeconomic volatility in several Latin American countries for at least two decades.[47] Understanding the 'initial conditions' which make an economy particularly vulnerable to 'sudden stops' is, therefore, part of the task of identifying the challenges of macroeconomic policy coordination. This involves understanding the internal and external economic and political factors that explain (fiscal and financial) policy postures. If the goal is to understand macroeconomic results, one needs to

> take into account some of the political or institutional realities that further constraint actual policy. Or going even further, one might want to take into account that policymakers have their own agenda, their own objective function. Policymakers may represent the interests of particular groups. At the same time they care about remaining in power, either because they want to be able to

implement their political agenda or simply because they enjoy it. Thus an alternative starting point is to derive the relevant objective function from the incentives and constraints faced by politicians. In the limit this approach becomes a purely positive analysis of policy in which the goal becomes one of explaining existing policy rather than to recommend changes (Blanchard and Fischer, 1992, p. 567).

It is from incentives and constraints faced by politicians that one has to approach the problem of the effectiveness of macroeconomic policy making.

> Economists have, for the most part, ignored these incentives and constraints and have analyzed optimal policy starting from a social welfare function, leaving to political scientists the job of explaining the characteristics of existing policy. This is not a completely satisfactory division of labor, nor is it strictly enforced (see Blanchard and Fischer, 1992, p. 567).

Sudden stops, because of their very nature, can only be identified after they occur. Preventing their occurrence or reducing their incidence is a daunting challenge, as they can come about from complex domestic and external circumstances which are difficult to anticipate and which can be different each time. It is, basically, an exercise that demands a balance between measuring risks and judging uncertainties. One of the few statements that can be made is largely tautological, that is that vulnerability is a function of risk. This *ex post* identity says that, after the fact, it could always be argued both ways that: (i) there was 'excessive' exposure to risk and, as a consequence, when the sudden stop came, a banking and macroeconomic crisis was precipitated and (ii) that the sudden stop came on its own and there was no amount of prudent policy measures that could have prevented its occurrence or the intensity of its consequences.[48] To go beyond this tautology and to develop a political economy theory on which to build specific preventive policies one avenue is to realize that external risk-taking may ultimately be a function of who policy makers can blame for the consequences of the sudden stops. If they can get away with blaming the external avatars for their own flaws, most likely they will not be able to resist such a strong incentive. After all, why go through the hassle of reform if the political process will not be able to hold policy makers accountable for the consequences of their opportunistic behavior?

XII. INFLATION TARGETING AS A MONETARY FRAMEWORK

During the last 15 years more than 25 countries in the world including Brazil, Chile, Colombia, Mexico and Peru have formally adopted inflation targeting as their preferred monetary policy framework. While it has been widely embraced by many countries and strongly endorsed (Bernanke et al., 1999, p. 308), it has not been adopted formally by the Federal Reserve Bank of the United States,[49] by Japan or by the European Central Bank. This probably means that these Central Banks feel confident about the political support for policies that will deliver a very low inflation level and variability. This strong tendency results from the search for a better anchor for monetary policy and the experience that intermediate targets have proved unreliable, exchange rate-based regimes ultimately fail and increased transparency about policy interventions is receiving particular support.

Generally speaking inflation targeting is a framework which seeks to stabilize inflation around a low average while also trying to stabilize growth around potential output (Svensson, 2003, p. 426). This approach has been called 'constrained discretion' (Bernanke and Mishkin, 1997; King, 1997; Bernanke et al., 1999). The constraint is the inflation target and the discretion is the scope to take account of short-run economic and financial considerations: 'The constraint and the discretion act together like a pair of scissors cutting through economic disturbances to produce a happy combination of low inflation and strong economy activity' (Truman, 2003, p. 5).

Has inflation targeting worked? If it has, does this confirm the wisdom of giving much larger independence to Central Banks? The answers to these questions have to be modulated. Although global inflation in developed and developing countries has dropped significantly since the early 1990s it may be premature to attribute all the improvement to better country-specific policies and to 'better' Central Banks. There are three subsequent questions to examine the context and characteristics of the disinflation observed particularly in Latin America: (i) is it possible that other factors drove down inflation?, (ii) if inflation dropped but it came with a collapse of GDP growth, can this be regarded as a success of macroeconomic policy coordination? and (iii) if there is strong political demand for macroeconomic stability does it extend to provide political support for the fiscal measures that deliver macroeconomic stability?

To the first question Kenneth S. Rogoff (2003, p. 54) observes that globalization has helped keep inflation down. 'Globalization, together with deregulation and privatization, increases competition, drives down inflation, both directly and indirectly'. In the case of Latin America two critical 'exogenous' events have helped keep inflation down or helped postpone fiscal corrections. First, much lower external rates of interest. Secondly, large inflows of capital which have contributed to exchange rate appreciation well beyond any durable improvement in international competitiveness.

In the case of Colombia, (1999), Mexico (1996) and Peru (1999) and even Chile (1999), the rapid disinflations came almost simultaneously with the severe economic recessions and exchange rate pressures. Under these circumstances, can it be concluded that inflation has been conquered? Particularly when 'hidden' fiscal deficits are looming large in the outlook of several countries? Can one really say that there is no significant 'fiscal dominance' in several countries in Latin America? The answer appears to be that although Central Bank independence and performance has been much better than in the past and the direction of their policies should be maintained, there is much work left to be done before it can be concluded that inflation has been fully tamed or brought to a one-digit level in a sustainable way. This cannot be achieved without a fiscal transformation equivalent to what took place in the area of monetary and exchange rate policies with Central Banks. This means, more independent fiscal institutions and more constitutional fiscal rules.

The major challenge is to improve distributive justice, to get political support for the policies that deliver gains in poverty levels and in initial access to the key public goods of education, health and social security in general. This is the road to 'fiscal rules' to complement inflation targeting and thus build a strong and fully consistent macroeconomic institutional framework. Latin America by and large is not quite there yet.

XIII. SUMMING UP: THE POLITICAL ECONOMY OF MACROECONOMIC POLICY MAKING IN LATIN AMERICA

The politics of macroeconomics or more precisely the politicization of macroeconomic issues leading to fiscal deficits, to inflationary periods, and to recurrent macroeconomic volatility has a long tradition in Latin America, albeit with some country variance. But on the whole, since the 1950s most policy makers have tended 'to ignore the existence of macroeconomic constraints' (Dornbush and Edwards, 1991, p. 9). They have embraced economic and social programs based on expansive fiscal and credit policies and overvalued exchange rates.[50] It is not easy to understand this proclivity towards macroeconomic mismanagement.[51] Is it lack of a real political demand for macroeconomic stability? Or lack of political incentives for those who have the political power to restrain fiscal excesses? Is it a real or alleged vulnerability to external shocks? Or, finally, not well understood distributional struggles? Could it be that what appears as inexplicable policy mistakes are perfectly rational political responses to distorted or imperfect incentives? According to Alesina (1991, p. 43): 'The political economy approach attempts to explain why certain apparent mistakes repeatedly occur. This approach underscores that one cannot correct "mistakes" without addressing the institutional features which make these so called "mistakes" likely to occur.'

If macroeconomic stability is not politically valued as a collective public good, there are scant political incentives for 'rational' political agents to use their resources to promote the policies that deliver macroeconomic stability (Wiesner, 2004b). To a large extent, Latin America on the whole has not yet fully politically considered that 'macroeconomic stability is a development issue' (Hausmann and Gavin, 1996, p. 29). Gavin and Perotti (1997, p. 55) offer a very suggestive explanation. In their view:

> The procyclicality of fiscal policy in Latin America has to do with a loss during macroeconomic bad times of the market access that would be required to support a more countercyclical fiscal policy. This is consistent with the fact that access to emergency credit is higher during bad times, and it also helps explain why fiscal policy is particularly procyclical in bad times, the cyclical behavior of inflation, and why policy is particularly procyclical for countries that enter a period with high deficits.

At the end of the day the more comprehensive answer to the question of why there is no more macroeconomic stability, or why macroeconomic policy coordination does not deliver better results at lower transaction costs, is because there is not sufficient political demand for these 'public goods'. The case of Chile, which is the exception, may largely be explained by the fact that since the 1980s there has been a growing political demand there for macroeconomic stability and for countercyclical fiscal rules. At the same time, rapid and substantial gains in reducing poverty levels have been achieved. It is here in this last development, together with Chile's particular history, that the explanation for the existence of a political demand for macroeconomic stability can be found in this country.

Whatever may have been the combination of reasons working in the past, the fact is that several countries (Mexico, Colombia, Ecuador, Argentina, Brazil, Venezuela and Peru) have had severe macroeconomic crises since the mid 1990s. Although they seem to have recovered and have made commendable progress,[52] particularly in terms of dramatically reducing inflation, it might be premature to conclude that the region has finally and firmly learnt to manage its macroeconomic policy realms better. After all, it continues to run relatively large fiscal deficits, it is not adequately covering for hidden fiscal and social security costs, and it is still exposed to highly likely adverse upcoming developments in international capital markets.

In brief, the real test of whether Latin America has finally come to terms with its 'own' macroeconomic responsibilities will be seen in the next few years. The test will come not so much by not having macroeconomic disturbances but by how this region is able to manage them. The challenge has been aptly summarized by Gaviria (2006, p. 20): 'The political economy of reforms in Latin America suggest that when the majority of the population cease to believe in the fairness and opportunities offered by the system the challenges of growth and equity cannot be tackled in sequence. They have to be resolved simultaneously.'

In a felicitous synthesis, Alesina and Rodrik (1994, p. 465) stated that: 'The distinction between economics and politics is that economics is concerned with expanding the pie while politics is about distributing it.' The political economy connection is that both depend on each other and on the expectations about how both processes will deliver on the promise to enlarge the pie and distribute it. To a large extent this a 'rational expectations' problem, one in which the history of the process determines its current credibility. This is a dynamic two period problem that can only be solved when 'there is consistency between how one treated the future yesterday and how one treats it today' (Drazen, 2000, p. 33).

Empirical studies point out that the initial configuration of resources shapes the political struggle for income and seems to hinder long-run growth. Alesina and Rodrik (1994, p. 465) have concluded: 'that inequality is conducive to the adoption of growth-retarding polices'. The real politics lies in the process through which self interested agents will compete for instant redistribution. The political challenge is to agree on collective rules that allow for the size of the pie to grow and for a large part of the marginal increment to go to reduce poverty and improve income distribution. Progress in terms of macroeconomic stability and poverty reduction requires institutional transformations at both interdependent fronts: first, at the macroeconomic level, where already 'decentralized' Central Banks have contributed to much lower inflation and to improved stability. At this level what is missing are fiscal rules for enhanced countercyclical capacity. Secondly, transformations are needed at the micro-institutional levels where there is still a long road to be traveled to change the incentives surrounding most public spending on education, health and social security in general.

These two reform fronts face daunting political challenges in Latin America today. Why? Because, in a way, they are mutually exclusive. The first macroeconomic front demands fiscal restraint. The second micro-institutional one is normally perceived as requiring more – not less – public spending. But more public spending has already been tried[53] in many countries in the last 10–15 years and has hardly worked. It has debilitated the macroeconomic frameworks and has not delivered enhanced equal opportunities or access by the poor to education, to health and to a modicum of social security. To really change initial conditions for the poor the micro-institutional incentive structure surrounding most social expenditures in the region would need to change. But those social expenditures have been 'captured' by public sector rent-seekers with immense political power. So we are nearly back at square one. Development in Latin America is basically a political economy problem, that is the balancing of economic and distributional needs.

In trying to put all this together there is one 'rational choice explanation'. If some Latin American politicians and policy makers can blame external shocks and avatars for the consequences of not doing their homework, and can often get away with this 'scapegoating', why not blame the external avatars? This would be the 'rational' posture for 'rational' agents to take. Disqualifying it as a 'mistake' is just normative *naïveté*. This would be the real 'non rational mistake'. It would not be 'positive' political analysis or economics. Furthermore, it seldom leads to effective corrections. This is precisely the point that Alesina (1991, p. 43) was making. Is this a defeatist conclusion? Does the political economy explanation for macroeconomic volatility and resistance to policy reforms in Latin America end and succumb here? Is there then no hope? Not in the least. Now that we know that the main restriction is a weak political demand for reform and for institutional transformation, we can go back to work on the underlying determinants of that demand. That is, the information markets, the diagnostics, the research agendas, and the incentives and interests behind the decision making processes. The circle is complete. This book began talking about rational choices and incentives. Back then, they may have looked like esoteric themes. Not any more.

NOTES

1. 'A complete understanding of the process of public finance requires an analysis of the political decision-making process that determines how governments will both raise and spend revenues. In other words, a complete understanding of public finance requires that it be analyzed from a public choice perspective'. See Holcombe (2000, p. 396).
2. The application of the theory of games to economics was 'originally' made by von Neuman and Morgenstern (1944). It deals with the strategies to maximize pay-offs given the risks in judging responses by others. Its applicability is widespread in situations in which there is no or little competition and one party's action induces a reaction from others.
3. Chari and Kehoe (2006, p. 5) observe that 'people's decision rules change when there is change in the way policy is conducted. Lucas (1976) forcefully argued that the question "How should policy be set today?" was ill-posed. In most situations, people's current decisions depend on their expectations of what future policies will be. Those expectations depend, in part, on how people expect policymakers to behave. Macroeconomists now agree, therefore, that any sensible policy analysis must include a clear specification of how a current choice of policy will shape expectations of future policies.'

4. 'Models of economic cycles induced by the political cycle are termed models of the political business cycle (PBC); models which focus on the desire to win elections as determinants of policy and the expected effect of such policies are termed models of the opportunistic PBC.' See Drazen (2000, p. 228).
5. Incentive theory emerges in all delegations and principal–agent situations and when actors have different objective functions. See Laffont and Martimort (2002, p. 7).
6. According to Dixit (1996, p. 56), transactions costs politics are very complicated. This is basically because 'the political process cannot use monitoring and incentive contracts to the same extent that they are used in economic relationships. Instead, we see much greater reliance on more blunt instruments – commitments and constraints.'
7. Following Baumol, the proximate causes of growth in a given country are basically its capital and investment, labor supply and productivity as well as its capacity for technological change. In 1987 Professor Solow received the Nobel prize for his contribution to growth theory by underscoring the importance of technological change as the factor that can contribute significantly to economic growth even if capital and labor are not increased. The issue, of course, is where does technological innovation come from if it is not from institutions propitious to research and to technological change? The long term causes of growth and equity are the institutions that determine how a society adopts the policies that lead to a given supply of capital and labor productivity.
8. On cliometrics see North (1997, p. 412).
9. See *The Economist* (2005, p. 82).
10. Nothing is really independent; Mistri (2003, p. 315) posits that 'one way to solve the question of how a norm forms is to take for granted that the agents already have some knowledge of how to solve problems of interaction'.
11. Wiesner (1998, p. xiii) argues that the problem is not getting the 'right' institutions but getting rid of the 'wrong' ones.
12. Mistri (2003, p. 314) posits that a common system of values 'outside the game' is necessary for a cooperative game to engender the 'right' institutions.
13. The received concept of 'transaction costs' normally includes those of organizing, maintaining and enforcing the rules of an institutional arrangement (Nugent, 1998, p. 11). Here it is conceptually extended to refer to the intended or unintended costs emerging from flaws in the interaction between the Central Banks, the Ministries of Finance and the financial sector regulators. An inefficient macroeconomic institutional arrangement would be one in which there are high transaction costs in terms of suboptimal macroeconomics results such as growth, inflation and distributive justice.
14. See Feeny (1993, p. 163).
15. This is what Barbados did. See IMF (2003).
16. On the political economy of the supply side of institutions see the work of Olson (1965) and also the views of Robert Mundell on the application of supply side economics to other problems in 'Interview with Robert Mundell' (Vane and Mulhearn, 2006, p. 102).
17. Rent-seeking is a legitimate activity not to be wished away by normative or ethical nostrums (Magee, 1997, p. 544). It results from endogenous protection and can be politically efficient. 'Rent-seeking is just a transaction costs of democracy' (Magee, 1997, p. 544). But that democracy will have to judge how high or low a transaction cost it is willing to accept.
18. For the case of Colombia see Wiesner (2004b).
19. 'The inefficiencies that arise when several groups or officials with redistributive aims have control over fiscal policy have been recognized in the literature. Weingast et al. (1981) and, more recently, Chari and Cole (1993) and Chari et al. (1994) show that having the supply of local public goods financed with national or federal revenues creates incentives for pork barrel spending.' See Velasco (1999, p. 39).
20. Alchian (1950) was one of the first scholars who used biological terms to refer to market processes.
21. It is interesting to remember that Charles Darwin wrote that he came to the idea of natural selection after reading Malthus' work on population.
22. According to Oliver Williamson (1996), it was Chester Barnard (1938) who really saw the importance of incentives in firms and organizations.

23. On the question of moral hazard, see Rogoff (2002). For a discussion of moral hazard issues in Latin America, see Ortiz (2002).
24. On the use of 'instrumental variables' (that may be linked to institutions but are entirely unconnected to economic success) see *The Economist* (2006c, p. 88).
25. See Morgan (1990, p. 220) for a particular approach on measurement errors and the method of instrumental variables.
26. For a summary of the methodology and result see Edison (2003, p. 35).
27. See Glaeser et al. (2004, p. 26), for a rigorous questioning of the role of institutions. To these scholars what matters the most is not so much institutions but human capital. In their view, 'The greater the human and social capital of a community, the more attractive its institutional opportunities. Institutions, in this framework, are points on this opportunity set, determined by efficiency, history, and politics. Our results have some implications for economic research and for economic policy. They suggest that research in institutional economics, and in particular on the consequences of alternative institutional arrangements, must focus on actual rules, rather than on conceptually ambiguous assessment of institutional outcomes. The results of this paper do not show that "institutions do not matter". That proposition is flatly contradicted by a great deal of available empirical evidence, including our own. Rather, our results suggest that the current measurement strategies have conceptual flaws, and that researches would do better focusing on actual laws, rules, and compliance procedures that could be manipulated by a policy maker to assess what works.'
28. Summers (1991, p. 143) posited that 'macroeconomics is an empirical science'.
29. In their view 'the natural rate of unemployment depended on labor supply, labor demand, optimal search times and other microeconomic considerations, not on the average rate of money growth'. See Mankiw (1990, p. 1647).
30. For a review of the 'state of nature' of macroeconomics see Solow (1997, p. 230); Taylor (1999); Blinder (1997); Taylor and Woodford (1999).
31. 'The way to model people's response or endogeneity of expectations is through the rational expectations approach although modifications to take account of the different degrees of credibility are necessary' (Taylor, 1997, p. 234). The key concept is that of the credibility on the real policies and on how that credibility affects actual outcomes.
32. See Taylor (1997, p. 234).
33. See Taylor (1997, p. 234, 235).
34. According to Talvi (2003, p. 670), this does not mean a change in the economic model.
35. Different macroeconomic management approaches between countries may explain different macroeconomic performances. See Calvo and Talvi (2005, p. 18).
36. See de Ferranti et al. (2004, p. 109), Chapter 4, 'Historical roots of inequality in Latin America'.
37. World Bank (2005, p. 2).
38. On the median voter theorem see Stallings et al. (2000, p. 105).
39. For an analysis of the impact of exchange rate, money supply and capital flows on poverty and income distribution, see Conway (2005, p. 39).
40. See Ocampo's (2004b, p. 84). See also Ocampo et al. (1998, p. 73). See also Berry (1998).
41. See Nuñez et al. (2005, p. 31).
42. See Keefer and Stasavage (2003, p. 60), for a discussion of the links between general social welfare and institutional political commitments to express it.
43. See Rogoff (2003, p. 54).
44. See Burnside (2005, p. 35) for the conditions for fiscal sustainability.
45. World Bank (2004b, p. 14).
46. See IMF, World Economic Outlook database. See Singh et al. (2005, p. xiv).
47. Gavin et al. (1996, p. 11), 'The volatility of Latin American fiscal expenditure is striking. Capital spending is twice, wage payments are four times, nonwage purchases of goods and services are six times, and transfer payments are nearly nine times as volatile as in the OECD. It is very hard to believe that the extremely high volatilities of real wage and transfer payments are the result of explicit fiscal decisions. It seems more likely that the very high volatility of real payments reflects the inflationary erosion of nominal

budgetary allocations due to unexpectedly high inflation. And indeed, the inflation tax rate has not only been much higher in Latin America averaging nearly 40 percent to the OECD's 6 percent – but also much more volatile, with a standard deviation of more than 20 percentage points in comparison with only 3 percentage points in the OECD.'

48. On the effectiveness of early warning systems see Goldstein et al. (2000, p. 21). See also Kaminsky and Reinhart (1999).
49. On inflation targeting in the United States see Goodfriend (2005, p. 311).
50. 'The interaction between loose fiscal and monetary policies, inflation and exchange rates has been especially destructive' (Fraga, 2004, p. 104).
51. To Velasco (1999, p. 38), delays are explained by 'fragmental fiscal policy-making'.
52. See Loser and Guerguil (2000, p. 9) for a review of the reforms of the 1990s and for pending challenges.
53. According to Clements et al. (2007, p. 24), 'primary expenditures have trended upwards for the past ten years as a share of GDP'.

PART II

Country Narratives and Comparative Economics

Institutional diversity is the underlying constant theme in all attempts to configure a fully robust causality theory of institutional development. In fact, dealing with diversity is the main theoretical and empirical challenge. This is one of the reasons why institutional economics quickly moves to incentive and information realms. To deal with diversity, 'new comparative economics' (Shleifer, 2002, p. 12) suggests a focus on 'institutional differences among countries' and Dixit (2004, p. 150) posits that: 'Country case studies show important links between good governance institutions and economic success.' Confronted with the difficulties of building rigorous econometric models to explain institutional development, Rodrik (2003, p. 3) opted for analytical country narratives 'to provide answers to selected growth puzzles and to explore the respective roles of microeconomic and macroeconomic policies, institutions, political economy and initial conditions in selected countries'.

The key questions guiding empirical research in institutional economics are: (i) 'Why do societies evolve along distinct institutional trajectories?' (ii) 'Why do societies often fail to adopt the institutional structure of more successful ones?' and (iii) 'How may we examine the interrelations between the implicit and informal aspects of societies' institutions, on the one hand, and their explicit and formal aspects, on the other?' To address these questions Greif (1998, p. 80) suggests the use of historical and comparative institutional analysis to 'explore the role of history in institutional emergence, perpetuation, and change'. This is the conceptual context framing the following 'Country narratives for Argentina, Brazil, Chile, Colombia, Costa Rica and Peru'.

As was indicated in the Introduction, these six countries were chosen mainly because of their potential capacity to inform policy principles in general and under specific different economic characteristics such as size, political structure, equity dynamics and policy responses to international or domestic volatility. It is an imperfect sample in the sense that there are situations and histories in countries like Mexico, Venezuela or Bolivia where their respective experiences also have great potential to inform policy and to provide guidance. However, it does not seem that the general conclusions drawn from this sample would not be broadly aligned with those likely to be derived from a wider and more varied group of countries.

These 'country narratives' are somewhat uneven in terms of their length but there is conceptual consistency in the treatment and analysis of the major political economy factors affecting their respective economic performances. The 'entry-point' into each country narrative is the particular political economy problem largely shaping the specifics of economic policies. The idea is to focus on that global political constraint before addressing why they end up with some policies and not others. The key issues of institutions, incentives, rules, information, political accountability and 'local' histories, in their relation to macroeconomic and distributive policy making, are examined in each country. However, some issues are treated in more depth in some countries than in others. It all depends on relative topical relevances. But there is general validity across countries. Issues such as the role of constitutional rules are reviewed in more detail in Colombia than in other countries, but the rules in general are a common thread. The issue of presidential re-election is part of the 'rules realm' all over the region. Compliance with fiscal nominal or real rules is also part of the macroeconomic governance structure of all countries. Distributive justice issues are covered in all countries of the 'sample'. In brief, these 'country narratives' hold together conceptually and are consistent in delivering broad policy messages.

It seems that, to a large extent, most countries have similar nominal policy objectives such as price stability, sustainable growth and employment. They also have macroeconomic institutional arrangements that share similar characteristics, such as Central Bank relative autonomy, inflation targeting as a monetary framework and an independent financial oversight regulator. But their actual results differ. What explains these different outcomes? The less imperfect answer with large validity across the region seems to be that there are different political incentives in each country to reward the achievement of those objectives. The political demand for those objectives is not strong enough in most of the countries. This conclusion is far from solving the problem and the question of why countries do not adopt the right reforms. But it changes the perspective and the priorities in the search for the specifics of the respective 'local' strategy for reform.

3.   Argentina: blinded by hindsight – the economics and politics of learning

'The rules!' shouted Ralph. 'You're breaking the rules!' 'Who cares?' Ralph summoned his wits. 'Because the rules are the only thing we've got!'

William Golding (1954, p. 83)

I.   FROM SCYLLA TO CHARYBDIS

A perennial quest and vexing dilemma of humanity has been the choice between rules, on the one hand, and discretion, on the other. Should choices be framed on rigid mandates or under discretionary flexibility? Since the myth of Ulysses[1] this pendulum has defined the extremes within which different social, political and individual choices have been pondered and made. At the beginning of 1991, and certainly not in an act of improvisation, Argentina chose the rule of a convertibility exchange rate arrangement as the anchor for its macroeconomic and fiscal policy. By doing so it was expressing its resignation to its capacity to judiciously exercise discretion and flexibility in the management of its fiscal and public expenditure policies. For decades it had been plagued by bouts of populism[2] and inflation.[3] Finally it came to the conclusion that to terminate this self imposed destiny it had to adopt a convertibility rule. Success came almost instantly. Inflation dropped from the thousands to low hundreds in 1991 and growth rebounded to 10.5 per cent. In 1992 inflation fell further to 24.9 per cent and growth remained very strong at 9.6 per cent. The convertibility regime was broadly seen as a major success. However, in that same year, in a clairvoyant article, Anna J. Schwartz wrote that 'the sustainability of the fixed exchange rate with the dollar was still to be tested' (1993, p. 179).

Over the following years up to 1999 Argentina lived 'the best and the worst of times'. With the exception of 1995, when growth was negative (−2.8 per cent), and resulted largely from a Mexican contagion-induced recession, its economy expanded robustly. In 1997 it grew by 8.1 per cent. But beginning in 1999 growth was negative by −3.4 per cent, followed by

−0.8 per cent in 2000, −4.4 per cent in 2001 and −10.9 per cent in 2002. From 1999 to the end of 2002 the poverty rate rose from 30 per cent to 58 per cent. The extreme poverty rate almost tripled, going from 10 per cent to 28 per cent.

In brief, in a short period of about eight years Argentina seemed to have overcome its traditionally fiscal and monetary weaknesses and graduated to a more orthodox and prudent macroeconomic management. But the initial triumph over history did not last.[4] Policy corrections did not come on time and from 1998 onwards the country descended into economic melt-down[5] and political collapse. The net balance was an immense welfare loss. This economic and political[6] debacle seems to be yet another example of the enormous difficulty that Argentina has had over many decades[7] to manage its fiscal, monetary and financial affairs well. Why and how did this happen? What explains developments that now appear to have been predictable? What did Anna Schwartz know that led her to express reservations on the convertibility regime eight years before it collapsed?[8] The broad answer that needs to be unbundled is why this unintended example of economic and political failure took place under such an extreme version of a collective action problem?

But are these the really ultimately relevant questions? After all, what rules were broken? Was breaking the fiscal rules the main policy flaw? If so, what explains that the fiscal rules were broken? The 'fiscal explanation' of the Argentina macroeconomic crisis has been well documented (Galiani et al., 2002, p. 1; Kenen, 2005, p. 51; IMF, 2004a).[9] One of the most insightful ones came even before the crisis. In 1997 Talvi (1997, p. 73), in an example of foresight, warned of the precariousness of an initial strong fiscal position as an anchor for a stabilization program.[10] But from a political economic perspective what explains these explanations?

This country narrative suggests as a possible complementary explicatory hypothesis that what tipped the balance of developments in the wrong direction was breaking the larger political rules[11] and accommodating a Constitutional change for the re-election of the incumbent President in 1993. This 'breaking of the rules within the game'[12] may well be the missing critical explicatory variable of developments since the mid 1990s, leading to the 2000–2001 debacle. The hypothesis is that the pervasive re-election climate during the decade changed the overall public sector incentive structure and decision making processes in favor of high expenditures, and induced an intended and unintended proclivity to take policy risks that gradually drained the macroeconomic framework of much-needed flexibility. This re-election incentive climate continued into 1998, surfaced again in 2003, and may even last into 2007 when the current President Kirchner may decide to seek re-election.

II. THE POLITICAL DEMAND FOR THE CONVERTIBILITY RULE

Within a conceptual context in which the effectiveness of a macroeconomic framework is mainly determined by the strength of the political demand for macroeconomic stability, the choice of a convertibility rule would imply the assumption that there was such political demand. But if the assumption was correct, why have the rule? You would not need the rule because the political process would already have engendered the policies that deliver macroeconomic stability. The tentative conclusion that emerges is then that there was something missing and that there was either not sufficient real demand for macroeconomic stability or insufficient political support for fiscal policies to anchor convertibility.

There might have been a dislike of hyperinflation and initial political support for the promise of its taming. But the first explicatory hypothesis is that *ab initio* there was a nominal repudiation of high inflation but insufficient political support for the policies that would contribute to macroeconomic stability. Such weak political support may originate in a nineteenth century 'constitutional design problem' (della Paolera and Gallo, 2003, p. 372). President Menem and Minister Cavallo, in supporting the convertibility rule, probably knew all this. Their strategy may have been to establish the rule and hope that if it delivered lower inflation the public would gradually come to support the other ancillary policies and Argentina would reach a completely different and positive development trajectory.

The literature on Argentina's crisis experience in 2000–02 is enormous. This country narrative will focus on the following three interdependent questions in the hope of making a contribution to the learning process from this tragic experience:

i.   What was the macroeconomic background[13] that may explain the early political acceptance and economic success of the convertibility system?
ii. What political economy factors changed in the 1990s which may have led to the 'wrong' incentives in the macroeconomic governance structure and to a collective action problem in the decision making process and in crisis management?[14]
iii. What are the main features of the current (mid-2007) emerging macroeconomic policy framework?

The first question aims at linking the pre-convertibility economic and political economy conditions, on the one hand, with the strength of the recovery in 2002 and 2003, on the other. In principle, the fast GDP rebound should not be surprising. The initial success in 2003 may have had more to

Table 3.1   Argentina: GDP growth, 1980–2006 (variation rate, %)

Year	GDP	Year	GDP	Year	GDP
1980	1.5	1989	−6.9	1998	3.9
1981	−5.4	1990	−1.8	1999	−3.4
1982	−3.2	1991	10.6	2000	−0.8
1983	4.1	1992	9.6	2001	−4.4
1984	2.0	1993	5.7	2002	−10.9
1985	−6.9	1994	5.8	2003	8.7
1986	7.1	1995	−2.8	2004	9.0
1987	2.6	1996	5.5	2005	9.2
1988	−1.9	1997	8.1	2006	8.5

Sources: For 1980–2003, Roberto Frenkel (2004, p. 34). For 2004–2005, Banco Central de la República Argentina (2006).

do with the possibility that the economy had reached bottom, after three years of contraction, than with the attributes of the convertibility arrangement. The importance of this issue is that the authorities at the time would have been more aware of the need to support the convertibility arrangement with fiscal measures. Neither convertibility nor fiscal constraint would be the main explanation for the initial success. It may well have been, in no small share, the 'free ride' of recovery (see Table 3.1). The importance of the second question is that it points out that what matters the most in any evaluation is not so much what was missing or what did not come about, but 'why' these developments occurred.[15] This is the path towards 'causality construction' and effective learning. The third question is the key one. It aims at putting the whole experience in perspective in the sense that it tries to establish how much has been learnt and what political economy restrictions may still be impeding the adoption of corrective pending macroeconomic reforms. Argentina's case contains a rich potential of lessons on the reasons why developing countries do not end up with the 'right' reforms.[16]

III.   EVALUABLE HISTORY AND THE POLITICAL ECONOMY OF LESSON TAKING

In principle, the awareness of the high welfare costs of the crisis experienced by Argentina in 2001 and 2002 should inform the public at large and engender a political demand for reform of the macroeconomic governance structure. That demand would provide the political incentives to support the fiscal and attendant reforms needed. Also, in principle, since the poverty levels reached by the end of 2002 are now declining, political support for the pending reforms should now be more forthcoming. But, although these, 'in principle', tenets have robust analytical and empirical support, there is not yet a direct causality relationship for all country experiences. If the current (mid-2007) emerging policy framework in Argentina is significantly different from those that came out of Brazil, Colombia, Mexico, Chile or Peru,[17] the question would be 'why is this so?' How could Argentina's learning process be that much different? Mario Teijeiro (2005) insightfully has observed that the 'failure' of the Convertibility arrangement may have led to political disenchantment with 'liberal' or orthodox policy frameworks. In his view this may already be pushing the Kirchner administration towards the left. Notwithstanding the fact that the collapse of the Convertibility arrangement was more than anything else a failure to meet its fiscal requirements, it may well be that it is still politically profitable to 'blame the external avatars' instead of searching for the right lessons and for domestic political accountabilities.

IV. MACROECONOMIC VOLATILITY 1980–1990, LEADING TO CONVERTIBILITY

The period before the adoption of the Convertibility arrangement in 1991 was highly volatile. All-out crisis had erupted in the early 1980s when 'an overvalued exchange rate had created a large cumulative balance of payments deficit, causing a serious debt service problem and an eventual loss of market access. Inflation accelerated, and real GDP declined by almost 10 percent from 1980 to 1982' (IMF, 2004a, p. 78). Later on a

> deep recession ensued, causing real GDP in 1989 to decline by 7 percent from the previous year. During the middle of this crisis, the ruling Radical party lost the national elections, and the administration of President Raul Alfonsín yielded power to the opposition Justicialist (Peronist) party, five months ahead of schedule. (IMF, 2004a, p. 78)

In June 1985 the 'Austral Plan' was tried as shock therapy and as a shift away from gradualist approaches. Then in 1988 the 'Plan Primavera' attempted to link wage and price controls with a fixed exchange rate. But supportive fiscal mechanisms were not sustained and this attempt also failed. In July 1989 the first Menem administration designed a fiscal and exchange rate package and in October requested a stand-by arrangement (SBA) with the IMF. But by the end of the year, policy control deteriorated and 'consumer prices rose by 90% during the last three weeks of December' (IMF, 2004a, p. 79).

President Menem's first period[18] began on 9 July 1989. In that year GDP declined by −6.9 per cent, and by −1.8 per cent in 1990. In both of these years inflation was above 2000 per cent. In April 1991, after having 'tried' three Ministers of Finance, President Menem appointed Domingo Cavallo. Under his inspiration Argentina adopted in April 1991 a macroeconomic regime anchored on the convertibility of the peso to the US dollar.[19] More broadly the government embarked on a wide ranging program of deregulation and privatization of state owned enterprises.

The answer to the first question on the macroeconomic and political conditions leading up to Convertibility can be summarized as follows. First, a GDP that had been falling for three consecutive years (−1.9 per cent in 1988; −6.9 per cent in 1989; −1.8 per cent in 1990). Secondly, inflation had reached above the thousands in 1989 and 1990. Thirdly, poverty rates in 1990 had more than doubled in five years. These were the conditions and antecedents nurturing a potential political demand for macroeconomic stability and for an institutional transformation of the macroeconomic governance structure.

V. MACROECONOMIC PERFORMANCE IN HISTORICAL PERSPECTIVE

Macroeconomic performance under a long term perspective has not turned out to be good in Argentina. Table 3.2 shows that as far back as 1900 Argentina's per capita income was one of the highest in the world and twice that of Latin America. This is a country that in 1913 had a higher per capita income than France and Germany (Blustein, 2005, p. 16).[20] From 1950 to 1960 its average annual rate of growth was as low as 1.1 per cent. During the 1980s it had a negative average rate of −2.4 per cent (Table 3.3). From 1960 to 2000 its average real per capita growth has lagged behind other Latin American and developing countries (Figure 3.1). Underlying this low growth record and high volatility there is persistent fiscal mismanagement. This was the historical context that inspired the adoption of the Convertibility arrangement. Namely, if the authorities could not print pesos there would not be fiscal deficits, and growth would be high and stable.

Macroeconomic performance measured in per capita terms in Argentina, as well as other Latin American countries, with the exception of Chile, has been lackadaisical or on a declining trend for well over the last 40 years. Figure 3.1 shows that for the period 1960–2000, Argentina's average real per capita GDP rate of growth has lagged behind Latin America as a whole and other developing countries as well.

Table 3.2   *Argentina's per capita income in regional and historical perspective*

	1900	1913	1950	1973	1992
Argentina	2756	3797	4987	7970	7616
Latin America (7)	1311	1733	3478	5017	5949
Western Europe (12)	2899	3482	5513	11694	17412
Western offshoots (4)	3868	5051	8083	13828	17475
Southern Europe (5)	1676	1788	2259	6770	10015
United States	4096	5307	9573	16607	21558
United Kingdom	4593	5032	6847	11992	15738
Japan	1135	1334	1873	11017	19425
South Korea	850	948	876	2840	10010
Taiwan	759	794	922	3669	11590

Notes:
Latin America (7): Argentina, Brazil, Chile, Colombia, Mexico, Peru, Venezuela.
Western Europe (12): Austria, Belgium, Denmark, Finland, France, Germany, Italy, Netherlands, Norway, Sweden, Switzerland, United Kingdom.
European New World (4 called 'Western offshoots' by Maddison): Australia, Canada, New Zealand, United States.
Southern Europe (5): Greece, Ireland, Portugal, Spain, Turkey.
Data in the table from Maddison (1995) in 1992 PPP-adjusted international dollars. The table shows incomes relative to a Western Europe arithmetic average equal to 1.0. The table shows relative rather than absolute economic performance.

Source: della Paolera and Taylor (2003, p. 4).

Table 3.3   *Argentina: equity evolution, 2001–2006*

Indicator	2001	2002	2003	2004	2005
Population below poverty line (%)	35.4	53.0	47.8	40.2	33.8
Population below extreme poverty line (%)	12.2	24.8	20.5	15.0	12.2
Unemployment	20.7	20.7	14.5	12.1	10.1
Inequality*	0.513	0.528	0.528	0.506	0.501

Note: * Gini coefficient, a higher value indicates an increase in inequality, 2001–2003 Gini are as of May; 2004 and 2005 Gini are as of the second semester.

Sources:
a.   IMF (2006, p. 4).
b.   For 'Inequality' source see World Bank (2006a, p. 17).
c.   Ginis for 1999 and 2000 come from IMF (2002, p. 36, Box 6).

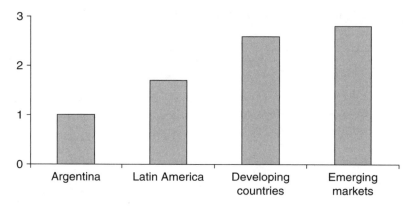

Source: IMF (2005a, p. 4).

*Figure 3.1   Argentina's average real per capita GDP growth relative to
other countries*

The main explanation for the declining long term trend has been a history
of high inflation, fiscal deficits and many failed attempts to establish credibility for economic policies. Behind these external systems there are fundamental political economy problems and weak fiscal and political institutions.

VI.   EQUITY AND POVERTY IN PERSPECTIVE

For decades Argentina could pride itself on being a country with relatively
low poverty rates in Latin America. But poverty has ratcheted up with
each crisis episode. Table 3.3 shows the enormous magnitude of poverty
increases resulting from the 2001–2002 crisis. From 35.4 per cent in 1991
poverty jumped to 53.0 per cent in 2002. The extreme poverty line doubled
from 2001 to 2002. Inequality as measured by Gini worsened slightly
between those two years.

VII.   THE 2001–2002 CRISIS IN REGIONAL
PERSPECTIVE

The Argentine crisis of 2001–2002 may well have been the most severe
one in Latin America during the last 20 years. Table 3.4 compares
the experience of Argentina with that of Mexico in 1995 and Chile in
1982. Neither of these countries had four consecutive years of GDP
contraction.

Table 3.4   Latin America: GDP economic shocks

Country	Year relative to crisis							
	−3	−2	−1	0	1	2	3	4
Argentina 2002	−3.4	−0.8	−4.4	−10.9	8.8	9.0	9.2	–
Argentina 2005	11.9	5.9	5.8	−2.8	5.5	8.1	3.8	−3.4
Mexico 1995	3.6	1.9	4.4	−6.2	5.1	6.8	5.0	–
Chile 1982	8.7	8.1	4.7	−10.3	−3.8	8.0	7.1	–

Source: World Bank (2000c, p. 50).

If one had to summarize the process that took place between 1995 and 2002, it would be done around the tension between the vulnerability of a convertibility regime and the pressures from 'fiscal dominance'.[21] At the end the arithmetics (Sargent and Wallace, 1981) of fiscal deficits and growing debt made convertibility unsustainable. From a Knightian[22] perspective the question that arises is why the authorities were not able to protect the inherent vulnerability of the convertibility with risk management of the probabilities of the occurrence of a particular hazard. An aeroplane is very vulnerable but by managing the risks of potential hazards, planes have become very safe.[23]

Another critical explanatory factor of the crisis was the role played by the IMF. According to Michael Mussa (2002, p. 3) the Fund incurred two important unintended mistakes: (i) 'Failing to press the Argentine authorities much harder to have a more responsible fiscal policy, especially during the three high growth years following the tequila crisis of 1995' and (ii) 'Extending substantial additional financial support to Argentina during the summer of 2001, after it had become abundantly clear that the Argentine government's efforts to avoid default and maintain the exchange rate peg had no reasonable chance of success.' However, these mistakes 'should not obscure the critical failure of Argentine economic policy to run a responsible fiscal policy. This is an old and sad story for Argentina. To satisfy various political needs and pressures, the government (at all levels) has a persistent tendency to spend significantly more than can be raised in taxes' (Mussa, 2002, p. 6).

But why did the Fund fail to establish the 'right' amount of conditionality and 'catalytic' financing? Part of the explanation lies in the double role of the Fund as 'a tough cop' and as a 'sympathetic' social worker (Mussa, 2002, p. 46). Wiesner (2004c, p. 337) observes that all multilaterals perform under 'Collective Action Restrictions, CAR's' which make it very difficult for them to meet what he calls the Resources-Restrictions-Condition (RRC). This

dual role is a political[24] conundrum resulting from the cooperative nature of
the collective action framework within which countries and 'their' multilateral institution are created (Tirole, 2002, p. 117). But in the end, it is the lack
of domestic political accountability that explains much of the 'wrong' risk
taking with which some developing countries manage their chosen or
endowed vulnerabilities. As long as Latin American developing countries
can blame the external avatars for their misfortunes and can do this with
political impunity there may not be sufficiently 'right' incentives to be more
judicious in managing sudden stops or business cycles. If Argentina now
draws the wrong conclusions and blames those avatars it will be because the
political incentives reward, at least in the short term, those policies.

VIII.   FISCAL DEFICITS WITHIN MACROECONOMIC COMPLEXITY

The role of fiscal deficits in compromising the sustainability of the
Convertibility arrangement is not a simple one. Guidotti (2005, p. 19)
argues that

> severely limited in terms of instruments by expenditure inflexibility, an inefficient
> tax system, and by a rigid exchange rate regime in the face of deteriorating exter-
> nal competitiveness, fiscal policy was confronted with serious difficulties in
> dealing with the dynamics imposed by the Brady deal, the pension reform, and
> *skeletons*[25] when international capital market turned volatile after the Asian
> crisis and the Russian default.

Figure 3.2 shows that of

> the increase in public debt of 64.1 USD billions in the period 1993–2000 – cor-
> responding to an average deficit of 2.9 percent of GDP per year – a share of
> 48.3 percent is explained by the pension reform – a contribution to the overall
> average yearly deficit equivalent to 1.6 percent of GDP – while a share of 40.5
> percent of the total is explained by the issue of BOCONes (Bonos de
> Consolidación or debt consolidating bonds, also known as 'skeletons'. These
> were compulsory bonds given to creditors and pensioners.). In sum, assuming
> an unchanged fiscal policy stance, the pension reform and skeletons can explain
> almost 99 percent of the increase in Argentina's public debt during 1993 and
> 2000. (Guidotti, 2005, p. 15)

Guidotti's conclusion (2005, p. 20) seems to be a major lesson and
warning for several Latin American countries. After all, fiscal reforms,
pension reforms and debt restructuring normally take place. What really
matters are liquidity constraints and vulnerability to sudden stops.

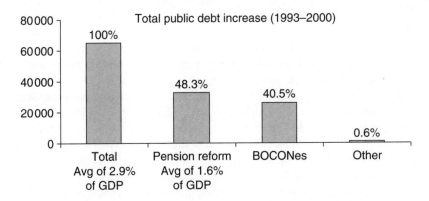

Source: Guidotti (2005, p. 15).

Figure 3.2 Argentina: accounting for the pension reform

IX. THE OCCULT FISCAL RE-ELECTION COSTS OR THE 'MENEM SYNDROME'

The search for a common thread spanning the whole decade of the 1990s that may help explain Argentina's March of Folly, from success to dismal failure, reveals one that seems to have the potential to do a considerable portion of that. It also illuminates some of the sources of the differences in the way macroeconomic crisis unfolded in other countries in Latin America. It could be called the 'Menem Syndrome'. In essence, it summarizes the changes that can take place in the whole incentive structure of a given public sector, and the effects those changes can have on the quality of economic policies, when the Constitutional rules of the political game are changed to allow, for instance, for the presidential re-election of the incumbent administration.

President Menem came to power in 1989 supported by Duhalde.[26] He sought his firm re-election in mid-1993 and then again in July 1998. In the first case he got it in 1995. In the second case he did not. Again in 2003 he also ran against Nestor Kirchner on the Peronista ballot. Duhalde, the outgoing President, supported Kirchner. Altogether Menem held the presidency for a total of over ten years, from July 1989 to December 1999. During the first period he and his team may have felt, in good faith, that he should remain in power to assure the continuity of, at the time, successful policies. But this meant a change in the incentive structure across the decision making process in the whole public sector. Controlling fiscal deficits and additions to public debt would have to compete with the need to obtain political support for the re-election.[27]

The question is, in which direction were the incentives stronger? In the often judgmental calls about fiscal risks, in which direction would the decision making process move? How would political accountability be traced back if the decision making process was taking place under ambiguous policy directives?

The hypothesis is that when an incumbent president and his party seek re-election they will have incentives to buy political support with, *inter alia*, public expenditures and particular favors to special groups. The possible political vigilance of those political forces that may oppose the expenditure policies, or the re-election itself, can be neutralized by short term interests. The vigilance or surveillance of multilateral institutions is also weakened by the 'cooperative nature'[28] of those institutions vis-à-vis a member country. The empirical and analytical support for this hypothesis comes from the fact that from 1994 through 2001 annual fiscal targets with the IMF were missed every year. They were missed by large margins, up to 2.0 per cent of GDP even when the economy was growing at rates exceeding the initial forecasts (IMF, 2004a, p. 24).

According to the IMF (2004a, p. 4), 'An election-driven increase in public spending led to a sharp deterioration in fiscal discipline in 1999. As a result, the stock of public debt steadily increased, diminishing the ability of the authorities to use countercyclical fiscal policy when the recession deepened.' But the fiscal problems had been brewing long before in the transfer system with the Provincias, in the issuance of debt to finance off-budget expenditures,[29] in the granting of wage increases and limiting downward flexibility, in focusing more on flow[30] fiscal concepts than on stock and debt concepts, and in the accounting for privatization revenues. All this explains 'why the stock of public debt doubled as a share of GDP between 1992 and 2001, when fiscal deficits appeared moderate and the government was receiving significant revenue from privatization' (IMF, 2004a, 80). Teijeiro (2001) opines that mistaken fiscal policy was the main explicatory factor for the 2001 crisis.

Not all re-election processes lead automatically to larger fiscal deficits. They lead more to higher public expenditures than to higher taxes to finance those expenditures. After all, higher taxes would have political resistance while other less transparent forms of financing have less opposition. In the case of Brazil, F.H. Cardozo was re-elected, and in his eight years of government, public expenditures grew much faster than GDP. President Lula has not done much that is different but Brazil has protected its overall fiscal balance by a 'tax and spend policy' which may explain why this country has been able to navigate the macroeconomic challenges of the last 10 years better. In Peru, Fujimori's re-election experience was also one in which public expenditures grew fast but tax revenues also did and the country has done very well in the last five years.

In brief, the net conceptual hypothesis is that changes in the Constitutional and political rules of presidential election games can have very deleterious effects on the incentive structure regulating fiscal balances and the accounting for stock changes of debt. It may affect the direction in which the management of fiscal risks is conducted by domestic authorities as well as by multilateral institutions. In the case of Argentina, the combination of vulnerability[31] coming from the Convertibility arrangement, and the re-election rules change, proved to be devastating.

X.   THE IMMEDIATE CAUSES OF THE CRISIS

Argentina's most severe economic and political crisis in several decades came about through the combination of three sets of factors:

i.   the failure of the Argentinian authorities to take early fiscal corrective measures to resolve the conflict between a fixed exchange rate, on the one hand, with fiscal profligacy and capital outflows, on the other;
ii.   a large part of the explanation for the 'fiscal failure' and for the loss of much-needed macroeconomic flexibility resulted from the re-election climate since the early 1990s and lasted well into the end of the decade. This political-intensive climate engendered intended and unintended 'wrong' incentives for higher public spending and for higher risk taking in the decision making process of key economic policies;
iii. the failure of the IMF in the pre-crisis period to resist political pressures to go on supporting a policy framework which had lost the confidence of the domestic and international markets. Between January and September 2001 the IMF made three decisions to provide exceptional financing support up to US$22 billion.

Notwithstanding the decisive importance of the fiscal related factors in gradually building up to the 2001 crisis, this assessment needs to be further illuminated by more precise answers to the following three interdependent questions:

i.   First, was the whole decade of the 1990s one of fiscal profligacy? Did things get out of hand by the end of the 1990s and if so why?[32]
ii.   Secondly, fiscal failure measured how? Above the line? Below the line? By debt stock changes that came from the recognition of hitherto

occult liabilities? By flow effects? (See Fernández, 2003, p. 348 and Guidotti, 2005, p. 19.)

iii. Thirdly, was the public sector facing a liquidity or a solvency problem or what possible interpretation or combination of the two? What are the fiscal implications of the relative importance of a liquidity vis-à-vis a solvency problem?

The literature[33] on the answers to these questions is already copious and will grow more over time, particularly as events continue to unfold in Argentina during 2007 and 2008. The hypothesis this book offers for further discussion is that in some critical judgments[34] about how to choose between the different risks inherent in all policy decisions, the political economy factors emerging from the presidential re-election syndrome throughout the decade may well have inclined the preferences in some sectors of the government towards protecting the interest of the incumbent president. Fortunately the task of apportioning causalities and relevant economic and political contexts has already begun within Argentina, in multilateral institutions and research centers across the world.[35]

XI.   THE EMERGING POST-CRISIS POLICY FRAMEWORK

The key guiding question to assess[36] the emerging post-crisis macroeconomic policy framework is to ask what has been learned. Since 'even under the best of circumstances systemic shocks cannot be entirely palliated' (Calvo and Talvi, 2005, p. 32), how should domestic policies be framed? All the pain and welfare loss of the crisis may largely be redeemed by history if, let's say, in 2010, and afterwards, events confirm that real learning took place.[37] If this were not to be the case, Argentina would prove again that it cannot put its political house in order. It would remain a country endowed with vast natural resources and very talented and hard working people but with arresting limitations to nurture the right political and fiscal institutions.[38] Martin Wolf (2005), examining the lessons of the debt restructuring of 2005, avers that 'Argentina is demonstrating once again why it has been both a serial defaulter and long-running economic failure. That may be the least important of the lessons. It is among the most depressing, all the same.'

In August 2003, Congress reformed the legal structure of the Central Bank and established the following institutional characteristics:

i.   It is an 'autarkic' institution whose primary function is to preserve the value of the currency.
ii. Board members are chosen by the President and approved by the Senate. They are appointed for 6-year periods and can be re-appointed indefinitely.
iii. In implementing its monetary and financial policy it is free from directives from the Executive National power.
iv. Before the beginning of each year it must publish its inflation target and the expected evolution of the flows of money.
v.   Quarterly, or each time there is inflation targeting deviation, it must publish an explanation as well as the program it intends to follow to correct the situation.
vi. It exercises financial oversight through the 'Superintendencia de Entidades Financieras y Cambiarias'.

These nominal characteristics indicate a large degree of Central Bank independence. They also suggest that there is a modality of inflation targeting as well as the authority for the Bank to issue a sort of 'Open Letter'[39] to the public whenever the inflation target is compromised. These characteristics suggest that the Bank has ample independence and can employ its open letter mechanism to use its credibility and to establish political accountability. But all this will need to be tested when difficult choices have to be made. After all, there are antecedents of Central Bank independence (a law passed by Congress in 1992) which in the end did not work out as expected.[40]

The question of whether there is inflation targeting is a complex one. In principle, yes, there is. The Central Bank annually announces annual targets but is not fully clear how much of an integrated analytical and operational framework is there to make monetary, fiscal and exchange rate mutually consistent. A very positive feature of the Central Bank's structures is that quarterly, or whenever it may be necessary, it has to issue to the public a statement explaining the causes of inflation targeting deviation and indicating what it will do to correct the situation.

The real long term reform has to be institutional and political, not so much in the sense of choosing to give independence to the Central Bank or to establish a fiscal surplus rule but in strengthening a culture[41] of legal property rights. One route with great potential to help in this endeavor is the dissemination of information to the public on the results of different interventions. The premise is that a well informed public minimizes the probability of political failures like the one that seems to explain the lamentable March of Folly from 1991 to 2002.

Table 3.5   Argentina: basic macroeconomic indicators, 2003–2006

Indicator	2003	2004	2005	2006
GDP growth rate	8.9	9.0	9.2	8.5
Inflation rate CPT end of period	3.7	6.1	12.3	9.8
Primary balance consolidated public sector	3.2	5.3	4.4	n.a.
Primary balance national public sector	2.3	3.9	3.7	3.5
Current Account (% GDP)	6.3	2.1	3.0	3.3
Unemployment rate end of period	14.5	12.1	10.1	8.7

Source: Banco Central de la República Argentina (2006).

XII.   THE RECOVERY PERIOD 2003–2006

Argentina continues to recover rapidly from the depths of the 2001–2002 crisis. Growth during the period 2003–2006 has averaged about 9.0 per cent, and has reached pre-crisis levels at the end of 2006. 'Export earnings are higher, tax revenues have increased substantially, fiscal accounts are in surplus, and the Government has restructured three quarters of its debt in default.' (World Bank, 2006a, p. 11). Table 3.5 shows that growth has been around 9 per cent on average for the last four years. The unemployment rate has been declining steadily from 14.5 per cent in 2003 to 8.7 per cent in 2006. But there are also reasons for concern. The inflation rate remains high and the primary balance of the consolidated public sector seems to be declining.

XIII.   THE POLITICAL ECONOMY OF THE 2001–2002 CRISIS

Fiscal deficits and fiscal misalignment are not the primary source of macroeconomic crisis. Weak fiscal and political institutions are. In the case of Argentina the traditional inclination to overspend and to overborrow[42] may have been exacerbated by the re-election environment since as early as 1993 when President Menem pressed the political institution for a constitutional change so that he could be re-elected. The question that emerges is what incentives were sent out to the political process. Again in 1998, President Menem pushed for a second re-election. What were the incentives behind fiscal decisions during these five years?

With the benefit of hindsight, it can be concluded that when 'convertibility' was adopted, the judgmental error was to assume that there was a political demand not only for low inflation but also for fiscal prudence. In

the event this was not the case. The results of the political process leading
to the crisis suggest that the public wanted, or was led to believe, that it was
possible to have it both ways: hardly any inflation and no fiscal constraints.
Now that factually this seems unrealistic, the key question is, what has been
learned from this painful experience?

The crisis of 2001–2002 is an example of the differences between nominal
and real institutional characteristics of macroeconomic governance frameworks. In effect, in Argentina in 1992 a law was approved granting independence to the Central Bank and mandating price stability as its main
objective. This was the nominal institutional characteristic. But was it the
real one? Judged by its results, and with the benefit of hindsight, it appears
that the Central Bank was not immune to political pressures to assume
more macroeconomic risks than a truly independent Central Bank probably would. In the last analysis, a Central Bank needs the support of a political demand for macroeconomic stability and the attendant political
support for fiscal and other policies that would deliver that macroeconomic
stability.

The political process in Argentina does not seem to have enough incentives to reward policies that have a higher probability of safeguarding the
general welfare than policies that imply high risks for society as a whole.
On the contrary, most of the political incentives seem to reward, or are seen
as potentially rewarding, 'opportunistic' behavior. Political institutions
appear to be misinformed or unaccountable for opportunistic interpretation of the information available. In terms of a principal–agent analytical
framework this suggests that the 'principal', that is the public at large, is an
'absentee principal', and that multiple agents can treat public goods such
as the credibility of the Central Bank or of the domestic currencies as a
'commons' to be dissipated.

Most countries and societies learn from their experiences, particularly
from the painful ones, and gradually seek to enhance control of their
political and economic institutions and processes. This is less the result of
particular philanthropy or gregariousness than of 'animal spirits' and of
rational self-serving choices to politically capitalize on what the public at
large demands. In the case of Argentina the question that arises is why
this learning process is still so protracted and fraught with insufficient
'right' incentives to politically reward appropriate lesson taking. This is
indeed a beguiling question, particularly in the case of a country so well
endowed with highly well trained economists and sophisticated research
capacity.

Blaming the external avatars, or the IMF, or capital markets and other
alleged fiendish actors, is part of the legitimate political game. All countries
do a share of that. But in the end, in some Latin American and other

developing countries, after a crisis, there is a modicum of domestic political accountability and potential positive incentives for politicians to capitalize from the errors of competitors. Why is this not fully the case for Argentina? Why do domestic and external Cassandras seem to fail so often, and so little learning take place in this country? The short and somewhat tautological answer is that there is little political accountability for results and that the rules of the political game are ambiguous and do not contain verifiability mechanisms to establish *ex ante* and *ex post* accountability. In brief, the crisis of 2001–02 was largely self-inflicted and largely the result of domestic political failure.

The Argentine political establishment and the public in general welcomed, by and large, the 1991 Convertibility proposal because they had been feeling the pain and welfare costs of hyperinflation and four consecutive years (1985 to 1990) of GDP decline. This was not a counterfactual argument for the costs of macroeconomic mismanagement. It was a potent source of 'real time information' on the high transaction costs of the hitherto existing macroeconomic governance structure. With the benefit of hindsight it can now be said that this political support for low inflation and for the promise of positive growth did not necessarily mean a firm support for the fiscal policies that would meet the indispensable fiscal condition for the sustainability of the Convertibility arrangement.

How much political support there was at the time for fiscal prudence, or for the illusion that the country could have it both ways, that is no inflation together with fiscal deficits, is not an easy matter to establish. But most likely there was a firm initial commitment by President Menem and Minister Cavallo to meet this fundamental requirement. After all, they were the ones who proposed and defended it and probably anticipated that there would be political dividends to be reaped from macroeconomic stability. But then, what political factors changed after the success of the initial years?

The tentative answer that this Country narrative offers for further research is that the Menem administration figured that its success should be rewarded (and perhaps its continuity be guaranteed) by immediate presidential re-election. The Olivos Pact in November 1993 by which Menem could be re-elected may have opened the Pandora's Box of the 'wrong' political incentives. From then on it would prove to be very difficult to resist political pressures and incentives to spend and to incur fiscal and monetary risks that would probably not take place under other conditions.

The rest is largely subsidiary. The technical or political misreadings that the International Monetary Fund may have made, the convoluted decision making process at the domestic and international level, and the failures in crisis management, were all important. However, all this would not have had the impact it had if the political incentives within Argentina had not been under the pressures, in mid-1998, of yet another attempt by President Menem to be re-elected. In brief, the overarching conclusion is that the 'wrong' political incentives, coming mostly from repeated presidential re-election dynamics, proved to be devastating for fiscal prudence and are the most important part of the explanation for Argentina's demise.

Under a more economic theory perspective, the above political economy explanatory hypothesis can be summarized as the triumph of 'fiscal dominance' over exchange rate convertibility. But then the question is, how can it be believed that fiscal issues do not have a political origin?[43] The real 'original sin' may well be not so much being unable to borrow abroad in domestic currency, but in issuing too much domestic currency based bonds in the domestic markets.

XIV.   THE POLITICAL ECONOMY IMPLICATIONS

An understandable but rather unhelpful conclusion would be to make a comprehensive judgment for the totality of the 1991–2002 experience and sum it up as an unmitigated overall failure. The demonizing of that decade does not seem to be the way to go about evaluating and learning from those years. The assessment has to be more specific both in terms of concrete policy measures and in the timing of those measures. Furthermore, the analysis would need to include the real options surrounding each circumstance. Referring to the debacle at the end of 2001, Machinea (2002) has observed that 'Once an economy has been fully dollarized it is almost impossible to abandon a hard peg without a financial crisis.' In this approach lies the enormous value of Claudio Loser's dialogue with Ernesto Tenembaum (Tenembaum, 2004) in which at each step of the way the crisis process unfolds, determined by a number of varied economic, political and almost personal circumstances. Surely, then, the question is, why was an earlier exit strategy not found before? This backward sequenced questioning of specific policy moments and decision making processes can go on for a long time. A final verdict will always need to be nuanced, contextualized and placed in counterfactual developments. Sebastian Edwards (2003, p. 632) puts it well when he warns against all-inclusive negative judgments which would end up missing some of the positive reforms that accompanied the convertibility regime.

A second misguided conclusion would be to say that the fault lies exclusively with fiscal mismanagement, largely with the IMF, with the 'convertibility' arrangement, with the global capital markets, with selected versions of the Washington Consensus, or with incompetent local politicians. It will take some time to attribute possible mistakes. Each actor will need to go on with its internal evaluation task. Each one will have different incentives driving those evaluations and the results will not be the same across institutions or experts. History seldom provides unequivocal answers. The learning comes from the emerging new questions.

A third, unwarranted conclusion would be to fall into the temptation of dismissing the role of markets, incentives and information in framing the direction in which 'human action' tends to evolve. At the end of the day, people respond to incentives. The challenge is to identify the incentives, the intended and the unintended ones, and frame policies that are consistent with those incentives. Navajas (2003, p. 356) has summarized it well when he discussed the meaning of a possible 'new macroeconomic'. His view seems to be that if there is a new macroeconomic in Argentina it has to do mainly with preserving general macroeconomic consistency and creating favorable conditions for investment.

The evaluation process of the Argentine experience and of its crisis in 2001–02 will go on for yet a number of years. On several fronts, particularly in the fiscal and financial ones, there are already well documented findings and conclusions because of the availability of data and significant 'evaluable history'. But in other areas, documenting and tracing back the decision making processes and figuring out the direction of causalities will prove to be very difficult. This will be the particular case of critical political judgments[44] made within the 'sanctum sanctorum' quarters of the IMF, its management, its Executive Board, the US Treasury and, of course, in the Casa Rosada at Buenos Aires. All those political judgments were legitimate and are made all the time. What may well be missing are the evaluability conditions for those judgments to be rigorously traced back to their respective origins. In brief, political accountability will not be easily established because of the unintended or intended ambiguity in those 'collective action' decision making environments. The policy implication and recommendation for the future is that enhanced *ex ante* 'evaluable political history' should become the incentive driving the competition for political rewards – or costs – to those whom history will judge to have been right on target or mistaken.

If the main conclusion is right, that is that the macroeconomic governance framework is particularly vulnerable to short term political opportunism, the policy implication is that underlying this situation there is political fragmentation and an information failure. The principal (the public at large) cannot hold its agents fully accountable for the results of their behavior, and the process does not generate sufficient information to engender a different incentive governance structure. That is, there is little political demand for institutional transformation because there is not sufficient awareness by the 'principal' that transaction costs are excessively high and are potentially lower and 'remediable'.[45] The response to an information market failure is not easy to figure out. One first step is to ascertain the relativities of the location of the failure. Is it more a demand failure than a supply failure? Which combination of the two? And perhaps more importantly, why is it that there are no incentives to reward the search for information and the use of information as a source of enhanced competitiveness?

The main policy implication of the conclusion that the macroeconomic governance structure has been, and still is, particularly vulnerable to short term political opportunism, is that underlying this situation there is political fragmentation and an information failure in the political and economic markets. These three factors are interdependent. Political opportunism is facilitated by a principal (the public at large) that is misinformed about what may have brought about the debacle of 2001–02 and is also misinformed about the causes that are currently bringing down the poverty and unemployment rates. In its turn the real political incentives will tend to reward political opportunism. The public is aware of the high transaction costs it ended up paying for macroeconomic mismanagement but is unclear as to whom to hold accountable. In addition, the temptation to 'blame the external avatars' (be they the IMF, the global capital markets or the economic model) is an attractive one to several actors. It can yield political dividends almost right away. It can also lead to 'interested searches' for a new macroeconomics. In spite of warnings that, more than a 'new macroeconomics', what is needed is to give priority to general equilibrium and to overall policy consistency (Navajas, 2003, p. 356 and Arriazu, 2003a, p. 320), the short term political incentives are there for, once again, the country failing to take advantage of the current recovery to nurture better policies.

Under these circumstances three recommendations emerge. First is a global one on the role of 'independent' information in completing political and economic markets. With regard to political markets and the hypothesis posed in this country narrative about the adverse effects of accommodating presidential re-elections, the recommendation is for the private sector and for 'think-tanks' to conduct or commission specific research programs on the actual results that Argentina has had with limiting political competition. Much more research is needed on the regulatory framework of political competition, that is on the constitutional rules that, as Persson and Tabellini (2004a, p. 94) insist, are the ones that shape economic policy. The second recommendation concerns the economic markets. Here again there is an information and an incentive problem. These problems are related to the evaluation of what happened, and why, and who can be blamed for it all. A spontaneous efficient market solution to these compet- ing interpretations and interests may well not yield the macroeconomic policy framework that best serves the long term welfare of Argentina. A major additional effort has to be made in universities, research centers and 'think-tanks' inside and outside Argentina to provide factual information and opinions on what happened, why and how the responsibilities should be attributed.

The third recommendation is for policy makers to focus more on the dis- tributive links between pro-growth and pro-poor policies. The premise is that since poverty reductions are currently taking place, some structural pro-growth reforms may find more political tolerance and a favorable envi- ronment. This is the time to adopt, as Artana (2003, p. 21) advocates, long term countercyclical fiscal rules and flexibility in the other key variables such as the exchange rate and the levels of public expenditure.

All research methodologies and attendant results can be questioned. It would be naïve to assume that an undisputed hypothetical tribunal can adjudicate causes and accountabilities. The point is that the more plural and varied the search for lessons, and the more intense the political com- petition for being able to 'prove to have been right', the higher is the prob- ability that the emerging policy framework will be the appropriate one. At worst, some 'falsifiability hypothesis' will emerge as well as more rigorous baseline scenarios on which to make more credible future evaluations.

NOTES

1. See Elster (2000).
2. For an examination of 'populism' in Argentina see Sturzeneger (1992, p. 142).
3. See Basco et al. (2006, p. 9) for an examination of the monetary causes of inflation in Argentina for 1970–2005.
4. Between 1945 and 1948 Argentina went from a situation in which it had abundant foreign exchange to one in which it practically defaulted on its external allegations. To Sourrouille (2005, p. 8) this change coincides with the role of Miguel Miranda in the Cabinet of President Juan Domingo Peron.
5. This meltdown is not much different from the one that took place in 1880. See della Paolera and Gallo (2003, p. 369).
6. Such macroeconomic volatility was accompanied by political volatility. In December 2001 protests led to the resignation of President De la Rua who had been in power just a few months. He was replaced on 19 December by the President of the Senate, Ramon Puerta. A few days later he was replaced by Adolfo Rodriguez Saa who, on 23 December, 2001, announced default on the government's debt to private foreign creditors. On 30 December, 2001, the presidency went, on an interim basis, to Eduardo Camano. Finally, in January 2002, Congress elected Eduardo Duhalde. On 6 January, the Duhalde admin- istration terminated the peso convertibility regime (Blustein, 2005, p. 242).
7. According to della Paolera and Gallo (2003, p. 372), it is in the arena of macroeconomic monetary and fiscal affairs from as early as 1810 that Argentina had serious constitu- tional design problems.

8. In the mid 1990s a World Bank Country Assistance Evaluation was already warning that 'the sustainability of the achievements remained in doubt'. See World Bank, (2000a, p. 1).
9. Galiani et al. (2002, p. 1) observe that 'Two arguments are often encountered in the discussion of the Argentine case: that fiscal policies were inconsistent with the fixed exchange rate (implying that the political system was incapable of adjusting itself to the discipline of budget constraints and let the public debt grow along an explosive path), and that the convertibility regime induced a sustained overvaluation of the currency, and thus was bound to end in a collapse. There are elements of validity in both arguments, but they are incomplete, and cannot provide by themselves the full picture.'
10. According to Talvi (1997, p. 73), 'In a model in which events are fully anticipated, the response of consumption and tax revenues to the announcement of an inconsistent exchange rate-based stabilization program generates the following pre-collapse dynamics: the rate of inflation falls dramatically, the balance of payments strengthens (the central bank accumulates reserves), the economy booms, (consumption rises), and as a consequence, the fiscal deficit improves and may eventually disappear altogether. In other words, the program will display all of the ingredients of a success story. Furthermore along the path towards the collapse of the stabilization program, the economy displays none of the usual early warning signals that it is headed toward a balance of payments crisis, since there is no fiscal deficit and international reserves are increasing. In contrast to the previous literature about inconsistent stabilization policy leading to a "Krugman type" balance of payments crisis, where the symptoms of an imminent crisis are visible all along, in this model the collapse of the program comes as a "surprise".'
11. On the political agreements between Menem and Alfonsin leading to the Olivos 1994 Pact on constitutional reform for re-election, see Grondona (2003, p. 138).
12. On the 'economics of self-control' see Buchanan (1991, p. 5). He opines that 'The "economics of self-control" has reached the status of a respectable, if minor, research program, which may be destined to become more important in this era of emphasis on diet, exercise, health and the environment.'
13. 'In the long run, macroeconomic policy choices can be viewed as a game between past, present and future generations of political rulers and economic agents. Like any other player in this game, a current government takes decisions subject to a set of bestowed restrictions, and will, in turn, bestow new restrictions on the next generation of government. It is here that the intertemporal fiscal constraints matter. In this conception, policymaking is not a static game in which current pay-offs are only affected by today's decisions. As Thomas Sargent (1986, p. 21) has shown, it is a dynamic game "that requires time to complete and whose current score depends on past actions of the various players".' See della Paolera et al. (2003, p. 46).
14. To Lavagna (2004, p. 115), it is in 'areas of crisis management and the decision making process' that some of the key lessons from the 2001–02 crisis can be drawn.
15. See De Gregorio (1992, p. 170).
16. Amongst those possible lessons, former Minister of Economy Roberto Lavagna is quoted by Blustein (2005, p. 200) as having said 'The lesson is, we must pay attention to bubbles.' See 'A pit too deep' in Blustein (2005).
17. For comparison between different country crisis experiences see Calvo and Talvi (2005). See also Calvo et al. (2004).
18. 'This was the first peaceful transfer of power from one democratically elected leader to another since 1928.' See Dominguez and Tesar (2005, p. 21).
19. From 1889 to 1929, Argentina had a very similar system based on a legal guarantee that paper pesos could be converted into gold pesos at a fixed rate. See Blustein (2005, p. 14).
20. In answering the question of 'what went wrong?', *The Economist* (2004, 5 June, p. 4), offers the following explanation. 'According to one school of thought the decline began in 1913, as the Pampas became fully settled: growth slowed because the country proved unable to industrialise and diversify effectively. Liberals, for their part, have traditionally blamed the governments of Juan Perón (1946–1955), with their quasi-fascist pursuit of

autarky and a state-run economy. Leftists have a more precise date: March 24th 1976, when the most vicious dictatorship of South America's recent history took power. In this view, shared by many of those close to Mr Kirchner, the dictatorship's economic policy prefigured Menemism, running up unsustainable debt and destroying the state's capacity to regulate the economy.'

21. For some of the rich literature on the puzzle of Argentina's economic development going back to 1820, see della Paolera and Taylor (2003, p. 1).
22. See Frank Knight (1921).
23. One can distinguish 'between vulnerability-based and risk-based approaches to management of extreme events. The word "vulnerability" describes inherent characteristics of a system that create the potential for harm but are independent of the probabilistic "risk" of the occurrence of any particular hazard or extreme event. One can also distinguish between the "risk" of an event and the "risk" of a particular outcome. The latter definition of "risk" integrates both the characteristics of a system and the chance of the occurrence of an event that jointly result in losses. The point is to consider separately vulnerability and risk, and the implications of such a distinction for thinking about the policy and politics of risk and vulnerability management.' See Sarewitz and Pielke (2002, p. 1).
24. See Wiesner (2003c).
25. 'Skeletons' result from the recognition 'by the government of arrears with pensioners and public suppliers'. See Guidotti (2005, p. 9).
26. According to Mariano Grondona (2003, p. 137), Menem made it to the Presidency thanks to Duhalde, who contributed with the political support of the Buenos Aires region. Duhalde may have thought that Menem would later on support his bid for the Presidency.
27. See *The Economist* (2004, p. 4), for references to Menem's 'quixotic drive to spend his way to an (unconstitutional) third term.'
28. Commenting on decision making under cooperative undertakings, Tirole (2002, p. 118) observes that 'Much recent research in economics has emphasized the difficulty of managing organizations on behalf of a highly heterogeneous constituency. Conflicts of interest among the board generate endless haggling, vote-trading and logrolling. They also focus managerial attention on the delicate search for compromises that are acceptable to everyone; managers thereby lose a clear sense of mission and become political virtuosos.' See his 'Institutional implications: What role for the IMF?' in Tirole (2002).
29. Teijeiro (2001) shows calculations of the fiscal balance implied by the increase in public debt that exceed the fiscal flow approach estimates.
30. According to the IMF (2004a, p. 24), 'The focus of the staff's analysis and discussion with the authorities was primarily on the fiscal deficit as a flow variable. Although total public sector debt was included as a performance criterion from the beginning, an assumption of overdue obligations was routinely accommodated. The staff did not produce a table providing a convincing connection between fiscal flow variables and the year-to-year change in the debt stock until July 1997. The debt stock per se became the main focus of briefing papers and policy discussions only in late 1999 or early 2000, when the debt-to-GDP ratio began to approach 50 percent. By then, the economy was in recession, and efforts to reduce the debt by running a fiscal surplus were difficult and possibly also counterproductive.'
31. Whether a convertibility rule makes an economy more vulnerable depends on how the risks associated with such convertibility are calculated, managed, and 'sold'. See IMF (2004a, p. 28, 35, 64).
32. See Webb (2003, p. 189), for the development of similar questions for the case of finances in Argentina's provinces.
33. According to Kochhar et al. (2003, p. 31), three features distinguish Argentina's crisis from that of other countries. First, the unilateral debt default. Secondly, the extended period of bank closures and deposit freeze. Thirdly, 'The forced conversion into pesos of US dollar loans and deposits'.
34. See Velasco (1997, p. 24), for a 'dynamic context' in which the level of one variable (for instance debt) determines the choices policy makers actually have.

35. See, for instance, the work conducted by FIEL, Mariano Tommasi at CEDI, The Universidad de San Andrés, the Centro de Estudios Públicos, CEMA Universidad, The Universidad Torcuato Di Tella, The Central Bank of Argentina and others.
36. See Berg et al. (2003, p. 3) on the question of how to achieve monetary policy credibility and price stability after a crisis. One of their key findings is that monetary policy alone cannot stabilize.
37. In Popper (1962, p. 1) he asserts that 'The essays and lectures of which this book is composed are variations upon one very simple theme – the thesis that we can learn from our mistakes.'
38. Teijeiro (2001) observes that Argentina's proclivity towards fiscal profligacy is a cultural trait with a long history. It will only change through learning from experience.
39. See Brazil's Country narrative on 'Open Letter utilization'.
40. In April 2001 the Central Bank Governor was replaced over an alleged money laundering charge.
41. Heymann (2004, p. 37) posits that further institutional development is needed. In his view Argentina 'faces an enormous credibility problem'.
42. For a well argued view that debt and convertibility were not the triggering factors in Argentina's crisis see Fernández (2004, p. 348).
43. See Wiesner (2004b, p. 14), on the political origins of fiscal deficits for the Colombian case.
44. Referring to conflicting institutional dilemmas Loser (2004, p. 67) observed that the IMF and the Argentinian authorities did not fully share a common analytical paradigm. When the IMF pressed for more fiscal correction the authorities resisted arguing in favor of alleged stronger growth. See Tenembaum (2004, p. 67).
45. According to Williamson (1996b, p. 379), 'A condition is held to be remediable if a superior feasible alternative can be described and implemented with net gains.'

4. Brazil: the market enhancing role of political economy factors

Research in institutional economics must focus on actual rules rather than on conceptually ambiguous assessment of institutional outcomes.

Glaeser et al. (2004, p. 26)

I. THE LULA FEARS IN REVERSE

Normally, distributive politics and political economy restrictions limit the role of markets and of competition in inducing efficient private and public outcomes. The case of Brazil since the mid-1990s may be the beginning of the reverse situation. In this country political economy factors appear to be the ones that increasingly enhance or protect the role of markets and restrict political opportunism. In 1994 with the Real Plan[1] this country finally tamed hyperinflation, bringing it down from 2000 per cent in that year to less than 4 per cent in 1998. Then in 1999 Brazil adopted an integrated macroeconomic policy regime anchored on inflation targeting which allowed it to manage a serious economic crisis successfully. Although there is still ample room for further macroeconomic improvement it appears that the public at large wants to preserve the lower inflation rates observed during the last ten years. Low inflation seems to have politically redeemed orthodox macroeconomic management in the eyes of a public hitherto very distrustful of markets. Early after having won the elections in 2002, the incoming Lula administration flirted with some populist policy postures which had to be quickly abandoned when market signals (spreads and the like) indicated the imminent costs of such an overture. The political demand for macroeconomic stability transformed itself into a demand for, or at least acceptance of, the role of markets. In brief, in Brazil there seems to be growing complementarity between some economic and political markets.

However, low inflation rates and the relative improved macroeconomic stability have not come about without costs and other serious imbalances. Those costs have come in the form of two interdependent processes, a very high level of public expenditure, which grew by an additional 7.5 per cent of GDP between 1991 and 2004 (Castelar and Giambiagi, 2006, p. 54) and very high real rates of interest. Both of these developments could be interpreted as the price, that is the political transaction costs to avoid even worse extreme populist postures.

Brazil's current challenge is then to preserve the current low inflation rate, while at the same time controlling the expansion of public expenditures and bringing down real rates of interest. More than a technical problem, this is a political economy challenge because there are immense pressures to continue to increase, and even to elevate, the level of social expenditures to allegedly bring about gains in distributive justice. But, at the same time, there is elusive political support for the policy reforms that would finance those expenditures and ease pressure on the interest rates. These reforms would nurture faster rates of growth and thus make possible additional gains in poverty reduction. Instead of a poverty trap or a vicious circle, a virtuous one of complementarity between growth and poverty reduction is the challenge.

To provide guidelines to enhance the effectiveness of the macroeconomic governance structure and Brazil's reform process in general, this Country narrative will focus on the following interdependent questions:

i.   After the successful management of the 1999 and 2002 crisis, what are the lessons learnt and pending policy challenges to enhance macroeconomic effectiveness in terms of faster rates of growth and enhanced distributive justice?
ii. What are the real and nominal institutional characteristics of the macroeconomic arrangement which may explain recent macroeconomic performance?
iii. What could be the elements of a strategy to enhance the role of political economy factors in deepening the macroeconomic and microeconomic reform processes?

The unifying premise is that political economy factors need to be further endogenized into economic policy making. The unifying objective is to discern policy implications and recommendations for Brazil and for Latin American countries in general.

II.   MACROECONOMIC PERFORMANCE IN HISTORICAL PERSPECTIVE

Between 1901 and 2000 Brazil had one of the fastest rates of per capita growth in the world, 4.4 per cent, 'few countries have done better' (World Bank, 2004c, p. 52). More recently, between 1950 and 1980, its GDP grew

Table 4.1   *Brazil: selected economic indicators, annual averages,*
              1950–2002

Period	CPI Inflation (average) (%)	GDP Growth (%)	Real fixed investment, 1980 prices (% of GDP)	Current account (US$ million)	Current account (% of GDP)	FDI (% OF GDP)	External debt (% of GDP)
1950–73	29.3	7.5	19.1	−354	−1.3	0.4	17.6
1974–80	41.6	6.8	24.0	−7 745	−4.5	0.8	27.0
1981–94	507.2	1.9	16.8	−2 716	−1.1	0.6	27.3
1995–99	16.6	2.3	17.0	−26 218	−3.7	2.7	42.5
2000	6.6	4.5	16.0	−24 225	−4.0	5.5	36.5
2001	5.7	1.5	16.5	−23 214	−4.6	4.5	41.7
2002	8.3	1.5	n.a.	−7 696	−1.8	3.5	45.0

Note: All variables are period averages except for external debt; 2002 figures are estimates.

Source: World Bank Operations Evaluation Department (OED) (2004, p. 2).

at the extraordinary rate of about 7 per cent, even when inflation was as high on average as 41.6 per cent for the years 1974–1980. Table 4.1 shows that during those fast growth years investment was near or above 20 per cent of GDP. Interestingly enough the Current Account deficit was low, −1.3 per cent for the period 1950–1973 and then −4.5 per cent for the years 1974–1980. Foreign direct investment was lower than the Current Account deficit and external debt grew from 17.6 per cent to 27.3 per cent by 1980.

Between 1981 and 1994 the previous expansionary period of GDP growth came down to 1.9 per cent. Inflation exploded to over 500 per cent and real fixed investment dropped from 24.0 per cent to 16.8 per cent. External debt remained at a 27 per cent level. GDP growth recovered somewhat to 2.3 per cent for the years 1995–1999 but the current account deficit tripled from −1 per cent to −3.7 per cent. Although foreign direct investment more than quadrupled from 0.65 per cent to 2.7 per cent, still external debt jumped from 27.3 per cent of GDP to 42.5 per cent. For the years 2000 to 2002 very high levels of foreign direct investment more than 'financed' the current account deficit. Notwithstanding this, external debt rose to 41.7 per cent in 2001 and then to 45.0 per cent in 2002. This suggests that the economy was 'absorbing' a high level of consumption well over its domestic savings.

Brazil's recent slower rates of growth compared to its own historical experience also occurs when compared to those of other countries in Latin

Table 4.2   Brazil's relative growth in perspective

Year	Brazil	Latin America	World Rate	Brazil/Latin America	Brazil/World Rate
1994	5.9	5.2	3.8	1.13	1.55
1995	4.2	1.1	3.7	3.82	1.14
1996	2.7	3.8	4.0	0.71	0.68
1997	3.3	5.5	4.2	0.60	0.79
1998	0.1	2.6	2.8	0.04	0.04
1999	0.8	0.4	3.7	2.00	0.22
2000	4.4	3.9	4.7	1.13	0.94
2001	1.3	0.3	2.4	4.33	0.54
2002	1.9	0.8	3.0	2.38	0.63
2003	0.5	2.0	4.0	0.25	0.13
2004	4.9	5.9	5.1	0.83	0.96
2005	2.3	4.3	4.3	0.53	0.53
2006	3.4				

Source: IPEA (2006, p. A-83, Table VIII).

America and of the world in general. Table 4.2 shows that since 2003 Brazil's growth rate has been much slower than that of its neighbors and of the rest of the world.

III.   THE FINANCIAL CRISIS OF 1998–1999 AND INFLATION TARGETING

In 1995 the first Cardoso administration inherited a long tradition of pop-ulist[2] expansionary policies going back to the Getulio Vargas era in the 1940s and 1950s with short-lived intervals of prudent monetary and fiscal policies (Rabello de Castro and Ronci, 1992, p. 176). The most initial conditions leading to the 1999 crisis were fiscal and Balance of Payments imbalances.

> In mid-1998, Brazil's consolidated fiscal position was showing a primary deficit as the government's expenditures, excluding interest payments, exceeded its income. The bulk of the government's domestic debt – which amounted to 40 percent of GDP – consisted of short-term financing. The current account deficit was approaching 5 percent of GDP, even as the economy was sliding into recession (Fraga, 2000, p. 1).

According to Edwards (2003, p. 35),

the real plan, launched in 1994, relied on a very slowly moving preannounced parity with respect to the U.S. dollar. In spite of repeated efforts, the authorities were unable to rein in a very large fiscal imbalance. By late 1998 the nation's consolidated nominal fiscal deficit exceeded the astonishing level of 8 percent of GDP.

When Brazil was consolidating the lower inflation levels that emerged out of the 1994 Real Plan it was hit in late 1998 by a sudden stop in capital flows. Russia had defaulted on its debt in August 1998 and external capital to Brazil came to a halt (Fraga, 2000, p. 1). The impact on the exchange market was extreme. 'In August and September alone the excess demand for US dollars was US$11.8 billion and US$18.9 billion respectively' (Baig and Goldfajn, 2000, p. 5). In September 1998 Brazil lost US$21.5 billion in foreign reserves.[3] The contagion from Russia was triggered by panicking foreign investors and local residents. Under immense pressures on the Real in January 1999 the Central Bank authorities floated the Real, which quickly depreciated from 1.20 at the beginning of the year to 2.15 to the dollar.[4]

What makes Brazil's currency collapse special is 'that it did not lead to a banking crisis'. Brazil's devaluation

> in effect, bailed out its banks and corporations before the crisis by using taxpayer resources to let them hedge their currency exposure. Indeed, many banks had bet that the Real would fall and obtained large profits out of the crisis. This avoided a banking/corporate crisis – a crisis that in all probability would have led to larger liquidation and output costs and required an even larger ex-post bailout (Roubini and Setser, 2004, p. 61).

IV.   THE 1999 POLICY REGIME CHANGE: THE 'POSSIBLE TRINITY'

The macroeconomic framework adopted during 1999 as a new 'policy regime change' comprised the following 'trinity': (i) inflation targeting as a 'rule' for monetary policy; (ii) a floating exchange rate system; and (iii) targets for fiscal primary balances through tax increases. This 'trinity' 'made the economy more resilient to shocks and enhanced growth prospects. While capital was flowing out of the region after the 1998 international capital markets crisis, it continued to flow into Brazil after its adjustment' (World Bank, 2004c, p. 548). But in the short term the economy practically stopped in 1998 registering a GDP growth of only 0.1 per cent. In 1998 it recovered to 0.8 per cent and jumped to 4.4 per cent in 2000 (Table 4.2).

After the exchange rate collapse in January 1999 most of the Central Bank's Board of Directors were replaced. The new Board took office in March 1999 and together with the Monetary Policy Committee (COPOM) raised the basic short term interest rate (SELIC) from 39 per cent to 45 per cent. Then the COPOM issued an unprecedented release stating that:

i.   Maintaining price stability is the primary objective of the Central Bank.
ii. In a floating exchange rate regime, sustained fiscal austerity together with a compatible monetary austerity support price stability.
iii. As fiscal policy is given in the short run, the control over inflationary pressures should be exerted by the interest rate.
iv. Observed inflation is due to the currency depreciation, and markets expect a further rise in the price level this month.
v.   The basic interest rate should be sufficiently high to offset exchange-based inflationary pressures.
vi. To raise the basic interest rate to 45 percent p.a., but with a downward bias, for if the exchange rate returns to more realistic levels, keeping the nominal interest rate that high would be unjustified.

By mid-1999 the crisis was under control. In March

in conjunction with a revised IMF program and in an environment in which a congress shocked by the currency collapse had finally moved to take important fiscal measures, the international banks agreed to a voluntary arrangement providing for the maintenance of trade and interbank credit lines, amounting to some \$25 billion. (Cline, 2003, p. 477)

A most important lesson or policy implication can be drawn from this 'voluntary' private sector involvement. The private international banks acted on their own and could have 'exited' without major institutional or legal hassle. But, by and large, they did not. The main reason can be presumed to be because they saw a feasible and largely credible policy package. By April of that year Brazil was able to return to capital markets. 'Brazil is perhaps the clearest case for the superiority of voluntary arrangements for private-sector involvement in crisis resolution over "dirigiste" alternatives. Brazil's authorities were right to be highly reluctant all along to be seen as seeking any type of a coercive rescheduling' (Cline, 2003, p. 477).

On 21 June 1999 the President of Brazil issued a Decree (No. 3088) instituting an inflation-targeting framework. Its main points were:

● The inflation targets will be established on the basis of variations of a widely known price index.
● The inflation targets as well as the tolerance intervals will be set by the National Monetary Council on the basis of a proposal by the Finance Minister.

- The Central Bank is given the responsibility to implement the policies necessary to achieve the targets.
- The price index that would be adopted for the purposes of the inflation targeting framework will be chosen by the National Monetary Council on the basis of a proposal by the Finance Minister.
- In case the targets are breached, the Central Bank's Governor will need to issue an Open Letter addressed to the Finance Minister explaining the causes of the breach, the measures to be adopted to ensure that inflation returns to the tolerated levels, and the period of time that will be needed for these measures to have an effect, and
- The Central Bank will issue a quarterly 'Inflation Report' which will provide information on the performance of the inflation targeting framework, the results of the monetary policy actions, and the perspectives regarding inflation. (Bogdanski et al., 2000, p. 5)

Although all these policy commitments were important, one in particular deserves special underscoring for its political accountability implications. The fact that the Central Bank's governor will need to explain to the Executive in an Open Letter why inflation targets may have been being breached, and how the situation should be remedied, is a major technical and political advancement. It established the 'evaluable history' of events and causal links so indispensable for political accountability to be established. This seems to be a unique institutional[5] characteristic of Brazil's macroeconomic regime not found in other Latin American countries; at least not with such unambiguous features. The enormous significance of this provision became evident in 2002 when President Lula was 'induced' to move back from the brink.

V.   THE POLICY REFORMS EMERGING FROM THE 1999 CRISIS

Just as 1994 with the birth of the Real was a watershed point in Brazil's modern economic history, so the crisis of 1999 spawned major reforms and institutional transformations in the management of macroeconomic policy. Three interdependent developments can be singled out: (i) inflation targeting within a comprehensive macroeconomic framework; (ii) the use of information as an incentive to enhanced political accountability for macroeconomic performance; and (iii) the strengthening of formal macroeconomic coordination through COPOM, the Monetary Policy Committee. The inflation targeting adopted was a triple regime change comprising switching to exchange rate flexibility, monetary rules and a strict fiscal policy anchored on the necessary primary surpluses to maintain consistency in the overall strategy. Although largely for political reasons this framework led in the subsequent years to a precarious balance between very high real interest rates, high levels of public expenditures and debt and some exchange rate difficulties, the reforms adopted represented a major institutional and political advancement (Castelar and Giambiagi, 2006, p. 284).

Worthy of special mention is the written mechanism through which the Central Bank Governor informs the Executive level of inflation targeting compliance and corrective measures if needed. This is in fact a transparent way to establish political accountability for macroeconomic performance. In a country where there is growing appreciation for macroeconomic stability and for low inflation rates this mechanism established political incentives for the political economy protection of prudent macroeconomic management. The triple regime has worked well, as the Monetary Policy Committee (COPOM) has demonstrated particular capacity to coordinate the different institutional instruments needed to design, implement and evaluate macroeconomic policy. Needless to say that what explains this coordination effectiveness is the fact that there is strong sharing of the conceptual paradigm guiding macroeconomic and financial management.

The Monetary Policy Committee (COPOM) is composed of the Minister of Finance, the Minister of Planning, the President of the Central Bank, and the Chief of the President's Cabinet and their respective Deputies. The COPOM is the highest economic policy making body in Brazil. Its institutional stature is even above that of the Central Bank's Board. But, of course, the Central Bank is the main coordination template for macroeconomic policy making. The members of the Central Bank's Board have to be approved by the Federal Senate through a two step process: first, a preliminary open hearing in the Committee of Economic Affairs; secondly, a discussion and voting session in which the 81 Senators decide by simple majority to approve or reject a given nominee (see Bogdanski et al., 2000, p. 2). Castelar and Giambiagi (2006, p. 301) consider that Brazil's reform agenda should include (i) reduction in external debt; (ii) fiscal reforms to strengthen the primary surplus and to improve the quality of public expenditures; and (iii) at the microeconomic level improvements in labor legislation, regulatory oversight and secondary education.

VI.   THE 2002 CRISIS: LULA FEARS AND THE ROLE OF POLITICAL ECONOMY FACTORS

After having grown by 4.4 per cent in 2000 the Brazilian economy slowed down rapidly to 1.3 per cent in 2001, to 1.9 per cent in 2002 and almost came to a standstill in 2003 with a mere 0.5 per cent rate of growth. This rapid slide was the result of a combination of factors, the first being the

*Table 4.3   Brazil: average rates of growth for central government
            expenditures*

Indicators	1995–1998	1999–2002	1955–2002	Accumulated/[a]
Primary expenditures[b]	7.0	5.0	6.0	59
Transfer to states and municipalities	6.6	11.3	8.9	98
Social security	7.4	5.2	6.3	63
Personnel	2.0	4.4	3.2	29
Other expenditures[b]	12.3	1.5	6.8	69
GDP growth	2.6	2.0	2.3	20

Notes:
[a] In eight years (%). Deflator: implicit deflator for GDP.
[b] Includes primary deficit of the Central Bank.

Source: Giambiagi (2004, p. 238).

consequences of the remaining vulnerabilities after the 1999 crisis. It had
lost half of its reserves, the stock of public debt rose from 40 per cent in
1997 to 72 per cent in 2002, and most of its debt was still indexed either to
the overnight rate or the dollar. 'As Argentina's crisis deepened Brazil
renewed issuance of large amounts of foreign currency linked debt to meet
the demand for hedging products and effectively intervene in the foreign
exchange market' (Roubini and Setser, 2004, p. 62). The Central government continued to spend at a very fast pace from 1999 to 2002 (Table 4.3).
Transfers to subnational jurisdictions grew at an average rate of 11.3 per
cent per annum.

   In the run-up to the presidential election in October 2002 the markets
became very worried. 'Lula had made statements that seemed to indicate
that once in office he would encourage expansionary fiscal policies and
would not reappoint the highly respected governor of the Central Bank
Arminio Fraga' (Mishkin, 2004, p. 18). The election of Lula in October
2002 led to a sharp depreciation[6] of the Real (up to 3.75 per cent) and to
an overshooting of the inflation target which had been 3.5 per cent for 2002
and rose to 12.5 per cent.The response of the Central Bank was to use its
faculty to declare openly what it would do to respond to the crisis and to
return to a credible inflation path. In January 2003 it sent an open letter to
the Minister of Finance with a comprehensive framework which included
escape clauses for a restructured inflation soft landing.

   It was a very transparent posture. Figuratively speaking, 'President Lula
went to China' (Cukierman and Tommasi, 1998, p. 180) and in August
2003 got Congress to pass legislation to partially reform the pension system

and pursued fiscal policies resulting in a 'primary surplus' of 4.3 per cent, which was above what had been agreed with the IMF. The markets believed this response. It was the triumph of the credibility principle. Referring to the Central Bank's role, Professor Mishkin called it 'a brilliant performance' (2004, p. 19).

VII.   UNEQUAL INEQUALITY AND DISTRIBUTIVE JUSTICE IN BRAZIL

The argument behind the observation that inequality is harmful for growth runs like this:

> Economic growth is largely determined by the accumulation of capital, human capital, and knowledge usable in production. The incentives for such productive accumulation hinge on the ability of individuals to appropriate privately the fruits of their efforts, which in turn crucially hinges on what tax policies and regulatory policies are adopted. In a society where distributional conflict is more important, political decisions are likely to result in policies that allow less private appropriation and therefore less accumulation and less growth. But the growth rate also depends on political institutions, for it is through the political process that conflicting interests ultimately are aggregated into public-policy decisions. See Persson and Tabellini (1994, p. 600).

Latin America, as was indicated before, is one of the most unequal regions in the world. Within Latin America, Brazil's inequality is one of the most extreme.

> Poverty incidence rates range from 3.1 in metropolitan Sao Paulo to more than 50% in the rural northeast. Income disparities in Brazil are significant not only across regions but also between metropolitan areas, non metropolitan urban centers, and rural areas. Moreover, inequalities across gender and racial groups are also important (Velez et al., 2004, p. xvii).

'With a Gini coefficient of 0.59 in the 1999 distribution of household income per capita Brazil has one of the highest levels of income inequality in the world'. In Brazil the richest 20 per cent have 25 times the income of the 20 per cent poorest group (Barros and de Carvalho, 2004, p. 436). Brazil's inequality is among the world's highest, whether it is measured by household income or consumption. Three sets of interdependent factors explain that inequality: (i) regressive public transfers; (ii) the unequal distribution of education; and (iii) high wage differentials.[7]

Within this context, two questions emerge. First, why did that inequality not seem to adversely affect past growth, which averaged about 7 per cent from 1950 to 1980? Secondly, why have recent growth rates been relatively so low and volatile over the last 10 years? The short answers to both questions would include the observation that normally fast rates of growth tend to have a direct redistributive effect which, in principle, would generate some modicum of political support for growth-intensive policies. As for the explanation for the recent low and volatile rates of growth, the answer would include that high real rates of interest, of taxation and of indebtedness adversely affect confidence and growth. All these three conditions have resulted mainly from the very fast rates of growth of public expenditures since the mid-1990s.

The political process in Brazil may have unintendedly constructed the perception that for approval by Congress of long term pro-growth policies, additional expenditures and targeted transfers are politically indispensable. This may be a simplifying fallacious equity versus growth dilemma – certainly an incomplete trade-off as long as the key issue of the redistributive effectiveness of the social expenditures is not included in the analysis. This is largely an information problem as significant portions of the additional expenditures and transfers are regressive. There is ample room for reducing poverty further and enhancing access to education and health by the poor without increasing the fiscal imbalance. In brief, Brazil seems to be going through the difficult processes of simultaneously trying to combine sufficient equity gains to elicit political support for the 'right' pro-growth policies, on the one hand, with sufficiently fast rates of economic growth to make redistributive policies sustainable in the long run, on the other.[8] It is trying to overcome what has been called '*assistencialismo empobrecedor*' (impoverishing social welfare) (Castelar and Giambiagi, 2006, p. 60) to return to much faster rates of economic growth. The distributive challenge is basically a political and informational one. After all,

> public transfers in Brazil, although less unequally distributed in that country than primary incomes, are still positively correlated with household income and do not contribute to a reduction in inequality. We found, for instance, that the greater inequality in the distribution of retirement pensions in Brazil than in the United States is responsible on its own for more than a third of the difference in the overall level of inequality between the two countries. (See Velez et al., 2004, p. 60)

The evolution of poverty and extreme poverty for 1981–2001 appears in Figure 4.1. It can be seen that poverty rates rose during the early 1980s and had a sharp and very substantial reduction. In the second half of the 1980s poverty rates rose again and remained above the 40 per cent level until the early 1990s. The Plan Real in 1994 helped in reducing poverty levels further.[9] In Brazil, the highest poverty rates may be found in the rural

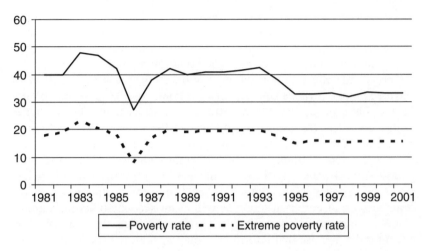

Source: World Bank Operations Evaluation Department (OED) (2004, p. 23, Figure 4.1).

Figure 4.1 *Brazil: evolution of poverty and extreme poverty in Brazil, 1981–2001 (percentage of population)*

Northeast but the highest poverty densities (the number of poor people) are found in the big cities, both north and south. This spatial distribution has profound policy implications. For instance, focusing on poor regions instead of on concentrations of poor people 'may actually decrease national growth' (Perry et al., 2006, p. 139).

VIII.   CONCLUSIONS AND POLICY IMPLICATIONS

The 'nominal' institutional characteristics of Brazil's macroeconomic arrangement would suggest the existence of a highly dependent Central Bank, one in which the President of the country has the legal power to remove at will the Governor, as well as all the members of the Executive Board. However, this prerogative has been exercised with prudence and discretion and, on the whole, the Executive has appointed highly qualified and independent members to the key positions. For this reason Brazil's Central Bank has ended up being one of the most independent of the dependent Central Banks of the world. The main reason behind this 'real' institutional characteristic appears to be the public's political demand for the preservation of low inflation rates and macroeconomic stability in general. This demand acts as a political incentive that rewards those policy choices that are perceived as having the capacity to deliver such stability. The transmission mechanism to inform both politicians and the public are market indicators such as 'spreads' and the judgments of independent risk and market evaluators. This may explain why the Lula administration won its second term. Good economic policies often have good political dividends.

One of the most important institutional characteristics of Brazil's macroeconomic arrangement is the legal power of the Governor of the Central Bank to send an Open Letter to the Minister of Finance if the former considers that he should divulge to the public what the Central Bank intends to do to manage a given inflation situation. This power was given to the Central Bank on 21 June 1999 through Decree No. 3080 and it came as part of the formal adoption of inflation targeting. This option has far-reaching policy implications. Perhaps the most important one is that it configures an incentive structure as well as an accountability mechanism that is *ex ante* and *ex post* evaluable. This is a major accomplishment. It is based on the premise that information matters and that the markets, economic and political ones, make rational choices on the basis of the information they are given. Institutional credibility is the organizing concept for all actors. The success in managing the 2002–03 crises is largely explained by the application of this mechanism and the letter which, in fact, was sent by the Governor of the Central Bank to the Minister of Finance in January 2003, stating what the policy was going to be. The markets gave credence to that commitment and in a rational expectations accompaniment lowered the costs of the adjustment.

From the crisis of 1997 and 1998 as well as from that in 2002 Brazil has come out with a remarkably resilient and credible macroeconomic policy framework that combines three sets of policy instruments within an effective institutional arrangement. 'In the Brazilian case, the construction of credibility was a process that combined reactions to inflationary pressures and increased transparency to the public' (Fraga et al., 2003, p. 20). This 'triple regime' is composed of a floating exchange rate system, inflation targeting as the main *ex ante* coordination template, and a strict fiscal policy of primary surpluses as needed to 'close' in a consistent manner the public sector accounts. But this triple macroeconomic regime is anchored on very high real rates of interest needed to protect the capital account and very high levels of taxes and public expenditure to respond to financing requirements and to distributive tension. These high rates of interest conspire against faster and less volatile growth, and the attendant slow GDP growth restricts distributive gains.

Brazil's main current economic and political challenge is to preserve the low inflation rate and to recapture faster rates of economic growth while at the same time curbing the rate of expansion of public sector expenditures and limiting public sector debt growth. More than a technical problem this is a political economy challenge because there are immense pressures to continue to increase public expenditures, particularly to finance social security and pensions. But, at the same time, there is scant political support for the reforms that would finance those expenditures and ease pressure on the interest rates. The conundrum is that the policies that are politically resisted are the ones that have the potential to deliver faster growth and sustainable equity gains. The 'tax and spend' political economy trade-off of the last ten years to protect the needed fiscal balances, on the one hand, and to appease distributive tension, on the other, may well have reached its limit. After all Brazil now has one of the highest rates of taxation and of real interest rates in the emerging economies. The political support for the pending macroeconomic and microeconomic reforms will need to come from sources different from additional expenditure and from costly social security concessions. It will need to come from a public better informed about the current transaction costs of appeasing short term and group-specific interests. It can come from political leadership and from the domestic and international markets signaling on which policies it can base the conditions of its support.

Although it could not be said that there is full 'fiscal dominance' restricting monetary policy and Central Bank independence, Brazil, with its current high levels of real interest rates, public expenditures and growing primary surpluses, may have unwittingly placed itself in a 'corner solution' amounting to a 'bad' or dysfunctional equilibrium. Fiscal deficits may not be determining the price level but the high real rates of interest, the exchange rate and external financing uncertainties only engender a damage control strategy, but not one without high transaction costs. Inflation may be under control but there may also be a latent 'sacrifice ratio' in terms of slow and volatile growth as well as in terms of loss of potential equity gains.

To get out of the unintended current 'bad' macroeconomic equilibrium, policy makers can make more intensive use of the enormously important asset represented by the existence of a political demand for macroeconomic stability. This indispensable requirement for reform is largely already there and could be extended beyond the theme of inflation targeting. What perhaps could be called the 'principle of the open letter to the public' has potential for use in the disentangling and institutional unbundling of the regressive public expenditures and distributive issues in general. After all, inequality has become a determinant of long term inflation targeting as well as of the rate of economic growth.

From a 'positive' political economy perspective a most telling development is that a substantial part of public expenditures and of pensions do not contribute to reduce income inequality or to reduce poverty levels. They worsen income inequality and poverty levels. They are actually regressive expenditures disguised as pro-poor. This is not totally surprising as it should be remembered that public markets are characterized by symmetric information and by the 'capture' of public resources by well organized rent-seekers. In principle, those resources could be either removed from the budget to increase the primary surplus or allocated to other real pro-growth uses. The political economy strategy to implement either one of these options would need to be based on better informing the public about these situations and finding political constituencies for the alternative use of the 'freed' resources. The unmasking of who really profits from social public expenditures is largely an informational and a political transaction costs problem. Although it is difficult to think of a complete solution to this problem, its worst consequences can be reduced by the use of information to the public and by the 'right' political use of political competition for the support of the 'real poor'.

Since the mid-1990s Brazil has increased social public expenditures at roughly twice the rate of GDP growth and has elevated in real terms social benefits and pensions to growing and large segments of the poor and middle income groups. It has done so for distributive justice reasons and to elicit political support for reforms in the fiscal, financial and social security areas. This has been 'a tax and spend' trade-off that has worked in terms of having prevented worse fiscal imbalances, the resurgence of high inflation and macroeconomic instability in general. The questions that emerge concern what the limits are of this political economy strategy and what may have been the costs of the relative neglect of, for instance, infrastructure or more generally faster growth. The time may have come when pending structural reforms will have to be politically 'bought' with new arguments and different policy options.

From a political economy perspective and from the premise that incentives are the main driving force behind behavior, a very important policy implication is that better informed diagnostics on the current pro-poor and pro-growth policies is the route to political accountability and to the adoption of the 'right' reforms. The Open Letter from the Central Bank to the Minister of Finance in January 2003 became the vehicle and the incentive to establish political accountability for the consequences of each political and institutional actor. In brief, the Lula administration, in its own political and rational choice calculation, came to the conclusion that it was a lower risk to support an orthodox macroeconomic management than the risk of following populist policies, even if it meant a 'sacrifice ratio' in terms of lost growth and income as it actually turned out to be.

Policy makers and political leaders in Brazil could build further on the currently existing political demand for macroeconomic stability to climb back from the 'dysfunctional equilibrium'. In the last analysis, what they confront is an asymmetric political economy information problem in which the country has cornered itself, putting itself into a vulnerable situation. The *assistencialismo* versus growth is a false dichotomy. Perhaps the time may have come for the Lula administration to 'go to China' again and further cement a long term place in the positive transformation of Brazil. If this were not to happen, the accountability political 'game' should be played in full, and those who favor the needed additional reforms should leave a transparent 'paper trail', as 'evaluable history' and evidence, on where and when they stood. This is the long term learning process which ends up explaining long term development.

NOTES

1. 'The Real Plan' of July 1994 succeeded in reducing inflation through an exchange-rate-based stabilization program that introduced a transitory unit of reference for prices. In March 1994, nominal prices wages, and other contracts were allowed to be quoted in a unit of real value (*Unidade Real de Valor*, or URV) that would be replaced by a new currency, the real, in July 1994.
2. On the relation between populism and democracy in Brazil see Rabello de Castro and Ronci (1992, p. 176).
3. For a detailed chronology of events see Baig and Goldfajn (2000, p. 41, Appendix IV).
4. The weak fiscal position was the broad context of the collapse of the Real but what may have prompted it was the moratorium on debt payments in January by the governor of Minas Gerais. See Mishkin (2004, p. 16).
5. Mishkin (2004, p. 19), 'The procedure followed by the Banco Central do Brasil was a textbook case for central bank response to shocks in emerging market countries.'
6. For an excellent analysis of developments during the Lula period see Giambiagi (2006, p. 4).
7. According to Bloom and Velez (2004, p. 269), 'Graduates from Brasilia College are highly rewarded for their education, the rising wage of workers with tertiary education exacerbate wage-inequality.'
8. For the links between inequality, growth and poverty reduction see Perry et al. (2006, p. 57).
9. 'This beneficial effect was due to: (i) economic growth and rising real wages; (ii) the end of inflation (salary erosion and inflation tax); (iii) a significant appreciation of the local currency shifting prices toward the service sectors in which most poor work; and (iv) a significant increase in the minimum wage to which important income sources, such as pensions, are tied.' See World Bank (2000b, p. ix).

5. Chile: the right mix of policies and institutions

> Chile has been able to grow faster than other Latin American countries since the mid 80's mainly thanks to its better institutions.
>
> Corbo et al. (2005, p. 3)

Chile's country narrative needs a special preface to explain its particular conceptual architecture. There are two distinct characteristics which separate this country's narrative from the others. First, the traditional question of what explains long term development takes a special meaning in the case of Chile. This results from the association that often links Chile's success with its undemocratic regime from 1973 to 1990. For this reason, the country narrative begins with a discussion of the relationship between public policies and the modality of political governance structures, in particular democracy. Secondly, although some aspects of the economic success of Chile may serve as a guideline to other developing countries, it would do so largely through the fundamentals of development policy and not necessarily through the specifics of each one of its policies. In other words, the 'endogeneity condition', that is each country's development, is somewhat unique, restricting the full replicability of Chile's particular case. On the other hand, Chile continues to face difficult problems which also challenge other Latin American countries. In this case, the cross country comparisons of experiences and approaches has enormous learning potential for all.

I. THE SEARCH FOR AN EXPLANATION FOR SUCCESS

Why and how has Chile been able to evolve so successfully along such distinct economic and institutional trajectories in contrast with other Latin American and developing countries? As Avner Greif (1998, p. 80) puts it more broadly, 'Why [do] some societies evolve in one direction and others fail to adopt more successful institutional structures?' Few questions have been asked more often with regard to Chile's development over the last two decades. Most of those questions can be grouped along the following lines:

- Can Chile's success be explained by the existence of an undemocratic regime which imposed policies and reforms that would not have been adopted under a democratic environment?
- Can it be explained by the rapid gains achieved in terms of poverty reduction? If so, why and how were these improvements possible?
- Can it be explained by the early policy postures and reforms adopted well ahead of most Latin American countries?
- Can it be explained by Chile's history and particular economic and social configuration?

The explanation for success[1] lies largely in a combination of Chile's particular political history and the institutional transformations and reforms that began in the mid-1960s and have by now evolved into an independent Central Bank, solid fiscal rules and other ancillary developments across the public sector. According to Corbo et al. (2005, p. 1), 'Chile's performance can be explained by the country's better institutions and better policies in equal shares.' These developments have resulted in remarkable gains in terms of growth and poverty reduction. Through the causal links between growth, distributive justice and political support for macroeconomic stability Chile appears to be on a self correcting and self sustaining long term trajectory for institutional transformation and for increasingly high levels of welfare.

The Dictatorship Hypothesis

The hypothesis that the success can be explained by the existence of an undemocratic regime is more a judgment on democracy[2] as a political framework for development than on the nature of the policies adopted. Moreover, this line of inquiry would need to explain the often 'bad' policies of many hardly democratic countries, or other 'good' and 'bad' policies in a whole gradient of political regimes (Persson and Tabellini, 2006, p. 319). Or, more specifically for the case of Chile, it would need to explain why those 'dictatorial' policies were not abandoned by the democratic government which assumed power in 1980. In addition, they have not been reversed by the following democratic administrations.[3] On the contrary: 'All three governments that have been in power since 1990 have strengthened the market economy model, accelerated the opening up process, consolidated the fiscal position and improved regulations, while at the same time, they have emphasized social policies and implemented new programs to alleviate poverty' (Corbo et al., 2005, p. 18).

Some of the empirical research on the relationship between political regimes and public policies has concluded that there are no significant differences between democracies and non-democracies. 'Democratic institutions have important effects on the degree of competition for public office, but otherwise have effects on public policies that are insignificant, or incidental to the struggle for political leadership' (Casey et al., 2004, p. 52). More recently Professors Acemoglu and Robinson (2005) have concluded that, by and large, democracies tend to be more viable where there is a robust middle class supporting them. The direction of causality here is between a strong middle class and democratic viability, while the causality in the dictatorship hypothesis is between the democratic or undemocratic origins of the characteristics of economic policies. The dictatorship hypothesis appears to assume that democratic regimes would fail to adopt economic policies with some given characteristics. This would be a curious judgment on the strength of democracy or a particular reading of what the defining characteristics of a democratic regime or a democratic process of reform are.

Long before the military rule, Chile had a tradition of good institutions.

> The success of reforms during General Augusto Pinochet's regime was not only the result of good economic policies supported by a dictatorial government; rather, the existence of strong institutions was key to this development and stands as a warning for countries that might consider rushing into reforms without a sound institutional framework. If Chile had had weak institutions, poor maintenance of the rule of law, and rampant corruption in the early 1970s, the orientation of the military government might well have been very different. The episode likely would have ended as did the corrupt dictatorships elsewhere in the region, with a lack of progress in all areas. (De Gregorio, 2004, p. 31)

The dilemma between democracy and dictatorship in the case of Chile has been summarized by Arturo Valenzuela (2005, p. 17), as follows:

> It was not the economic reforms of the Pinochet regime (the so-called first generation reforms) alone that explain Chile's ability to grow its economy while cutting poverty levels in half. Rather, it was the strength of its established political institutions – particularly high levels of transparency and acceptance of the rule of law, coupled with the ability of strong and disciplined parties able to forge enduring governing coalitions that generated and implemented public policies – that enabled the country to break the mold.

The Political Economy of Equity

Another major source of the explanation for success may lie in the large reductions in poverty levels which Chile has achieved during the last 20 years. This line of explanation seeks to understand the links and causalities between poverty and income distribution, on the one hand, with support for the 'right' reforms, on the other. Thus far the political economy of reform and equity has come to the appreciation that 'inequality is conducive to the adoption of growth retarding policies' (Alesina and Rodrik, 1994, p. 465).

> Democracy, political stability and executive constraints all appear to be more feasible in more equal societies. Public policies towards redistribution and human capital can make societies more equal. Unequal societies have less redistribution, and we have little idea whether this relationship is caused by redistribution reducing inequality or inequality reducing redistribution. (Glaeser, 2005, p. 2)

The developmental implication of these messages is that poverty and income distribution should be endogenized in a consistent approach at all levels of policy reform. This should certainly be at the macroeconomic level, as it is the encompassing framework from which the overall incentive climate is created. It should also be at the social sectors as they are the specific transmission mechanisms to deliver equality of access[4] and of opportunity to all members of society, but particularly to the lower income groups (Ferranti et al., 2004, p. 35). This is a good way to enfranchise the poor and the low income groups in the political process of reform in Latin America, to make them stakeholders in macroeconomic stability. This is what Chile seems to have done. It is here where most of the explanation for Chile's performance may lie (Williamson and Haggard, 1994). Here too is where some of Chile's experience may offer guidance to other Latin American countries.

The Early Budget and Trade Reforms of the 1960s

The so-called 'first generation reforms' began early in Chile largely[5] during the Frei Montalvo administration (1964–1970). Some of the key budget process reforms were introduced in 1970, before the military rule. They 'greatly limited the scope for vested interests to lobby in fiscal affairs' (Foxley, 2003; Foxley and Sapelli, 1999). In essence, these reforms led to a budget process 'dominated by the Executive Branch rather than by the Legislature, and by the Ministry of Finance rather than by spending ministries' (Espinoza-Vega and Phillips, 2004, p. 10). In other words this was a hierarchical system instead of a collegiate one as Marcel (1999, p. 49) has aptly summarized it. Since the mid-1970s Chile began a process of opening its economy. According to De Gregorio (2004, p. 25): 'The opening of the Chilean economy was one of the most important, if not the most important reform undertaken by the military regime of the 1970s and 1980s.' After the return of democracy in 1990 Chile continued its open trade policy with two further unilateral tariff reductions.

Chile thus became the first country in the region to break away from the import substitution approach so prevalent in Latin America. Why did they do it? How was Chile able to mitigate the classic trade policy problems of rent-seeking and lobbying? There are two combined answers. First, the early reformers favored the role of markets. Their policy approach dated back to the late 1960s and early 1970s. The so-called 'El Ladrillo' document, a liberal economic program drawn up mainly under the leadership of Sergio de Castro, already called for trade liberalization and for a strategy of tariff reduction. This visionary document[6] also called for a social security system that would be largely private and regulated by the state.[7] The second reason why Chile sought 'openness' was because it saw clearly that as a small country with a very limited domestic market, it had to reach out to bigger external ones. This view was not the case in other countries whose domestic markets were also relatively small.

History and the Political Demand for Stability

The explanation for Chile's success is better sought in its history, at least since 1925, when a strong presidential vision on how to organize the country prevailed, and over the following decades in which a particular fiscal culture evolved.[8] After many years of macroeconomic volatility (Lüders, 2005, p. 11), Chile gradually evolved into an inflation-afraid and a fiscally conservative country. Chile finally understood or discerned a critical insight, which Harberger summarized: 'people must perceive real costs in order to reduce them' (1998, p. 21). Chile felt those costs probably more deeply than any other country in the region. It had a recession in the 1930s, another in 1975 and the one in 1982–1983 in which GDP is estimated to have fallen by about 16.4 per cent (cumulative). The 1980 Constitution reaffirmed the principle that only the Executive power can exercise public expenditure initiatives. This historical value has been strengthened by different regimes and has become a politically demand driven rule. It is real because it is shared by a large segment of the population even though it is not a formal 'constitutional' mandate.

The Institutions and Incentives Explanation

In brief, Chile's success can largely be explained by the relative strength of this country's political demand for macroeconomic stability[9] as well as by the political support for the attendant institutions and fiscal and monetary policies that deliver such stability. Without this political demand for the 'right' institutional transformations there would not be sufficient political incentives to develop those institutions. The key factor is the alignment of the 'right' policy reforms with the political incentives to deliver those reforms. This is a rare case in which the politics of economics and the economics of policies, through positive growth and distributional links, are yielding a largely self sustaining and self correcting political and economic system. This system is not immune to internal or external shocks but it appears well prepared to respond adequately to those uncertainties. As William Easterly (2001, p. 289) aptly summarized it: 'We have learned once and for all that there are no magical elixirs to bring a happy ending to our quest for growth. Prosperity happens when all players in the development game have the right incentives.' The political and institutional demand hypothesis does not bring closure to the fundamental developmental questions but sets the discussion on the right heuristic track, namely, the search for strategic relevance and for better understanding the direct and reverse causalities between macroeconomic stability and growth, on the one hand, with redistribution and equity outcomes, on the other.

II.   MACROECONOMIC PERFORMANCE IN HISTORICAL PERSPECTIVE

Chile's twentieth century growth trajectory has been marked by three deep recessions in the 1930s, 1975 and 1982–1983. These recessions were all triggered by external shocks, but internal vulnerabilities were the main sources of the large economic and welfare losses that ensued after the shocks. After each recession the recovery rates were very fast and then tended to stabilize around a more 'structural' production frontier (Coeymans, 1999a, p. 548). During the 1960–2000 period Chile's per capita GDP grew at an average rate of 2.4 per cent, while the rest of Latin America grew at 1.4 per cent. A huge difference (Table 5.1).

Table 5.1   Chile: GDP per capita in regional perspective

Countries	1960s	1970s	1980s	1990s	1960–2000
Chile	2.2	1.2	1.3	4.8	2.4
Latin America*	2.2	2.5	−0.9	1.8	1.4
East Asia**	4.7	5.4	4.5	4.0	4.6

Notes:
* The 15 countries with the largest GDP: Argentina, Bolivia, Brazil, Chile, Colombia, Costa Rica, Dominican Republic, Ecuador, El Salvador, Guatemala, Mexico, Paraguay, Peru, Uruguay, Venezuela.
** China, Hong Kong, Indonesia, Korea, Malaysia, Philippines, Singapore, Taiwan and Thailand.

Source: De Gregorio (2004, p. 6).

III.   MACROECONOMIC PERFORMANCE, 1998–2006

Table 5.2 summarizes Chile's macroeconomic performance for 1998–2006. It is a remarkable one. One of the most comprehensive 'metrics' of Chile's macroeconomic performance is provided by the 'Mortgage Interest Rate', which has come down from 8.3 per cent in 1998 to 4.1 per cent in 2005. This particular 'metric' subsumes in the least imperfect way the effectiveness of a country's macroeconomic policy coordination.[10] It expresses ongoing market realities as well as expectations. It is not an infallible measurement but in relative terms is more 'satisficing'[11] than most other alternatives. It also has the immense advantage of informing policy makers how the markets tend to perceive what those policy makers think they are doing. In brief, interest rates, particularly long term, appear to be the less ambiguous metric of the appropriateness of economic policy.

IV.   THE MACROECONOMIC IMPLICATIONS OF DISTRIBUTIONAL GAINS

If 'inequality is conducive to the adoption of growth retarding policies', as Alesina and Rodrik (1994, p. 465) aver, it may follow that reductions in poverty levels and improvements in access to education and health by low income groups are conducive to a modicum of political support by these groups for macroeconomic stability.

> New analytical work and country experiences have identified channels explaining why economic growth and reduced inequality can go together. These mechanisms emphasize: (i) the reduced social tensions associated with less income and wealth inequality; (ii) the potential for greater savings among the poor; (iii) an education-mediated positive correlation between economic growth and social equity; and (iv) the positive effects of more equalitarian distribution on aggregate demand, capacity utilization, and investment (Solimano, 2000, p. 11).

This is what seems to have happened in Chile where poverty reduction is the main priority as part of a broader concept of social equity (Váldes, 1999, p. 260). Adequate macroeconomic and microeconomic institutional transformations have provided a propitious environment for macroeconomic stability, growth and reductions in poverty levels. In its turn, the equity gains appear to have made some low income groups stakeholders in economic reforms conducive to macroeconomic stability. Table 5.3 shows that between 1987 and 1996 Chile's poverty rate fell from 45.1 per cent to 23.2 per cent, a reduction of 48.6 per cent in less than 10 years. Chile has continued to reduce poverty to levels below 20 per cent but the Gini

Table 5.2 Chile: key macroeconomic indicators, 1998–2006 (% GDP)

Indicator	1998	1999	2000	2001	2002	2003	2004	2005	2006
A. GDP real growth rate	3.2	−0.8	4.5	3.4	2.2	3.7	6.1	6.3	5.2
B. Inflation rate, CPI, end of period	4.7	2.3	4.5	2.6	2.8	1.1	2.4	3.7	3.4
C. Exchange rate (US$LCU)	460.3	508.8	539.5	634.9	688.9	691.4	609.5	580.0	n.a
D. Mortgage interest rate	8.3	7.5	7.2	6.6	5.9	5.1	4.4	4.1	n.a
E. Current account balance (% GDP)	−4.9	0.1	−1.2	−1.6	−0.9	−1.5	1.5	0.6	2.0
F. Overall fiscal bal. central gov. (% GDP)	0.4	−2.1	−0.6	−0.5	−1.2	−0.4	2.2	4.7	5.9
G. Gross external debt (% GDP)	41.1	47.6	49.4	56.2	60.2	58.7	46.0	39.0	33.8
H. Gross international reserves (billions US$)	16.0	14.7	15.1	14.4	15.4	15.9	16.0	17.0	16.6
I. Unemployment rate	6.3	9.8	9.2	9.1	9.0	8.5	8.8	8.0	7.7
J. Structural balance (% GDP)	0.6	−0.8	0.1	0.9	0.5	0.7	1.0	1.0	1.0
K. Terms of trade (var. % annual)	−2.7	2.6	2.8	−4.3	3.3	7.8	20.1	12.5	17.6

Source: Central Bank, MIDEPLAN, Finance Ministry, INE IMF (2006, p. 24).

Table 5.3 Change in the poverty rate and decomposition of the change in growth and redistribution effects

	Period	Poverty line	Initial Poverty Rate	Final Poverty Rate	Total Change	Percentage of the change due to:		
						Growth	Redistribution	Residual
Brazil	1985–95	Extreme	10	11.1	10.2	–40	145	–5
		Moderate	30.4	28	–7.9	–40	–70	10
Bolivia	1990–95	Moderate	52.4	47.1	–10.1	–147	44	3
Chile	1987–96	Moderate	45.1	23.2	–48.6	–85	–7	–8
Colombia	1991–95	Moderate	58.5	58.5	–0.1	–103	6	–3
Costa Rica	1986–95	Moderate	29.4	25.6	–12.9	–117	17	0
Peru	1985–96	Moderate	43.1	50.5	17.2	99	–27	28

Source: Attanasio and Székely (2005, p. 46, Table 6).

coefficient remains around 0.57 per cent. According to Váldes (1999, p. 231), 'The entire distribution function has been shifting to the right with nearly all people earning higher incomes in the same relative ranks.'

V.   THE POLITICAL ECONOMY OF MACROECONOMIC STABILITY IN CHILE

There are two broad sets of interdependent key institutional characteristics that explain a large portion of the effectiveness of Chile's macroeconomic overall performance: (i) the existence of a real political demand for macroeconomic stability and (ii) the supply of political support for the policies which deliver stability. The point to be emphasized here is that both sides of this equation are political in nature. These two sides, of what could be regarded as an identity or as a tautology, have a political origin and a political outcome. After all, if there is political demand for macroeconomic stability, in principle it would follow that the political supply of support for that goal will be forthcoming. Why? Basically because there would be a political incentive to respond to that demand. But this is not always the case in Latin America. If such political support does not materialize (or does, but in the 'wrong' supply response) it could be argued, in retrospect, that there had not been real political demand for reform and macroeconomic stability. Likewise, if the result is macroeconomic stability one could argue, again *ex post*, that this outcome 'proves' the validity of this political-intensive explanation for Chile's development and for developing countries at large.

Notwithstanding these restrictions a tentative theorem could be ventured as follows: 'The lower (higher) the real demand for macroeconomic stability the higher (lower) will be the transaction costs of coordination between fiscal and monetary policy and the less (more) macroeconomic stability will result.' Although this does not yet solve the identification or tautological problems, the analysis can proceed with the tentative hypothesis that the 'independent variable' is the political demand for macroeconomic stability and for reforms in general. The dependent variables, on which policy seeks to have effects, are the real (not the nominal) characteristics of the institutional arrangements that define such governance structures.

VI.   KEY CHILEAN SPECIFIC INSTITUTIONAL CHARACTERISTICS

Within the broad context of a propitious political environment, there are six distinct Chilean institutional characteristics that explain a large portion of the effectiveness of this country's macroeconomic policy formulation: (i) A credible independent Central Bank; (ii) strong and independent banking regulatory agencies; (iii) countercyclical fiscal rules; (iv) the unique role of Congress; (v) behind the veil outsourcing; and (vi) an effective 'informal' coordination mechanism.

The current macroeconomic arrangement between the Central Bank and the Ministry of Finance was born in the difficult transition period between the Pinochet regime and the incoming Aylwin democratic administration in 1990. It could have failed to deliver an effective institutional arrangement, one, for instance, without strong political legitimacy. But both sides decided to 'cooperate', to bet on a higher political game, and agreed to let the democratic incoming regime be the one to father the 'autonomous Central Bank'. These unique developments responded more to institutional hysteresis than to short term political interests or to individual autonomous preferences. After all, it should be remembered that eight years before democracy returned to Chile there had been a political agreement on a Constitution and on rules to govern a transition to an elected government. At that time, in the late 1980s, a unique compromise was made to have a credible Central Bank and for a smoothing of the political transition. This was remarkable and speaks well for the parties involved in the political transition and in the 1980 planning for it. History will laud the wisdom involved and the compromises made.

Conscious of the importance of a strong financial sector regulatory capacity the government enacted in 1986 (and then upgraded in 1997) a new banking law granting more 'powers to the supervisory agencies, while updating specific regulations to keep up with international standards and best practices' (Corbo et al., 2005, p. 18). As the review of the 1999 'stress test' experience reveals, the importance of a strong and credible Banking and Financial regulatory Commission cannot be exaggerated. It is here at this front that most Latin American countries have proven to be particularly vulnerable (Carstens et al., 2004, p. 30).

In 2001 the government adopted a fiscal rule of maintaining a 1.0 per cent structural fiscal surplus. Under this commitment, government expenditures are set to be 1 per cent of GDP less than the Government's structural revenues, which are defined as the revenues that would occur in steady state. In other words, expenditures are 1 per cent less than the revenues that would occur if the economy were on its long-term path (after eliminating cyclical variations in taxes and other key variables, such as the price of copper and the level of international interest rates). 'This rule is intended to guarantee that the government will remain solvent in the long run' (Marcel et al., 2001, p. 8). One of the advantages of a structural fiscal surplus is that such a policy improves the country risk perception and lowers the spreads on public debt. The costs saved engender what Eyzaguirre (2004, p. 20) calls 'a fiscal social dividend'.

Chile's fiscal rule is a successful attempt to self-insure against macroeconomic risk at the country level.

> It adjusts for the business cycle and for cyclical fluctuations in the copper price and thus, like a stabilization fund, transfers resources from good to bad states. By pursuing debt-sustainability and communicating a clear signal of fiscal discipline to the markets, the new fiscal framework should help to protect against fiscal crises and help lower the costs of external financing. To the extent that the Chilean rule signals credible fiscal discipline to financial markets, it also has the potential to serve as a self-protection measure against financial contagion. (Fiess, 2005, p. 196)

A structural surplus rule is not targeted at a specific budget level. Unlike fiscal rules that specify a given budget balance, or an expenditure ceiling, in the case of a structural surplus it is difficult to forecast the implications for the size and composition of future public spending. After all, if taxes are increased or the tax base expands, 'structural' revenues will expand. This is fine. Flexibility for budget allocations remains all within the structural surplus.

In the case of Chile, the Congress, through its Economic Commission, plays a major role in support of the traditional macroeconomic institutional arrangement. This contrasts with other Latin American countries where Congress tends to be a destabilizing factor or at least one that may raise the transaction costs of the macroeconomic policy coordination exercise. This means that countries end up with higher inflation, lower growth, less employment and longer recovery periods. What explains this arrangement or, more precisely, what explains the way it works in Chile? After all, most countries have formal or informal 'coordination' mechanisms. So, what distinguishes Chile's format? The 'reduced form' answer is that in Chile there is 'political incentive compatibility' and most relevant actors have agreed on the rules to seek growth and equity within a time consistent framework. The political demand for macroeconomic stability coming from the 'overarching principal', that is the public at large, leaves the details to be worked out formally and informally by the 'agents' in their different roles and relative comparative advantages.

All Latin American countries face difficult monetary and fiscal policy decisions which are subject to pressures from political and vested interests. One example of those decisions is the definition of a future price for a commodity or the assessment of a future flow of income around which there can be all sorts of assumptions and complex consequences. This happens when countries have to calculate revenues for a budget or for a given institution.

Chile has been able to 'decentralize' some of those tasks to committees of 'neutral' experts who are credible and who conduct the best possible estimates. This is a very delicate task in a country that has a fiscal rule which *inter alia* means that a 'structural budget' has to be calculated. From this estimate several expenditures are determined. Calculating the future price of copper has immense public repercussions and yet these estimates are accepted as part of the rules 'behind the veil'.

It should be remembered that Chile's structural surplus rule is not a structural balance rule. The rule does not aim at a given budget balance or level. Any fiscal rule that is based on the structural balance rather than on the actual balance poses difficult methodological problems. After all, 'structural balance' is a latent concept. Neither the structural balance nor its main determinants (potential output and the long-run copper price) are observable. Here 'There are no unique ways to measure the structural balance and different estimation techniques will derive different estimates' (Fiess, 2005, p. 196). The choice of any methodology can become a major political issue but Chile has been able to handle it well basically through transparency and an open approach. This reflects much more than the delegation of a complex technical task. It reveals the political trust in these delegations and the confidence that, while those estimates are not infallible, they represent the best possible 'solution' for society as a whole. It is an extension of the principle of the division of powers and of the convenience of checks and balances.

Central Banks, Ministries of Finance and even financial sector regulatory agencies have *de facto* or *de jure* 'coordination mechanisms'. In the case of Chile the heads of the Central Bank and the Ministry of Finance meet normally for lunch at least once a month. Only one senior advisor from each institution attends these meetings. An informal exchange of views takes place. There are no minutes or formal decisions taken. These meetings have been found to be very useful in Chile. The underlying cause of this result is that there is a large convergence of views on the fundamentals of macroeconomics management. Formal or informal 'coordination mechanisms' serve little purpose if the parties have different policy frameworks.[12]

VII.   THE 'STRESS TEST' OF 1998–1999

Just as the origins of a crisis are important to understand what may have caused it, its consequences are critical to discern what was learned. After all, crises happen and what matters is learning from them. To do this, one should examine the following sequenced developments: (i) the initial conditions prior to the onset of the crisis; (ii) the policy response during the crisis; and (iii) the measures taken following the resolution of the crisis. The underlying question in this approach is to establish the relative causalities and accountabilities involved in the process or episode as a whole. After all, vulnerability is a function of exposure, but risk is a function of information and very importantly of expected political attribution for unexpected outcomes. In brief, vulnerability and political risk are ultimately a function of how well informed a society is and of how effectively it can apportion political accountabilities for predictable or unpredictable outcomes. In Latin America what often happens is that some political actors can blame external volatility for the vulnerability which could have been reduced if better and more complete information had forced them to be more accountable for remediable unpreparedness.

Initial Conditions in 1998

The initial conditions[13] before the 1998 and 1999 crisis were the following: (i) a high rate of GDP growth (8.5 per cent) on average for 1990–1996; (ii) strong expansion in domestic demand financed by large capital inflows of close to 10 per cent of GDP in 1997; (iii) low interest rates from the Central Bank; from 7.5 per cent at the beginning of the year and 6.5 per cent by December 1997; (iv) an expansionary fiscal stance although still within a positive balance; (v) inflation falling from 27.0 per cent in 1990 to 6.6 per cent in 1996 but a Central Bank committed to even lower rates for 1997 and 1998.[14] In other words, when the crisis occurred, inflation was above the Central Bank's announced target for 1998. This added to the 'fears of floating';[15] and (vi) Low downward flexibility resulting from large minimum wage increases set by government for 1998 (12.7 per cent) and for 1999 (12.4 per cent).

The Policy Response to the Sudden Stop

The policy response focused on the interest rates as the main (shock absorber) policy instrument to 'protect' the established inflation objectives, to reduce the current account deficit, and to mitigate pressures on the exchange rate.[16] On 8 January, 1998, the Central Bank raised the interest rate by 50 basis points. But as the pressures on the exchange rate continued, the Central Bank of Chile intervened via non-sterilized operations. As a consequence, the inter-bank interest rate reached values over 90 per cent in real annual terms at the end of January, 1998.

On 3 February, 1998 the Central Bank of Chile raised the 'Monetary Policy Rate' by 150 basis points and announced its intention of bringing the Current Account deficit to around 5 per cent of GDP. It also announced that the interest rate it was targeting was the Monetary Policy Rate. There was not to be a ceiling to the 'inter-bank rate' which was to be determined by market forces. In general terms the policy posture of the Central Bank was to reduce volatility in the financial markets and in the exchange rate. The 'fear of floating' was explained by the fear of a possible 'inflation pass-through'. The CBC's signal was that it would protect its credibility by maintaining its commitment to its previously established inflation target.

During the second half of 1998 speculative attacks continued as news from Asia and Russia worsened. In September the Central Bank responded by increasing the 'Monetary Policy Rate' to an unprecedented level of 14 per cent in real annual terms. Also, the Central Bank widened the exchange rate band width to +/− 3.5 per cent, establishing a gradual increase from 3.5 per cent to 5 per cent by the end of 1998. In December of 1998 the Central Bank widened the band to +/− 8.0 per cent (Céspedes et al., 2005, p. 23). The combination of external shocks and a contractionary monetary policy resulted in a GDP growth in 1998 of only 3.2 per cent (compared to 6.6 per cent in 1977) and a reduction of −0.8 per cent in 1999. The Central Bank's inflation target for 1998 (4.7 per cent) was reached while inflation in 1999 was 2 per cent lower than the target fixed in September 1998. The Current Account deficit fell to 4.9 per cent in 1998 and to −0.1 per cent in 1999.

In brief, the coordinated policy response and the dynamics of the domestic and external events may have led to a possible 'overshooting' of the interest rate, to a lower inflation than the targeted one, to a lower than expected Current Account deficit and to an unintended lower rate of growth of GDP. These judgments can only be made with the benefit of hindsight.[17] However, behind the 'fear of high inflation pass-through' was the overarching goal of preserving the institutional credibility of the Central Bank.[18] This led Chilean policy makers to the dilemma of 'rules vs flexibility' and the difficulty of calculating trade-offs around a Taylor curve,[19] between deviations from an inflation target and deviations from potential output. 'In the case of Chile, the gains in credibility allowed the economy to move toward a more flexible inflation-targeting regime with well-anchored inflation expectations around the long-run level of 3 percent' (Céspedes et al., 2006, p. 160).

The general problem behind these circumstances is one of incentives and of rational choices affecting decision making processes under uncertainty. A decision making process in which baseline scenarios are volatile and difficult to ascertain and accountabilities may be lost in ambiguous collective action problems. Central Banks will tend to give priority to the protection of their credibility and will risk overshooting the interest rate. The

Ministries of Finance will want to protect growth and the financial system. Hence they will prefer 'lower' interest rate rises, a 'controlled' exchange rate depreciation and some 'room' or wider range for the inflation target. Both preferred positions have excellent *ex ante* arguments. But these incentives are not really fully compatible. The Central Bank will probably insist on protecting its 'inflation target', or range, so that it builds a positive rational expectations credibility in the markets. This is, of course, a most desirable objective. The fiscal side will prefer that the Central Bank errs on the side of its inflation target and will warn of the risk of financial sector problems and of lost output potential. The elusive Taylor curve trade-offs between deviations from an inflation target and deviations from potential output are not easy to establish.

Carstens and Jácome (2005, p. 27) suggest that

> Central Banks should seek to achieve price stability while minimizing the potentially adverse effect of their policies on output. A key ingredient of such a strategy is to make central bank policies more transparent and predictable. This may help bring interest rates down, thereby encouraging investment and production. While central banks in the region – especially those that practice inflation targeting – have increased transparency, there is still room for improvement in many countries. Measuring the transparency of monetary policies by region, Latin America ranks behind Europe, Asia and the Middle East and Central Asia.

At the end of the day, what emerges is the well known 'flexibility versus credibility' dilemma. When credibility is *ex ante* perceived as somewhat weak or in any case as the main priority to be protected, inflation flexibility may need to be sacrificed. These are very high costs to pay for past errors. But, in principle, there will be lower future costs for corrected or mended history. One of the key policy implications of this analysis is that countries with more rigid market (labor markets for instance) and micro-institutional restrictions end up having a larger cumulative loss. Court or legal decisions can have very deleterious consequences as may have happened in the case of Colombia, where the Constitutional Court intervened in the real state and banking crisis in ways which may have aggravated the situation.

The Emerging Restructured Policy Framework

Although it would be difficult to establish precise attribution to the different causes (external vs domestic policy 'preparedness') of the crisis of 1998–1999, the fact is that Chile restructured its policy framework by adopting the following four major changes: (i) the adoption of a free floating exchange rate regime; (ii) the total opening of the Capital Account in 2001; (iii) the use of an explicit fiscal policy rule for the central government; and

(iv) an enhanced inflation-targeting framework. The lessons learned by Chile are subsumed in these four interdependent and mutually reinforcing changes. They configure a 'first-best policy regime' for a medium sized country that needs to be integrated into the international financial and trade system to be able to grow at faster rates. This is by and large the case for most Latin American countries. The implementation of something close to this 'first-best' policy regime is a major challenge to all Latin American countries. It is not something that can be decreed or dictated, nor can it be installed in a short period of time. But it sets the direction of the steps and building blocks to arrive there.

With regard to the floating of the exchange rate, Morande and Tapia (2002, p. 90) observe that it was not really a major policy change but part of a transition from a previous ongoing evolution. Since the early 1990s the existing band had mimicked a flexible rate regime. In brief, the floating was the 'natural' evolution of recent history as well as a step to avoid a potential conflict of policy objectives. In 2000 the government announced that for the following six years

> it would follow a rule for determining total expenditures. The rule, known as the one-percent structural surplus rule, aimed at ensuring a 1 percent surplus for the central government every year considering structural revenues, measured as cycle-adjusted tax revenues and what could be considered a 'normal' copper price. The 1 percent target was explained as necessary to cover for the recurrent CBC deficit, as a means to save copper wealth for future generations and as insurance against contingent liabilities. The rule allowed better communication of the fiscal position, separating cyclical from structural changes. It was accompanied by an important fiscal restraint, and it helped to improve credibility. (Céspedes et al., 2006, p. 26)

The importance of the adopted fiscal rule cannot be exaggerated. Singh and Collyns (2005, p. 11), when explaining Chile's success, answered by saying that: 'Prudent fiscal policies, a move to inflation targeting, a freely floating exchange rate, and trade openness tell much of the story.'[20]

VIII.   CONCLUSIONS AND POLICY IMPLICATIONS

Chile's success can largely be explained by the relative strength of this country's political demand for macroeconomic stability as well as by the political support for the attendant institutions and fiscal and monetary policies that deliver such stability. Without this political demand for the 'right' institutional transformations there would not be sufficient political incentives to develop those institutions. The key factor is the alignment of the 'right' policy reforms with the political incentives to deliver them. There are five key institutional characteristics that Chile has been able to nurture since the late 1960s and to put in place since the mid-1980s.

- A largely independent Central Bank with credible inflation targeting and a flexible exchange rate band.
- A 'fiscal policy rule' of having a 1 per cent 'structural fiscal balance' surplus adjusted for cyclical effects and for copper price movements.
- A Congress that through its special Economic Commission supports prudent monetary and fiscal policies.
- The development since 1986 of new banking and bankruptcy laws giving strong independent power to the supervisory and regulatory agencies to keep up with international standards and best practices.
- An effective 'informal coordination mechanism' between the Central Bank and the Ministry of Finance.

With the benefit of hindsight the policy response by the Central Bank of raising the interest rate to unprecedented levels and intervening to protect the exchange rate, could now be seen as somewhat 'excessive'. However, behind the 'fear of high inflation pass-through' was the powerful argument of protecting the Central Bank's institutional credibility and investing to build this capital for the future. This brought policy makers to the dilemma of 'rules versus discretion', the dilemma of handling the crisis via exchange rate or via interest rates.

In retrospect it could be argued that there might have been an 'overshooting' of the interest rate and that more flexibility might have reduced deviations from potential output. There are good arguments on both sides of the alleged divide. But there is not sufficient empirical evidence on the costs of the overshooting or of the gains in lower lost output. The counterfactuals are difficult to quantify. However, from a long-term perspective, and even for a country with a good reputation for its economic management, as Chile is, the judgmental call to favor future dividends of a strengthened Central Bank's credibility seems to have been the right policy posture. In principle, the markets, next time around, will 'smooth' the adjustment process out even more. After all, this is the promise of rational expectations.

The key lesson to be extracted from the 1997–1998 crisis can be summarized by saying that the 'initial macroeconomics conditions' are the crux of the costs of an external shock. All the fundamental challenges and all the agonizing choices between rules, credibility and flexibility are mitigated if the initial macroeconomic conditions provide institutional and financial resilience. In the last analysis:

The optimal degree of flexibility may also depend on the initial macroeconomic conditions. In the first-best world, countries with a high degree of pass-through probably stand to gain more from a flexible approach to inflation targeting than those with low pass-through. Given that these countries are likely to demonstrate more short-term volatility in their inflation rate, additional flexibility increases the probability that they will not be drawn into the type of sub-optimal policy responses discussed above. However, again the difficulty arises where credibility is weak. In such cases, the needed flexibility cannot be used for fear of undermining confidence in the regime (Céspedes et al., 2005, p. 35).

Findings from empirical studies on the effectiveness of 'early warning systems' point out that banking and financial crises do not typically arrive without some sort of warning (Goldstein, 2005, p. 31). There are often recurrent behavior patterns in the period leading to crises. However, it is also true that each crisis may bring or come from unanticipated developments. In current times global capital markets, in particular, appear in need of constant in-depth examination. 'The ongoing globalization of goods and capital promises to bring profound changes to the global economy and to individual economies' (Fischer, 2004, p. 497). For the particular case of Chile, Caballero (2001, p. 161) warns that when 'financial development rises so does leverage and, with it, vulnerability'.

NOTES

1. Chile's case is particularly instructive because as Espinosa-Vega and Phillips put it, this country was not always so successful. 'Over the period 1940–70, Chile was in many ways typical of much of Latin America, in following an import-substitution strategy, giving a heavy role to the state in the economy more generally, rationing foreign exchange, and experiencing high and unstable inflation. Moreover, after major reforms of this old regime began in the 1970s, Chile exemplified a problem that has been familiar elsewhere, with its severe financial crisis of the early 1980s' (IMF, 2004d, p. 6).
2. According to Besley and Coate (1998, p. 139), 'One of the crowning achievements of neoclassical economics is a rigorous appreciation of the performance of markets in allocating resources. However, for resources allocated in the public sector, our understanding is much less complete. In part this reflects the lack of a satisfactory theoretical framework to analyze policy choice in representative democracies. Despite the vast volume of research on public choice, there is no clear consensus on the ability of representative democracy to produce efficient outcomes. At one extreme are writers in the Chicago tradition, such as George Stigler (1982), Gary Becker (1985), and Donald Wittman (1989), who argue that political competition will bring about efficient policy choices. At the other extreme are James M. Buchanan, Gordon Tullock, and their followers (the "Virginia School"), who see "political failures" as pervasive.'
3. Santiso (2006, p. 102), 'Under the new democratic regime, monetary and fiscal orthodoxy continued in place'. See his 'The Chilean trajectory: From liberalism to possibilism' in Santiso (2006).
4. Income distribution tends to be determined by market forces while poverty levels and equity of access are more the result of the effectiveness of specific policy interventions and particularly the quality of public expenditures. See Váldes (1999, p. 261).

5. Even before, during the Alessandri Rodriguez (1958–1964) government, the 'Oficina de Evaluación de Proyectos' was created in 1963 under the leaderships of Sergio Molina and placed within the Ministry of Finance. According to Ernesto Fontaine (1997, p. 67), this office, and its role over many years, explains why 'Chile has been quite free of white elephants and other wasteful uses of public investment funds'.

6. See Aidunate Arturo Fontaine (1988, p. 38), for the political background and events surrounding the 'El Ladrillo' document and its main contributors.

7. Harberger (1993b, p. 345) posits that for the subsequent revolution in Chilean economic policy 'El Ladrillo' 'played a role not unlike that of the *Federalist Papers* in shaping the constitutional framework of the United States.'

8. For a summary of Chile's fiscal and budgetary history see Petrei (1997, p. 295).

9. According to Valdés (1995), Chilean economists subscribed to economics as a science; to a cult of rationality. On the influence of the Chicago School of Economics on Chile see Barber (1995, p. 1941).

10. 'Long-term yield curves represent the market's expectations for future short-term rates'. See *The Economist* (2006d, p. 69).

11. Simon (1982) states that in economics, optimal conceptual and operational solutions are seldom possible, nor necessary, and that progress is achieved gradually by marginal 'satisficing' improvements.

12. Mistri (2003, p. 314) posits that a common system of values 'outside the game' is necessary for a cooperative game to engender the 'right' institutions.

13. These initial conditions references are taken from Céspedes et al. (2006) and Caballero et al. (2004).

14. Countries with declining inflation targets may lose flexibility when hit by an unexpected shock. The authorities may fear missing the inflation target and putting their institutional credibility at risk. They may misjudge the costs of the attendant policy trade-offs.

15. See Hausmann et al. (2001, p. 389) for a discussion on exchange rate management under floating regime by different countries. Emerging countries seem to shy away from exchange rate volatility probably because of their limitations to borrow in their own currencies. This is the so-called 'original sin' defined by Roubini and Setser (2004, p. 412) as 'an economic theory arguing that structural impediments in global capital markets make it difficult for emerging economies to borrow abroad in their own currencies. Countries that have to denominate their external debt in another country's currency suffer from "original sin".'

16. Calvo and Mendoza (1999, p. 52) call into question the effectiveness of interest rate policy as an anti-inflationary device. They quote Robert Lucas as follows 'Central bankers and even some monetary economists talk knowledgeably of using high interest rates to control inflation, but I know of no evidence from even one economy linking these variables in a useful way . . .' (Lucas, 1966).

17. Caballero and Krishnamurthy (2003) argue that optimal monetary policy should be countercyclical even if it does little to reduce the real impact of a sudden stop.

18. Aninat (2000b, p. 21) points out that Chile also protected its social spending programs.

19. Trade-offs between deviations from an inflation target and deviation from potential output are associated with a loss function resulting from Taylor rules. See Truman (2003, p. 85).

20. This policy action seems to fit well within the Chang and Velasco framework (2000, p. 75), namely 'the evaluation of exchange-rate policy should move away from the "fix versus flex" dichotomy, and toward the characterization of optimal monetary policy in well-specified analytical frameworks. Inflation-targeting is one such framework, though not the only one.'

6. Colombia: fairness perception and the political tolerance for macroeconomic policy reform

> Constitutional rules appear to shape economic policy and largely determine economic performance.
>
> Persson and Tabellini (2004a, p. 94)

I. THE PRIMACY OF CONSTITUTIONAL RULES

Colombia seems to be the typical case in which Constitutional rules determine economic policies and the politics of those policies (Persson and Tabellini, 2003; Acemoglu, 2005b, p. 1025).[1] In effect, no other set of factors better explains this country's economic, political and social developments over the last fifteen years[2] than the rules that emanated from its 1991 Constitution and from the basic conceptual and philosophical perspective under which it was framed. This is the 'first-order-context-necessary-condition' to avoid excessive and unnecessary focus on particular or specific episodes thus running the risk of missing the structural nature of the problems at hand. In brief, understanding Colombia's recent macroeconomic performance, in terms of growth, inflation, volatility and distributional outcomes, requires careful consideration of its *ab initio* 'Constitutional normative philosophy' and delving into at least the following two 1991 constitutional mandates:

i.   Articles 356 and 357 established a formula driven transfers[3] system which more than doubled the revenue transfers from the national level to the subnational level, to the states, to municipalities[4] and to some sectors.
ii. Articles 371, 372 and 373 mandated the creation of an autonomous Central Bank with the instruction to lower inflation and to maintain price stability in coordination[5] with the general social and economic policies of the government.[6]

There were other Constitutional mandates with enormous fiscal, economic and political economy implications, such as Article 350, with its instruction that social public expenditures would have priority over any other budget allocation, and Article 359, which prohibited 'ear-marked' funds except in the case of social investment. These two articles and other related provisions have introduced a high degree of inflexibility in budget allocations (Cárdenas and Mercer-Blackman, 2006, p. 2; Echeverry et al., 2003). Such inflexibility is not an accident. It has deep political economy and 'fairness perception' historical origins. It reflects the feelings of some political actors or groups to have guarantees for the public entitlements they feel they deserve. It reflects the feeling of unfairness that some 1991 'constitutional actors' felt characterized Colombia's social structure.[7] To them 'people should get what they deserve' and a Constitution should guarantee them that. Whether they deserve what they get was a question hardly addressed. This is a major issue. After all, it is of the essence of distributive justice to balance equality and fairness of opportunity, on the one hand, with equity and fairness of outcomes, on the other (Solimano, 2000, p. 33).

The 1991 Constitution was framed under an overarching 'Estado Social de Derecho' precept which provides room[8] for normative and value judgments[9] and for ad hoc rulings by the Constitutional Court. These rulings have, in some cases, superseded legislation duly processed by Congress (Pinilla, 2006, p. 27).[10] According to the former Minister of Finance of Colombia, Alberto Carrasquilla (2006, p. 73), if the government tries to lower tax rates because high levels can be detrimental to investment, this proposal runs the risk of being perceived, by some judges of the Constitutional Court, as potentially inimical to its own and particular interpretation of how it affects distributive justice and thus may be deemed unconstitutional. To Carrasquilla this poses difficult trade-offs in economic policy making.

Under the views of some Constitutional judges, such welfare and distributionally-intensive legislation is the relevant subject matter of the principle of the 'Estado Social de Derecho'. As such it is part of the Court's jurisdiction and duty to verify if the legislation is consistent with the precepts (and interpretations) of the 'Estado Social de Derecho' philosophy.[11] All this can take place independently of what Congress or the Executive level may have intended or included in the respective legislation. However, Echeverry (2006, p. 29) avers that it is possible to reconcile economic principles with the 'values' implicit in the Estado Social de Desarrollo framework.

Having personal preferences over what should be the 'fair' welfare function of Colombia and specific views about how to achieve it is, of course, a legitimate personal and political position. However, this is not the issue. Nor is it if economics should or should not be concerned with ethics (González, 1998, p. 32). The problem is allowing these subjective personal welfare notions to influence Constitutional rulings beyond what Congress may have established, or what is fiscally, financially or institutionally possible. Unfortunately, some of the well intentioned distributive Constitutional Court rulings have had unintended consequences[12] and have led to welfare losses by the poor and by the middle class. There are arguments that such was the consequence of the Court's ruling in 1998 on the way to manage the real state crisis. Such rulings aggravated the situation and contributed to the collapse of the legal and financial system of the housing market in Colombia in 1999.

Constitutional Articles 356 and 357, on revenue transfers, and 371, 372 and 373 on the creation of an independent Central Bank with the responsibility of lowering inflation, have been the main source of enormous institutional, political and policy tension[13] which the country has been trying to manage and resolve since the early 1990s. It has been a severely trying period. It has put to test the effectiveness of macroeconomic policy making and of all major national and subnational[14] reform processes across the whole spectrum of Colombia's public policies.[15] Moreover, to Kugler and Rosenthal (2005, p. 97), the Constitution of 1991 'while well intentioned, has left Colombian institutions with a diminished capacity to govern in a manner that promotes economic efficiency and growth.'

The first mandate, together with other related expenditures, led to an increase of about 50 per cent in terms of GDP in the level of public expenditures, excluding interest payments, by the non-financial public sector from 1990 to 2001.[16] Transfers to the decentralized and territorial level increased from 3.6 per cent of GDP in 1994 to 5.9 per cent in 2002. The second mandate[17] led to Law No. 31 of 1992 and to an enhanced Central Bank institution which took its responsibilities very seriously and has delivered much lower rates of inflation,[18] albeit through severe but unanticipated disinflation and macroeconomic volatility, particularly in 1998–1999 when an unprecedented severe recession took place.

These two truly historical mandates appear to have been in conflict with each other, admittedly not an intended one. They were adopted by a choice that did not explicitly involve establishing the institutional fiscal infrastructure or the political mandate to finance the additional expenditures. Although a difficult stand to understand, it may have had the underlying political economy rationale of increasing social expenditures hopefully to remedy social injustice[19] and to build a minimum of fairness into Colombia's social fabric. As Alesina (1991, p. 43) would probably aver, there is often an occult political economy rationale for policy postures which, at first sight, appear as evident 'mistakes'. In any case, it unsettled the previous political economy compromise[20] through which the state and the citizenry had traded off an inflationary[21] tax for alleged macroeconomic and political[22] stability. According to Carrasquilla (1999, p. xxxiii), this

'Pacto Social reflected a fiscal problem in the sense that it linked the collections and distribution of the inflationary tax'. It worked because idiosyncratically Colombians did not abuse this political agreement.[23] It seemed to work for many years.[24]

These two paradigmatic changes were on a collision course with each other right from the beginning. Between 1974 and 1990 the average annual inflation rate had been 23.9 per cent (Carrasquilla, 1999, p. xxxiv). To this initial condition the Constitution simultaneously added an enormous fiscal and transfer[25] burden and the instruction to its new Central Bank to lower inflation. Indeed a major political economy coordination problem.[26] Why the Constitutional Assembly adopted this contradictory position[27] and why the Gaviria[28] administration apparently did not object to – or was unable to correct – this anomaly,[29] is still a subject of research.[30] Another key question is whether a historical opportunity may not have been missed to nurture an institutional fiscal transformation analogous (*mutatis mutandi*) to the one adopted with regard to monetary policy and to the Central Bank. However, there were other policy areas like deregulation in which the Gaviria administration took important initiatives (Montenegro, 1995, p. 20).[31]

Part of the explanation for the 'omission' of a Constitutional fiscal rule, analogous to the Central Bank one, can be found in Alesina and Tabellini (2007, p. 177) who observe that politicians will tend not to delegate redistributive tasks to an independent albeit highly technical 'decentralized' institution.[32] 'If the Constitution is designed by politicians, rather than chosen by voters behind a veil of ignorance, then the politician will never choose to delegate redistributive tasks to an independent bureaucrat.' This is so because redistribution enables a politician to build winning coalitions of voters, increasing his incumbency advantage. While this observation is soundly based on the different incentives and accountabilities distinguishing the decision making process between a high level bureaucrat and a politician, it seems that a general aggregate fiscal 'Constitutional rule' could be proposed within the behind the veil framework to limit the size of the 'fiscal pool' allowing for political competition for redistributive purposes but without infringing on the overall budget constraint. For the case of Colombia this could mean, for instance, a Rawlsian rule to have a primary surplus of, let's say, 4–5 per cent over the next ten years. Chile's current fiscal rule to have a 'structural' surplus is a variant of this approach, which combines desirable long term intertemporal consistency with political realism to negotiate redistribution mechanisms and results, but within a stable macroeconomic environment.

Another part of the answer which future economic historians[33] will give to the above questions will come from a political economy perspective on the real origins of the initiative to have an independent Central Bank.[34] What were those origins?[35] Was there a firm political demand for less inflation and for an autonomous Central Bank?[36] Was there a real demand for macroeconomic stability meaning low interest rates[37] and low inflation rates and no seignorage?[38] If so, how come all administrations since 1990 have not been able to obtain sufficient political support for much-needed fiscal and financial reforms and restraint? Surely the political incentives were there in 1991 to decree additional public expenditures but were they equally present to support the measures needed to bring inflation down under a controlled process? According to Wiesner (1999, p. 86), the separation of responsibilities between the Central Bank and the Ministry of Finance assumed *inter alia* that when fiscal imbalances led to interest rate increases, a sort 'of logic of collective action' would engender political support for fiscal correction. The general public would understand that if the most comprehensive 'price' of all rose, then there would be political clamor to correct such a situation. It is now history that, as Olson (1971) and Cournot (1897) said, there is little logic of collective action, and the meaning of interest rates increases (or their sources) is not yet fully comprehended by the general public. Although their consequences are felt by all. Particularly their mismanagement.

One possible explicatory hypothesis is that, to some extent, the origin of the independent Central Bank was more supply driven from the technical side than demand driven from the political side;[39] that it was driven mostly by serious and competent economists and some political leaders who knew how welfare costly inflation[40] can be, and how dangerous it is to believe that you can always keep it under a short leash.[41] Once the hypothesis of insufficient political demand for macroeconomic stability is brought into the picture, the puzzle becomes less beguiling. From then on it is clear why the original conflict and contradiction since 1990 still remains a major challenge that continues to test macroeconomic stability and questions the alleged political compromise which Colombia is supposed to have had for decades.

In reality, Colombia's hitherto political economy compromise began to unravel at the beginning of the 1990s.[42] It would probably be unwarranted to say that the severe crisis at the end of the 1990s had been seeded in this particular contradiction[43] of the 1991 Constitution. But it would be difficult to argue that these two developments were unrelated. For a while the economy even prospered, public expenditures grew fast,[44] higher taxes were collected in the early 1990s, but by the mid-1990s gradually weakened, ran into fiscal deficits, became highly indebted and, finally, collapsed in 1998 and 1999.[45] The bursting of the real estate bubble and the attendant constitutional and legal obfuscation made everything more welfare costly.

One of the more rigorous examinations of the economic implications of the 1991 Constitution (Cárdenas et al., 2006, p. 55) concluded that it brought some 'positive changes but the main problems were associated with fiscal policies'. Mishkin and Savastano (2001) found that Colombia's post-Constitutional anti-inflationary strategy was a failure. The average annual rate of inflation for 1991–1998 was basically the same on average as that of the 1980s. According to Kalmanovitz (2001a, p. 10) by '1993 fiscal and monetary policy should have been concretionary'.

In any case it would be difficult to characterize Colombia's last 10 to 15 years as a period of macroeconomic stability (Partow, 2003, p. 147).[46] After all, these were the years when GDP growth was highly uneven,[47] the unemployment rate rose above 20 per cent, fiscal results worsened, public debt almost doubled and the financial sector suffered a major crisis. After the GDP collapse of 1999 and the protracted recovery, poverty levels increased and the middle and low income groups suffered major setbacks. Finally the period 2003–2006 has shown remarkable recovery with an average GDP growth rate above 5 per cent. If macroeconomic volatility has been the predominant characteristic over the last 15 years, 'constitutional volatility' has also been high. The balance shows 22 amendments since the 1991 Constitution was adopted (Castro, 2006, p. 6).

II. DISINFLATION AND THE EFFECTIVENESS OF MONETARY POLICY

The laudable achievement of low, single-digit inflation since the early 2000s raises the question of to what extent this result may not have been more the consequence of the abrupt and unexpected – and unintended – disinflation of the years 1998 and 1999 than the unqualified success of monetary policy.[48] Inflation dropped by over seven points from 16.70 in 1998 to 9.20 in 1999 but GDP was 5.7 in 1998 and became negative, −4.29, in 1999. According to Echeverry (2005) it would not be fully accurate to attribute a drop in the inflation rate of such magnitude to monetary policy.[49] In his words, 1999 'was an infernal year and the inflation target was missed by a wide margin', meaning there was an inflation target 'overshooting'.

This question, posed with the benefit of hindsight, is not intended as a criticism or judgment on the competence or wisdom of the policy makers at the time.[50] They had to make extremely difficult decisions under very limited information and uncertain domestic and external environments. In most similar circumstances in Latin America and Asia, crises made unexpected turns, triggering unanticipated policy restrictions and collateral costs. In the end, the measurements that have been made of the 'sacrifice ratios' in Latin America for the crisis of the 1990s show that although Colombia may have paid a high 'output forgone' for its lower inflation it was not one of the worst.

Be that as it may, the current low, single-digit inflation is unquestionably one of the most valuable collective assets of the country. The best way to protect it is to fully understand how it came about, what information may have been missing to make better decisions and what coordination failures there might have been. In brief, what follows is an examination of what can be learned from history and to see what lessons should be converted into new policies.[51] This country narrative does not pretend to be an exhaustive examination of the crisis of 1998–1999. It merely hopes to be a contribution to that research agenda which Hommes (2005, p. 47)[52] rightly posed to the academic community.

III.   MACROECONOMIC PERFORMANCE IN PERSPECTIVE, 1970–2007

Colombia's GDP per capita rate of growth has been on a declining trend for the past 35 years. This has happened even though the population rate of growth itself has been declining. Table 6.1 shows that for the period 1970–1980, per capita GDP grew at 2.9 per cent, then at 1.19 per cent in 1980–1990, declining further to 0.78 per cent in 1990–2000. This trend changed for the better in 2000–2004 when per capita GDP grew at 1.15 per cent. What explains this trend? Cárdenas (2005, p. 52) finds the explanation in worker productivity which has been declining since the early 1970s. He posits that illicit drug traffic may explain some of this trend. Ocampo (1991, p. 49) calls this a 'structural crisis'.

Figure 6.1 shows a growth cycle of 5.2 per cent for 1951–1979, followed by a 3.0 per cent growth period during 1980–2002. The overall picture is one of considerable volatility.[53] For 2003–2008, the projection is for an average growth of about 5.0 per cent. Whether this will become a reality

Table 6.1   Colombia: per capita GDP rates of growth, 1970–2004

Indicators	1970–1980	1980–1990	1990–2000	2000–2004
PIB	5.51	3.40	2.72	2.90
Population	2.52	2.18	1.93	1.73
GDP per capita	2.92	1.19	0.78	1.15

Source: Cárdenas (2005, p. 50).

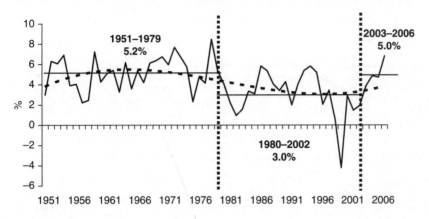

Source: Cárdenas (2007).

Figure 6.1   Colombia's long-term growth cycles

Table 6.2   Colombia: key macroeconomic indicators, 1997–2006

Indicator	1997	1998	1999	2000	2001	2002	2003	2004	2005	2006
A. GDP real growth rate	3.43	0.57	−4.20	2.92	1.47	1.93	3.86	4.78	5.7	6.8
B. Inflation rate, CPI	17.70	16.70	9.20	8.80	7.60	7.00	6.49	5.50	4.86	4.7
C. Unemployment rate	11.30	14.10	18.00	17.30	18.20	17.60	16.70	15.40	13.90	13.4

Source: Central Bank of Colombia.

depends on two interdependent processes. First, how abrupt the reversal of the global business cycle will be and, secondly, how effective the Colombian authorities will be in managing such development.

During the last ten years (1997–2006) two distinct periods can be discerned in terms of GDP growth and macroeconomic performance. First, the 1997 to 1999 period shows a declining trend culminating in 1999 with a GDP drop of −4.2 per cent. Secondly, an upward trend for 2000–2006 with a dip in 2001 and 2002. During the last four years, 2003–2006, GDP growth has strengthened, reaching 6.8 per cent in 2006. Inflation came down from 17.7 per cent in 1997 to 4.7 per cent in 2006. The collapse of GDP growth in 1999 was so pronounced that the *ex ante* inflation targets for that year were met with a 'surplus', a typical abrupt disinflation with a high 'sacrifice ratio'. Unemployment, which rose during the crisis years has

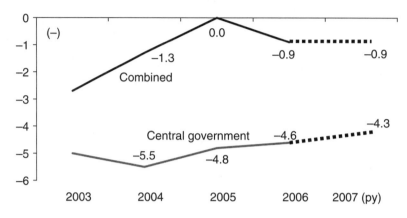

Source: CONFIS, Ministerio de Hacienda y Crédito Público.

Figure 6.2   Colombia: fiscal balances, 2006

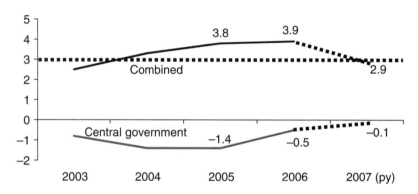

Source: CONFIS, Ministerio de Hacienda y Crédito Público.

Figure 6.3   Colombia: primary fiscal balances, 2006

come down in the recovery after 2003. But it has been a somewhat 'jobless growth' in 2005 and 2006.

The fiscal performance for 2003–2007 appears in Figures 6.2 and 6.3 and Table 6.3. At the end of 2006 Colombia had a primary positive balance of 4.0 per cent for its consolidated public sector and a positive one of 0.2 per cent for its Central Government. Total fiscal balance was −0.4 per cent for the Consolidated Public Sector and −3.8 per cent for the Central Government. Figures 6.2 and 6.3 also show a projected weakening of fiscal performance for 2007.

Table 6.3   Colombia: fiscal balances, 2006 (% GDP)

Sector	Primary balance	Fiscal balance
Consolidated public sector	4.0	−0.4
Central government	0.2	−3.8

Source: ANIF, CONFIS, Ministry of Finance.

IV.   THE POLITICAL ECONOMY OF EQUITY IN COLOMBIA

In their pioneering work on income distribution in Colombia, Urrutia and Berry (1975, p. 11) found something very telling about the early tradition of linkages between equity and political economy in Colombia. This tradition, although it has evolved significantly in the last 30 years, is still short of having been fully comprehended and unbundled in its current causal relationships. Urrutia and Berry were disconcerted to find 'Clear evidence that some public policies have contributed to worsen income distribution or to slow down potential avenues for improvement.' This was not so much an intended purpose but the result of insufficient understanding of the real incentive causalities involved. The point is that back then as well as today Colombia still needed to understand better the inner intended or unintended incentive structures that actually regulate the interaction between deliberate or implicit pro-growth and pro-poor policies. Gaviria (2004, p. 11) has underscored the apparent contradictions between those policy makers that believe that fiscal adjustment and social expenditure are inherently incompatible. This may have been the contradiction underlying the social welfare function that the 1991 Constitution tried to define.

Poverty matters in many ways but particularly in influencing political preferences towards or against some specific modalities of distributive justice.[54] Alejandro Gaviria (2006, p. 20) has found that for Latin America high poverty levels and the perception of limited social mobility have become severe restrictions for the adoption of pro-growth policies.[55] The political insistence seems to be for some particular modalities of alleged pro-poor policies. Under these circumstances the challenge for policy makers is to deliver, simultaneously, faster and more redistributive growth as well as more equitable and pro-growth distributive policies. If this daunting challenge is valid for Latin America it is particularly apt for Colombia. After all, this is a country that has just recently learned how unsettling it can be to have a crisis as severe as the one experienced in 1998–1999. Colombia may well fit into the group of those countries where fairness

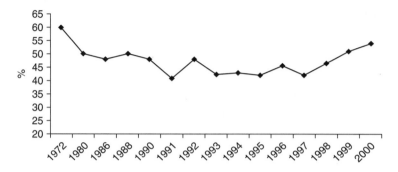

Source: Ocampo et al. (2004, p. 12).

Figure 6.4   Colombia: households below the poverty line, 1972–2000

perception is not helping in making pro-growth or pro-poor policies more
effective. After all, 'fairness perception impacts aggregate outcomes and
individual attitudes' (Alesina and Angeletos, 2005, p. 963).[56]

Poverty levels are determined jointly by macroeconomic and microeconomic conditions. Amongst the first, growth and rates of employment are
the more important ones. Amongst the second conditions, the level of
education in the household, the size of the household and its characteristics (rural vis-à-vis urban, for example) and access to market opportunities, are the critical factors. In this country narrative the emphasis is
on the macroeconomic determinants of the evolution[57] of poverty in
Colombia.[58]

'Halfway through the twentieth century, when it was possible to assess
social conditions globally for the first time, the country's social indicators
were disastrous' (Ocampo and Tovar, 2000, p. 273). Figure 6.4 provides an
overview of the evolution of Colombia's poverty for the period 1972–2000.
It can be appreciated that there was a decline in poverty levels in the 1970s
(Urrutia, 1984, p. 195) and up to the mid-1980s. Then there was some
increase, a further decline and a worsening in the early 1990s. The terrible
negative impact of the 1999 crisis actually began in 1996 when unemployment began to rise. According to Cárdenas and Urrutia (2004, p. 155) the
crisis of 1998–1999 reversed the poverty reduction of the previous decade.
After 2003 there was a fast decline in poverty levels down to 45.1 per cent
in 2006 (Table 6.4). Hugo López (2006, p. 2) finds this decline to be the
result of fast growth and low inflation since 2003.

Figure 6.5 shows the evolution of the Gini coefficient for the period
1991–2005. Income concentration rose steadily from 1991 and reached its
highest level in 1999.

Table 6.4   Colombia: national poverty lines, 1995–2006

Year (Sept.)	Poverty line	Extreme poverty
1995	49.5	15.5
1996	50.9	17.2
1997	52.7	18.5
1998	55.3	20.8
1999	57.5	25.4
2000	55.0	19.0
2001	55.2	18.7
2002	57.0	20.7
2003	50.7	15.8
2004	52.7	17.4
2005	49.2	14.7
2006*	45.1	12.04

Note: * Refers to June. SISD: Sistema de Indicadores Sociodemográficos del Departamento Nacional de Planeación.

Source: Cárdenas and Urrutia (2004, p. 151).

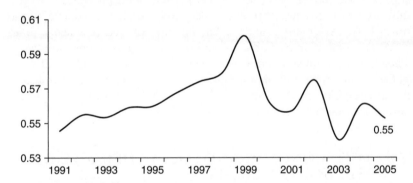

Source: Clavijo (2006, p. 2).

Figure 6.5   Colombia: income Gini coefficient evolution, 1991–2005

V.   FAIRNESS PERCEPTION IN COLOMBIA AND EQUITY CHALLENGES

'Colombians regard income distribution as unfair' (Velez, 2004, p. 61) and Alejandro Gaviria (2002, p. 2) posits that 'Colombia's levels of social mobility are lower than those in the United States, Mexico and Peru and comparable to those in Brazil'. This is the political economy baseline scenario. As such, the current policy challenge to enhance equity in general and to reduce poverty levels in particular in Colombia is to reconcile and balance over time the political pressures to increase social public expenditures with the need to make such public expenditures more effective. The political economy nature of the problem arises for two reasons. First, because there is strong and well organized opposition by public sector rent seekers to changing the incentive structure of the micro-institutional arrangements where social public expenditure (particularly education)[59] takes place. Secondly, because there are larger fiscal and budget restrictions limiting public expenditures over the whole of the public sector.

This political economy problem exists largely as a result of information asymmetries. They allow public sector rent-seekers to defend and tout their interests in the name of public interest. Information asymmetries also lead the general public to believe that only additional public expenditure can respond to its very legitimate expectation of equal initial conditions to all members of society. This is an information problem that can only be mitigated by deliberate efforts by the government and the private sector to conduct and support research on the real redistributive capacity of current subsidies and budget arrangements. The key to making progress in this very difficult distributive justice problem is to emphasize that Colombia, just as other Latin American countries, has already traveled (Clements, 2007, p. 25) the road of more public expenditure in the last ten or more years. Therefore it cannot show convincing evidence to warrant additional social public spending without first adopting reforms in the micro-institutional incentive and information frameworks in sectors such as education, health and social security in general.

VI.   THE ECONOMIC AND SOCIAL DEBACLE OF THE 1998–1999 CRISIS

The 1998–1999 economic crisis in Colombia was a major social, political, financial and distributional debacle. Probably not since the 1930s had the country experienced anything as severe and disrupting. This was a country that, by and large, had not experienced anything as severe and institutionally disrupting. Colombia had not gone through explosive macroeconomic turmoil as some other Latin American countries had done (Kalmanovitz, 2001b, p. 272).[60] Perhaps not having known such disasters may partly explain its having come to live those circumstances. After all, it is not easy for the political process to adopt difficult decisions largely on the basis of a theoretical counterfactual without any real experience of the trouble it forecasts. It was not just a drop in GDP, which is always a major problem; it had a devastating and prolonged effect on employment, poverty, the financial sector and the housing market (Arias, 2000, p. 27).[61] It may even have adversely affected the role and the division of political responsibilities between governmental bodies, including the Constitutional Court,[62] and their decisions on public issues such as fiscal, monetary, wages and financial policies.

The policy evolution from mid-1991 onwards has been summarized as follows:

> When the Board of the Central Bank took office in August 1991, its stance in terms of monetary and exchange rate policy was substantially modified. Monetary policy was somewhat relaxed, interest rates were drastically reduced, and an important nominal appreciation was allowed for, followed by a decline in the rate of nominal depreciation, which became the main tool in the effort to reduce inflation. To tackle the problem of large intermediation margins, quantitative restrictions on capital inflows were removed in order to provide competition to the domestic financial system. Since inflation diminished only gradually ex post real interest rates fell in a dramatic fashion. In addition, the Central Bank adopted a variety of measures in relation to capital flows. In an initial phase, with quantitative restrictions on the capital account still in place, capital inflows were sterilized. In a second stage, which began in 1992 and was consolidated in 1993, quantitative controls were removed, some price-based disincentives to capital inflows were introduced, and sterilization was largely abandoned (Cárdenas and Steiner, 2000, p. 211).

The 'initial conditions' for the crisis of 1998–1999 have distant origins, intermediate ones and immediate 'triggering' ones. Amongst the first 'distant' origins is the *ab initio* 'macroeconomic coordination tension' seeded by the 1991 Constitution in attempting to reconcile the need to reduce inflation with the political aspiration to improve distributive justice through transfers to the subnational level and through higher levels of public expenditure. This vision soon proved unsustainable when external and internal financial flows became unbalanced and led to an asset or stock fundamental disequilibrium.[63] According to Ocampo (2005a, p. 75), 1992–1995 were 'euphoric years of expenditure' which became unsustainable when private financing, particularly external debt, began to recede in 1995. The financial system became very sensitive to interest rate increases and to exchange rate depreciation.[64] In the event, both occurred and the private sector incurred large losses. Gómez (2006, p. 39) has concluded that 'the most important factors explaining the 1999 crisis originated in the financial sector'. To Hernández (2003, p. 4), the genesis of the crisis was the opening of the Capital Account at the beginning of the 1990s.[65] To González (2003, p. 27) there was double volatility during the 1990s; real and monetary volatility.

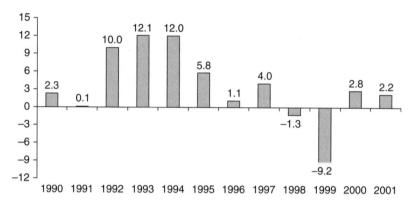

Source: Uribe and Vargas (2002, Figure 8).

Figure 6.6   Colombia: domestic demand annual growth rate (%)

Given the magnitude of the 1998–1999 crisis, some observers may miss the key point that the markets and the long term GDP growth tendency had, since late 1996 and early 1997, already indicated that the economy was on a declining trend. Figure 6.6 shows that domestic demand had reached its peak in 1994 and then dropped to 5.8 per cent in 1995 and to 1.1 per cent in 1996.

Although the Samper administration did not want to increase fiscal deficits but to conduct an orderly expansion of the public sector (Ocampo, 2004a, p. 108), the government's response to the 1995–1996 demand down-turn (Figure 6.6) was basically a Keynesian strategy on the basis that the fault was on the demand side. On the fiscal side expenditures were increased, the interest rate was lowered and added liquidity was injected into the system as multilateral loans flowed in (Montenegro, 2007, p. 16A).[66] For a while the 'reactivation strategy' seemed to work. Aggregate demand rebounded to a 4.0 per cent growth in 1997. But the fundamental flow and asset balances of the public sector and of the financial system were deeply misaligned. The deficit in the trade account doubled to US$4 billion between 1996 and 1998. The public turned the 'excess' domestic liquidity into purchases of foreign exchange and began to put pressure on the exchange rate. The combination of unbalanced public and private flows created a major problem, namely, a stock or asset disequilibrium. After the implosion of the real estate sector, households were finding it difficult to service their mortgages. In 1991 they allocated 10 per cent of their savings to servicing those debts. By 1998 this proportion rose to 60 per cent (Echeverry, 2002, p. 58).

One of the most challenging questions for economic historians is whether the crisis might have been averted or pre-empted by a different macroeconomic policy during 1996 and 1997. More specifically, instead of trying to revert the declining GDP growth trend, which had already begun in 1995 (Figure 6.7), with expansionary policies and growing fiscal deficits (Figure 6.8), what if more opportune corrective fiscal and credit actions had been taken? Figure 6.7 shows that the declining GDP trend which had begun since late 1994 was not avoided or diverted by the 'Keynesian'[67] expansion of expenditures that took place (Figure 6.8) in 1995 and 1996.

An argument can be made for a countercyclical expansionary policy to confront the rapidly declining GDP and aggregate demand. In principle, a largely Keynesian response may be called for. But this would be an incomplete argument. It would miss the critical point that to turn around a market-declining demand process, corrective public policies have to be credible to those markets. 'Credit constraints make it hard or impossible for developing countries to borrow exactly when they need it more, in bad times' (Alesina and Tabellini, 2005, p. 23). As it turned out, the total public policy package was not credible to the markets and the Keynesian response may well have worsened the final outcome.[68]

In terms of the political economy of macroeconomic policy coordination, the conceptual paradigm and policy approach followed by the incoming Samper administration (1994–1998) became the predominant view on the Board of the Central Bank. The President was able to appoint three members; including the Finance Minister this defined a majority. There was 'coordination' with the Central Bank but the question is whether it responded to the impending downturn with the 'right' policy. History now seems to suggest that trying to manage a deflating bubble with an another expansionary bubble may not have been the 'right' response.

Against this interpretation, Ocampo (2005a, p. 77) offers the view that the Central Bank's raising of interest rates may have been a mistake. He bases his argument on the fact that aggregate demand was already falling in 1997. There was then no reason to have 'fear of floating' and 'pass-through effects on inflation'.[69] This is indeed a powerful argument. But who knew this in the 'real time' of decision making at the *ex ante* juncture? Who knew for sure that the banking sector, particularly the public banks, were so fragile? Who knew that the real estate bubble would explode and that the Constitutional Court would interfere with 'normative' enforcements severely limiting the capacity of the system to contain the loss of confidence?

Perhaps the key lesson learned, with the benefit of hindsight, is that policy makers and even the Constitutional Court were forced to take measures as best they could but with limited 'real time' information. The one factor that multiplied the costs was the insufficient real time information. Once the crisis unraveled, the need for instant information was even more

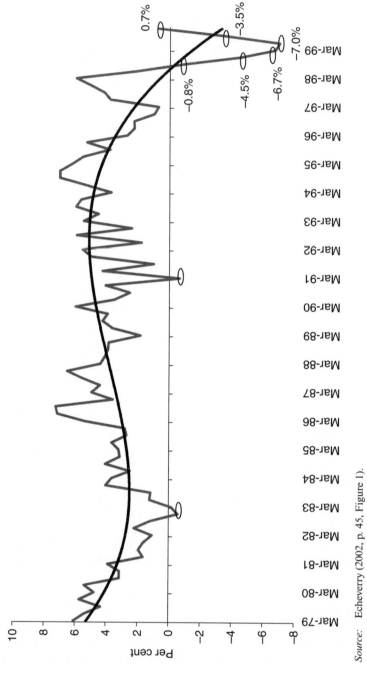

Source: Echeverry (2002, p. 45, Figure 1).

Figure 6.7 Colombia: quarterly real GDP growth, 1979–1999

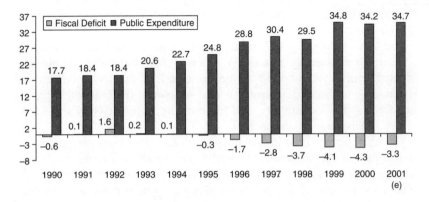

Source: Uribe and Vargas (2002, Figure 9).

Figure 6.8   *Colombia: fiscal deficit and public expenditure excluding interest payments (% of GDP)*

urgent but was not available as needed. If one had to choose one single variable that would have helped reduce the 'sacrifice ratio', that would be to have had better information on the macroeconomic conditions and on the fragility of the financial sector, in particular of some public banks.

No crisis comes without a warning. The problem lies in the *ex ante* decision making process and the incentives behind the interpretation of incomplete information under uncertain domestic and external scenarios.[70] Well trained Colombian economists and policy makers had taken notice since the mid-1990s of the worrisome fast growth of domestic and external credit, of rising public expenditures as well as the growing size of the Current Account deficit (Posada, 1996). And yet no one anticipated the intensity of the peremptory process of adjustment that followed.

VII.   THE POLICY RESPONSE TO THE 1998–1999 CRISIS

Monetary policy which in 1996 and 1997 had been targeted to expand domestic demand was tightened in early 1998 'In an effort to contain exchange rate pressures' (IMF, 1999, p. 9). As a result, interest rates rose, weakening economic activity and revealing the full extent of the fragility of the financial sector. To Ocampo (2005a, p. 77), this Central Bank-led process to protect the exchange rate engendered considerable costs. In his view, raising the interest rate to defend the exchange rate resulted in a capital or assets loss in the private sector and precipitated an unprecedented recession (Ocampo, 2005, p. 77).

The view that the Central Bank should not have raised the interest rates to protect the exchange rate (Tenjo, 2006, p. 36)[71] but rather should have 'floated' earlier would need to be examined in the wider context of: (i) undergoing fiscal developments and prospects; (ii) inflation targeting and Central Bank credibility; and (iii) exchange rate flexibility and 'sticky prices' in labor and other markets.

In other words, it is in the integrality and interdependencies of the restrictions of the 'impossible trinity'[72] that a particular policy preference needs to be postulated and evaluated. It is in the explicit or implicit trade-offs of the totality of one policy package and proposal, vis-à-vis another, that an evaluation of the decision making process that took place in real time can be made. With the benefit of hindsight it is not so difficult to establish what might have been a better course of action. A 'softer' and earlier exchange rate floating appears now, in retrospect, to have been a realistic and better policy option. But this is largely because we now know that the fiscal front was not going to emit to the markets credible signals of its strengthening. It is also because now we know that the financial sector was extremely fragile and vulnerable to interest rate rises and to external capital outflows. In addition, we now know that fear of a 'pass through inflation effect' would have been minimal under an economy which was already declining rapidly. What we do not know is what unintended consequences there might have been under a different policy response.

Instead of trying to establish responsibility, or worse, blame, what clearly emerges at this juncture is the near consensus lesson that if better 'real time information' had been available on the actual situation in the financial sector and on its vulnerability to internal and external shocks, policy makers would have been able to mitigate some of the more severe consequences of the crisis. Further and more profound research on the crisis experience should be carried out to inform the general public and to strengthen a political constituency that is in favor of macroeconomic stability and willing to support the fiscal and financial policies that deliver such stability. In brief, the decisive element is information and the technical capacity to interpret it to make policy decisions. There will always be other important factors and complex occult incentives at work, but improving the information framework is the one first choice route to reduce ambiguity and to strengthen technical and political accountability.

Colombia has had difficult macroeconomic coordination problems since the mid-1990s, not only between the Central Bank and the Ministry of Finance but also with regard to understanding the real situation in the financial sector. Finally, there was a tense and difficult political economy environment as presidential elections were scheduled for mid-1998. To make things even more challenging, policy makers had to make decisions under the pressures of international financial turmoil. The Pastrana administration took over in August 1998 and proceeded to take the following measures:

i.   In early September 1998 the exchange rate was depreciated by 9.0 per cent.[73]
ii.   A fiscal package to raise revenues and lower expenditures was put in place.[74]
iii. From November 1998 onwards the Central Bank began a series of interventions which brought the 'asset' interest rate from 30 per cent at the end of 1998 to 18 per cent in May 1999.
iv.   In November 1998 the government declared a 'state of emergency' basically to prevent further deterioration of the financial sector.[75]
v.   In September 1999 the exchange rate band regime was abandoned in favor of a much softer floating.[76]

The policy response continued along the line of a real depreciation which amounted to 24 per cent year-on-year to August 1999. The external trade account shifted to surplus in the first nine months of 1999. But exchange rate pressures re-emerged in mid-1999 and the band was again depreciated and widened from 7 to 10 per cent on each side of the mid-point. The government had earlier asked for an IMF arrangement which culminated in December 1999 with the signing of a Letter of Intent. 'The attendant IMF credit was taken by the Central Bank as it was not intended to finance public expenditures but to strengthen the international reserve position of the country' (Restrepo, 2006, p. 39).

VIII.   THE RESTRUCTURED POLICY FRAMEWORK AFTER THE CRISIS

Colombia's 1998–1999 crises were the combined result of mostly domestic flaws, external shocks and unresolved analytical and political economy interpretations of economic and social developments and about how to manage them within a consistent policy framework. Since the late 1990s there has been no analytical ambiguity about the fundamentals of the policy framework to be followed. In essence, this has meant the adoption of the following innovations:

i.   The development of a largely shared conceptual paradigm to guide specific policy action.

ii.   The adoption of a less 'fear of floating' exchange rate regime.[77]
iii. The enhanced utilization of inflation targeting as the main 'coordination template'.[78]
iv.   The growing awareness of the complementarities of fiscal and monetary policy for sustainable macroeconomic stability.
v.   Consolidation and strengthening of financial oversight and 'financial deepening' in general.
vi.   The 'balancing' of different policy and instrument 'shock absorbers'.[79]

From the perspective of trying to identify the key institutional characteristics that might explain macroeconomic performance over time, the sharing of a given conceptual and policy paradigm,[80] in this case, the preservation of low inflation has been the main source of the consistency that Colombia's economic management has exhibited over the last five years. In brief, the key institutional characteristic is sharing, by and large, a conceptual paradigm that minimizes coordination and transaction costs and maximizes macroeconomic performance even under domestic or external stress. This does not mean that all macroeconomic policy coordination tension has disappeared. There will probably never be a 'macroeconomic policy game'[81] in which each 'principal' will not try to optimize its own main political and technical mandate. The existence of such tension can be discerned, for instance, from the particular semantics of the Reports on Inflation or on Financial Stability by the Central Bank and by the separate texts which are the main responsibility of the technical staff. Subtle caveats and elaborate analytical messages can be found as possible future references to trace back a given policy posture. This is fine. Over time this will build 'a track record' and 'evaluable history' as an incentive to enhance overall accountability.

The second innovation is consistent with the approach suggested by Chang and Velasco (2000, p. 75) namely, that 'exchange rate policy should move away from the "fix versus flex" dichotomy and toward the characterization of optimal monetary policy in a well specified analytical framework. Inflation targeting is one such framework, though not the only one.' However, what used to be 'fear of floating' was meant to be 'fear of floating upwards' because of pass-through inflation. Nowadays the concern seems to be more fear of floating downwards because of fear of exchange rate appreciation. In the end, it may be fear of somewhat unwarranted and unsustainable 'overshooting' inflation target compliance. This may explain why the Central Banks of Peru and Colombia have intervened to slow down exchange rate appreciation. In interesting contrast, the Central Bank of Chile has decided not to intervene. The relevance of the inflation targeting framework can be appreciated in the difficulties encountered in

September 1992 and in mid-2006 when overall long term policy advised a rise in the domestic interest rates. On this occasion the macroeconomic policy framework responded well and inflation targeting worked as an effective coordination template. Policy makers were able to manage different instruments to deal with difficult changing domestic and international circumstances. Although these circumstances will probably remain volatile, the economy seems in a much better position to deal with it than was the case in the late 1990s.

IX.   THE LESSONS FROM THE CRISIS

With the benefit of hindsight and not wishing to criticize the policy makers who were in charge, it could be said now that there were the following flaws and specific restrictions for a better outcome.

i.   Insufficient information on banks (particularly public banks and CAVs) and financial sector fragility.
ii.   The large inflows and outflows of external capital made monetary policy very difficult (Uribe and Vargas, 2002, p. 22; Urrutia and Fernández, 2003, p. 16).
iii.   Regulatory failures with the Savings and Loan Associations (CAVs), public banks and 'financial cooperatives'.
iv.   The 'interventions' by the Constitutional Court.[82]

From a heuristic perspective the broad question that emerges is if the governance regime[83] adopted in the 1991 Constitution for the macroeconomic framework was part of the problem, part of the solution, or in what proportions, a combination of the two. From the particular perspective of the Central Bank the following questions could be asked. Did it help to have an autonomous Central Bank? Did it make things more difficult to manage? One possible answer could be that it did not help. After all, there was an economic and a social crisis in 1998–1999. However, this first judgment would fail to meet the most elementary requirements of attribution. Most likely, under possible counterfactuals, the collapse would have had even worse consequences with a less independent Central Bank. As Kalmanovitz has put it, 'It would be parochial to accuse the Central Bank' (2005, p. 2).

But, is the first question the more relevant one? Not really; the larger question would be, why did the Central Bank, together with the Ministry of Finance, fail to pre-empt and contain the process leading to the crisis? Was there macroeconomic institutional failure? Future economic historians and refined cliometrics work will address these questions with full rigor. In the meantime, the following preliminary explanation may be offered. Neither the Central Bank nor the Ministry of Finance made major mistakes, beyond some specific misreading of what was actually happening in the real sector at large and in the financial sector in particular. The real problem may have arisen more out of two failed assumptions for which there were insufficient grounds.

The first assumption concerns the definition and requirements of real institutional transformations, that they be: (i) more demand driven than supply driven; (ii) self-correcting; and (iii) resulting in lower transaction costs. Colombia's 1991 emerging macroeconomic governance structure may not have met the requirements of this assumption. Secondly, it was largely assumed that the general public as well as the political process would understand the full extent and import of the message that raising real interest rates can have in informing about impending crisis (Wiesner, 1999, p. 86). The colossal capacity of unanticipated high levels of real interest rates to precipitate a disorderly process of adjustment may well have been underestimated. If these two assumptions had been fully met since the 1990s, the moment the inevitability of interest rate rises became evident there would have been political clamor and support for opportune fiscal, monetary and financial correction. There would have been little hesitation in reining in the public sector expenditure, tightly overseeing the flows of short term external financing and scrutinizing the real state vulnerability of the public banks more vigorously. There would have been a more structured framework to manage the challenges of the 'impossible trinity'. Commenting on the political economy of the monetary management of the crisis, Cárdenas and Urrutia (2004, p. 144) opine that there was severe political criticism for the loss of international reserves. In their view the lesson for the future is that 'reserves have the function of avoiding abrupt depreciations and excessive interest rises'.

In brief, as the crisis began to loom on the horizon there may have been some judgment calls and technical readings that now, with the benefit of hindsight, may seem not to have been the best ones. Once a crisis starts, its management tends to be untidy. What may have been the most important failing of the whole 1991 policy and political regimes was to assume that there was a strong political demand for much lower inflation and attendant political support for fiscal, financial and labor reforms. If this conclusion is not warranted why then has it been so difficult over the last ten years to get political approval for fiscal, social security and transfer reforms?

The major conclusion and lesson that emerges is that policy makers may have underestimated the full importance of the political demand for policy change and for macroeconomic institutional transformation. The policy implication is that reforms need to be inchoate and nurtured right at the beginning from the political level upwards. In this process, information to the public on existing transaction costs will play a critical role. The political demand for new institutions and for policy reform can hardly come just from normative nostrums. It has to be based on 'positive' arguments backed by credible data and information.

X. THE SUSTAINABILITY OF GROWTH IN 2008 AND BEYOND

Table 6.5 shows the differences between the high growth-rate of the mid-1990s and the one ten years later. It can be appreciated that the 2004–2005 expansion has more solid anchors. The Current Account deficit at 1.3 per cent is less than a third of what it was in 1994–1995. Bank provisions are also much stronger; so is the level of international reserves. In terms of external sustainability several indicators show the large differences between 1994–1998 and 2005. Practically all indicators show a strengthening of basic solvency indicators. However, although there is data to suggest that the economy's 'fundamentals' are well aligned there is never a guarantee that an unanticipated internal or external event will not come to test the ongoing positive growth and investment cycle. The dynamics of macroeconomic developments can create unexpected vulnerabilities. Echeverry et al. (2002, p. 40) insightfully opined that 'Colombia faces a new vulnerability' basically because of its capital account. In 2007, most likely, there will be a growth slowdown as the rises in interest rates begin to dampen a demand that was growing at over 9 per cent in the first half of that year.

Table 6.5   Colombia: the differences in growth episodes (%)

Indicator	1994–1995	2004–2005
GDP growth	5.5	5.0
Current account deficit/GDP	4.7	1.3
Bank provisions/total loans	1.7	5.4
Bank provisions/non-performing loans	28.4	127.8
International reserves/GDP	9.5	12.9
International reserves/short-term external debt	170.0	260.0
External debt/GDP (2 year change)	−0.6	−17.6

Source: DANE, Banco de la República and Superintendencia Financiera de Colombia, in Ministerio de Hacienda (2006, p. 10, Table 1).

XI. CONCLUSIONS AND POLICY IMPLICATIONS

Beyond the short term specific financial and economic developments that may take place in the immediate future, Colombia's most important challenge as of mid-2007 is, and will remain for several years, a political economy intensive one. Namely, this will involve the nurturing of sufficient political support for much-needed long term structural fiscal,[84] financial, trade liberalization, social security and pension reforms. The political demand for these reforms seems to depend mainly on the continued improvements in poverty and equity conditions. Furthermore, the fate of these structural reforms largely depends on the 'fairness' perception that most Colombians, in particular the low income groups, may have about their country.[85] As usual, the response to these long term challenges will be conditioned by what happens in the short term. Notwithstanding the positive developments mentioned above, there are three interdependent reasons for serious concern about this country's vulnerability to domestic financial uncertainties, to external volatility and to a sudden stop.

In mid-2007 Colombia is facing three ominous interdependent circumstances. First, there is an unresolved Central Government fiscal deficit and a still large internal and external public sector debt.[86] In mid-2007 an independent and high-level 'Commission on Public Expenditures', chaired by a former Minister of Finance, Rodrigo Botero, unambiguously stated that there was a serious fiscal problem and that total public debt should be substantially reduced (Botero et al., 2007, p. 16). Secondly, there are growing commercial and current account deficits in the Balance of Payments. And thirdly, there are immense exchange rate appreciation pressures.[87] The combined effect of these weaknesses does not augur well. Few countries have been able to overcome these triple challenges without going through intense economic and political turbulence. In the case of Colombia the search for solutions[88] is putting to test the independence of the Central Bank. This has led to policy inconsistencies such as establishing capital controls to external financing to reduce exchange rate appreciation while trying to raise interest rates to slow down credit expansion and to protect medium term inflation targets.[89] At the same time the political climate favors continued public expenditures.[90]

The initial response of the government to the core of the Botero Commission's recommendations was that politically they would be very hard to adopt. However, some experts (Echeverry, 2007, p. 17) insisted that a serious crisis was likely in late 2008 or 2009. To Gomez (2007, pp. 1–23) the fiscal adjustment should be conducted precisely when the economic cycle is favorable. Other economists compared the mid-2007 situation as not too different from the one preceding the crisis of 1999 (Sarmiento,

2007, p. 3B). But other experts find that these concerns are exaggerated and fail to see that what matters the most is not the Central Government's fiscal deficit but the consolidated one. They see no major exchange rate risk because private capital and foreign equity investments are financing the bulk of the commercial and current account deficits (Carrasquilla, 2007, pp. 1–19).

Fortunately, there is little disagreement about the importance of maintaining the existing inflation goals. But whether this will be achieved over the next few years is contingent upon the capacity of Colombia's policy makers and politicians to fully understand the causes that brought about the current macroeconomic rigidities in 2006 and 2007. Professor Allan Drazen (2000, p. 33) summarized the immense complexities of these types of situations when he said that the credibility of policy makers today depends considerably on what they said and did yesterday. Short of being able to change the past, the challenge then is to interpret it correctly and to learn from it.

The laudable achievement of a low, single-digit inflation is now probably the most valuable collective asset of the country. It should be protected. To do this, the roots of its origin and the conditions for its sustainability should be further examined. This should be a clinical exercise conducted under an ample policy context including the attendant high 'sacrifice ratio' and the unintended disinflation that took place together with the collapse of GDP growth in 1999. For mistakes not to be repeated it is important to examine history and to see the links between macroeconomics and poverty (Hommes, 2005). The process of reducing the 'crisis information gap'[91] should be mainstreamed as a central component of the research and basic studies of all the three major 'macroeconomic principals', that is the Central Bank, the Ministry of Finance and the Superfinanciera. Preparedness is a constant watch. A sort of 'Taylor rules' might be attempted to include financial, public banks and exchange rate appreciation and current account balances.

The first policy implication from Colombia's macroeconomic experience since the mid-1990s and particularly from the 1998–1999 crisis is that there should be a great deal of prudence before characterizing the existing low, single-digit inflation as an unqualified achievement of monetary policy. Although there are many aspects of monetary policy management that deserve recognition and praise, this interpretation would not augur well for future policy as some of the underlying political and institutional factors leading to the crisis may still lie largely unchanged. After all, the distributional and political tension[92] is still there and policy reforms have met with strong political intolerance, as Hirschman's (1973, p. 545) brilliant early insight shows. The risk would be to believe that inflation has been permanently tamed, that exchange rate stability[93] is assured and that there is no need for further fiscal,[94] pension,[95] and social security reform.[96] The real risk would be to believe that distributional tension has been substantially reduced. The enormous difficulties that have emerged since 2001 and in 2007 to change the transfer system to the subnational sector suggest that such tension is still strong and that protecting macroeconomic stability is not yet a widely held political priority. It does not seem to be a priority held by most Colombians.

The 1991 Constitution and the macroeconomic developments that followed it have led to the renewed or enhanced emergence of the Constitutional Court as a more pro-active member of the classical tripod comprising a macroeconomic institutional arrangement, namely, a Central Bank, a Ministry of Finance and the entity in charge of financial supervision. Although there has always been a role for 'constitutional oversight', the conceptual perspective[97] from which the Court now seems to intervene is largely new and has had enormous fiscal, political[98] and economic consequences.[99] It certainly has changed the conditions under which macroeconomic policy making has taken place in the last few years.[100] According to Clavijo (2001, p. 39), 'The Constitutional Court has created Constitutional instability.' Its interventions have actually become detrimental to income distribution and make inflation control more difficult.

This 'Constitutional' development has enormous policy implications. It is difficult to fully anticipate the unfolding of the different political economic and social scenarios that may follow from it. It could lead to an improvement of economic policies if redistributive Constitutional concerns engender appropriate changes in the micro-institutional incentive frameworks governing social and pro-poor policies and expenditures. It could also lead to more redistributive tension if public social expenditures end up not being more effective and fiscal restrictions impede further rises in expenditures. Better information and more rigorous diagnostics is the path to restrict value judgments and ideology-inspired Court rulings. Value judgments are a 'personal right' but the incorporation of those values in Court rulings and in policies has to follow the political process. Otherwise they have no political legitimacy.

On the whole the policy response by the 'macroeconomic principals' after the 1999 crisis was the appropriate one all along. This was basically a countercyclical monetary policy while strengthening the fiscal and financial fronts. This policy was aided by substantial external financing and by a very favorable international economic cycle. These conditions will change and it is not clear under what particular path the business cycle will revert and the US dollar will smooth out its current external account imbalance. At the Colombian domestic level there is the challenge of fine-tuning interest rate policy and long term exchange rate competitiveness[101] while protecting inflation targets and financial stability.

The macroeconomic volatility Colombia has experienced in the last 15 years is ultimately explained more by the lack of sufficient political demand for macroeconomic stability and for fiscal reform than by actual market developments. After all, the ultimate policy response to market volatility is conditioned by the political support that corrective measures can elicit from the political markets. All the high political, institutional and social transaction costs which all actors incurred would have been much lower if there had been enough political incentives for those actors to compete in the delivery of macroeconomic stability. Although the 1991 Constitution put the country in a difficult macroeconomic predicament it was not the original source of instability. It merely reflected that there was insufficient political demand for that stability. It reflected distributional tension. There was demand for public expenditures but little political support for the fiscal measures to finance those expenditures and to engender macroeconomic stability.

If there was fault, it lay in failing to see fully why more social spending, without changing the micro-institutional conditions under which it was to take place, would not engender significant welfare gains for the poor. Raising the quality of social services to the poor, particularly to poor children, is something that can be done with the current level of available resources (Hommes, 2006, p. 15). Without changes in the incentive structures governing social expenditures and determining its distributional effectiveness, higher spending levels will not engender the indispensable political support for fiscal, labor and social security reforms. On the other hand, the approach followed often worsens the fiscal imbalances. If history informs policy, the first policy implication for Colombia is to appreciate that at the bottom of the lack of sufficient political demand for macroeconomic stability there is an equity and 'fairness perception' problem that needs to be urgently addressed. A large segment of the Colombian population, at all levels of income, do not perceive that the system is sufficiently fair,[102] even after the recent increases in social spending (Gaviria, 2006, p. 287). They may have arrived at this perception for some 'wrong' reasons and may draw the 'wrong' conclusions but surely there are a number of well documented factual reasons for holding that view. According to Gaviria (2002, p. 22) 'the data suggest that Colombia is far from being a just society'. Amongst the latter:

a. Public education and even private education are not providing sufficient social mobility nor real access to work opportunities and further development.

b. Poverty levels, although they have declined, are still very high.
c. Social public infrastructure in terms of collective public goods is still very limited.
d. A large part of public subsidies are going to middle and even high income groups.[103]
e. Health services to the poor are still very limited.

The second policy implication is that it does not help much to insist in the 'righteousness' of competing in artificially structured ideological dichotomies (the neo-liberals versus the truly socialists versus the conservatives versus the democrats). An empirical approach is more productive; to learn from history and to understand why things did not work as expected. The challenge is more to identify the political economy restrictions than to insist on purely 'normative' ideological or philosophical nostrums. Cárdenas (2004, p. 129) puts it well by saying that 'from a strict social point of view it is better to avoid recessions than to substantially increase public expenditure even if it is oriented towards social sectors'.[104]

The third policy implication is that macroeconomic problems can hardly originate in the enhanced independence of the Central Bank. If anything, its institutional and technical autonomy should be enhanced at the same time that its political accountability should be made more transparent and rules framed. The problems do not lie in the orthodoxy of the Ministry of Finance or in alleged insufficient social public spending. This type of expenditure has nearly doubled in the last 15 years and there is no corresponding result in terms of improved equity or poverty condition. The problem, in the end, lies in the ineffectiveness of the 'social public sector' and in the general public not drawing the 'right' policy implications for which policy reforms to support. This is ultimately an information problem. It is not a problem with the economic model.[105]

Ocampo (2004c, p. 72) makes a strong case for enhancing the political accountability of the current technocratic governance structure of the Central Bank. He aptly argues from a broad principle perspective, which makes it difficult to question his contention. Basically he posits that the current framework is in want of more political scrutiny and political accountability. In his view, an enhanced political process is indispensable to giving political legitimacy to the governance structure of the Central Bank. He is indeed correct. All functional and institutional or regulatory 'delegations' should be derived from a transparent political process and be politically accountable for its results. The question that arises, however, is how specifically the political accountability would be disaggregated between the different political actors. How will specific results be attributed to multiple actors? After all, is there not the very real risk of a collective action problem? For instance, in the Congress, where ambiguous political accountabilities (and interests) may diffuse further precisely the enhanced accountability that Ocampo seeks. Perhaps 'political accountability' is too broad a concept to use without going further into the devilish details that, in principle, would deliver it. Under a repeated game perspective this problem may be somewhat mitigated.

Finally, from a political economy perspective, one of the key policy implications is that Colombia now has a recent history of an economic and social debacle in the fresh memory of the crisis of 1998–1999. This painful experience has the potential to contribute to the 'right' pro-poor and pro-growth reforms. This experience is a credible counterfactual and may engender political support for pending fiscal and financial reforms. More research on this experience and more dissemination of information will help in eliciting the 'right' political demand for the most urgent reforms.

XII. POLICY RECOMMENDATIONS

The main recommendations for Colombian policy makers address the following highly interdependent areas: (i) the redistributive effectiveness of social expenditures and the political demand for macroeconomic policy stability; (ii) the need to protect the low, single-digit existing level of inflation; and (iii) the strengthening of some particular 'constitutional' and institutional characteristics which determine the effectiveness of macroeconomic policy formulation, in particular the fiscal anchor.

The first recommendation can be disaggregated into the following specific steps. Change the micro-institutional incentive framework under which most of the social public expenditure takes place. This means shifting to more demand-driven and results-based budgeting instead of the current largely supply-driven 'earmarked' financing. The central idea is to assure that low income groups actually gain access to better education, health and employment opportunities. In brief, lowering poverty levels and enhancing the effectiveness of government subsidies[106] in the financing of public goods should be the first priority. The key conceptual premise is that public resources have the highest positive redistribution impact and do not subsidize the middle or upper income groups. If income inequality is conducive to growth-retarding policies, lowering poverty levels and improving access by the poor to public and private goods should engender political support for pro-growth policies. And also for the 'right' pro-poor policies. But information is the most important factor. Even if public policies improve poverty conditions, this result has to be disseminated to public opinion in general.

The second recommendation deals with the need to protect macroeconomic stability and to keep inflation under tight control. Inflation targeting is much more than a strict monetary rule (Bernanke and Mishkin, 1997). As López (2006, p. 71) nicely put it 'it involves an analytical and institutional framework'. The current single-digit level is the most valuable collective public good of the country and it needs to be protected.[107] This is not a politically easy task as most of the political incentives favor precisely the policies which conspire against price and financial stability. In this respect the main recommendation is to seek countercyclical fiscal capacity, and a reduction of 'fiscal dominance'. The recommendation of the 2007 'High level Expenditure Commission' of adopting a fiscal rule of a 'primary surplus' for the Central Government of about 2 per cent of GDP is a fundamental component of any strategy to protect macroeconomic stability (Botero et al., 2007, p. 19). However, as was said at the beginning of this chapter, such surplus may well need to be higher in the face of growing fiscal uncertainties.

The third recommendation deals with the need to strengthen macroeconomic institutional characteristics such as credibility, transparency, independency and technical and political accountability. For these characteristics to be fully effective in delivering macroeconomic stability they have to emerge in response to the political demand for that stability. They cannot be fully effective if they are largely the result of a decree or a law. The best technical design is a necessary condition but is not enough. In fact, the appropriate ultimate design comes guided by the requirements flowing out of the political demand. Developing those characteristics will include the following: (i) enhancing the technical independence of the Central Bank; (ii) strengthening the legal and technical capacity of the Superintendencia Financiera; (iii) building long term fiscal rules and a decentralized 'Fiscal and Budget Authority'; and (iv) developing a more intensive use of independent evaluations of macroeconomic and microeconomic inflation targeting related issues.

Enhancing the independence of the Central Bank would involve developments in the following four interdependent fronts: (i) at the Executive Board[108] level and appointment procedures;[109] (ii) at the conflict resolution level or political accountability level; (iii) in its role in debt management and long term capital markets development; and (iv) transparency and disclosure.

The fundamental collective interest of the country is best served when a Central Bank is given full (within limits) technical independence of instruments to perform the delicate task of assuring the best possible economic climate for private and public organizations to conduct their business. For this to work, that independence needs to be largely free from ambiguous or opportunistic interference from other interests. Otherwise the technical and political accountability of that Central Bank as well as its effectiveness may end up being impaired. This does not mean that Central Banks have no political accountability. Of course they do. But to ascertain it the indispensable condition is that each party (the Central Bank, the Executive level and even the Legislative levels) cannot play an intended or unintended ambiguous role. A traceable 'evaluable history' for the position each party took vis-à-vis a given public issue is needed so that a learning process and a repeated game sequence each time better informs the political process.

The independence of Colombia's Central Bank needs to be strengthened and certainly at least restored to the original level contemplated in the 1991 Constitution. The original restrictions limiting the power of the President were *de facto* if not *de jure* changed by the re-introduction of the re-election option for the incumbent president and for other ex-presidents (see Castro, 2005, p. 143).[110] ANIF (2006, p. 3) suggests that Central Bank Board members should be appointed for 12 years without re-election. Another possibility would be to appoint Board members for a six-year period, instead of the current four-year one, with the limit of one re-election for a maximum of 12 years for anyone in the Executive Board including the President of the Central Bank.

One key recommendation would be to formally establish what could be called the 'Open Letter Option' by which the Governor of the Central Bank can send an open letter to the Minister of Finance or to the President of Colombia detailing why and how he (she) will pursue a given macroeconomic policy, in particular a given inflation targeting framework. This would follow what the Brazilian inflation targeting regime is contemplating and has so successfully utilized in 1999 and 2003. In the case of Colombia, although there is nothing forbidding a similar process, it would be much better to have this faculty adopted legally. Just to have the political debate around it would already be a further positive step.[111] Credibility, transparency and political accountability are the principles underpinning this central recommendation.

One of the clear lessons emerging from the 1998–1999 crises[112] is that the financial sector needs to be 'deepened' and strengthened legally and technically.[113] The costs of a crisis largely depend on how fragile the financial sector is at the time of the onset of the crisis. The institutional restructuring process is already under way and financial sector reform is now on the agenda of the government.

One of the strengths of developed countries is the high technical level of competence of their 'macroeconomic principals'. In those countries there is actually intense academic and technical competition for effective information generation and analysis of data on public issues. In the case of

Colombia, the Ministry of Finance needs to be given a 'more level long term playing field' vis-à-vis the Central Bank. These two institutions need to develop further a long term institutional and technical partnership. This does not mean that they should subsume their respective and distinct responsibilities but that they constantly nurture deeper, formal and informal, 'research protocols' to inform their individual and joint long term work agendas. One critical step in this direction would be the development of a 'Decentralized Fiscal and Budget Authority' similar (*mutatis mutandis*) to the one that evolved over the years for the management of monetary policy.[114] The current CONFIS is already a fine basis on which to build the new fiscal and 'budget institution'. Castellanos (2004, p. 31) has proposed specific rules for the budgetary process and for its sequenced phases.

This is a structural institutional transformation that will take some time to come into full fruition. Its specific design is more than a complex technical task. It is, above all, a political economy challenge as it will never come into full being until there is a political demand for it, until the general public, particularly the low income groups, become stakeholders in macroeconomic stability and decide to politically support a fiscal transformation as fundamental as the configuration of an autonomous 'Fiscal and Budget Authority'.

The overall policy goal is to build greater political accountability through the careful and strategic development of new and independent sources of information. There is almost unanimous agreement among the experts and even within those directly involved at the highest level in the management of the crisis of 1998–1999 that if they had had better and more opportune information on, for instance, the actual precariousness of the financial sector (public and private banks) or on the degree of international 'contagiousness', or on the real estate bubble, the immense welfare and economic losses which the country incurred might have had a chance to be very substantially reduced. Academic and inter-institutional (domestic and international) competition should be the foundation supporting the generation of new information[115] on macroeconomic and microeconomic performance. This means there would be, for example, rigorous examinations of fiscal issues by the Central Bank and of monetary policy by the Ministry of Finance. The Superfinanciera should be a major source of research on financial deepening and stability. National and international research centers should compete amongst themselves and with public institutions in the provision of information and of evaluation results on public sector performance. Colombia does not seem to be making adequate political use of information to strengthen its 'right' pro-poor and pro-growth policies.

It should be said that this line of preparedness has already been adopted by the Central Bank with its 'new' research on, for instance, 'output-gaps' (*brechas de producto*), or *brechas de desempleo*[116] on financial sector oversight and on risk assessment in general. This development should be further supported to include 'Sacrifice Ratios' as well as research on the macroeconomic implications of microeconomic 'downward rigidities' in labor markets, for instance on indexation mechanisms in the long term mortgage markets.[117] In brief, new knowledge is constantly needed as the private and public markets in pursuit of their own self interests find new avenues for non-market gains. All this may sound like naïve normative nostrums that assume that the government is a benevolent guardian of the public welfare and seldom 'captured' by special interests.[118] However, in some countries in Latin America and in other regions, it has been possible for some politicians to find 'positive' political incentives to take political positions to actually enhance the effectiveness of public interventions in general and expenditures in particular. This is not so much out of altruism or social enlightenment but because the political incentives and potential rewards for self-interested[119] reasons have become attractive enough.

In conclusion, the source of the demand for reforms and for institutional transformation, on the one hand, and for the eventual supply response of (the 'right') institutions, on the other, is the awareness of excessively high transaction costs. This has been the experience at the industry and firm levels in public and private markets in developed and some developing countries. These recommendations are not naïve. They aim at nothing else than meeting what North (1990, p. 108) calls the 'institutional rationality postulate of neoclassical theory' in the sense that all interventions have the information and institutional framework necessary for achieving the 'desired ends'. Another distinguished Nobel prize winner puts it in these terms: 'One of the most important determinants of the pace of growth is the acquisition of knowledge' (Stiglitz, 2002a, p. 483). Finally, Rodrik (2006, p. 986) makes the perceptive point that to understand the economics of reform one should 'be skeptical of top-down, comprehensive, universal solutions – no matter how well intentioned they may be. And it reminds us that the requisite economic analysis – hard as it is, in the absence of specific blueprints – has to be done case by case.'

NOTES

1. On this literature see Persson and Tabellini (2004a, p. 94). On this subject see also Acemoglu et al. (2001, 2002); Acemoglu and Robinson (2005); Persson and Tabellini (2000); Persson (2003); Persson et al. (1997); Persson et al. (2000) and Weingast et al. (1981).
2. Under a longer term perspective Montenegro (2006, p. 4) opines that Colombia's economic model may not have been the most adequate one as it responded to a political model which perpetuated regional and sectoral privileges.
3. For the evolution of these transfers see Cárdenas and Urrutia (2004, p. 156).

4. For an early warning on the consequences of these 'automatic' and formula driven transfers, see Wiesner (1992, p. 324). See also his *La Descentralización, el Gasto Social y la Gobernabilidad en Colombia* (1995, p. 26).

5. See Vargas (1994, p. 38), for the conditions under which 'coordination' between the government and Central Bank is mutually advantageous.

6. The Constitutional Court's Ruling No. C-481 of 1999 established that the autonomy of the Central Bank did not preclude the obligation to 'coordinate' its policies with other major policies of the government. See Hernández Correa (1999, p. 4). See also Salomón Kalmanovitz (2001a, p. 1).

7. Alesina and Angeletos (2005, p. 960) posit that: 'Different beliefs about the fairness of social competition and what determines income inequality influence the redistributive policy chosen in a society.'

8. See Wiesner (2004b, p. 20), for a discussion of the implications of the difficult interpretation of the 'preferred' social welfare function.

9. According to Harsanyi (1991, p. 704), most disagreements about value judgments 'are about the relative weights and the relative priorities to be assigned to different basic values'.

10. Nelson Pinilla (2006, p. 27), a former member of Colombia's Supreme Court, thinks that the Constitutional Court 'has unduly grabbed away legislative powers from Congress'.

11. Manuel José Cepeda (2004, p. 357) posits that Court rulings to provide guarantees to political minorities go way back before the 1991 Constitution.

12. On the power and influence of intended but unrealized efforts, Hirschman (1997, p. 131) observes that 'There is no doubt that human actions and social decisions tend to have consequences that were entirely unintended at the outset. But, on the other hand, these actions and decisions are often taken because they are earnestly and fully expected to have certain effects that then wholly fail to materialize. The latter phenomenon, while being the structural obverse of the former, is also likely to be one of its causes; the illusory expectations that are associated with certain social decisions at the time of their adoption help keep their real future effects from view.'

13. An example of that tension was the discussion that arose in mid-2006 when a study by the CID (Centro de Investigaciones) of the National University questioned the alleged advantages of lower inflation and posited that inequitable growth is not sustainable (González and Bonilla, 2006, p. 8). For a response, see Juan Mauricio Ramirez (2006, p. 1.19).

14. The 1991 Constitution established transfers as the main transmission mechanism for decentralization. Since then there has been an enormous tension around how much those transfers really enhance 'local' development or compromise macroeconomic stability. See Bird and Acosta (2005, p. 265), on 'The dilemma of decentralization in Colombia'.

15. Roberto Junguito (1994, p. 337) provides a fine example of the challenge of coordination between macroeconomic policies (for example lower inflation) and energy sector specific developments.

16. According to Juan Pablo Córdoba (1997, p. 32), '90% of the growth of expenditures in the period 1990–96 originated in the dynamics generated by the 1991 Constitution'.

17. Palacio Eduardo Sarmiento (1996, p. 124) considers that this mandate was based on a wrong diagnostic of the Colombian economy.

18. Jaramillo Luis Alberto Zuleta (1999, p. 45) considers that inflation would have been higher without an independent Central Bank.

19. Former President Cesar Gaviria (1994, p. xi) stated that the goal of his administration was to 'provide a better standard of living by guaranteeing universal coverage in education, health and basic public services'.

20. For an analysis on the idiosyncrasies of economic policy making in Colombia and of implicit social and political pacts between the private sector and the political class, see Marulanda (1999, p. 34).

21. An inflationary tax and seignorage are two related concepts, but they are not identical. The first one refers to a capital loss resulting from price increases or inflation. The

second one refers to the net income accruing to whoever has the monopoly to issue currency. See Hernando Zuleta (1995, p. 15) for estimates of the importance of each in the case of Colombia.

22. On Colombia's tradition of political stability see Posada Carbó (2001).
23. See Adolfo Meisel (1996, p. 21).
24. Rodrigo Botero (2005, p. 17).
25. In the view of José Dario Uribe (2000, p. 4), 'a share of the increase in government's expenditures is represented by transfers to the regions. These transfers, on the whole, have discouraged local tax effort and led to negative owned savings. The government does not seem particularly active in rapidly transferring responsibilities and attendant expenditures to the regions. Moreover, it has increased expenditures in some levels of the public administration where there is institutional and organizational disorder.'
26. According to Sergio Clavijo (2000, p. 4), this remit could be achieved. To him 'the crucial issue in terms of achieving dynamic economic growth and low inflation hinges on curtailing public expenditure, along the lines above mentioned. Under these circumstances, neither the number of the Board Members nor its chairing by the Minister of Finance (with no veto power or tie-breaking vote) are serious obstacles to maintaining single-digit inflation, while recovering fast economic growth.'
27. Cárdenas and Urrutia (2004, p. 156) consider that the 1991 Constitution with its emphasis on specifics led to a greater degree of interventions by the Constitutional Court in public policies.
28. Armando Montenegro (1994, p. 13), reviewing the policies of the Gaviria administration, argued that this 'apparent contradiction' could be resolved through privatizations and higher public sector effectiveness.
29. Whether this is indeed an anomaly depends, of course, on the perspective on these issues. For a different view see Uprimny and Rodríguez (2005, p. 29).
30. See Perry (2005, p. 110). See also Echeverry (2002); Ocampo (2005a); Clavijo (2000); Hernández and Florez (1999); Villar (2001); Clavijo (2004b).
31. Montenegro (1995, p. 20).
32. The literature on the political processes leading to policy and task delegation began in earnest with Rogoff's (1985) insistence in an independent Central Bank to run monetary policy and to minimize intertemporal policy inconsistency. Societies seem more inclined to allocate monetary policy to an independent institution than to assign fiscal policy to a similar institutional arrangement. This is so even though fiscal policy is also marred by time inconsistency and many other problems. The explanation seems to lie in the different accountabilities and incentives between top-level politicians and top-level bureaucrats. Alesina and Tabellini (2007, p. 169) aver that 'Politicians are held accountable by voters at election time. Top-level bureaucrats are held accountable to their professional peers or for the public at large. These different accountability mechanisms induce different incentives.' But society's preferences are changing and the delegation to some forms of fiscal rules to independent arrangements are becoming more politically viable. Alan S. Blinder (1997) has argued in favor of the delegation of some aspects of fiscal policy in an agency operating like an independent Central Bank.
33. Ocampo (2004a, p. 105) has already begun this task pointing out specific 'contradictions' between the 1991 Constitution, the 2000–2004 Development Plan and the trade liberalization that followed in the early 1990s.
34. Alesina (2004a, p. 3) posits that this Constitution 'was the result of a complex bargaining process that led to a document containing something for everyone. Further, since some groups did not trust others, extremely detailed prescriptions were added to ensure that the application of the Constitution would be strict'.
35. Alesina et al. (2005, p. 347) aver that 'the reform of the Central Bank achieved within the Constitutional reform of 1991 was part of a more comprehensive set of reforms that included, among others, trade liberalization, the elimination of most capital controls and the elimination of a monopoly on the part of mortgage banks, for index deposits.
36. Rodrigo Botero (1992, p. 45) considers that there were pragmatic reasons for moving away certain critical policy areas from short term political pressures.

37. See Posada and Misas (1995, p. 31) for the determinants of interest rates for the period 1958–1992.
38. See Villar (2004) on the yield and fiscal implications of seignorage in Colombia.
39. According to Alesina et al. (2005, p. 348), 'It is clear from the documentary evidence that the Central Bank was the main advocate of independence. A paper entitled "Proposal for a monetary regime in the constitutional reform" was written by the staff of the Bank and circulated to the government in 1990. This draft was the fundamental proposal which, by and large, dominated the discussion.'
40. Carrasquilla et al. (1994, p. 9) concluded that 'lowering inflation from 22% to 5% would raise welfare by 7.8%.' See also Uribe (1994, p. 15) who posits that 'inflation levels of two digits raises growing costs over time'.
41. Rudolf Hommes (1995, p. 33) posits that the proposal for an autonomous Central Bank reflected 'the long held dream and aspirations of the Bank's management to isolate the institution from short term politics and even from the Minister of Finance when he turned excessively assertive'.
42. See Salomón Kalmanovitz (2001a) for a review of the initial conditions and challenges of the Central Bank.
43. Ocampo (2004c, p. 17) finds that it was a historical contradiction to have a Constitutional mandate for more State, on the one hand, with a concurrent National Plan advocating a more limited public sector, on the other. But in his view these two perspectives are not necessarily antagonistic.
44. Santiago Herrera (1994, p. 37) has pointed out that public sector expenditures grew substantially between 1990 and 1993; from 11.1 per cent of GDP to 15 per cent.
45. In an evaluation of the policies adopted in the early 1990s Molina et al. (1992, p. 137) opined that by and large they would 'contribute to long term growth and would tend to lower poverty'.
46. Zeinab Partow (2003, p. 147) shows how Colombia's volatility in macroeconomic and fiscal terms nearly doubled in the 1990s compared to the previous two decades.
47. See Andrés Escobar (2005, p. 84) for an analysis of GDP deviations from structural trend.
48. Sergio Clavijo (2002, p. 43) refers to 'a fortuitous disinflation that fails to recognize unemployment and the collapse of the real sector'.
49. Echeverry (2005).
50. One of the members of the 1991 Constitution in an article written in July 2006 offers the following balance 'We, as members of the 1991 Constitutional Assembly, may have made the mistake of mandating an excessively fast transfer system without first assuring an equivalent transfer of responsibilities.' See Perry (2006, pp. 1–23).
51. This task has already begun, see for example Echeverry (1999, p. 93); Ocampo (2005a, p. 74); Lora (2005, p. 41); Rentería (2005, p. 145).
52. Hommes (2005, p. 47).
53. According to Escobar (2005, p. 83), the average duration of each economic cycle has been four years for the expansionary ones and seven years for the recessionary ones.
54. According to Solimano (2000, p. 32), 'The modern theory of distributive justice distinguishes between "outside" (or morally arbitrary) factors (gender, race, initial assets, talent) and "personal responsibility" elements (effort, risk-taking attitudes) in shaping the level of income, wealth, and welfare of the individual in society. Social inequality is a reflection of individual differences in these two sets of wealth-creating factors.'
55. Gaviria's findings are based on empirical research conducted by the Corporación Latinobarometro, an entity that has the support of the IDB (Gaviria, 2005).
56. Alesina and Angeletos (2005, p. 960) posit that: 'Different beliefs about the fairness of social competition and what determines income inequality influence the redistributive policy chosen in a society. But the composition of income in equilibrium depends on tax policies. We show how the interaction between social beliefs and welfare policies may lead to multiple equilibria or multiple steady states. If a society believes that individual effort determines income, and that all have a right to enjoy the fruits of their effort, it will choose low redistribution and low taxes. In equilibrium, effort will be high

and the role of luck will be limited, in which case market outcomes will be relatively fair and social beliefs will be self-fulfilled. If, instead, a society believes that luck, birth, connections, and/or corruption determine wealth, it will levy high taxes, thus distorting allocations and making these beliefs self-sustained as well. These insights may help explain the cross-country variation in perceptions about income inequality and choices of redistributive policies.'

57. See Nuñez et al. (2006, p. 42) for an examination of the role of inherited characteristics in influencing poverty, social mobility and income distribution in the case of Colombia.

58. See Lora and Ocampo (1986, p. 109), for a review of the relationships between macro-economic policy and income distribution for 1980–1990.

59. On the importance of education to reduce income concentration and to increase savings, see Sarmiento (1998, p. 220).

60. Salomón Kalmanovitz (2001b, p. 272) has pointed out that Colombia had been able to avoid severe macroeconomic crisis because of its relatively small public sector. But from the early 1990s on, its private and public sectors became highly indebted to finance-growing expenditures. When conditions changed in 1998, disaster struck.

61. In the view of Andrés Felipe Arias (2000, p. 27), 'it would take about five years for the economy to fully recover'.

62. See Sergio Clavijo (2004a, p. 5) on the 'activist' role of the Constitutional Court in monetary policies.

63. In early 1998 the then Technical Manager of the Central Bank, Alberto Carrasquilla, warned the Board of the Central Bank about an impending stock or asset imbalance in contrast to a 'flow' imbalance. See Echeverry (2002, p. 71).

64. According to the IMF (1999, p. 8) 'To allow for greater flexibility in the operation of monetary policy, the authorities replaced the "crawling peg" exchange rate arrangement in early 1994 with a 14 percentage point band. Following a steady depreciation over the preceding seven years, the real effective exchange rate appreciated considerably from 1990 through mid-1997 owing to the large capital inflows, rapid increase in public sector spending (particularly on nontradables), faster productivity growth in the tradables than in the nontradables sector, and terms of trade gains.'

65. 'The genesis of the crisis can be found in the early 90s when Colombia followed a Capital Account opening policy. This policy stated: whoever has dollars, irrespective of its origin can bring them to the country without restrictions. Was this the Gaviria liberalization? The Hommes liberalization? The result was an avalanche of dollars which, together with import liberalization and lower tariffs, delivered a mortal blow to the industrial and agricultural sectors. This was the beginning of the crisis' (Hernández, 2003, p. 111).

66. Armando Montenegro (2007, p. 16A) has observed that in the mid-1990s, when fiscal deficits exploded, loans from the World Bank and the Inter-American Bank rose substantially. The more fiscally and financially weak a country is, the more it will tend to resort to multilateral credit.

67. See Escobar (2005, p. 85) for comments on the origins of economic cycles. See also Ocampo (1989a and 1989b) for a structural view on economic cycles. Finally, there is Austrian business-cycle theory. 'Unlike Keynes, who thought recessions were caused by insufficient demand, these economists put them down to excess supply brought about by overinvestment. As a result of mutually reinforcing movements in credit, investment and profits, each boom contains the seeds of the subsequent recession and each recession the seeds of the subsequent boom' (*The Economist*, 2002, pp. 8 and 9).

68. Leonardo Villar (2006) argues that fiscal procyclicality in Colombia has changed over time. It was countercyclical before 1982 and turned procyclical afterwards. The reasons are related to (i) the transfer system and fiscal decentralization; (ii) high fiscal dependency on oil revenue; (iii) fiscal populism.

69. Ocampo (2005a, p. 77) considers that there were not sufficient grounds to argue – or to expect – that some exchange rate depreciation would accelerate the rate of inflation. In the event, this reading of the dynamics of the variables involved was confirmed. In his view, the Central Bank was able to manage well the unfolding Real depreciation.

70. This is not only the case in economics or in financial contexts. In several other realms of individual and social conduct there are problems restricting the *ex ante* adoption of *ex post* recognized failures. All the usual issues related to 'counter factuals' are involved as well as the incentives for 'waiting' for the crisis or for acting pre-emptively. On counter factuals see Donald McCloskey (1991, p. 153). See also Jon Elster (1978).

71. According to Fernando Tenjo (2006, p. 36), the increases in the Central Banks intervention regarding interest rates were not aimed at keeping inflation under control but to defend the exchange rate band against speculative attacks and to soften the effects of capital outflows.

72. The 'impossible trinity' principle holds that when capital is mobile – and it always tends to be – it is nearly impossible to fix simultaneously the rate of interest and the rate of exchange. According to Vargas (2006, p. 8), 'with high capital mobility monetary and exchange rate policy are not independent'.

73. The band Exchange rate regime had been established in January 1994. It appreciated in December 1994 and remained stable until September 1998. See Juan Camilo Restrepo (2003, p. 410).

74. In a 2 November 1998 Memorandum to the President, the then Minister of Finance Juan Camilo Restrepo said 'that to control the fiscal deficit two strategies are needed: a tax reform and a reduction in public expenditures'. See his *Memoria de Hacienda 1998–1999* (1999, p. 28).

75. See Restrepo (1999, p. 183).

76. Restrepo (2000, p. 75) considers that the abandonment of the exchange rate on 25 September, 1999, can be 'considered as the last phase of a flexibilization which had begun in 1994'.

77. Echabarria et al. (2005, p. 63) aver that 'the government has to lower its public expenditure and its external debt levels to achieve a higher real exchange rate to foster growth'.

78. See Clavijo (2002, p. 13) for a detailed analysis of the monetary strategy following the 'softer floating'.

79. On the use of 'shock absorbers', see Mauricio Avella (2005, p. 20).

80. For a discussion reflecting different nuances on economic paradigms around Colombia's debt management, see Hernández et al. (2000, p. 149). See also Cabrera and González (2000, p. 185).

81. On policy games between macroeconomic authorities, see Hernando Vargas (1994).

82. The Constitutional Court may have revealed animosity towards the private sector when it prohibited the use of public emerging resources to help them manage the crisis (Kalmanovitz, 2001c, p. 159).

83. Robert E. Lucas, Jr (1990) distinguishes a policy regime change from a policy action on a specific occasion within the regime.

84. To Ramírez Fabio Villegas (2004, p. 46), the real fiscal problem is the deficit of the Central Government even if it is partly caused by its own transfers to other entities. This is the essence of the financial problem.

85. Bird et al. (2005, p. 7) observe that in Colombia 'the need to promote a perception of fairness can in some cases make it difficult to implement efficient taxes'.

86. According to Clements et al. (2007, p. 25), 'debt burdens remain a challenge to entrenching macroeconomic stability'. Some experts consider that an emerging country's public debt should not exceed 25 per cent of GDP. Colombia's ratio of 55 per cent at the end of 2006 is well above the 'prudent' level.

87. Ocampo (2006, p. 6) observes that a similar exchange rate appreciation took place in 1992–1994. This makes the economy vulnerable to external volatility.

88. According to Villar (2003, p. 44), an effective way to reduce exchange rate appreciation pressures is to restrict external debt.

89. Hernando Vargas (2007, p. 14) warns that inflation targeting is now restricted by a 'weak' interest rate pass-through in the channel credits.

90. The Botero Commission rightly pointed out that 'instead of focusing on the appreciation of the exchange rate the priority of the discussion should be on the rate of growth

of public expenditures. To incur debt to finance interest payments goes against economic theory and basic principles of prudent economic management' (Botero et al., 2007, p. 9).

91. See Montenegro (2004, p. 37) for a summary of the evaluation and information challenges faced by Colombia.

92. According to Acemoglu and Robinson (2006a, p. 329), 'the appearance of change in certain dimensions of specific institutions does not necessarily mean a change in economic institutions that are essential for the allocation of resources in a society.'

93. Kalmanovitz (2007, p. 14A) argues that exchange rate appreciation is largely the result of an expansionary fiscal policy and excessive external borrowing.

94. R. Guillermo Perry (2005, p. 109) observes that the current fiscal imbalances 'correspond to a large and unsustainable unbalance in the finances of the Central Government, particularly in the transfers to the subnational level and to finance pensions.'

95. According to Urrutia (2004, p. 35), a pension reform is necessary to eliminate privileges and to have a more equitable system.

96. Sergio Clavijo (2004c, p. 47) estimates that contingent liabilities in the form of pensions or health cover will add about 1.3 per cent of GDP each year to budget expenditures.

97. In its Sentence C-481-99 the Constitutional Court stated that the independence of the Central Bank was limited by or to the Development Plan. See Alesina et al. (2005, p. 350).

98. From a political perspective, the 1991 Constitution has inspired a discussion on social choice theory and practice in Colombia. See Valenzuela and Arregocés (2005, p. 21).

99. According to Vargas and Uribe (2002, p. 22), 'The response of the State (particularly the Constitutional Court) to the S&Ls crisis may have created serious moral hazard problems.'

100. Alesina (2004b, p. 68) posited that 'he cannot think of a country in which the Constitutional Court makes judgements on whether the Central Bank should be concerned with inflation, interest rates and unemployment'.

101. Echabarria and Arbelaez (2005, p. 43) find that real devaluations tend to have a positive effect on investment.

102. Gaviria (2006, p. 285) and (2002) indicates that social mobility seems to have increased from 1970 to 1980. However, most Colombians appear to regard the socio-economic order as 'unfair' and lacking in justice. This perception tends to engender political pressures for redistribution (Alesina and La Ferrara, 2005). Gaviria holds that social expenditures should aim at increasing mobility but finds that politically this is difficult as the citizenry has yet to endogenize the fiscal restrictions.

103. See Velez (1997, p. 23).

104. Cárdenas (2004, p. 129).

105. On the question of whether Colombia's problems originate from its 'model', see Echeverry (2002, p. 27), 'El Siglo del Modelo de Desarrollo'.

106. See Valenzuela (2003, p. 140) for a criticism of the 'wrong' subsidies on public policies.

107. For some of the remaining inflation risks, see Javier Guillermo Gómez (2006, p. 51).

108. Sergio Clavijo (2000, p. 4) posits that 'The crucial issue of achieving economic growth and low inflation hinges on curtailing public expenditure, along the lines above mentioned. Under these circumstances, neither the number of the Board Members nor its chairing by the Minister of Finance (with no veto power or tie-breaking vote) are serious obstacles to maintaining single-digit inflation, while recovering fast economic growth.'

109. Alesina et al. (2005, p. 350) have observed that 'The ambiguity between independence and government control is exemplified by a number of precepts. Consider, for example, the so-called appointed directors. With only one exception the original members (appointed in 1992) came from outside the government, but today only one of the five appointed members comes from outside the government.'

110. Jaime Castro (2005, p. 143) observes that the overall 'checks and balances' of the 1991 Constitutional text were changed by the introduction of the immediate presidential re-election. He calls this the opening of Pandora's Box.

111. 'Making government processes more open, transparent, and democratic, with more participation and more efforts at consensus formation is likely to result not only in a process that is fairer, but one with outcomes that are more likely to be in accord with the general interests. Maybe eventually we will be able to bring Coase to the public sector, so that Pareto improvements will actually be adopted' (Stiglitz, 1998, p. 21).
112. Javier Guillermo Gómez (2006, p. 25) concluded that the depth of the 1999 crisis was largely caused by financial factors.
113. In the early 1990s the Gaviria administration put in place a financial reform through Law 45 of 1990 and Law 35 of 1993. A second round of structural changes took place in 1997.
114. See Alesina (2000, 2002, 2005) and Bird et al. (2005, p. 24) for some suggestions on fiscal and budget reforms in Colombia.
115. For a good example of such evaluation, see Attanasio (2004, p. 173).
116. See Misas and Lopez (2001, p. 25).
117. On the critical importance and destabilization capacity of some indexation mechanisms particularly in the real estate market, see Uribe and Vargas (2002, p. 11).
118. 'Interests' may well be balancing factors in the complex process of social interaction. Hirschman quotes Montesquieu's sentence in *L'esprit des lois*. 'It is fortunate for men to be in a situation where, though their passions may prompt them to be wicked (mechants), they have nevertheless an interest in not being so.' See his 'Preface to the Twentieth Anniversary Edition' (Hirschman, 1997, p. xxii).
119. The literature on narrow self-interests as a potential social regulator found in Hirschman (1997, p. 119) its most brilliant rendition. See also Buchanan and Tullock (1962, p. 18), on Wicksell's (1896) 'non-tuism'.

7.   Costa Rica: the effectiveness of political economy compromise

Institutions cannot absolutely prevent an undesirable outcome, nor ensure a desirable one, but the way that they allocate decision making authority makes some policy outcomes more probable and others less likely.

Cukierman et al. (1992, p. 353)

I.   THE SUSTAINABILITY OF HISTORY

Few countries in Latin America can claim more political economy wisdom than Costa Rica. For decades this country has deservedly prided itself on its capacity to maintain political stability together with the record of having had positive rates of GDP growth for the last 20 years (Table 7.1). In addition, Costa Rica has had amongst the best indicators of social welfare in Central America and Latin America in general. These results have been attributed to the country's capacity to compromise and to reconcile competing interests and views about the role of the state and markets. Avoiding

Table 7.1   Costa Rica: GDP rates of growth, 1980–2005

Year	GDP rate	Year	GDP rate
1984	6.2	1996	0.9
1985	1.0	1997	5.6
1986	5.8	1998	8.4
1987	6.9	1999	8.2
1988	3.8	2000	1.8
1989	5.1	2001	1.1
1990	3.9	2002	2.9
1991	2.6	2003	6.4
1992	9.2	2004	4.1
1993	7.4	2005	4.1
1994	4.7	2006	7.9
1995	3.9		

Source: Central Bank of Costa Rica.

open confrontation and seeking consensus has been the generally preferred option.[1] It is difficult to argue against the effectiveness of this particular political economy arrangement. It has worked well for Costa Rica. However, against this positive backdrop the following interdependent questions emerge:

i.   How sustainable is this historical framework in the face of rapidly changing domestic and international circumstances and outlook?
ii.   How effective has the 'consensus' approach really been in terms of resolving public issues in general and macroeconomic policy problems in particular?
iii. How sustainable is the recent excellent macroeconomic performance for 2003–2006?

The first two questions have already been posed by Costa Rican policy makers together with proposals to reduce the country's vulnerability to macroeconomic challenges (Lizano and Zuñiga, 1999, p. 5; Garnier and Blanco, 2006; Gutierrez, 2005b, p. 214). Some have observed that Costa Rica may be dysfunctional and that a new constitutional architecture may be needed (Casas, 2006, p. 3). There are a number of interdependent specific developments to substantiate these concerns.

First, for years Costa Rica has tried to resolve the interdependent problem of the losses of the Central Bank and the attendant fiscal and monetary implications. Political economy considerations have been offered since the mid-1980s to explain why this problem has become intractable within Costa Rica and a continued source of tension with multilateral institutions. Just in the middle of the presidential transition in March 2006, the 'Sala Cuarta' of the Constitutional Court declared unconstitutional the law that was 'finally' addressing this problem. Independently of the reasons supporting this decision, it could be interpreted within the context of the long history of compromises between alleged efficiency and equity trade-offs. Some observers will wonder if this event is not yet another example of a costly political economy compromise.

The Court's ruling may reflect that there is insufficient political demand for this particular macroeconomic correction. In good faith the Court may have found real flaws in the process of the fiscal reform. At the same time, this outcome may not be far away from what the real political incentives were. After all, the Constitutional Court perhaps in some analogy to the one in Colombia may feel that there is a preferred social welfare function which it is responsible for upholding. Whether this interpretation is valid or not will be established in the future when the government reconfigures its original proposal.

The second question is whether the framework hitherto followed may not have had hidden costs in terms of forgone growth and undercapitalization of overall physical and even social infrastructure (Garnier and Blanco, 2006, p. 55). Some observers of Costa Rica's political scene ask whether the real political power in Costa Rica has rested more with the public sector rent-seekers and labor unions than with public officials and the established constitutional political bodies. After all, those unions have often been able opportunistically[2] to extract non-market rents precisely from the general political inclination to avoid confrontation and strikes or 'intransigent' demands.[3] Behind the cover of political compromise some actors may follow more the rational choice of their interests than the alleged collective choice of compromise. At some point in time Costa Rica may have to face and resolve some difficult policy choices where earlier historical trade-offs may now be too costly in terms of future growth and equity.

A third indication that the traditional political economy arrangement may need to be reviewed comes from the recent evolution of poverty and income distribution results. Table 7.2 shows that the poverty level of 2003 (18.5 per cent) has not been recovered even though the economy has since been growing very fast. The Gini coefficient, which had been declining up to 2005, grew in 2006 up to 0.4218.

Table 7.2   Costa Rica: poverty evolution, 1991–2005

Year	Poverty	Extreme poverty	Gini
1991	31.9	11.7	0.3932
1992	29.4	9.3	0.3799
1993	23.2	6.9	0.3800
1994	20.0	5.8	0.3891
1995	20.4	6.2	0.3790
1996	21.5	6.9	0.3952
1997	20.7	5.7	0.3820
1998	19.7	5.3	0.3909
1999	20.6	6.7	0.4019
2000	20.6	6.1	0.4131
2001	20.3	5.9	0.4345
2002	20.6	5.7	0.4321
2003	18.5	5.1	0.4266
2004	21.7	5.6	0.4195
2005	21.2	5.6	0.4079
2006	20.2	5.3	0.4218

Source: See World Bank (2004a, p. 10).

A fourth consideration regarding the effectiveness of the established political compromise culture is the question of why Costa Rica's economy is in a process of growing dollarization. In 1990, 33 per cent of bank deposits were in US dollars. By 2004 this proportion had risen to 54 per cent (Jiménez, 2004, p. 32). A fifth and last reason why an overhaul of the system may be needed comes from the declining trend in Costa Rica's terms of trade. Gutierrez (2005b, p. 233) has summarized the implications of these five interdependent challenges as follows: 'To avoid a crisis we need major fiscal and financial transformations.'

II. ECONOMIC AND SOCIAL DEVELOPMENT IN PERSPECTIVE, 1980–1999

Few countries in Latin America have enjoyed more political stability in the last 50 years than Costa Rica. Few countries have had more prudent macroeconomic policies and better growth and distributional results. However, in the early 1980s it went through a difficult process of adjustment. Its GDP per capita for the period 1980–1989 declined on average by −0.8 per cent. As a consequence of following an outward-oriented export-led growth strategy, the economy recovered, and during 1990–1999 grew at 4.4 per cent, and its per capita GDP at 2.2 per cent (Table 7.3). After a low rate of growth in 2001, 1.1 per cent, the economy has grown rapidly, reaching 5.9 per cent in 2005 and 7.9 per cent in 2006 (Table 7.1).

These macroeconomic developments have been accompanied by a particular social policy which has resulted in poverty and equity indexes which are better than the average for Central America and better than most Latin American countries.[4] Costa Rica 'has already met or is well on its way to meeting the Millennium Development Goals'.[5] Notwithstanding these

Table 7.3   Costa Rica: overall macroeconomic performance

Indicator	1980–1989	1990–1999
GDP	2.2	4.4
GDP per capita	−0.8	2.2
Overall fiscal balance	−6.3	−3.5
Tax rev central gov.	14.2	15.6
Current account balance	−7.2	−4.7

Source: Cardemil et al. (2000, p. 35).

social accomplishments, Costa Rica's progress in some areas remains somewhat incomplete or with still relatively ample room for improvement. Inflation appears still high, at just below 10 per cent for 2006, total public debt is over 50 per cent of GDP, the operating losses of the Central Bank continue to burden monetary policy, financial dollarization appears to have increased and tax reform has been slow.

It has been observed[6] that this may be the political economy price, or trade-off, that needs to be paid to achieve the social and political progress observed. It has also been observed that having political stability and relatively low poverty levels could be the reward for the high transaction costs of less than desirable macroeconomic performance.

> Costa Rica's government and politics have long placed a high premium on achievement of wide socio-political consensus on major policies. While sometimes delaying decisions, this emphasis on consensus has the advantages of creating a broad social base, enhancing the sustainability of economic and social reforms and helping to maintain the credibility and accountability of public institutions (World Bank, 2004, p. 1).

This interpretation would need to go into the conceptual specifics as well as into its concrete situations or experiences to substantiate such a particular version of the transaction costs of politics and policy making. In principle, there is no inherent incompatibility between 'good' macroeconomic performance and equity gains. On the contrary: there is complementarity.

The underlying premise is that a process of enhancing the effectiveness of macroeconomic policy coordination between the Central Bank, the fiscal authorities and the financial sector is not incompatible with the existing relatively favorable distributional situation. An evaluation of Costa Rica's health system provided the following view on how results can be improved without necessarily higher public spending. Marquez (2004, p. 2) has posited that:

> Costa Rica has transformed its health system from a supply-based to a population-based model. It has introduced performance contracts for health providers and a clearer division of responsibilities among institutions, thereby increasing accountability. The coverage of primary healthcare has been expanded. At the same time, public health spending has been reduced from 6.7 percent of GDP in 1990 to a more affordable 5.3 percent. The reform has increased the share of health spending allocated to poor neighborhoods and to primary healthcare.

If fiscal restrictions were to limit the expansion of public spending, Costa Rica's tradition of consensus-seeking would be tested to assure the sustainability of the macroeconomic performance together with social and equity gains. The challenge would be to change the micro-institutional frameworks under which social spending takes place and to change the incentive structure underpinning the education and health sectors.

III. RECENT MACROECONOMIC DEVELOPMENTS, 1998–2006

Costa Rica's recent overall macroeconomic performance can be divided into three short periods: the years 1998 and 1999 when the country grew at a very fast pace, over 8.2 per cent on average; from 2000 to 2002 when average growth dropped below 2.0 per cent; and from 2003 to 2006 when average growth has climbed back to over 6 per cent. This is a remarkable rate of growth. In addition it has been attained while the authorities have brought down the rate of inflation from 13.1 per cent in 2004 to 9.43 per cent in 2006. This growth has also brought down the rate of unemployment to 6.0 per cent in 2006. Finally, the overall fiscal balance was more than halved to 0.7 per cent. In brief, this has been a commendable macroeconomic performance for the last four years (Table 7.4).

From this broad look at recent macroeconomic developments a key question emerges. Should Costa Rica continue to make a major political effort to reduce its inflation rate even further? Peter J. Montiel (2005, p. 31) suggests the following strategy to phase Costa Rica out of its inflation tradition.

> A Chilean-like transition to inflation targeting may make sense for Costa Rica: keep the real exchange rate targeting regime in place, as Chile did during the 1980s, while working on the institutional and technical conditions that are required to implement full-fledged inflation targeting. The most important of these are institutional reforms in the domestic financial sector in the areas of regulation and supervision. While these are desirable in general to enhance the efficiency of the financial system, they are needed in particular to achieve the important goal of reducing the system's vulnerability to exchange rate fluctuations as the result of currency mismatches. Reducing the incidence of such mismatches, and ensuring that domestic financial institutions are sufficiently well capitalized so as to cope with any residual risks that may remain, will allow the BCCR more latitude to permit exchange rate fluctuations under a future inflation-targeting regime.

In its 'Informe de Inflación' (January, 2006, p. 28) the Central Bank articulates a strategy to move monetary policy to inflation targeting. This is a well structured proposal.

Table 7.4 Costa Rica: key macroeconomic indicators, 1999–2006

Indicator	1999	2000	2001	2002	2003	2004	2005	2006
A. GDP real growth rate	8.2	1.8	1.1	2.9	6.4	4.3	5.9	7.9
B. Inflation rate, CPI, end of period	10.1	10.2	11.0	9.7	9.9	13.1	14.1	9.43
C. Current account balance (% GDP)	-4.3	-4.3	-3.7	-5.1	-5.0	-4.3	-4.9	4.9
D. Total tax revenue (% GDP)	11.9	12.3	13.2	13.3	13.3	13.3	13.5	14.14
E. Overall fiscal balance	-3.1	-3.8	-2.9	-5.4	-4.3	-2.61	-1.6	-0.7
F. Total external debt (% GDP)[1]	19.3	20.5	20.3	19.8	21.4	20.9	18.2	16.1
G. Total public sector debt (% GDP)	58.7	57.6	56.7	59.3	60.6	59.3	55.0	51.2
H. Net international reserves US$billion	1.5	1.3	1.3	1.5	1.8	1.9	2.3	3.3
I. Unemployment rate	6.0	5.2	6.1	6.4	6.7	6.5	6.6	6.0
J. Terms of trade variation	-1.6	-7.9	-1.8	-1.6	-2.7	-2.0	-3.7	-1.9
K. Total exports, US$billion	6.7	5.8	5.0	5.3	6.1	6.3	7.0	8.2

Note: [1] Refers only to public sector external debt.

Source: Central Bank of Costa Rica.

IV. THE MACROECONOMIC FRAMEWORK AND THE 2001 STRESS TEST

Costa Rica's macroeconomic institutional framework is composed of the following entities: (i) the Ministry of Finance; (ii) the Central Bank; and (iii) the Consejo Nacional de Supervisión del Sistema Financiero (CONASSIF). The Central Bank's main objective is to preserve a balance between growth and stability of the financial system (Lizano, 2004, p. 86). Within this objective the Central Bank is participating in the CONASSIF. According to Lizano (2004, p. 86), the Central Bank's encompassing objective does not stop at monetary stability, 'Economic development is also its concern and responsibility.'

Costa Rica's 'crisis' in 2000–2001 requires that the word be put between quotation marks because GDP did not turn negative as was the case in other Latin American countries. But it was an abrupt adjustment. The initial (previous) conditions were a GDP growth above 8.0 per cent in 1999. There was a combination of factors contributing to the 'crisis' of 2000–2001, the end of the construction phase of a large foreign direct investment project, a deterioration of the terms of trade and the effects of high real interest rates on domestic demand. According to the Central Bank's 2001 Memoria Annual Report (Banco Central de Costa Rica, 2001, p. 8), the abrupt 2000 slowdown was largely caused by an external shock originating in the United States, Costa Rica's main trading partner.

The 'crisis' of 2000–2001 is important for several reasons but one is particularly significant. Inflation did not subside, even when GDP fell in such magnitude. There was no 'disinflation'. Although Costa Rica's case is not identical to other countries in the region, this inflation rigidity suggests strong macroeconomic inflexibility. This point was understood by the Central Bank, which stated in its 2001 Report (page 9) that 'inflation has reached a plateau and it is difficult to lower it further'. Few things can be more revealing than a crisis. The conditions leading to a crisis may be obscured by many factors and interests. But a crisis brings out underlying weakness to the surface and opens a new political economy game. In Costa Rica's case the fiscal and the current account imbalances worsened in conjuction with the crisis. The fundamental point is that there was no significant disinflation. This suggests several things but one stands out, that is indexation is limited downwards and inflexibility is strong.

V. EQUITY AND POLITICAL ECONOMY MACROECONOMICS

The literature on equity and growth seems to converge on the general view that 'inequality is conducive to the adoption of growth retarding policies' (Alesina and Rodrik, 1994, p. 465). Given Costa Rica's 'commendable' relative indexes of poverty and income distribution, it would follow that adopting more long term pro-growth policies would be less difficult than in countries where those indexes are less favorable. However, the curious argument in some quarters, inside and outside Costa Rica, is the insistence that some particular pro-growth and pro-poor policies might jeopardize its social gains. How can these opposing views be reconciled?

A political economy explanation would assign to special interest groups[7] the real opposition to some reforms. It may well be that it is not so much that inequality or poverty retard or thwart reforms, but that well organized public or private rent-seekers are better able, under those equity conditions, to 'capture'[8] the political sentiment of the country through opportunistic manipulation of information on its collective perception of 'fairness'. Alesina and Angeletos (2005, p. 960) posit that: 'Different beliefs about the fairness of social competition and what determines income inequality influence the redistributive policy chosen in a society.' Well organized public sector rent-seekers can influence the public's perception of fairness and manipulate policy making.

The case of Costa Rica may be one in which early (in the 1960s and 1970s) long term 'structural' factors such as gains in political and relative macroeconomic stability together with education and health reforms yielded overall equity gains. These 'structural factors' have been helped in the last 10 years by 'cyclical factors', such as fast rates of growth and employment, which yield reductions in poverty levels. But the 'traditional' structural factors may be entering declining marginal productivity. Perhaps reconfigured structural reforms are needed. Further, inflation reduction may be one of such reforms. If inflation is mostly a tax on the poor why not bring it down precisely in response to social priorities? After all,

> The costs of inflation are borne most heavily by the poor, who lack the wealth needed to diversify into inflation-proof assets. The fact that the colón is a less than perfect store of value encourages local currency disintermediation and shortens the maturities of claims denominated in local currency, which limits the financial system's capacity to contribute to economic growth. Bringing down inflation to low single-digit levels – and keeping it there – could therefore help improve welfare in Costa Rica (Carstens, 2004).

VI.   CONCLUSIONS AND POLICY IMPLICATIONS

At this juncture in early 2007 Costa Rica's traditional consensus-seeking political economy formula is being put to the test by redistributive tension, political fragmentation and reform dithering. Close to two-thirds of the country's citizens did not participate in the 2006 presidential elections. The key policy question for Costa Rica is then not whether it has been well managed in the last 20 or more years (the answer is, on balance, yes) but what are the strategic adjustments it must make to deepen its social and economic accomplishments within a rapidly changing global economy perspective.

In the area of social progress the key policy implication is that further fiscal corrections are compatible with maintaining progress in terms of poverty reductions. The issue is not the sophistical dilemma of 'more public spending or equity losses' but the micro-institutional framework within which social public spending takes place. It is a false dichotomy to frame the problem in terms of either more spending or more poverty. This is an example of a rational 'opportunistic' approach which would need to be supported empirically or analytically across developing countries.

Few problems epitomize as well the political economy interpretation of Costa Rica as the long-standing problem of the losses of the Central Bank. The administration of President Pacheco was close to resolving this problem. But something happened on the way to the forum and, at the end, once again, the process was politically inconclusive. Now the Arias administration will surely try hard to move this agenda forward in the Assembly. Only time will tell what the outcome will be. The history of this emblematic issue augurs a formidable test, not so much of political wills but of the use of information to induce political and institutional transformation. A well known observer of Costa Rica's institutional scenary has summarized Costa Rica's challenges as follows: 'We urgently need a deep state reform to finally resolve our chronic fiscal problem' (Casas, 2004).

The really relevant political economy question is not, why are there not further fiscal and macro-institutional incentive corrections, but where are the real political incentives to do so? In a deeper sense, the key question is, why is it often assumed that whenever something is not performing there is in place an autonomous corrective mechanism in process? This is an 'idealized' view of the political and economic markets working in tandem under perfected informational conditions. This assumes the 'logic of collective action'. This assumes that the incentives of the logic of individual rational choice are not the predominant ones under a limited information framework. The key policy implication is that the restriction is the limited information on the existing high transactions costs and on who profits most from these circumstances. Better information on those transaction costs is a major component of the reform process in Costa Rica, as in many other developing countries.

NOTES

1. It has been said that Costa Rica's approach is to do things *De a poquitos, a raticos y a medias*. A former Central Bank Governor, Eduardo Lizano (1999, p. 5) asks 'Why is it we have not done so bad and not so good either?' See also Garnier et al. (1991).
2. There is nothing morally or legally wrong with this behavior. It is a legitimate posture which simply follows 'rational choice' and self-serving interests. The concept of rent seeking was introduced in economics by Gordon Tullock (1967). See also Krueger (1974). For the Colombian case see Eduardo Wiesner (1997, p. 93).
3. This is what some observers argue with regard to the attempts by the government to privatize the telecommunications sector.
4. To the question of why Costa Rica's experience appears to be different, Albert Berry (1998, p. 28) observes 'One broad interpretation of the Costa Rican experience is that it shares many elements with other LAC countries but includes differences in degree, timing, and abruptness.'
5. See World Bank (2004a).
6. See World Bank and Inter-American Development Bank (2005, p. 1).
7. IMF (2004f, p. 5).
8. The term 'rent-seekers', which was developed by Tullock (1967) and Krueger (1974), refers to legitimate actions by individuals who seek to capture rents and revenues from government through non-market choices on contracts, tariffs, regulation, quotas, and earmarking in general.

8. Peru: from macroeconomic volatility to credibility building

Fairness perception impacts aggregate outcomes and individual attitudes.
Alesina and Angeletos (2005, p. 963)

I. PERU'S POLITICAL ECONOMY PREDICAMENT

Why did it take a Fujimori to adopt a Vargas Llosa reform program in 1991 to bring Peru back from the depths of a −20 per cent GDP collapse in 1988–1989? Why did the Peruvian voters shun Vargas Llosa's proposed economic orthodoxy and elect an obscure Fujimori as their new president in 1991? What may explain Fujimori's volte face in adopting a rigorous stabilization program that engendered fast rates of growth in the mid-1990s and brought Peru back from the cold? And, finally, why was Alan García able to get elected again in June 2006? These questions seek to identify the conditions under which policy shifts come about from the most improbable sources. Cukierman and Tommasi (1998, p. 180) point out that

> The history of public policy contains several episodes in which structural reforms or important economic or foreign policy shifts were implemented by parties or policy makers whose traditional position was to oppose such policies. Argentina under (Peronist) Menem, Peru under Fujimori, and Bolivia under (populist) Paz Estenssoreo underwent profound market-oriented economic reforms.

The reasons why apparently only Fujimori could have adopted Vargas Llosa's program may have been because a large segment of Peruvians, particularly the low income groups, felt that they could trust Fujimori to protect their interests against what they largely perceived as an 'unfair'[1] system. In May 2006 the voters preferred Alan García in spite of his dismal record in the second half of the 1980s and the fact that Peru had been very well managed in the last five years. One possible interpretation of this phenomenon is that, again, a large segment of Peru's population continues to feel that their interests are better served by one who claims to care for the poor and who will 'defend' the country from external exploitation.

The relevant political economy question is, what will García's economic program turn out to be? Will he be a Nixon going to China? If political economy conditions (that is, asymmetric information, individual rational choices and collective action problems) are the main forces driving Peru's actual choices, the direction and substance of the new administration will be more determined by global capital markets and by the intensity of the change in the current economic cycle than by ideology or political postures. This may augur well for Peru. After all, policy makers and politicians may find it difficult not to succumb to the syndrome of blaming the external avatars for the consequences of what they may fail to do, or for what they will actually have to do, once an external change of wind hits.

This is the essence of political economy, that is to be able to elude political accountability and to be able to survive with the minimum political cost. This can be done if information is asymmetrically distributed between the public and the political leadership and if the former can be manipulated within much bounded interpretations. If this political economy context is an apt guide to assess the outlook of policy direction in Peru, it will not be ideology (a left or a right position) but the 'opportunistic' use of the 'blame the external avatars syndrome' that will largely determine the direction of policy. This strategy will find a receptive ear in the many who consider that the system or economic model in Peru is 'unfair'. The extension of this perception to an 'unfair' international system would not be difficult to accept. However, blaming the external avatars can also be a good excuse to adopt hitherto 'delayed reforms' and to find a 'scapegoat for doing it'. At the end García may yet go to China just as Fujimori did 15 years ago.

II.   PERU'S HISTORY OF MACROECONOMIC AND POLITICAL VOLATILITY

Peru has known political[2] and macroeconomic volatility in varied manifestations.[3] Between 1967 and 1968, during the last year of President Belaunde's first administration, there were seven Ministers of Finance (Kuczynski, 1997, p. 303). After Belaunde was deposed in October 1968 by General Juan Velasco, Peru went through an intensive period of macroeconomic volatility. One of the worst occurred 'between 1987 and 1988 when GDP plummeted by over 20%, real salaries decreased by 60% and inflation surpassed 2000 percent in 1989' (Lago, 1991, p. 354). The immediate cause of this particular crisis was President Alan García's attempt to 'stimulate the economy through public expenditure and wage increases while freezing prices and neglecting to provide fiscal resources to match the increase in spending' (Kuczynski, 1990, p. 86).

This turbulent macroeconomic episode in the late 1980s is an example of what happens when policy reforms are delayed and transaction costs politics[4] makes it very difficult to coordinate[5] competing interests. Political polarization leads to non-cooperative macroeconomic postures and to costly economic and social crisis. It is not only that without growth it is nearly impossible to reduce poverty, but that without equity gains political support for pro-growth and even pro-poor reforms often fails to come through.

III. MACROECONOMIC PERFORMANCE IN PERSPECTIVE, 1950–1996

From 1950 until 1975 Peru's growth was rather robust and sustained (Table 8.1). During 1950–1962, GDP grew at an average rate of 6.1 per cent. Then it grew at an average of 4.6 per cent between 1963 and 1968. From 1969 until 1975 the average rate of growth accelerated to 5.5 per cent. From then on until 1990, growth was particularly volatile and weak. During the period from 1963 to 1975 inflation rates were around 10 per cent, and budget deficits were kept at around 3–4 per cent. Then inflation rates exploded in 1976–1979 to 48.6 per cent, to 94 per cent in 1980–1985 and to 445.8 per cent in 1986–1989 (see Table 8.1).

During the 1980s the economy had years in which growth collapsed to −12.9 in 1983, rose to 9.2 per cent in 1986 and had two devastating years in 1988 and 1989 when growth was negative by −7.9 per cent and −11.3 per cent, respectively (Table 8.2). The immediate cause of this last monumental collapse was President Alan García's attempt to 'stimulate the economy through public expenditure and wage increases while freezing prices and neglecting to provide fiscal resources to match the increase in spending' (Kuczynski, 1990, p. 86).

Table 8.1   Peru: growth rates, budget deficits and inflation, 1950–1989

Period	GDP	Budget deficit (% of GDP)	Annual inflation
1950–62	6.1	−0.2	7.9
1963–68	4.6	2.9	11.6
1969–75	5.5	3.9	10.6
1976–79	0.7	6.8	48.6
1980–85	0.5	6.0	94.2
1986–89	−1.5	5.9	445.8

Source: Hamman and Paredes (1991, p. 61).

Table 8.2 Peru: GDP rates of growth, 1983–1996

Year	GDP rate	Year	GDP rate
1983	−12.9	1990	(−5.1)
1984	4.8	1991	2.2
1985	2.3	1992	−0.4
1986	9.2	1993	4.8
1987	8.5	1994	12.8
1988	−7.9	1995	8.6
1989	−11.3	1996	2.5

Source: Cáceres and Paredes (1991, p. 99); Banco Central del Perú, Memorias.

From 1975 to 1989 there were at least 10 stabilization attempts, 17 ministers of finance, and seven Presidents of the Central Bank, not including two periods during the García administration when the Presidency of the Central Bank was vacant. These are all examples of the political instability underpinning – and resulting from – the macroeconomic instability. In July 1980 democracy returned to Peru with the advent of Fernando Belaunde's second administration. He inherited a relatively stable macroeconomic situation. But in the 'first two years he indulged in a strange mixture of neoliberal rhetoric and the implementation of populist measures' (Hamman and Paredes, 1991, p. 70). The budget deficit rose to 9.7 per cent of GDP in 1982 and external conditions weakened. The El Niño weather turbulence precipitated a 12.9 per cent GDP collapse in 1983 and caused inflation to climb to three digits. Within this context Alan García was elected president and assumed power in July 1985. In his inaugural address he announced a

> unilateral reduction in foreign debt service to 10% of total export revenues. The new economic team abandoned previous diagnoses of excess aggregate demand as the primary cause of domestic price increases. Instead, it considered cost pressures and inflationary expectations to be main causes. Its solution was to freeze and in some cases reduce the so-called basic prices (exchange rate, interest rates, and fuel prices) to cut down production costs.

The rest is well known history (Cáceres and Paredes, 1991, p. 83).

In 1991 Richard Webb, a keen observer of Peru's development, insightfully posited that

> The most striking result of Peru's fifteen-year economic crisis has been de facto privatization. The public sector has undergone massive compression. The state is withering away, and surprisingly the process has been independent of any political program. The government is shrinking despite the politicians, the

bureaucrats, and the broad preferences of the Peruvian polity as a result of what could be called environmental change. The tax base, the public sector's access to credit, and the polity are changing faster than the state itself. The government's food supply is running out, and more and more it is being outmaneuvered and even outmuscled by privatize citizens. But the state is not going quietly. In fact, the monetary instability, distorted prices, loss of production, and bankruptcy that have characterized the years since 1975 are more easily understood as the desperate final thrashings of a largely predatory state. (Webb, 1991, p. i)

The environmental change alluded to by Richard Webb continued to take place in the second half of 1991 with the adoption of President Fujimori's stabilization program.

The main components of this program were a huge increase in the prices of goods and services supplied by state-owned enterprises and the introduction of emergency taxes; the establishment of a public sector cash-management committee and an announcement that the Central Bank would cease financing the fiscal deficit; the unification of the various exchange rates and the establishment of a managed floating exchange rate system; a very tight domestic credit policy; and a significant reduction in price controls, including de facto elimination of ceilings on interest rates. (Paredes, 1991, p. 299)

IV.   RECENT MACROECONOMIC DEVELOPMENTS, 2000–2006

Economic performance during (2002–2006) was remarkable. GDP grew at an average rate of over 5 per cent per annum. Inflation declined to 1.5 per cent in 2005 and to 1.1 per cent in 2006. The overall fiscal balance declined to −0.7 per cent in 2005 but rose to 1.4 per cent in 2006. The Current Account was in a surplus of 1.3 per cent. The unemployment rate was stable at around 10 per cent. Total external debt declined from 52.5 per cent of GDP in 2000 to 36.5 per cent in 2005 and to 30.4 per cent of GDP in 2006 (Table 8.3). Although this remarkable performance has been supported by very favorable terms of trade, it is also the result of good economic management. Most likely the outcome of an economic team sharing a common economic paradigm.

V.   THE POLITICAL ECONOMY OF EQUITY

Following the Alesina and Rodrik (1994, p. 465) premise that inequality is not propitious to growth enhancing policies, it would be relevant to observe what has happened in Peru in terms of poverty reduction and income

Table 8.3 *Peru: key macroeconomic indicators, 2000–2006*

Indicator	2000	2001	2002	2003	2004	2005	2006
A. GDP real growth rate	2.9	0.2	5.2	3.9	5.2	6.4	8.0
B. Inflation rate, CPI, end of period	3.7	−0.1	1.5	2.5	3.5	1.5	1.1
C. Current account balance (% GDP)	−2.9	−2.3	−2.0	−1.6	0.0	1.4	2.6
D. Tax revenue (central gov.) (% GDP)	12.2	12.4	12.0	12.8	13.1	13.6	14.9
E. Total expenditure (central gov.) (% GDP)	18.0	17.3	16.5	16.7	16.2	16.5	15.9
F. Overall fiscal bal. central gov. (% GDP)	−2.8	−2.8	−2.1	−1.8	−1.3	−0.7	1.4
G. Total external debt (% GDP)	52.5	50.4	48.9	48.1	44.8	36.1	30.4
H. Net international reserves US$bl ms	8.18	8.61	9.60	10.19	12.63	14.10	17.3
I. Unemployment rate*	7.8	8.8	9.7	10.3	10.5	11.4	n.a
J. Combined public sect. primary bal.	−0.8	−0.2	−0.1	0.4	1.0	1.6	3.9

Note: * Refers to Metropolitan Lima.

Source: World Bank, CAS, 19 August 2002. IMF, Article IV Consultation, Staff Report, 10 February 2004. 'Encuesta de Hogares Especializada de Niveles de Empleo', Ministerio de Trabajo.

213

Table 8.4   Peru: poverty evolution (% of population)

Indicator	2001	2002	2003	2004
National poverty level	54.3	53.8	52.2	51.6
Lima and Callao	31.8	34.2	33.7	36.6
Other provinces	63.3	61.8	59.6	57.7
Western provinces	70.6	70.0	68.6	67.7
Extreme national poverty	24.1	24.2	21.9	19.2

Source: INE, ENAHO 2001–2002 (IV Trimester), 2003 (May–December) and 2004 (annual 19 590 households).

distribution in recent years and to see what implications can be derived for future policy making. Table 8.4 shows that poverty at the national level declined from 54.3 per cent in 2001 to 51.6 per cent in 2004. A relatively more intensive decline took place, 'extreme poverty' coming down from 24.1 per cent to 19.2 per cent in the same period. The improvement was countrywide with the exception of Lima and Callao, where poverty worsened from 31.8 per cent to 31.6 per cent.

Complementing this data it should be remembered that in Peru 80 per cent of the indigenous population are poor and 50 per cent of the non-indigenous population are poor. That is, poverty is highly concentrated. The rate of extreme poverty is three times higher among indigenous peoples than the rest of the population. If growth were to return to more long term structural rates, the challenge would be to protect the poor while preserving an adequate 'countercyclical' fiscal stance together with measures to maintain the cost-effectiveness of social public spending.[6] This will be the real test of the political leadership, that is to provide social protection without discarding the need to be cost-effective while doing it.[7]

VI.   THE MACROECONOMIC INSTITUTIONAL FRAMEWORK

The current macroeconomic institutional framework has been anchored on the following developments since the early 1990s: (i) an independent Central Bank; (ii) law of fiscal responsibility and transparency; (iii) the superintendence of banks and prudential regulation; (iv) the national council of fiscal decentralization; and (v) the multiyear macroeconomic policy framework. In January 1993 an independent Central Bank was created with the explicit purpose of assuring monetary stability.[8] This was in contrast with the previous central bank law, which stipulated that the central bank had to manage credit conditions and promote output and employment growth while fostering the development of the banking sector. In October 1993 a new banking law was enacted extending the supervisory and regulatory framework to nonbank financial intermediaries, improving capitalization requirements to Basilea levels, and establishing a system of deposit insurance. The banking law of December 1996 improved and broadened the previous one.[9]

The new Central Bank has a seven-member Board appointed for five years. The Executive power appoints four members, including the Bank's President. Congress ratifies the President and appointed three Board members. The Bank enjoys full budget independence. Article 77 of the Bank's Organic Law forbids direct lending to the Treasury or issuing financial guarantees. No multiple exchange rate regimes are allowed. During 2003 it strongly defended its policy of intervening in the foreign exchange rate market. Since 2002 the Bank adopted inflation targeting. For 2005 the range was 1.5 to 3.5 and the result was 1.5 per cent.

There is an amended (2003) Law of Fiscal Responsibility and Transparency which now: (i) allows for a longer adjustment period to the medium-term fiscal target following a recession; (ii) requires the authorities to adjust fiscal policy when it is off-track in non-recessionary years; and (iii) extends rules of fiscal discipline to all levels of government.

The Superintendency of Banks (SBS) has strengthened norms on provisioning and loan classification (taking into account currency mismatches); introduced Value-at-Risk models for measuring exchange rate risk; and legislation was recently approved to implement credit exposure limits and strengthen the definition and measurement of capital (by deducting goodwill), in line with the recommendations of the Financial Sector Assessment Program (FSAP).[10]

The National Council of Decentralization is charged with the oversight for the implementation of Peru's decentralization scheme. Peru is a sort of late bloomer in joining Latin America's interest in fiscal and political decentralization.[11] Its late arrival may help it avoid some of the errors of its neighbors. The current framework appears to be fiscally sound. Law No. 27680 established the conditions to assure that the decentralization process does not affect macroeconomic stability adversely. Currently, local governments get resource transfers from the National level through the 'Fondo de Compensación Municipal' (FONCOMUN).[12] Finally, a major institutional transformation in the area of macroeconomic policy formulation was the adoption of the Multiyear Macroeconomic Framework, which guides monetary and fiscal policy for three-year periods. This policy framework is approved in the Council of Ministers and is designed to assure overall consistency on all major policy fronts.

VII.   THE STRESS TEST OF 1998–1999

Toward the end of 1997 economic activity slowed down owing mainly to the impact of the El Niño weather phenomenon, and output growth fell to 1.5 per cent in the first quarter of 1998. In the second half of 1998 Peru's financial sector was hit by the sudden withdrawal of foreign financing. To understand the policy implications, this episode should be examined with regard to the following three questions: (i) what were the initial macroeconomic and financial conditions; (ii) what was the policy response during the crisis; and (iii) what policy changes were adopted following the 'resolution' of the crisis?

When the sudden stop hit Peru in 1998 the economy was growing at a very high rate, 6.8 per cent for the year 1997. Inflation was coming down from 11.8 per cent in 1996 to 6.5 per cent in 1997, the Current Account balance had been negative in 1995 (−8.6), in 1996 (−6.5) and in 1997 (−5.7). The broad trust of fiscal policy was expansive, and hardly counter-cyclical 'as a result of increases in expenditures in goods and services, wages and investment'.[13] In the banking and financial sector there was a large degree of 'informal dollarization'. As a result of the 1999 crisis in December 1999 Congress approved the Law on Fiscal Responsibility.

> It sets limits to the deficit, the growth of general government expenditure, and the increase in public debt. In addition, it provides for the creation of a fiscal stabilization fund to generate savings during boom periods that would be utilized in times of recession or emergency. Also, the law requires that the public sector budget be prepared within a three-year macroeconomic framework, and it contains other features aimed at fostering fiscal transparency. For the purpose of fiscal transparency, plans for assisting individual sectors will avoid contingent fiscal costs, and so will channel fiscal support through the budgetary accounts.[14]

A very important change was the adoption of a 'softer' exchange rate regime. This decision to move to a 'softer' exchange rate regime reveals less 'fear of floating' and probably more trust on the fiscal and interest rate instruments (as shock absorbers) to deal with severe challenges.

VIII.   INFORMAL DOLLARIZATION AND LEARNING FROM HISTORY

The concept of dollarization needs to be disaggregated into its different modalities. Basically there are three forms of local currency substitution for a foreign currency dollarization: (i) substitution as a means of payment; (ii) substitution as a store of value or assets or portfolio; and (iii) full real dollarization. Either form introduces restrictions on macroeconomic policy making and implies risks and external vulnerability. One of these risks is the so-called balance sheet risk (Eichengreen et al., 2003), which emerges when financial agents hold liabilities in foreign exchange although their revenues come in local currency. In the case of Peru and referring to the 1990s, Morón and Castro (2004, p. 9) posit that in the 1990s dollarization increased.

At this juncture the question is not so much if informal dollarization has been reduced but if it has been reduced enough to protect the economy against a sudden or rapid change in the global capital markets. The problem is that public banks, and in Peru they continue to be important, may end up being 'protected', and this leads to moral hazard contagion and to general imprudent policies. This may be induced or perceived as being induced by government behavior – in the past – or possibly in the future. The 'best practice' advice to deal with a banking crisis is then to 'intervene early and address problems comprehensively and credibly' (Claessens, 2005, p. 17).

IX.   CONCLUSIONS AND POLICY IMPLICATIONS

If political factors largely shape the demand for reforms, policy developments in Peru will be conditioned by the unfolding in 2007 and 2008 of answers to the following questions.

i.   Do the very good macroeconomic performance and equity gains of the last five years (2001–06) confirm the existence of a strong political demand for macroeconomic stability and ancillary fiscal and sectoral reforms? Or was it rather, the felicitous coincidence of extraordinary external conditions with a minimum of political support for those reforms?

ii.   Have the last five years built the mechanisms for a countercyclical capacity to minimize the costs of an adjustment when more 'steady state' conditions return in the commodities and global capital markets?

iii.   How vulnerable to external shocks may Peru still be? How should the ongoing reforms be strengthened to limit 'informal dollarization'? What strategy should be put in place for the moment a sudden stop triggers domestic and financial volatility?

The most probable answer to the first 'either-or question' is that both sets of factors have played in favor of performance and reforms, but with one caveat. Perhaps there were more technical considerations on the government's supply side than widespread political demand for reforms. And clearly, there was a very favorable economic cycle providing a propitious environment for reform. This was fine. After all, it is much easier to adopt reforms in 'good times' than otherwise. But the fact is that in the mid-2006 elections, the 'incumbent policies' did not win the day. Perhaps there is still insufficient political acceptance and demand for reforms which are generally perceived as not 'poor-friendly'.

The answer to the second question will depend on the actual counter-cyclical capacity that *inter alia* the Law on Fiscal Responsibility and Transparency may be able to actually deliver if called upon. The answer will also depend on the credibility which the Central Bank may be willing and able to exercise in the search for a balanced trade-off between its inflation target, on the one hand, and managing a 'soft landing' of the economy, on the other.

The answers to the third set of questions hinge on the authorities' actual capacity to reduce external vulnerability. That capacity will depend on how politically and technically accountable they may feel they are when external shocks emerge. Following recent findings on 'rational expectations macroeconomics', that capacity will depend on whether there is still the syndrome of 'why really be concerned if you can always blame the external avatars?' If the answer is that this syndrome is still valid, then there will probably be severe macroeconomic and social volatility. This will probably happen as long as there is weak political demand for reforms and a fragmented and inconsistent policy response on the supply side. It will also happen if most Peruvians feel that their society is 'unfair' and does not assure equitable aggregate and individual outcomes.

Peru's society may well be an 'unfair' one. With all its immense importance, this condition matters less in terms of long term historical significance than the actual policies that will be adopted to correct this situation. Those policies are going to largely depend on the success of different interpretations of the causes of development competing with each other in the political arena of Peru. Peru has evolved in the right direction in the last five years. Although history moves slowly, this recent 'path dependency' augurs well for this country's response to the remaining challenges of its development.

NOTES

1. Alesina and Angeletos (2005, p. 960) posit that: 'Different beliefs about the fairness of social competition and what determines income inequality influence the redistributive policy chosen in a society.'
2. For an examination of the causes of recent political instability see McMillan and Zoido (2004, p. 89).

3. Scartascini (2006, p. 9) underscores how 'cabinet coalescence' can affect policy making and even legislative voting behavior.
4. Drazen (2000, p. 97), 'There has been interesting recent research exploring a transaction cost approach to politics, spearheaded by North (1990) and explored in a recent book by Dixit (1996). In transaction cost politics, the basic relation is a political transaction, trading votes (or contributions) for promised policies, or sometimes simply votes for votes. North argues that transaction costs – problems of information, specification or enforcement of a political transaction – are even higher in politics than in economics.'
5. Professor Barry R. Weingast (2005, p. 96) calls this situation 'the citizen coordination dilemma' or the difficulty for a society to 'create a focal solution . . . so that citizens can act in concert.'
6. See Anwar Shah (2005, p. xxiv) for a discussion on how to link fiscal allocation with specific results and targets.
7. See Fiszbein and Lowden (1999, p. 15) for ways in which poverty reduction can be tackled through public–private partnerships.
8. See Article 2 of the Bank's Organic Law and the Decreto Ley No. 26123.
9. IMF (1998, p. 22).
10. IMF (2004b, p. 10).
11. During the first Fernando Belaunde period (1963–1968) there was a program called 'Cooperación Popular' which, borrowing from an old Inca tradition, applied somewhat intuitively decentralization concepts and subsidiarity principles. See Kuczynski (1997, p. 41).
12. See Ministerio de Economía y Finanzas (2005, p. 11).
13. See Ministerio de Economía y Finanzas (2005, p. 36).
14. See IMF (2005b).

References

Acemoglu, Daron (2003a), 'Why not a political Coase Theorem? Social conflict, commitment and politics', Cambridge, MA: Department of Economics, Massachusetts Institute of Technology, MIT Press.

Acemoglu, Daron (2003b), 'Root causes', *Finance & Development*, June, Washington, DC: International and Monetary Fund, IMF.

Acemoglu, Daron (2005a), *Lecture Notes for Political Economy of Institutions and Development, 14773*, Cambridge: Massachusetts Institute of Technology, MIT Press.

Acemoglu, Daron (2005b), 'Constitutions, politics, and economics: a review essay on Persson and Tabellini's "The Economic Effects of Constitutions"', *Journal of Economic Literature*, **XLIII**(4), 1025–48.

Acemoglu, Daron (2007), 'Is democracy the best setting for strong economic growth?', *Wall Street Journal* (online edition), 12 March, New York.

Acemoglu, Daron and James A. Robinson (2000), 'Political economy, governance, and development: political losers as a barrier to economic development', *American Economic Review*, **90**(2), 126–30.

Acemoglu, Daron and James A. Robinson (2005), *Economic Origins of Dictatorship and Democracy*, New York: Cambridge University Press.

Acemoglu, Daron and James A. Robinson (2006a), 'De facto political power and institutional persistence', *American Economic Review*, **96**(2), 325–30.

Acemoglu, Daron and James A. Robinson (2006b), 'Persistence of power, elites and institutions', *NBER Working Paper No. 12108*, March, Cambridge, MA: National Bureau of Economic Research, NBER.

Acemoglu, Daron, Simon Johnson and James A. Robinson (2001), 'The colonial origins of comparative development: an empirical investigation', *American Economic Review*, **91**(5), 1369–401.

Acemoglu, Daron, Simon Johnson and James A. Robinson (2002), 'Reversal of fortune: geography and institutions in the making of the modern world income distribution', *Quarterly Journal of Economics*, **117**(4), 1231–94.

Acemoglu, Daron, Simon Johnson and James A. Robinson (2006), 'Institutions as the fundamental cause of long-run growth', in Philippe Aghion and Steven Durlauf (eds), *Handbook of Economic Growth*, Amsterdam: North-Holland.

Akerlof, George A. (2002), 'Behavioral macroeconomics and macroeconomic behavior', *American Economic Review*, **92**(3), 411–33.

Akitoby, Bernardin, Benedict Clements, Sanjeev Gupta and Gabriela Inchauste (2006), 'Public spending, voracity, and Wagner's Law in developing countries', *European Journal of Political Economy*, **22**, 908–24.

Alchian, Armen A. (1950), 'Uncertainty, evolution and economic theory', *Journal of Political Economy*, **58**(3), 211–22.

Alcorn, Stanley and Ben Solarz (2006), 'The autistic economist', *Yale Economic Review*, **2**(3), a Yale college publication.

Alesina, Alberto (1991), 'Comment' on 'The political economy of Latin American populism', by Roberto R. Kaufman and Barbara Stallings in *The Macroeconomics of Populism in Latin America*, edited by Rudiger Dornbusch and Sebastian Edwards, Chicago and London: The University of Chicago Press.

Alesina, Alberto (1999), 'Budget deficit and budget institutions', in J.M. Poterba and J. von Hagen (eds), *Fiscal Institutions and Fiscal Performance*, National Bureau of Economic Research, NBER, Chicago and London: The University of Chicago Press.

Alesina, Alberto (2000), *Institutional Reforms in Colombia*, Working Paper No. 21, Fundación para la Educación Superior y el Desarrollo, FEDESARROLLO, Bogotá, Colombia.

Alesina, Alberto (2002), *Reformas Institucionales en Colombia*, Bogotá, Colombia: Alfaomega Colombiana S.A.

Alesina, Alberto (2004a), *Institutional Reforms: The Case of Colombia*, Cambridge, MA: MIT Press.

Alesina, Alberto (2004b), 'Entrevista a Alberto Alesina', *Carta Financiera No. 127*, Asociación Nacional de Instituciones Financieras, ANIF, Bogotá, Colombia.

Alesina, Alberto (2005), *Institutional Reforms: The Case of Colombia*, Cambridge, MA: MIT Press.

Alesina, Alberto and George-Marios Angeletos (2005), 'Fairness and redistribution', *American Economic Review*, **95**(4), 960–80.

Alesina, Alberto and A. Drazen (1991), 'Why are stabilizations delayed?', *American Economic Review*, **81**(5), 1170–88.

Alesina, Alberto and Eliana La Ferrara (2005), 'Preferences for redistribution in the land of opportunities', *Journal of Public Economics*, **89**(5), 897–931.

Alesina, Alberto and Roberto Perotti (1994), 'The political economy of growth: a critical survey of the recent literature', *The World Bank Economic Review*, **8**(3), 351–71.

Alesina, Alberto and Roberto Perotti (1995), 'The political economy of budget deficits', IMF Staff Papers.

Alesina, Alberto and Dani Rodrik (1994), 'Distributive politics and economic growth', *The Quarterly Journal of Economics*, **CIX**(2), published for Harvard University, Cambridge, MA: MIT Press.

Alesina, Alberto and Guido Tabellini (2005), 'Why is fiscal policy so often procyclical?', *NBER Working Paper No. 11600*, Cambridge, MA: National Bureau of Economic Research, NBER.

Alesina, Alberto and Guido Tabellini (2007), 'Bureaucrats or politicians? Part I: a single policy task', *American Economic Review*, **97**(1), 169–79.

Alesina, Alberto, Alberto Carrasquilla and Roberto Steiner (2005), 'Toward a truly independent Central Bank in Colombia', in Alberto Alesina (ed.), *Institutional Reforms: The Case of Colombia*, Cambridge, MA and London: MIT Press.

Alesina, Alberto, Edward Glaeser and Bruce Sacerdote (2005), 'Work and leisure in the US and Europe: why so different?', Mimeo, Harvard University.

Alesina, Alberto, Nouriel Roubini and Gerald Cohen (1997), *Political Cycles and the Macroeconomics*, Cambridge, MA: MIT Press.

Alesina, Alberto, Ricardo Hausmann, Rudolf Hommes and Ernesto Stein (1996), 'Budget institutions and fiscal performance in Latin America', *NBER Working Paper No. 5586*, Cambridge, MA: National Bureau of Economic Research, NBER.

Anderson, Lisa R. (2001), 'Public choice as an experimental science', in William F. Shughart II and Laura Razzolini (eds), *Public Choice*, Cheltenham, UK and Northampton, MA, USA: Edward Elgar Publishing.

ANIF (2006), 'El Banco de la República, su independencia y los a justes institucionales', *Informe Semanal*, No. 842, ISSN 1794-2616, Bogotá, Colombia: a Asociación de Instituciones Financieras, ANIF.

Aninat, Eduardo (2000a), 'Economic growth, social equity, and globalization: the Chilean case', in Andrés Solimano, Eduardo Aninat and Nancy Birdsall (eds), *Distributive Justice & Economic Development: The Case of Chile and Developing Countries*, Ann Arbor: The University of Michigan Press.

Aninat, Eduardo (2000b), 'Chile in the 90s: development opportunities', *Finance and Development*, March, International Monetary Fund, IMF.

Aninat, Eduardo (2000c), 'Closing remarks', High Level Seminar: Implementing Inflation Targeting, Washington, DC: International Monetary Fund, IMF.

Arias, Andrés Felipe (2000), 'The Colombian banking crisis: macroeconomic consequences and what to expect', *Borradores de Economía*, No. 157, Banco de la República, Bogotá, Colombia.

Arriazu, Ricardo Héctor (2003a), 'Introducción', *Argentina: Crisis, Instituciones y Crecimiento*, Conferencias FIEL 2003, 40 Aniversario, Tomo 1, Buenos Aires, Argentina: Fundación de Investigaciones Económicas Latinoamericanas, FIEL.

Arriazu, Ricardo Héctor (2003b), *Lecciones de la Crisis Argentina*, Buenos Aires, Argentina: Editorial el Ateneo.

Arrow, Kenneth J. (1951), *Social Choice and Individual Values*, New York: John Wiley.

Arrow, Kenneth J. (1985), 'Economic history: a necessary though not sufficient condition for an economist', *American Economic Review*, Papers and Proceedings, **75**(2).

Artana, Daniel (2003), '¿Qué Aprendimos de la Crisis y qué Desafíos nos Esperan?', *Argentina Crisis, Instituciones y Crecimiento*, Conferencias FIEL 2003, 40 Aniversario, Tomo 1, Buenos Aires, Argentina: Fundación de Investigaciones Económicas Latinoamericanas.

Attanasio, Orazio (2004), 'Evaluación de familias en acción y hogares comunitarios, por qué evaluar el gasto público?', Seminario Internacional, Departamento Nacional de Planeación, DNP, Banco Interamericano de Desarrollo, BID, BIRF, Bogotá, Colombia.

Attanasio, Orazio and Miguel Székely (2001), 'Going beyond income: redefining poverty in Latin America', in Orazio Attanasio and Miguel Székely (eds), *Portrait of the Poor: An Assets-Based Approach*, Baltimore: Johns Hopkins University Press.

Attanasio, Orazio and Miguel Székely (2005), Table 6, in Vittorio Corbo, Leonardo Hernández and Fernando Parro (eds), 'Institutions, economic policies and growth: lessons from the Chilean experience', *Working Paper No. 317*, Central Bank of Chile, April, p. 46.

Avella, Mauricio (2005), 'The shock absorber role of the internal public debt in Colombia, 1923–2003', *Borradores de Economía*, No. 342, Banco de la República, Bogotá, Colombia.

Baig, Taimur and Ilan Goldfajn (2000), 'The Russian default and the contagion to Brazil', *IMF Working Paper No. 00/160*, International Monetary Fund, IMF.

Banco Central de Costa Rica (2001), 'El Banco Central de Costa Rica y su participación en la economía nacional', *Memoria Anual*, San José, Costa Rica: Banco Central de Costa Rica.

Banco Central de la República Argentina (Central Bank of Argentina) (2006), 'Economic indicators', *Macroeconomic Radar*, 10 December 2006.

Bannock, Graham, R.E. Baxter and Evan Davis (1989), *Dictionary of Economics*, London: Hutchinson Business in association with The Economist Books.

Barber, William (1995), 'Chile con Chicago: a review essay', *Journal of Economic Literature*, December, **XXXIII**(4), 1941–9.

Bardhan, Pranab (2001), 'Distributive conflicts, collective action, and institutional economics', in Gerald M. Meier and Joseph E. Stiglitz (eds), *Frontiers of Development Economics: The Future in Perspective*, Washington, DC: The World Bank and Oxford University Press.

Barnard, Chester (1938), *The Functions of the Executive*, Cambridge, MA: Harvard University Press.

Barros, Ricardo and Mirela de Carvalho (2004), 'Desafíos para a politica social Brasileira', *Reformas no Brazil: Balanco e Agenda*, Rio de Janeiro, Brazil: Nova Fronteira.

Basco, Emiliano, Laura D'Amato and Lorena Garegnani (2006), 'Crecimiento monetario e inflación: Argentina 1970–2005', *Documentos de Trabajo 2006*, **12**, Investigaciones Económicas, Banco Central de la República Argentina.

Bénabou, Roland and Jean Tirole (2006), 'Incentives and prosocial behavior', *American Economic Review*, **96**(5), 1652–78.

Berg, Andrew and Eduardo Borensztein (2000), 'The dollarization debate', *Finance & Development*, March, International Monetary Fund, IMF.

Berg, Andrew G., Christopher J. Jarvis, Mark R. Stone and Alessandro Zanello (2003), 'Re-establishing credible nominal anchors after a financial crisis: a review of recent experience', *IMF Working Paper, No. 03/76*, Washington, DC: International Monetary Fund, IMF.

Bergsten, Fred (2006a), 'A new steering committee for the world economy?', in Edwin M. Truman (ed.), *Reforming the IMF for the 21st Century*, Washington, DC: Institute for International Economics.

Bergsten, Fred (2006b), 'Preface', in Edwin M. Truman (ed.), *Reforming the IMF for the 21st Century*, Washington, DC: Institute for International Economics.

Bergsten, Fred and John Williamson (2003), *Dollar Overvaluation and the World Economy*, Washington, DC: Institute for International Economics.

Bernanke, Ben S. and Frederic S. Mishkin (1997), 'Inflation targeting: a new framework for monetary policy?', *Journal of Economic Perspectives*, **11**(2), 97–116.

Bernanke, Ben S. and Michael Woodford (2006), 'Introduction', in Ben S. Bernanke and Michael Woodford (eds), *The Inflation-Targeting Debate*, National Bureau of Economic Research, NBER, Chicago and London: The University of Chicago Press.

Bernanke, Ben S., Thomas Laubach, Frederic Mishkin and Adam Posen (1999), *Inflation Targeting; Lessons from the International Experience*, Princeton, NJ: Princeton University Press.

Berry, Albert (1998), 'Confronting the income distribution threat in Latin America', in Albert Berry (ed.), *Poverty, Economic Reform, and Income Distribution in Latin America*, Boulder, CO: Lynne Rienner Publishers, Inc.

Berry, Albert (ed.) (1998), *Poverty, Economic Reform, and Income Distribution in Latin America*, London: Lynne Rienner Publishers.

Besley, Timothy and Stephen Coate (1998), 'Sources of inefficiency in a representative democracy: a dynamic analysis', *American Economic Review*, **88**(1), 139–56.

Bhagwati, J. and T.N. Srinivasan (1980), 'Revenue seeking: a generalization of the theory of tariffs', *Journal of Political Economy*, **88**(6), 1069–87.

Bird, Richard (2003), 'Taxation in Latin America: reflections on sustainability and the balance between equity and efficiency', *International Tax Program Paper 0306*, Joseph L. Rotman School of Management, University of Toronto, Toronto, Ontario: Institute for International Business.

Bird, Richard (2006), 'Fiscal flows, fiscal balance, and fiscal sustainability', in Richard M. Bird and François Vaillancourt (eds), *Perspectives on Fiscal Federalism*, Washington, DC: World Bank Institute.

Bird, Richard and Olga Lucia Acosta (2005), 'The dilemma of decentralization in Colombia', in Richard M. Bird, James M. Poterba and Joel Slemrod (eds), *Fiscal Reform in Colombia: Problems and Prospects*, Cambridge, MA and London: MIT Press.

Bird, Richard, James Poterba, Juan José Echabarria and Joel Slemrod (2005), 'Introduction', in Richard M. Bird, James M. Poterba and Joel Slemrod (eds), *Fiscal Reform in Colombia*, Cambridge, MA: MIT Press.

Birdsall, Nancy (2005a), 'Rising inequality in the new global economy', *2005 Wider Annual Lecture*, United Nations University.

Birdsall, Nancy (2005b), 'The world is not flat: inequality and injustice in our global economy', *Wider Annual Lecture 9*, World Institute for Development Economics Research.

Birdsall, Nancy and Kemal Dervis (2006), 'A stability and social investment facility for high-debt countries', *Working Paper No. 77*, January, The Center for Global Development.

Blanchard, Oliver Jean and Stanley Fischer (1992), 'Monetary and fiscal policy issues', *Lectures on Macroeconomics*, Cambridge, MA and London: MIT Press.

Blinder, Alan S. (1997), 'Is there a core of practical macroeconomics that we should all believe?', *American Economic Review*, **87**(2), 240–43.

Bloom, Andreas and Carlos Eduardo Velez (2004), 'The dynamics of the skill-premium in Brazil: growing demand and insufficient supply?',

Inequality and Economic Development in Brazil, a World Bank Country Study, Washington, DC.

Blustein, Paul (2005), *And the Money Kept Rolling in (and Out): The World Bank, Wall Street, the IMF, and the Bankrupting of Argentina*, New York: Public Affairs.

Bogdanski, Joel, Alexandre Antonio Tombini and Sérgio Ribeiro da Costa Werlang (2000), 'Implementing inflation targeting in Brazil', *Working Paper No. 1*, Central Bank of Brazil.

Botero, Rodrigo (1992), 'Rodrigo Botero habla sobre Tecnocracia y Desarrollo Económico', *Carta Financiera No. 110*, January–March 1999, Bogotá, Colombia: Asociación Nacional de Instituciones Financieras, ANIF.

Botero, Rodrigo (2005), 'Una nota sobre la tecnocracia Colombiana', *35 Años FEDESARROLLO*, Segundo Semestre de 2005, **XXXV**(2), Bogotá, Colombia: Editora Coyuntura Económica.

Botero, Rodrigo, Mauricio Cárdenas, Alejandro Gaviria, Armando Montenegro and Gabriel Rosas (2007), *Comisión Independiente de Gasto Público*, 20 May–5 June, Bogotá, Colombia.

Brennan, Geoffrey and Alan Hamlin (2001), 'Constitutional choice', in William F. Shughart II and Laura Razzolini (eds), *Public Choice*, Cheltenham, UK and Northampton, MA, USA: Edward Elgar Publishing.

Bruno, Michael, Martin Ravallion and Lyn Squire (2000), 'Equity and growth in developing countries: old and new perspectives on the policy issues', in Andrés Solimano, Eduardo Aninat and Nancy Birdsall (eds), *Distributive Justice & Economic Development: The Case of Chile and Developing Countries*, Ann Arbor: The University of Michigan Press.

Buchanan, James (1991), 'The domain of constitutional political economy', *The Economics and the Ethics of Constitutional Order*, Ann Arbor: The University of Michigan Press.

Buchanan, James and Gordon Tullock (1962), *The Calculus of Consent: Logical Foundations of Constitutional Democracy*, Ann Arbor: The University of Michigan Press.

Burnside, Craig (2005), 'Some tools for fiscal sustainability', in Craig Burnside (ed.), *Fiscal Sustainability in Theory and Practice: A Handbook*, Washington, DC: The World Bank.

Caballero, Ricardo (2001), *Macroeconomic Volatility in Reformed Latin America*, Washington, DC: Inter-American Development Bank.

Caballero, Ricardo and A. Krishnamurthy (2003), 'Excessive dollar debt: financial development and underinsurance', *Journal of Finance*, **58**(2), 867–93.

Caballero, Ricardo, Eduardo Engel and Alejandro Micco (2004), 'Flexibilidad macroeconómica en América Latina', *Economía Chilena*, 7(2), August.

Caballero, Richard, Kevin Cowan and Jonathan Kearns (2004), 'Fear of sudden stops: lessons from Australia and Chile', *Financial Dollarization: Policy Options*, Conference at the Inter-American Development Bank, IDB, December 2003.

Cabrera, G. Mauricio (2006), '¿Quién le cree al FMI?', *Portafolio*, 29 August, Bogotá, Colombia.

Cabrera, G. Mauricio and Jorge Iván González (2000), 'La disyuntiva no es pagar o sisar la deuda, es pagarla a sobreprecio o a un precio justo', *Economía Institucional*, No. 3, Segundo Semestre, Bogotá, Colombia: Universidad Externado de Colombia.

Cáceres, Armando and Carlos E. Paredes (1991), 'The management of economic policy, 1985–1989', in Carlos E. Paredes and Jeffrey D. Sachs (eds), *Peru's Path to Recovery: A Plan for Economic Stabilization and Growth*, Washington, DC: The Brookings Institution.

Calderon, Cesar and Rodrigo Fuentes (2005), 'Characterizing the business cycles of emerging economies', Preliminary Version, August, The World Bank and Central Bank.

Calvo, Guillermo (2006), 'Region focus', *Federal Reserve Bank of Richmond*, Summer, 44–8.

Calvo, Guillermo and E. Mendoza (1999), 'Empirical puzzles of Chilean stabilization policy', in G. Perry and Danny Leipziger (eds), *Chile: Recent Policy Lessons and Emerging Challenge*, Washington, DC: World Bank Institute, World Bank.

Calvo, Guillermo and Carmen M. Reinhart (2000), 'Fear of floating', *NBER Working Paper No. 7993*, National Bureau of Economic Research, NBER.

Calvo, Guillermo and Ernesto Talvi (2005), 'Sudden stop, financial factors and economic collapse in Latin America: learning from Argentina and Chile', *NBER Working Paper No. 11153*, Cambridge, MA: National Bureau of Economic Research, NBER.

Calvo, Guillermo and Carlos Végh (1999), 'Inflation, stabilization and BOP crisis in developing countries', in John Taylor and Michael Woodford (eds), *Handbook of Macroeconomics*, North-Holland: Elsevier.

Calvo, Guillermo, Alejandro Izquierdo and Ernesto Talvi (2003), 'Sudden stops, the real exchange rate and fiscal sustainability: Argentina's lessons', Washington, DC: Inter-American Development Bank.

Calvo, Guillermo, Alejandro Izquierdo and Ernesto Mejía (2004), 'On the empirics of sudden stops: the relevance of balance-sheet effects', *NBER*

Working Paper No. 10520, Cambridge, MA: National Bureau of Economic Research, NBER.

Calvo, Guillermo, Alejandro Izquierdo and Ernesto Talvi (2006), 'Sudden stops and phoenix miracles in emerging markets', *American Economic Review*, **96**(2), 405–10.

Calvo, Guillermo, Leonardo Leiderman and Carmen M. Reinhard (1993), 'Capital inflows to Latin America: the role of external factors', *IMF Staff Papers*, March, No. 40, 108–51.

Calvo, Guillermo, Leonardo Leiderman and Carmen M. Reinhard (1994), 'Capital inflows to Latin America: the 1970s and 1990s', in Edmar L. Bacha (ed.), *Economics in a Changing World, Volume 4: Development, Trade, and the Environment*, London: Macmillan, pp. 123–48.

Calvo, Guillermo, Leonardo Leiderman and Carmen M. Reinhard (1996), 'Inflows of capital to developing countries in the 1990s', *Journal of Economic Perspectives*, **10**(2), 123–39.

Cardemil, Leonardo, Juan Carlos Di Tata and Florencia Frantischek (2000), 'America Central ajuste y reformas durante los años noventa', *Finance & Development*, March, International Monetary Fund, IMF.

Cárdenas Enrique, José Antonio Ocampo and Rosemary Thorp (2000), 'Introduction', in Enrique Cárdenas, José Antonio Ocampo and Rosemary Thorp (eds), *An Economic History of Twentieth-Century Latin America*, Palgrave, Vol. 3.

Cárdenas, Mauricio (2004), 'Evaluación y gasto público en Colombia', *Por qué Evaluar el Gasto Público?*, Seminario Internacional, Departamento Nacional de Planeación, DNP, Banco Interamericano de Desarrollo, BID, Banco Mundial.

Cárdenas, Mauricio (2005), 'Crecimiento económico en Colombia: 1970–2005', *35 Años FEDESARROLLO*, Segundo Semestre de 2005, **XXXV**(2), Bogotá, Colombia: Editora Coyuntura Económica.

Cárdenas, Mauricio (2007), 'Crecimiento económico Colombiano: ¿cambio de suerte?', *Ensayos sobre Política Económica*, **25**(3), Bogotá, Colombia: Banco de la República.

Cárdenas, Mauricio and Eduardo Lora (2006), 'La reforma de las instituciones fiscales en América Latina', *Working Paper No. 559*, April, Washington, DC: Banco Inter-Americano de Desarrollo, BID.

Cárdenas, Mauricio and Valerie Mercer-Blackman (2006), 'Descripción del sistema', *Análisis del Sistema Tributario Colombiano y su Impacto Sobre la Competitividad*, Cuadernos FEDESARROLLO, No. 19, June, Bogotá, Colombia.

Cárdenas, Mauricio and Robert Steiner (2000), 'Private capital flows in Colombia', in B. Felipe Larrain (ed.), *Capital Flows, Capital Controls and*

Currency Crises: Latin America in the 1990s, Ann Arbor: The University of Michigan Press.

Cárdenas, Mauricio and M. Miguel Urrutia (2004), 'Impacto social del ciclo económico en Colombia: 1989–2004', *Coyuntura Social*, No. 30, June, Bogotá, Colombia: Fundación para la Educación Superior y el Desarrollo, FEDESARROLLO.

Cárdenas, Mauricio, Roberto Junguito and Mónica Pachón (2006), 'Political institutions and policy outcomes in Colombia: the effects of the 1991 constitution', *Research Network Working Paper No. R-508*, Inter-American Development Bank, IDB, Fundación para la Educación Superior y el Desarrollo, FEDESARROLLO, Department of Political Science, University of California, February.

Carrasquilla, Alberto (1999), 'Introducción', *Estabilidad y Gradualismo: Ensayos sobre Economía Colombia*, Banco de la República, Bogotá, Colombia: Tercer Mundo Editores.

Carrasquilla, Alberto (2006), 'Sobre la calidad del debate económico en Colombia', *Carta Financiera, No. 132*, January–March, Entrevista, Bogotá, Colombia: Asociación Nacional de Instituciones Financieras, ANIF.

Carrasquilla, Alberto (2007), '¿De cuáles piernas?', *El Tiempo*, 18 May, Bogotá, Colombia, pp. 1–19.

Carrasquilla, Alberto, Arturo Galindo and Hilde Patron (1994), 'Costos en bienestar de la inflación en teoría y una Estimación para Colombia', *Borradores de Economía*, No. 3, Banco de la República, Bogotá, Colombia.

Carstens, Agustin G. (2004), 'Twenty years without a crisis in Costa Rica', Conference at the Academy of Central America, 12 July.

Carstens, Agustin G., Daniel C. Hardy and Celia Pazarbasioglu (2004), 'Avoiding banking crises in Latin America', *Finance & Development*, September, Washington, DC: International Monetary Fund, IMF.

Carstens, Agustin G. and Luis I. Jácome H. (2005), 'Taming the monster', *Finance and Development*, December, Washington, DC: International Monetary Fund, IMF.

Casas, Kevin (2004), *Revista Actualidad Económica 18 Aniversario No. 307*, Año XVIII del 5 al 28 de November, San José, Costa Rica.

Casas, Kevin (2006), 'Gobierno atacará los "cuellos de botella" que merman control del poder ejecutivo', *La Prensa Libre*, 15 June, San José, Costa Rica.

Casey, Mulligan B., Ricard Gil and Xavier Sala-i-Martin (2004), 'Do democracies have different public policies than nondemocracies', *Journal of Economic Perspectives*, **18**(1), 51–74.

Castelar, Armando and Fabio Giambiagi (2006), *Rompendo o Marasmo: A Retomada do Desenvolvimento no Brasil*, Rio de Janeiro: Elsevier Editora Campus.

Castellanos, Daniel (2004), 'Algunas causas y remedios del déficit presupuestal', *Revista ESPE* (Ensayos sobre Política Económica), Bogotá, Colombia.

Castro, Jaime (2005), *Postdata a la Re-elección*, Bogotá, Colombia: Fundación Foro Nacional por Colombia.

Castro, Jaime (2006), 'El congreso vuelve colcha de retazos la carta del 91' (Universidad Nacional) *Un Periódico*, No. 98, 15 October, Universidad Nacional de Colombia, Bogotá, Colombia.

Cepeda, Manuel José (2004), 'Las sentencias de la corte con implicaciones económicas: reflexiones con ánimo constructivo', *Memorias*, XXVIII Jornadas Colombianas de Derecho Tributario 18, 19, 20 de Febrero de 2004, Cartagena de Indias, ICDT, Colombia.

Céspedes, Luis Felipe, Ilan Goldfajn, Phil Lowe and Rodrigo Valdés (2006), 'Policy responses to external shocks: the experiences of Australia, Brazil and Chile', in Ricard J. Caballero, Cesar Calderón and Luis Felipe Céspedes (eds), *External Vulnerability and Preventive Policies*, Santiago de Chile: Central Bank of Chile.

Chang, Roberto and Andrés Velasco (2000), 'Exchange policy for development countries', *American Economic Review*, **90**(2), 71–5.

Chari, V.V. and Harold Cole (1993), 'A contribution to the theory of pork barrel spending', *Staff Report 156*, Federal Reserve Bank of Minneapolis.

Chari, V.V. and Patrick J. Kehoe (1999), 'Optimal fiscal and monetary policy', in John Taylor and Michael Woodford (eds), *Handbook of Macroeconomics*, Vol. 1C, North-Holland: Elsevier.

Chari, V.V. and Patrick J. Kehoe (2006), 'Modern macroeconomics in practice: how theory is shaping policy', *Journal of Economic Perspectives*, **20**(4), 3–28.

Chari, V.V., Larry Jones and Ramón Marimón (1994), 'On the economics of split voting in representative democracies', paper presented at the Conference on Political Economy, Mass, New York University.

Chhibber, Ajay (2006a), 'Effectiveness of policies and reforms', in Ajay Chhibber, R. Kyle Peters and Barbara J. Yale (eds), *Reform & Growth: Evaluating the World Bank Experience*, New Brunswick and London: Transaction Publishers.

Chhibber, Ajay (2006b), 'Overview', in Ajay Chhibber, R. Kyle Peters, and Barbara J. Yale (eds), *Reform & Growth: Evaluating the World Bank Experience*, New Brunswick and London: Transactions Publishers.

Claessens, Stijn (2005), 'Theories of currency and banking crises: a literature review', in Asian Development Bank (ed.), *Early Warning Systems for Financial Crises*, Basingstoke: Palgrave Macmillan.

Clavijo, Sergio (2000), 'Central banking and macroeconomic coordination: the case of Colombia', *Borradores de Economía*, No. 159, Banco de la República, Bogotá, Colombia.

Clavijo, Sergio (2001), 'Fallos y fallas económicas de las altas cortes: el caso de Colombia 1991–2000', *Borradores de Economía*, No. 173, Banco de la República, Bogotá, Colombia.

Clavijo, Sergio (2002), 'Política monetaria y cambiaria en Colombia: Progresos y desafíos 1991–2002', *Borradores de Economía*, No. 201, Banco de la República, Bogotá, Colombia.

Clavijo, Sergio (2004a), 'Descifrando la nueva corte constitucional', Bogotá, Colombia: Alfaomega.

Clavijo, Sergio (2004b), 'Monetary and exchange rate policies in Colombia: progress and challenges', *IMF Working Paper No. 04/166*, September, Washington, DC: International Monetary Fund, IMF.

Clavijo, Sergio (2004c), 'Requisitos para la estabilidad fiscal: un balance en la agenda', *Revista del Banco de la República*, **LXXVII**(919), May, Bogotá, Colombia.

Clavijo, Sergio (2006), *ANIF Informe Semanal*, June, ISSN 1794–2626, Bogotá, Colombia.

Clements, Benedict, Christopher Faircloth and Marijn Verhoeven (2007), 'Public expenditure in Latin America: trends and key policy issues', *IMF Working Paper No. 07/21*, Washington, DC: International Monetary Fund, IMF.

Clements, Benedict, Sanjeev Gupta and Gabriela Inchauste (2004), 'Fiscal policy for development: an overview', in Sanjeev Gupta, Benedict Clements and Gabriela Inchauste (eds), *Helping Countries Develop: The Role of Fiscal Policy*, Washington, DC: International Monetary Fund, IMF.

Cline, William R. (2003), 'The role of the private sector in resolving financial crises in emerging markets', in Martin Feldstein (ed.), *Economic and Financial Crises in Emerging Market Economies*, Chicago: The University of Chicago Press.

Coase, Ronald (1937), *The Nature of the Firm*, Economica N.S. 4, pp. 386–405. Reprinted in Oliver E. Williamson and Sidney Winter (eds) (1991), *The Nature of the Firm: Origins, Evolution, Development*, New York: Oxford University Press, pp. 18–33.

Coase, Ronald (1960), 'The problem of social cost', *Journal of Law and Economics*, **3**(October), 1–44.

Coase, Ronald (1994), 'The institutional structure of production', *Essays on Economics and Economists*, Chicago and London: The University of Chicago Press.

Coeymans, Juan Eduardo (1992), 'Productividad, salarios y empleo en la economía Chilena: un enfoque en la oferta agregada', en *Cuadernos de Economía*, **29**(27), 229–63, August.

Coeymans, Juan Eduardo (1999a), 'Ciclos y crecimiento sostenible a mediano plazo en la economía Chilena', *Cuadernos de Economía*, **36**(107), 545–96, April.

Coeymans, Juan Eduardo (1999b), 'Determinantes de la productividad en Chile: 1961–1997', *Cuadernos de Economía*, **36**(107), 597–637, April.

Coeymans, Juan Eduardo and Yair Mundlak (1993), *Sectoral Growth in Chile*, Research Report No. 95, Washington, DC: International Food Policy Research Institute.

Cole, Harold L., Lee E. Ohanian, Alvaro Riascos and James A. Schmitz Jr (2004), 'Latin America in the rearview mirror', *Research Department Staff Report 351*, Federal Reserve Bank of Minneapolis, November.

Collyns, Charles V. and Russell G. Kincaid (2003), *Managing Financial Crises: Recent Experience and Lessons for Latin America*, IMF Occasional Paper No. 217, Washington, DC: International Monetary Fund, IMF.

Conway, Patrick (2005), 'Monetary and exchange rate policy reforms', in Aline Coudouel and Stefano Paternostro (eds), *Analyzing the Distributional Impact of Reforms*, Washington, DC: The World Bank.

Cooper, Richard (1988), 'To coordinate or not to coordinate?', in N. Fieleke (ed.), *International Payments Imbalances in the 1980s*, Federal Reserve Bank of Boston.

Corbo, Vittorio and Klaus Schmidt-Hebbel (2001), 'Inflation targeting in Latin America', *Working Papers No. 105*, September, Santiago de Chile: Central Bank of Chile,

Corbo, Vittorio, Leonardo Hernández and Fernando Parro (2005), 'Institutions, economic policies and growth: lessons from the Chilean experience', *Working Paper No. 317*, April, Santiago de Chile: Central Bank of Chile.

Córdoba, Juan Pablo (1997), 'Ajuste fiscal: Cuando y cómo?', *Debates de Coyuntura Económica*, Fundación para la Educación Superior y el Desarrollo, FEDESARROLLO, y Fondo Social, Junio.

Cortés, H. (1984), 'Lecciones del pasado: recesiones económicas en Chile: 1926–1982', *Cuadernos de Economía*, **21**(63), 137–68, August.

Cournot, Augustin (1897), *Researches into the Mathematical Principles of the Theory of Wealth*, trans. Nathaniel T. Bacon, New York: Macmillan, especially chap. VII, pp. 79–90.

Cukierman, Alex and Mariano Tommasi (1998), 'When does it take a Nixon to go to China?', *American Economic Review*, **88**(1), 180–97.

Cukierman, Alex, S. Webb and B. Neyapti (1992), 'Measuring the independence of central banks and its effects on policy outcomes', *World Bank Economic Review*, **6**(3), 353–98.

De Gregorio, José (1992), 'Comentarios al Artículo de Roque B. Fernandez', in Rudiger Dornbusch and Sebastián Edwards (eds), *Macroeconomía del Populismo en la América Latina*, Fondo de Cultura Económica México.

De Gregorio, José (2004), 'Economic growth in Chile: evidence, sources and prospects', *Working Paper No. 298*, December, Santiago de Chile: Central Bank of Chile.

De la Torre, Augusto and Sergio Schmukler (2004), 'Developments in capital markets', *Whither Latin American Capital Markets?*, October, Office of the Chief Economist Latin America and the Caribbean Region, The World Bank.

De Larosiere, Jacques (2004), 'How should the IMF be reshaped?', *Finance and Development*, September, Washington, DC: International Monetary Fund, IMF.

Debreu, G. (1959), *The Theory of Value*, New York: John Wiley & Sons.

Debrun, Xavier and Manmohan Kumar (2007), 'The discipline-enhancing role of fiscal institutions: theory and empirical evidence', *IMF Working Paper No. 171*, WP 07/171, Washington, DC: International Monetary Fund, IMF.

della Paolera, Gerardo and Ezequiel Gallo (2003), 'Epilogue: the Argentine puzzle', in Gerardo della Paolera and Alan M. Taylor (eds), *A New Economic History of Argentina*, New York: Cambridge University Press.

della Paolera, Gerardo and Alan M. Taylor (2003), 'Introduction', in Gerardo della Paolera and Alan M. Taylor (eds), *A New Economic History of Argentina*, New York: Cambridge University Press.

della Paolera, Gerardo, Maria Alejandra Irigoin and Carlos G. Bózzoli (2003), 'Passing the buck: monetary and fiscal policies', in Gerardo della Paolera and Alan M. Taylor (eds), *A New Economic History of Argentina*, New York: Cambridge University Press.

Dervis, Kemal (2006), 'Effectiveness of policies and reforms', in Ajay Chhibber, R. Kyle Peters and Barbara J. Yale (eds), *Reform & Growth: Evaluating the World Bank Experience*, New Brunswick and London: Transaction Publishers.

Di Tella, Rafael and Robert MacCulloch (2006), 'Some uses of happiness data in economics', *Journal of Economic Perspectives*, **20**(1), 25–46.

Dixit, Avinash (1996), *The Making of Economic Policy: A Transaction-Cost Politics Perspective*, Cambridge, MA: MIT Press.

Dixit, Avinash (2004), *Lawlessness and Economics: Alternative Modes of Governance*, Princeton, NJ and Oxford: Princeton University Press.

Dixit, Avinash (2006), 'Evaluating recipes for development success', *Policy Research Working Paper 3859*, World Bank.

Dominguez, Kathryn M.E. and Linda L. Tesar (2005), 'International borrowing and macroeconomic performance in Argentina', *NBER Working Paper No. 11353*, Cambridge: National Bureau of Economic Research, NBER.

Dornbusch, Rudiger and Sebastian Edwards (eds) (1991), *The Macroeconomics of Populism in Latin America*, Chicago: University of Chicago Press.

Drazen, Allan (2000), *Political Economy in Macroeconomics*, Princeton, NJ: Princeton University Press.

Drazen, Allan and William Easterly (1999), 'Do crises induce reform? Simple empirical tests of conventional wisdom', Mimeo, University of Maryland and World Bank.

Easterlin, Richard (1974), 'Does economic growth improve the human lot? Some empirical evidence', in P. David and M. Reder (eds), *Nations and Households in Economic Growth: Essays in Honour of Moses Abramovitz*, New York: Academic Press.

Easterly, William (1999), 'When is fiscal adjustment an illusion?', *Economic Policy No. 28*, April, pp. 57–86.

Easterly, William (2001), *The Elusive Quest for Growth: Economists' Adventures and Misadventures in the Tropics*, Cambridge, MA: MIT Press.

Echabarria, Juan José and Maria Angelica Arbelaez (2005), 'Tasa de cambio y crecimiento económico en Colombia durante la ultima década', *Borradores de Economía*, No. 338, Banco de la República, Bogotá, Colombia.

Echabarria, Juan José, Diego Vasquez and Mauricio Villamizar (2005), 'La tasa de cambio real en Colombia: muy lejos del equilibrio?', *Borradores de Economía*, No. 337, Banco de la República, Bogotá, Colombia.

Echeverry, Juan Carlos (1999), 'La recesión de fin de siglo en Colombia: flujos, balance y política anticíclica', *Revista Planeación y Desarrollo, Estudios Macroeconómicos*, **30**(2), April–June, Departamento Nacional de Planeación, DNP.

Echeverry, Juan Carlos (2002), 'La recesión de fin de siglo', *Las Claves del Futuro: Economía y Conflicto en Colombia*, Bogotá, Colombia: Editorial Oveja Negra.

Echeverry, Juan Carlos (2005), 'Los devaluadores', *El Tiempo*, 4 March, Bogotá, Colombia.

Echeverry, Juan Carlos (2006), 'El conflicto entre constitución y economía es exagerado', *Ambito Jurídico*, 19 June–2 July, p. 29.

Echeverry, Juan Carlos, Andrés Escobar and Mauricio Santa Maria (2002), 'Tendencia, ciclos y distribución del Ingreso en Colombia: una critica al concepto de modelo de desarrollo', *Archivos de Economía*, No. 186, Bogotá, Colombia: Departamento Nacional de Planeación, DNP.

Echeverry, Juan Carlos, Leopoldo Fergusson and Pablo Querubín (2003), 'La batalla política por el presupuesto de la nación: inflexibilidades o supervivencia fiscal', *Documentos CEDE No. 1*, ISSN 1657-5334, Universidad de los Andes, Facultad de Economía, Bogotá, Colombia: Centro de Estudios sobre Desarrollo Económico, CEDE.

The Economist (2001), 'Does inequality matter?', 16–22 June.

The Economist (2002), "Of shocks and horrors', 28 September–4 October.

The Economist (2004), 'Becoming a serious country', 5–11 June.

The Economist (2005), 'Economics focus: war games', 15–21 October.

The Economist (2006a), 'Economic focus', 20–26 May.

The Economist (2006b), 'Love Lula if you're poor, worry if you're not', Special Report Brazil, 30 September–6 October.

The Economist (2006c), 'Winds of change', 4–10 November.

The Economist (2006d), 'Inverted yield curves', 7–13 January.

Edison, Hali (2003), 'Testing the links', *Finance & Development*, June, Washington, DC: International Monetary Fund, IMF.

Edwards, Sebastian (1995), *Crisis and Reform in Latin America: From Despair to Hope*, Washington, DC: The World Bank.

Edwards, Sebastian (2003), 'Introduction', *Argentina: Crisis, Instituciones y Crecimiento*, Conferencias FIEL 2003, 40 Aniversario, Tomo 1, Buenos Aires, Argentina: Fundación de Investigaciones Económicas Latinoamericanas, FIEL.

Edwards, Sebastian (2007), 'Crises and growth: a Latin American perspective', *NBER Working Paper No. 13019*, Cambridge, MA: National Bureau of Economic Research, NBER.

Eichengreen, Barry and Alan M. Taylor (2003), 'The monetary implications of a free trade area of the Americas', University of California, Berkeley, Mimeo, March.

Eichengreen, Barry, Ricardo Hausmann and Ugo Paniza (2003), 'Currency mismatches, debt intolerance and original sin: why they are not the same and why it matters', *NBER Working Paper No. 10036*, National Bureau of Economic Research, NBER.

Elson, Anthony (2006), 'What happened?', *Finance & Development*, June, **43**(2), Washington, DC: International Monetary Fund, IMF.

Elster, Jon (1978), *Logic and Society: Contradictions and Possible Worlds*, New York: Wiley.

Elster, Jon (2000), *Ulysses Unbound*, New York and Cambridge: Cambridge University Press.

Engerman, Stanley L. and Kenneth L. Sokoloff (1997), 'Factor endowments, institutions, and differential paths of growth among new world economies', in Stephen Haber (ed.), *How Latin America Fell Behind*, Stanford, CA: Stanford University Press.

Engerman, Stanley L. and Kenneth L. Sokoloff (2000), 'Institutions, factor endowments, and paths of development in the new world', *Journal of Economic Perspectives*, **14**(3), 217–32.

Engerman, Stanley L. and Kenneth L. Sokoloff (2002), 'Factor endowments, inequality, and paths of development among new world economics', *Economía*, **3**: 41–109.

Escobar, Andrés (2005), 'Los ciclos externos en Colombia', *Coyuntura Económica*, Segundo Semestre, Fundación para la Educación Superior y el Desarrollo, FEDESARROLLO, Bogotá, Colombia.

Eslava, Marcela (2006), 'Political influences on monetary and fiscal policy', Ph.D. Dissertation, University of Maryland.

Espinoza-Vega, Marco A. and Steven Phillips (2004), 'The role of institutions in Chile', in E. Kalter (ed.), *Chile: Institutions and Policies Underpinning Stability and Growth*, Washington, DC: International Monetary Fund, IMF.

Esteban, Joan and Ray Debraj (2006), 'Inequality, lobbying, and resource allocation', *American Economic Review*, **96**(1), 257–79.

Eyzaguirre, Nicolas (2004), 'Estado de la hacienda pública', Ministerio de Hacienda, Santiago, Chile.

Favero, Carlo A. and Francesco Giavazzi (2004), 'Inflation targeting and debt: lessons from Brazil', *NBER Working Paper No. 10390*, Cambridge, MA: National Bureau of Economic Research, NBER.

Feeny, David (1993), 'The demand for and supply of institutional arrangements', in Vincent Ostrom, David Feeny and Hartmut Picht (eds), *Rethinking Institutional Analysis and Development*, San Francisco, California: Institute for Contemporary Studies.

Feinstein, Osvaldo and Rema N. Balasundaram (2003), 'Evolution of OED's evaluation partnerships', in Patrick G. Grasso, Sulaiman S. Wasty and Rachel V. Weaving (eds), *World Bank Operations Evaluation Department: the First 30 Years*, Washington, DC: The World Bank.

Feldstein, Martin (1979), 'The welfare cost of permanent inflation and optimal short run economic policy', *Journal of Political Economy*, **87**(4).

Feldstein, Martin (2002), 'Argentina's fall: lessons from the latest financial crisis', *Foreign Affairs*, **81**(2), (March/April), 8–14.

Feldstein, Martin (2003), 'Economic and financial crises in emerging market economies', National Bureau of Economic Research, *NBER Working Paper No. 8837*, edited by Martin Feldstein, Chicago and London: The University of Chicago Press.

Ferguson, Niall (2001), 'Introduction', *The Cash Nexus: Money and Power in the Modern World, 1700–2000*, New York: Basic Books.

Fernández, Roque (2004), *Argentina Crisis, Instituciones y Crecimiento*, Conferencias FIEL 2003, 40 Aniversario, Tomo 1, Buenos Aires, Argentina: Fundación de Investigaciones Económicas Latino-americanas.

Fernández, R. Javier (2006), 'La descolgada de la DTF', *Prospectiva Económica y Financiera*, No. 567, Bogotá, Colombia.

Ferranti, David de, Guillermo E. Perry, Francisco H.G. Ferreira and Michael Walton (2004), *Inequality in Latin America: Breaking with History?*, Washington, DC: The World Bank.

Ffrench-Davis, Ricardo (2005), 'Reformas financieras y desarrollo', *Reformas para América Latina Después del Fundamentalismo Neoliberal*, Argentina: Siglo veintiuno editores Argentina S.A.

Fiess, Norbert (2005), 'Chile's fiscal rule', in Craig Burnside (ed.), *Fiscal Sustainability in Theory and Practice: A Handbook*, Washington, DC: The World Bank.

Fischer, Stanley (2000), 'Opening remarks by Stanley Fischer, Acting Managing Director', March, Washington, DC: International Monetary Fund, IMF.

Fischer, Stanley (2004), *IMF Essays from a Time of Crisis*, Cambridge, MA: MIT Press.

Fiszbein, Ariel and Pamela Lowden (1999), 'A partnerships-based approach to poverty reduction: an empirical exploration', in *Working Together for a Change: Government, Civic and Business Partnerships for Poverty Reduction in Latin America*, Economic Department Institutions, Washington, DC: The World Bank.

Fontaine, Ernesto (1997), 'Project evaluation training and public investment in Chile', *American Economic Review*, **87**(2), 63–7.

Fontaine, Aldunate Arturo (1988), *Los Economistas y el Presidente Pinochet*, Santiago de Chile: Zig-Zag.

Foxley, Alejandro (2003), 'Development lessons of the 1990s: Chile', paper presented at the World Bank Conference Series, 'Practitioners of development', Washington, DC.

Foxley, Alejandro and Claudio Sapelli (1999), 'Chile's political economy in the 1990s: some governance issues', in G. Perry and D. Leipziger (eds), *Chile: Recent Policy Lessons and Emerging Challenges*, Washington, DC: The World Bank.

Fraga, Arminio (2000), 'Monetary policy during the transition to a floating exchange rate: Brazil's recent experience', *Finance & Development*, March, Washington, DC: International Monetary Fund, IMF.

Fraga, Arminio (2004), 'Latin America since the 1990s: rising from the sickbed?', *Journal of Economic Perspectives*, **18**(2), 89–106.

Fraga, Arminio, Ilan Goldfajn and André Minella (2003), 'Inflation targeting in emerging market economies', *NBER Working Paper No. 10019*, Cambridge, MA: National Bureau of Economic Research, NBER.

Frenkel, Roberto (2004), 'Real exchange rate and employment in Argentina, Brazil, Chile and Mexico', Principal Researcher Associate at the Centro de Estudios de Estado y Sociedad (CEDES) and Professor at the Universidad de Buenos Aires, draft 24 August.

Friedman, Milton (1953), *Essays in Positive Economics*, Chicago: University of Chicago Press.

Friedman, Milton (1969), 'The optimum quantity of money', *The Optimum Quantity of Money and Other Essays*, Chicago: Aldine, pp. 1–50.

Galiani, Sebastián, Daniel Heymann and Mariano Tommasi (2002), 'Missed expectations: the Argentine convertibility', December, CEPAL, Universidad de Buenos Aires, Universidad de San Andres and CEDI, Buenos Aires, Argentina.

Galindo, Arturo, Alejandro Micco and Ugo Panizza (2007), 'Two decades of financial reforms', in Eduardo Lora (ed.), *The State of State Reform in Latin America*, Washington, DC: Inter-American Development Bank and Stanford University Press.

Garnier, Leonardo and Laura Cristina Blanco (2006), 'Costa Rica: un país subdesarrollado casi exitoso', San José, Costa Rica.

Garnier, Leonardo, Roberto Hidalgo, Guillermo Monge and Juan Diego Trejos (1991), *Costa Rica: Entre la Ilusión y la Desesperanza: Una Alternativa para el Desarrollo*, San José, Costa Rica: Editorial Guayacán.

Gavin, Michael and Ricardo Hausmann (1996), 'The roots of banking crises: the macroeconomic context', in Ricardo Hausmann and Liliana Rojas-Suarez (eds), *Banking Crises in Latin America*, Baltimore, MD: Inter-American Development Bank, IDB, and Johns Hopkins University Press.

Gavin, Michael and Roberto Perotti (1997), 'Fiscal policy in Latin America', *Macroeconomics Annual 1997*, National Bureau of Economic Research, NBER, Cambridge, MA and London: MIT Press.

Gavin, Michael, Ricardo Hausmann, Roberto Perotti and Ernesto Talvi (1996), 'Managing fiscal policy in Latin America and the Caribbean: volatility, procyclicality and limited creditworthiness', *Working Paper No. 326*, March, Inter-American Development Bank, IDB.

Gaviria, Alejandro (2002), *Los que Suben y Los que Bajan: Educación y Movilidad Social en Colombia*, Bogotá, Colombia: Fundación para la Educación Superior y el Desarrollo, FEDESARROLLO, and Alfaomega Colombia S.A.

Gaviria, Alejandro (2004), 'Del romanticismo al realismo social: lecciones de la década del 90', *Documentos CEDE*, No. 21, Bogotá, Colombia: Centro de Estudios sobre Desarrollo Económico, CEDE.

Gaviria, Alejandro (2006), 'Movilidad social y preferencias por redistribución en América Latina', *Documentos CEDE*, No. 3, Facultad de Economía, Universidad de los Andes, Bogotá, Colombia: Centro de Estudios sobre Desarrollo Económico, CEDE.

Gaviria, Cesar (1994), 'Prologo', in Rudy Hommes, Armando Montenegro and Pablo Roda (eds), *Una Apertura Hacia el Futuro*, Bogotá, Colombia: Tercer Mundo Editores.

Giambiagi, Fabio (2004), 'A agenda fiscal', in Fabio Giambiagi, José Guilherme Reis and André Urani (eds), *Reformas no Brasil: Balanco e Agenda*, Rio de Janeiro: Editora Nova Fronteira.

Giambiagi, Fabio (2006), 'A politica fiscal do goberno Lula em perspectiva historica: qual e o limite para o aumento do gasto publico?', *Revista do Planeamento*, IPEA.

Glaeser, Edward L. (2005), 'Inequality', *NBER Working Paper No. 11511*, June, Cambridge, MA: National Bureau of Economic Research, NBER.

Glaeser, Edward L., Rafael La Porta, Florencio López-de-Silanes and Andrei Shleifer (2004), 'Do institutions cause growth?', *NBER Working Paper No. 10568*, Cambridge, MA: National Bureau of Economic Research, NBER.

Golding, William (1954), *Lord of the Flies*, Wideview/Perigee Books are published by the Putnam Publishing Group.

Goldstein, Morris (2005), 'Predicting financial crisis: an overview', in Asian Development Bank, *Early Warning Systems for Financial Crisis*, Basingstoke: Palgrave Macmillan.

Goldstein, Morris (2006), 'Currency manipulation and enforcing the rules of the international monetary system', in Edwin M. Truman (ed.), *Reforming the IMF for the 21st Century*, Washington, DC: Institute for International Economics.

Goldstein, Morris, Graciela L. Kaminsky and Carmen M. Reinhart (2000), *Assessing Financial Vulnerability: An Early Warning System for Emerging Markets*, Washington, DC: Institute for International Economics.

Gómez, Javier Guillermo (2006), 'La política monetaria en Colombia', *Revista del Banco de la República*, **LXXIX**(940), June, Bogotá, Colombia.

González, Jorge Iván (1998), 'Arrow: la elección, los valores y la ideología del mercado', *Cuadernos de Economía No. 28*, Bogotá, Colombia: Universidad Nacional de Colombia.

González, Jorge Iván (2003), 'La volatilidad acentúa la vulnerabilidad', *Innovar Revista de Ciencias Administrativas y Sociales*, Facultad de Ciencias Económicas, January–June, No. 21, Bogotá, Colombia: Universidad Nacional de Colombia.

González, Jorge Iván (2004), 'La dicotomia micro-macro no es pertinente', *Revista de Economía Institucional*, **6**(11), Bogotá, Colombia: Universidad Externado de Colombia.

González, Jorge Iván and Ricardo Bonilla González (2006), 'Bien-estar y macroeconomía 2002–2006', *El Tiempo*, 2 July, p. 8; for a response Juan Mauricio Ramirez (2006), *El Tiempo*, 30 June, 2006, Bogotá, Colombia.

González, G. Andrés, Luis Fernando Melo V and Carlos Esteban Posada (2006), 'Inflación y dinero en Colombia: otro modelo P-estrella', (Figure 4) *Borradores de Economía*, No. 418, Banco de la República, Bogotá Colombia.

Goodfriend, Marvin (2005), 'Inflation targeting in the United States?', in Ben S. Bernanke and Michael Woodford (eds), *The Inflation-Targeting Debate*, National Bureau of Economic Research, NBER.

Graham, Carol and Moises Naim (1998), 'The political economy of institutional reform in Latin America', in Nancy Birdsall et al. (eds), *Beyond Trade-Offs: Market Reforms and Equitable Growth in Latin America*, Washington: Brookings Institution Press.

Greif, Avner (1998), 'Historical and comparative institutional analysis', *American Economic Review*, **88**(2), 80–84.

Griffith-Jones, Stephany and José Antonio Ocampo (1998), *What Progress on International Financial Reform? Why so Limited?*, Prepared for the Expert Group on Development Issues, Sweden.

Grondona, Mariano (2003), *Argentina Crisis, Instituciones y Crecimiento*, Conferencias FIEL 2003, 40 Aniversario, Tomo 1, Buenos Aires, Argentina: Fundación de Investigaciones Económicas Latinoamericanas.

Guidotti, Pablo E. and Carlos A. Rodríguez (1992), 'Dollarization in Latin America: Gresham's Law in reverse?', *IMF Staff Papers*, **39**(3), September, International Monetary Fund, IMF.

Guidotti, Pablo E. (2005), 'Argentina's fiscal policy in the 1990s: a tale of skeletons and sudden stops', Universidad Torcuato Di Tella, March.

Gutiérrez, Francisco de Paula (2005a), 'Reflexiones sobre política económica para el 2006', Seminario ECONOÁNALISIS 7 December, San José, Costa Rica.

Gutiérrez, Francisco de Paula (2005b), 'Áreas prioritarias de acción', in Grettel C. López and Reinaldo A. Herrera (eds), *Volatilidad y*

Vulnerabilidad: El Caso de Costa Rica, Veinte Años (1984–2004) Sin Crisis, San José, Costa Rica: Academia de Centroamérica.

Hamman, Javier and Carlos E. Paredes (1991), 'The Peruvian economy: characteristics and trends', in Carlos E. Paredes and Jeffrey D. Sachs (eds), *Peru's Path to Recovery: A Plan for Economic Stabilization and Growth*, Washington, DC: The Brookings Institution.

Hands, D. Wade (2001), 'The breakdown of the received view within the philosophy of science', in D. Wade Hands (ed.), *Reflection Without Rules: Economic Methodology and Contemporary Science Theory*, Cambridge, UK: Cambridge University Press.

Harberger, Arnold C. (1993a), 'The search for relevance in economics', *American Economic Review*, **83**(2), 1–16.

Harberger, Arnold C. (1993b), 'Secrets of success: a handful of heroes', *American Economic Review*, **83**(2), 343–50.

Harberger, Arnold C. (1998), 'A vision of the growth process', *American Economic Review*, **88**(1), 1–32.

Harsanyi, John C. (1991), 'Value judgments', in John Eatwell, Murray Milgate and Peter Newman (eds), *The World of Economics*, New York, London: W.W. Norton.

Hausmann, Ricardo (2001), 'A way out for Argentina: the currency board cannot survive much longer', *Financial Times*, 30 October.

Hausmann, Ricardo and Michael Gavin (1996), 'Securing stability and growth in a shock-prone region: the policy challenge for Latin America', *Working Paper Series 315*, January, Washington, DC: Inter-American Development Bank.

Hausmann, Ricardo and Andrés Velasco (2002), 'Hard money's soft underbelly: understanding the Argentine crisis', 2 May, Brookings Trade Forum.

Hausmann, Ricardo, Ugo Panizza and Roberto Rigobon (2004), 'The long-run volatility puzzle of the real exchange rate', *NBER Working Paper No. 10751*, September, Cambridge: National Bureau of Economic Research, NBER.

Hausmann, Ricardo, Ugo Panizza and Ernesto Stein (2001), 'Why do countries float the way they float', *Journal of Development Economics*, **66**(2), 387–414.

Hausmann, Ricardo, Dani Rodrik and Andrés Velasco (2006), 'Getting the diagnosis right', *Finance & Development*, March, Washington, DC: International Monetary Fund, IMF.

Heilbroner, Robert and William Milberg (1995), *The Crisis of Vision in Modern Economic Thought*, Cambridge: Cambridge University Press.

Hernández, Gamarra Antonio (2003), *EL TIEMPO*, Lecturas Dominicales, 25 May, p. 3D, Bogotá, Colombia.

Hernández, Gamarra Antonio and L.B. Florez (1999), 'Aclaración de voto de los co-directores: sesión del 25 de Septiembre de 1999', *Revista del Banco de la República*, Bogotá, Colombia, October.

Hernández, Gamarra Antonio, Luis I. Lozano Espitia and Martha Misas Arango (2000), 'La disyuntiva de la deuda pública: pagar o sisar', *Economía Institucional*, No. 3, Segundo Semestre, Bogotá, Colombia: Universidad Externado de Colombia.

Hernández Correa, Gerardo (1999), 'The bank's autonomy and the constitutional court's ruling', unpublished internal memorandum, 6 August, by the Legal Department, Banco de la República, Bogotá, Colombia.

Herrera, Santiago (1994), 'Comentarios sobre la política fiscal 1990–1994', in Olga Lucia Acosta and Israel Fainboim Yaker (eds), *Las Reformas Económicas del Gobierno del Presidente Gaviria: Una Visión desde Adentro*, Bogotá, Colombia: Ministerio de Hacienda.

Heymann, Daniel (2004), 'Introduction', in *Argentina: Crisis, Instituciones y Crecimiento*, Conferencias FIEL 2003, 40 Aniversario, Tomo 1, Buenos Aires, Argentina: Fundación de Investigaciones Económicas Latinoamericanas, FIEL.

Hicks, John (1963), *The Theory of Wages*, London: St Martin's Press.

Hirschman, Albert O. (1973), 'Changing tolerance for inequality in development', *Quarterly Journal of Economics*, **LXXXVII**(4).

Hirschman, Albert O. (1981), 'The turn to authoritarianism in Latin America and the search for its economic determinants', *Essays in Trespassing Economics to Politics and Beyond*, Cambridge: Cambridge University Press.

Hirschman, Albert O. (1997), *The Passions and the Interests: Political Arguments for Capitalism before its Triumph*, Twentieth Anniversary Edition, Princeton, NJ: Princeton University Press.

Hoff, Karla and Joseph E. Stiglitz (2001), 'Modern economic theory and development', in Gerald M. Meier and Joseph E. Stiglitz (eds), *Frontiers of Development Economics: The Future in Perspective*, The World Bank and Oxford University Press, pp. 389–459.

Hofstetter, Marc (2005), 'Why have so many disinflations succeeded?', *Documentos CEDE*, ISSN 1657-5334, November, Bogotá, Colombia: Centro de Estudios sobre Desarrollo Económico, CEDE.

Holcombe, G. Randall (2000), 'Public choice and public finance', in William F. Shughart II and Laura Razzolini (eds), *The Elgar Companion to Public Choice*, Cheltenham, UK and Northampton, MA, USA: Edward Elgar Publishing.

Hommes, Rudolf (1995), 'El proyecto del gobierno y su evolución durante la constituyente', in Roberto Steiner (ed.), *La Autonomía del Banco de la República*, Bogotá, Colombia: TM Editores.

Hommes, Rudolf (2005), 'Una lección para tener en cuenta', *Portafolio*, 19 December, Bogotá, Colombia.

Hommes, Rudolf (2006), 'Ideas alternativas para pensar en grande', *El Tiempo*, 28 July, Bogotá, Colombia.

International Monetary Fund (IMF) (1998), 'Peru selected issues', SM/98/108/, 20 May, C-525, 0450, Washington, DC: International Monetary Fund, IMF.

International Monetary Fund (IMF) (1999), 'Overview', *Colombia: Selected Issues and Statistical Appendix*, IMF Staff Country Report No. 99/6, January, Washington, DC: International Monetary Fund, IMF.

International Monetary Fund (IMF) (2002), 'Staff report for the 2002 Article IV Consultation', Washington, DC: International Monetary Fund, IMF.

International Monetary Fund (IMF) (2003), 'Economic resilience with an exchange rate peg: the Barbados experience, 1985–2000', *IMF Working Paper No. 03/168*, DeLisle Worrell, Harold Codrington, Roland Craigwell and Kevin Greenidge, Washington, DC: International Monetary Fund, IMF.

International Monetary Fund (IMF) (2004a), 'The IMF and Argentina, 1991–2001', Evaluation Report, Independent Evaluation Office, Washington, DC: International Monetary Fund, IMF.

International Monetary Fund (IMF) (2004b), 'Executive summary', 'Staff report for Peru's 2004 Article IV Consultation, fourth review under the stand-by arrangement, and request for waiver of nonobservance of performance criterion', prepared by Western Hemisphere Department, 10 February

International Monetary Fund (IMF) (2004c), 'The IMF and Argentina, 1991–2001', Evaluation Report, Evaluation Office, Washington, DC: International Monetary Fund, IMF.

International Monetary Fund (IMF) (2004d), 'The role of institutions in Chile', Marco A. Espinoza-Vega and Steven Phillips, in Eliot Kalter, Steven Phillips, Marco A. Espinosa-Vega, Rodolfo Luzio, Mauricio Villafuerte and Manmohan Singh (eds), *Chile Institutions and Policies Underpinning Stability and Growth*, Washington, DC: International Monetary Fund, IMF.

International Monetary Fund (IMF) (2004e), 'Argentina and the IMF prior to 1991', *The IMF and Argentina, 1991–2001 Evaluation Report*, Independent Evaluation Office, Washington, DC: International Monetary Fund, IMF.

International Monetary Fund (IMF) (2004f), 'Staff report for Costa Rica's 2004 Article IV Consultation', September, IMF Country Report 04/298, Washington, DC: International Monetary Fund, IMF.

International Monetary Fund (IMF) (2005a), 'Argentina 2005 Article IV Consultation–Staff Report; Staff Supplement; Public Information Notice on the Executive Board Discussion; and Statement by the Executive Director for Argentina', IMF Country Report No. 05/236, July.

International Monetary Fund (IMF) (2005b), 'Letter of Intent (May 20th, 2005), Memorandum of Economic and Financial Policies, and Technical Memorandum of Understanding', Lima, Peru: International Monetary Fund, IMF.

International Monetary Fund (IMF) (2006), 'Public Information Notice (PIN) on the 2006 Article IV Consultation', Washington, DC: International Monetary Fund, IMF.

IPEA (2006), *Boletin de Cojuntura No. 72*, March, Brazil: Instituto de Pesquisa Economica Aplicada, IPEA.

Jiménez, R. Ronulfo (2004), 'La economía Costarricense durante el 2004', in Eduardo Lizano and Grettel López (eds), *La Economía Costarricense y la Evolución del Sistema Financiero en el 2004*, San José, Costa Rica: Academia de Centroamérica.

Jones, Mark A., Pablo Sanguinetti and Mariano Tommasi (1999), 'Politics, institutions, and public-sector spending in the Argentine provinces', in James M. Poterba and Jürgen von Hagen (eds), *Fiscal Institutions and Fiscal Performance*, Chicago and London: The University of Chicago Press.

Junguito, Roberto (1994), 'Comentarios' on Perry Guillermo, Eduardo Lora and Felipe de Barrera (1994), 'Cusiana y la política macro-económica', *Cusiana un Reto de Política Económica*, Bogotá, Colombia: Departamento Nacional de Planeación, DNP, and The World Bank.

Kahneman, Daniel and Amos Tversky (1979), 'Prospect theory: an analysis of decision under risk', *Econometrica*, **47**(2), 263–91.

Kahneman, Daniel and Amos Tversky (1986), 'Rational choice and the framing of decisions', in Robin M. Hogarth and Melvin W. Reder (eds), *Rational Choice: The Contrast between Economics and Psychology*, Chicago and London: The University of Chicago Press.

Kalmanovitz, Salomón (2001a), 'El Banco de la República como institución independiente', *Borradores de Economía*, No. 190, Bogotá, Colombia: Banco de la República.

Kalmanovitz, Salomón (2001b), *Las Instituciones y el Desarrollo Económico en Colombia*, Bogotá, Colombia: Editorial Norma.

Kalmanovitz, Salomón (2001c), 'Las consecuencias económicas de la corte constitucional', in *Las Instituciones y el Desarrollo Económico en Colombia*, Bogotá, Colombia: Grupo Editorial Norma.

Kalmanovitz, Salomón (2005), 'Interview', *El Tiempo*, Bogotá, Colombia, 24 January.

Kalmanovitz, Salomón (2007), 'Paños de agua', *El Espectador*, Bogotá, Colombia, 8 April.

Kaminsky, Graciela and Carmen Reinhart (1999), 'The twin crises: the causes of banking and balance of payments problems', *American Economic Review*, **89**(3), 473–500.

Kaminsky, Graciela, Saul Lizondo and Carmen M. Reinhart (1997), 'Leading indicators of currency crises', *IMF, Working Paper No. WP/97/79*, Washington, DC: International Monetary Fund.

Keefer, Philip and David Stasavage (2003), 'Checks and balances, private information, and the credibility of monetary commitments', in William T. Bernhard, J. Lawrence Broz and William Roberts Clark (eds), *The Political Economy of Monetary Institutions: An International Organization Reader*, Cambridge, MA and London: MIT Press.

Kenen, Peter B. (2005), 'Book reviews', *Finance and Development*, September, Washington, DC: International Monetary Fund.

Kiguel, Miguel A. (2002), 'Structural reforms in Argentina: success or failure?', *Comparative Economic Studies*, **44**(2), 83–102.

King, Mervyn (1997), 'Changes in UK monetary policy: rules and discretion in practice', *Journal of Monetary Economics*, **39**, 81–7.

Knight, Frank (1921), *Risk Uncertainty and Profit*, Boston: Houghton Mifflin.

Kochhar, Kalpana, Timothy Lane and Miguel Savastano (2003), 'Macroeconomic consequences of a financial crisis', in Charles Collyns and G. Russell Kincaid (eds), *Managing Financial Crises: Recent Experience and Lessons for Latin America*, Washington, DC: International Monetary Fund.

Konow, James (2003), 'Which is the fairest one of all? A positive analysis of justice theories', *Journal of Economic Literature*, **XLI**(4), 1188–239.

Krueger, Anne O. (1974), 'The political economy of the rent-seeking society', *American Economic Review*, June, pp. 291–303.

Krueger, Anne O. (2002), 'Crisis prevention and resolution: lessons from Argentina', National Bureau of Economic Research Conference, 'The Argentina Crisis', Cambridge, MA, 17 July.

Kuczynski, Pedro-Pablo (1990), 'Peru', in John Williamson (ed.), *Latin American Adjustment: How Much has Happened?* Washington, DC: Institute for International Economics.

Kuczynski, Pedro-Pablo (1997), *Democracia Bajo Presión Económica: El Primer Gobierno de Belaunde*, Lima: Ediciones Treinta y tres y Mosca Azul Editores.

Kugler, Maurice and Howard Rosenthal (2005), 'Checks and balances: an assessment of the institutional separation of political powers in Colombia', in Alberto Alesina (ed.), *Institutional Reforms*, Cambridge, MA: MIT Press.

Kuhn, Peter and Fernando Lozano (2006), 'The expanding workweek? Understanding trends in long work hours among US men, 1979–2004', *NBER Working Paper No. 11895*, National Bureau of Economic Research, NBER, July.

Kuhn, T.S. (1970), *The Structure of Scientific Revolutions*, Chicago: University of Chicago Press.

Lachman, Desmond (2006), 'How should IMF resources be expanded?', in Edwin M. Truman (ed.), *Reforming the IMF for the 21st Century*, Washington, DC: Institute for International Economics.

Laffont, Jean-Jacques and David Martimort (2002), *The Theory of Incentives: The Principal–Agent Model*, Princeton, NJ and Oxford: Princeton University Press.

Lago, Ricardo (1991), 'La ilusión de una redistribución por medio de la política macroeconómica: la experiencia heterodoxa del Perú', in Rudiger Dornbusch and Sebastián Edwards (eds), *Macroeconomía del Populismo en la América Latina*, National Bureau of Economic Research, NBER, Chicago and London: The University of Chicago Press.

Larrain, Felipe (ed.) (2000), *Capital Flows, Capital Controls and Currency Crisis*, Ann Arbor: The University of Michigan Press.

Lavagna, Roberto (2004), 'Statement to the Executive Board Members from the Governor for Argentina, his Excellency Roberto Lavagna', on the IEO Evaluation of the Role of the Fund in Argentina, 1991–2001, *Evaluation Report: The IMF and Argentina, 1991–2001*, Independent Evaluation Office, Washington, DC: International Monetary Fund.

Levy, Joaquín (2006), 'Comments on middle-income country programs: Brazil', in Ajay Chhibber, R. Kyle Peters and Barbara J. Yale (eds), *Reform and Growth: Evaluating the World Bank Experience*, New Jersey: Transaction Publishers.

Lindbeck, Assar (2006), 'Sustainable social spending', *International Tax and Public Finance*, **13**(4).

Lizano, Eduardo (1999), 'Why is it we have not done so bad and not so good either?', in Eduardo Lizano and Norberto Zuñiga (eds), *Evolución de la Economía de Costa Rica*, Documento No. 2, San José, Costa Rica: Academia de Centroamérica.

Lizano, Eduardo (2004), 'Introducción: el Banco Central y el Desarrollo Económico', in Eduardo Lizano and Grettel López (eds), *La Economía Costarricense y la Evolución del Sistema Financiero en el 2004*, San José, Costa Rica: Academia de Centroamérica.

Lizano, Eduardo and Norberto Zuñiga (1999), *Evolución de la Economía de Costa Rica durante 1983–1998*, Documento No. 2, San José, Costa Rica: Academia de Centroamérica.

Londoño, J.L. and M. Székely (2000), 'Persistent poverty and excess inequality: Latin America, 1970–1995', *Journal of Applied Economics*, **3**(1), 93–134.

López C., Hugo (2006), 'Imputación de ingresos y medición de la pobreza', *Un Periódico*, Universidad Nacional, 9 April, Bogotá, Colombia.

López, Martha (2006), 'Algunos criterios para evaluar una meta de inflación de largo plazo', *Revista del Banco de la República*, **LXXXIX**(940), February, Bogotá, Colombia.

Lora, T. Eduardo (2004), 'Los efectos sociales de las reformas estructurales de los noventas', *Coyuntura Social*, No. 30, June, Bogotá, Colombia: Fundación para la Educación Superior y el Desarrollo, FEDESARROLLO.

Lora, T. Eduardo (2005), 'Dos pasos adelante y uno atrás: 35 años de reformas estructurales en Colombia', *35 Años FEDESARROLLO*, Segundo Semestre de 2005, **XXXV**(2), Bogotá, Colombia: Editora Coyuntura Económica.

Lora, T. Eduardo (2007), 'State reform in Latin America: a silent revolution', in Eduardo Lora (ed.), *The State of State Reform in Latin America*, Inter-American Development Bank and Stanford University Press.

Lora, T. Eduardo and José Antonio Ocampo (1986), 'Política macroeconómica y distribución del ingreso en Colombia: 1980–1990', *Coyuntura Económica Análisis y Perspectivas de la Economía Colombiana*, **XVI**(3), October, Bogotá, Colombia: Fundación para la Educación Superior y el Desarrollo, FEDESARROLLO.

Loser, Claudio (2004), *Enemigos*, Buenos Aires: Grupo Editorial Norma.

Loser, Claudio and Martine Guerguil (2000), 'El largo camino hacia la estabilidad financiera', *Finanzas & Desarrollo*, March, Washington, DC: International Monetary Fund.

Lucas, Robert E., Jr (1976), 'Econometric policy evaluation: a critique', *Journal of Monetary Economics*, Supplementary Series, **1**(2), 19–46.

Lucas, Robert E., Jr (1990), 'Supply-side economics: an analytical review', *Oxford Economic Papers*, **42**, 293–316.

Lucas, Robert E., Jr (1996), 'Monetary neutrality', *Journal of Political Economy*, **104**(4), August, 661–82.

Lüders, Rolf (2005), '¿Podemos tener mayor estabilidad de precios y un fisco más eficiente?', *Administración y Economía No. 59*, Facultad de Ciencias Económicas y Administrativas Universidad Católica de Chile, Santiago de Chile.

Machinea, José Luis (2002), 'Currency crises: a practitioner's view', Brookings Trade Forum, May, Washington: Brookings Institution.

Machinea, José Luis (2004), 'Reestructuración de la deuda: nuevas propuestas para viejos problemas', in José Antonio Ocampo and Andras

Uthoff (eds), *Gobernabilidad e Integración Financiera: Ámbito Global y Regional*, Santiago, Chile: Comisión Económica para América Latina y el Caribe, CEPAL.

Maddison, Angus (1995), *Monitoring the World Economy*, Paris: Organisation for Economic Cooperation and Development, OECD.

McMillan, John and Pablo Zoido (2004), 'How to subvert democracy: Montesinos in Peru', *Journal of Economic Perspectives*, **18**(4), 69–72.

Magee, Stephen (1997), 'Endogenous protection: the empirical evidence', in Dennis C. Mueller (ed.), *Perspectives on Public Choice: A Handbook*, Cambridge, UK: Cambridge University Press.

Malan, Pedro (2005), 'Comment', on 'A half-century of development', by Richard N. Cooper and 'The evaluation of development thinking: theory and practice', by Gustav Ranis, *Lessons of Experience*, Annual World Bank Conference on Development Economics.

Malan, Pedro (2007), 'Committee Report on the Bretton Woods Institutions', Washington, DC: The World Bank, International Monetary Fund.

Mallaby, Sebastian (2005), 'Class matters', *Washington Post*, 14 November, p. A-21.

Mankiw, Gregory N. (1990), 'A quick refresher course in macroeconomics', *Journal of Economic Literature*, **XXVIII**(4), December.

Mankiw, Gregory N. (2006), 'The macroeconomist as scientist and engineer', *Journal of Economic Perspectives*, **20**(4), 29–46.

Manski, Charles F. (2003), 'Identification problems in the social sciences and everyday life', *Southern Economic Journal*, **70**(1), 11–21.

Marcel, Mario (1999), 'Effectiveness of the state and development: lessons from the Chilean experience', in Guillermo Perry and Danny M. Leipziger (eds), *Chile: Recent Policy Lessons and Emerging Challenges*, Washington, DC: The World Bank.

Marcel, Mario, Marcelo R. Tokman, Rodrigo P. Valdés and Paula S. Benavides (2001), 'Balance estructural: la base de la nueva regla de política fiscal Chilena', *Economía Chilena*, December, **4**(3).

Margo, Robert (2006), 'Review of *Economic Origins of Dictatorship and Democracy*, by Daron Acemoglu and James A. Robinson', *Journal of Economic History*, **66**(2), 532–4.

Marquez, José (2004), 'Costa Rica and El Salvador: finding the appropriate role for the public and private sectors in poverty reduction', paper presented at the 'Scaling Up Poverty Reduction: A Global Learning Process' Conference, Shanghai, 25–27 May, The World Bank.

Marshall, Alfred (1930), *Principles of Economics*, eighth edition, London: Macmillan.

Marulanda, Gómez Oscar (1999), *Economía Política del Manejo Macroeconómico en Colombia*, Universidad Jorge Tadeo Lozano, Colección Estudios de Economía, Bogotá, Colombia.

McCloskey, Donald (1991), 'Counterfactuals', in John Eatwell, Murray Milgate and Peter Newman (eds), *The World of Economics*, Hong Kong: The Macmillan Press Ltd.

Meisel, Adolfo (1996), 'Why no hyperinflation in Colombia?', *Borradores de Economía*, No. 54, Banco de la República, Bogotá, Colombia.

Meltzer, Allan H. (2005), 'Origins of the great inflation', *Federal Reserve Bank of St. Louis Review*, **87**(2), Part 2, March/April.

Meltzer, Allan H. and Charles I. Plosser (1993), 'Introduction', in Allan H. Meltzer and Charles I. Plosser (eds), *Carnegie-Rochester Conference Series on Public Policy*, **39**, December, Amsterdam: North Holland.

Ministerio de Economía y Finanzas (2005), 'Marco macro-económico mul-tianual 2006–2008', Lima, Peru: Ministerio de Economía y Finanzas.

Ministerio de Hacienda (2006), *Colombia is on the Way to Sustainable 5% Growth: How Vulnerable is the Recent Recovery?*, April, Bogotá, Colombia: Ministerio de Hacienda y Crédito Público.

Misas Arango, Martha and Enrique López Enciso (2001), 'Desequilibrios reales en Colombia', *Borradores de Economía*, No. 181, Banco de la República, Bogotá, Colombia.

Mishkin, Frederic S. (1996), 'Understanding financial crises: a developing country perspective', *NBER Working Paper No. 5600*, Cambridge, MA: National Bureau of Economic Research, NBER.

Mishkin, Frederic S. (2004), 'Can inflation targeting work in emerging market countries', Graduate School of Business, Columbia University and National Bureau of Economic Research, 'Festschrift in Honor of Guillermo A. Calvo', 15–16 April.

Mishkin, Frederic S. and Miguel A. Savastano (2001), 'Monetary policy strategies for Latin America', *Journal of Development Economies*, **66** (October), 415–44.

Mistri, Maurizio (2003), 'Procedural rationality and institutions: the production of norms by means of norms', *Constitutional Political Economy*, **14**(4).

Mokyr, Joel (2006), 'Economics and the biologists: a review of Geerat J. Vermeij's *Nature: An Economic History*', *Journal of Economic Literature*, **XLIV**, December, pp. 1005–13.

Molina, Carlos Gerardo, Eduardo Lora and Miguel Urrutia (1992), 'Un plan de desarrollo humano de largo plazo para Colombia', *Coyuntura Social: Gasto Social y Crecimiento*, Bogotá, Colombia: Fundación para la Educación Superior y el Desarrollo, FEDESAR-ROLLO.

Montenegro, Armando (1994), 'El sector privado y la reforma del estado', in Olga Lucía Acosta and Israel Fainboin (eds), *Las Reformas Económicas*, Bogotá, Colombia: Ministerio de Hacienda.

Montenegro, Armando (1995), *Economic Reforms in Colombia: Regulation and Deregulation, 1990–94*, Economic Development Institute of the World Bank, EDI, Working Papers No. 95-04, Washington, DC: The World Bank.

Montenegro, Armando (2007), 'Tigres de papel', *El Espectador*, 22–28 April, Bogotá, Colombia.

Montenegro, Armando and Rafael M. Rivas (2006), 'Las piezas del rompecabezas: Desigualdad, pobreza y crecimiento', *Ambito Juridico*, Bogotá, Colombia: LEGIS.

Montenegro, Santiago (2004), 'Retos y perspectiva de la evaluación y la información en Colombia', *Por qué Evaluar el Gasto Público?*, Seminario Internacional, Departamento Nacional de Planeación DNP, Banco Interamericano de Desarrollo BID, BIRF, Banco de la República, Bogotá, Colombia.

Montenegro, Santiago (2006), 'Geografía y modelo político', *Lecturas de Fin de Semana*, *El Tiempo*, 24 June, Bogotá, Colombia.

Montiel, Peter J. and Williams College (2005), 'A disinflation strategy for Costa Rica', Draft, November.

Montiel, Peter J. and Luis Servén (2006), 'Macroeconomic stability in developing countries: how much is enough?', *The World Bank Research Observer*, **21**(2).

Morande, Felipe L. and Matías G. Tapia (2002), 'Política cambiaria en Chile: el abandono de la banda y la experiencia de flotación', *Economía Chilena*, **5**(3), December.

Morgan, Mary S. (1990), *The History of Econometric Ideas: Historical Perspectives on Modern Economics*, New York: Cambridge University Press.

Morón, P. Eduardo and Juan F. Castro C. (2004), 'Desdolarizando la economía Peruana: un enfoque de portafolio', *Estudios Económicos No. 12*, Banco Central de Reserva del Perú, Consorcio de Investigación Económica y Social, December.

Mulligan, Casey B., Ricard Gil and Xavier Sala-i-Martin (2004), 'Do democracies have different public policies than nondemocracies', *Journal of Economic Perspectives*, **18**(1), 51–74.

Mussa, Michael (2002), *Argentina and the Fund: from triumph to tragedy*, Washington, DC: Institute for International Economics.

Mussa, Michael (2006), 'Reflections on the function and facilities for IMF lending', in Edwin M. Truman (ed.), *Reforming the IMF for the 21st Century*, Washington, DC: Institute for International Economics.

Naim, Moises (2000), 'Washington consensus or Washington confusion?', *Foreign Policy*, Spring.

Navajas, Fernando (2003), 'Introducción', *Argentina: Crisis, Instituciones y Crecimiento*, Conferencias FIEL 2003, 40 Aniversario, Tomo 1, Buenos Aires, Argentina: Fundación de Investigaciones Económicas Latinoamericanas.

Nelson, Richard R. and Sidney Winter (1982), *An Evolutionary Theory of Economic Change*, Cambridge: Belknap Press.

North, Douglass C. (1990), 'Institutions, economic theory and economic performance', in Douglass C. North, *Institutions, Institutional Change and Economic Performance*, New York: Cambridge University Press.

North, Douglass C. (1997), 'Cliometrics – 40 years later', *American Economic Review*, **87**(2), 412–14.

North, Douglass C., John Joseph Wallis and Barry R. Weingast (2006), 'A conceptual framework for interpreting recorded human history', *NBER Working Paper No. 12795*, National Bureau of Economic Research, NBER.

Nugent, Jeffrey (1998), 'Institutions, markets and development outcomes', in Robert Picciotto and Eduardo Wiesner (eds), *Evaluation and Development: The Institutional Dimension*, New Brunswick and London: Transaction Publishers.

Nuñez, Jairo, Juan Carlos Ramírez and Bibiana Tabeada (2006), 'Desigualdad de ingresos, esfuerzos y oportunidades: un estudio del caso Colombiano', *Documentos CEDE No. 11*, February, Bogotá, Colombia: Centro de Estudios sobre Desarrollo Económico, CEDE.

Nuñez, Jairo, Juan Carlos Ramírez and Laura Cuesta (2005), 'Determinantes de la pobreza en Colombia, 1996–2004', *Documento CEDE No. 60*, October, Bogotá, Colombia: Centro de Estudios sobre Desarrollo Económico, CEDE.

Ocampo, José Antonio (1989a), 'Ciclo cafetero y comportamiento macroeconómico en Colombia', *Coyuntura Económica*, **XIX**(3), 125–54.

Ocampo, José Antonio (1989b), 'Ciclo cafetero y comportamiento macroeconómico en Colombia', *Coyuntura Económica*, **XIX**(4), 147–83.

Ocampo, José Antonio (1991), 'Determinantes y perspectivas del crecimiento económico en el mediano plazo', in Eduardo Lora (ed.), *Apertura y Crecimiento: El Reto de los Noventa*, Tercer Mundo Editores.

Ocampo, José Antonio (2004a), 'Economía, conflicto y gobernabilidad en Colombia', *Entre la Reformas y el Conflicto: Economía y Polítice en Colombia*, Bogotá, Colombia: Grupo Editorial Norma.

Ocampo, José Antonio (2004b), 'Latin America's growth and equity frustrations during structural reforms', *Journal of Economic Perspectives*, **18**(2), 67–88.

Ocampo, José Antonio (2004c), 'Reforma del estado y desarrollo económico y social en Colombia', *Entre las Reformas y el Conflicto: Economía y Política en Colombia*, Bogotá, Colombia: Grupo Editorial Norma.

Ocampo, José Antonio (2005a), 'Por qué fue tan severa la crisis económica de fines de los 90s', *35 Años FEDESARROLLO*, Segundo Semestre de 2005, **XXXV**(2), Bogotá, Colombia: Editora Coyuntura Económica.

Ocampo, José Antonio (2005b), 'Executive summary', *The Inequality Predicament*, Report on the World Social Situation 2005, New York: United Nations.

Ocampo, José Antonio (2005c), 'A broad view of macroeconomic stability', *Economic & Social Affairs, Working Paper No. 1*, ST/ESA/DWP/1, October.

Ocampo, José Antonio (2005d), 'Overview', *World Economic and Social Survey 2005*, New York: United Nations; Department of Economic and Social Affairs, DESA.

Ocampo, José Antonio (2006), 'Expuestos a repetir la historia de los 90s', *Portafolio*, 20 October, Bogotá, Colombia.

Ocampo, José Antonio and Camilo Tovar (2000), 'Colombia in the classical era of inward-looking development, 1930–1974', in Enrique Cárdenas, José Antonio Campo and Rosemary Thorp (eds), *Industrialization and the State in Latin America: The Postwar Years; An Economic History of Twentieth-Century Latin America*, Volume 3, Basingstoke, UK and New York: Palgrave and St Martin's Press.

Ocampo, José Antonio, María José Pérez, Camilo Tovar and Francisco Javier Lasso (1998), 'Macroeconomía, ajuste estructural y equidad en Colombia, 1978–1996', in Olga Lucía Costa (ed.), *Coyuntura Social: Análisis y Perspectivas de Empleo Educación en Santafé de Bogotá Demografía Salud Evolución de la Reforma Pensional*, No. 18, May, Bogotá, Colombia: Fundación para la Educación Superior y el Desarrollo, FEDESARROLLO.

Ocampo, José Antonio, Fabio Jose Sanchez, Gustavo A. Hernandez and Maria Fernanda Prada (2004), 'Crecimiento de las exportaciones y sus efectos sobre el empleo, la desigualdad y la pobreza en Colombia' (Figure 5), *Documentos CEDE*, ISSN 1657-5334, February, Bogotá, Colombia: Centro de Estudios sobre Desarrollo Económico, CEDE.

Olson, Mancur (1965), *The Logic of Collective Action: Public Goods and the Theory of Groups*, Cambridge, MA: Harvard University Press.

Olson, Mancur (1971), *The Logic of Collective Action*, Cambridge, MA: Harvard University Press.

Olson, Mancur (1996), 'Distinguished lecture on economics in government: big bills left on the sidewalk: why some nations are rich, and others poor', *Journal of Economic Perspectives*, **10**(2), 3–24.

Ortiz, Guillermo (2002), 'Solving debt crisis', *The Financial Times*, 20 September.

Ostrom, Elinor (2000), 'Collective action and the evolution of social norms', *Journal of Economic Perspectives*, **14**(3), 137–58.

Ostrom, Elinor and James Walker (1997), 'Neither markets nor states: linking transformation processes in collective action arenas', in Dennis C. Mueller (ed.), *Perspectives on Public Choice: A Handbook*, New York: Cambridge University Press.

Paredes, Carlos E. (1991), 'Epilogue: in the aftermath of hyperinflation', in Carlos E. Paredes and Jeffrey D. Sachs (eds), *Peru's Path to Recovery: A Plan for Economic Stabilization and Growth*, Washington, DC: The Brookings Institution.

Partow, Zeinab (2003), 'Macroeconomic and fiscal frameworks', in Marcelo Giugale, Oliver Lafourcade and Conny Luff (eds), *Colombia: The Economic Foundation for Peace*, Washington, DC: The World Bank.

Perotti, Roberto (1993), 'Political equilibrium, income distribution, and growth', *Review of Economic Studies*, September.

Perotti, Roberto (2005), 'Public spending on social protection in Colombia: analysis and proposals', in Alberto Alesina (ed.), *Institutional Reforms: The Case of Colombia*, Cambridge, MA: MIT Press.

Perry, Guillermo (2005), 'Finanzas públicas: evolución y agenda pendiente', *35 Años FEDESARROLLO*, Segundo Semestre de 2005, **XXXV**(2), Bogotá, Colombia: Editora Coyuntura Económica.

Perry, Guillermo (2006), 'La constitución del 91 qué funcionó y qué no', *El Tiempo*, 23 July.

Perry, Guillermo and Luis Servén (2002), 'The anatomy of a multiple crisis: why was Argentina special and what can we learn from it?', Washington, DC: The World Bank.

Perry, Guillermo, Omar S. Arias, J. Humberto López, William F. Maloney and Luis Servén (2006), *Poverty Reduction and Growth: Virtuous and Vicious Circles*, Washington, DC: The World Bank.

Persson, Torsten and Guido Tabellini (1994), 'Is inequality harmful for growth?', *American Economic Review*, **84**(3), 600–621.

Persson, Torsten and Guido Tabellini (1999), 'The size and the scope of government: comparative politics with rational politicians, 1998 Alfred Marshall Lecture', *European Economic Review*, April (43), 699–735.

Persson, Torsten and Guido Tabellini (2000), *Political Economics: Explaining Economic Policy*, Cambridge, MA: MIT Press.

Persson, Torsten and Guido Tabellini (2002), 'Foreword', *Political Economics: Explaining Economic Policy*, Cambridge, MA: MIT Press.

Persson, Torsten and Guido Tabellini (2003), *The Economic Effects of Constitutions: What do the Data Say?*, Cambridge, MA: MIT Press.

Persson, Torsten and Guido Tabellini (2004a), 'Constitution and economic policy', *Journal of Economic Perspectives*, **18**(1), 75–98.

Persson, Torsten and Guido Tabellini (2004b), 'Constitutional rules and fiscal policy outcomes', *American Economic Review*, **94**(1), 25–45.

Persson, Torsten and Guido Tabellini (2006), 'Democracy and development: the devil in the details', *American Economic Review*, Proceedings, **96**(2), 319–24.

Persson, Torsten, Gérard Roland and Guido Tabellini (1997), 'Separation of powers and political accountability', *Quarterly Journal of Economics*, **112**(4), 1163–202.

Persson, Torsten, Gérard Roland and Guido Tabellini (2000), 'Comparative politics and public finance', *Journal of Political Economy*, **108**(6), 1121–61.

Peters, R. Kyle (2006), 'Lessons from country program evaluations', in Ajay Chhibber, R. Kyle Peters and Barbara J. Yale (eds), *Reform & Growth: Evaluating the World Bank Experience*, New Brunswick and London: Transaction Publishers.

Petrei, Humberto (1997), *Presupuesto y Control: Pautas de Reforma para América Latina*, Washington, DC: Banco Interamericano de Desarrollo, BID.

Phelps, Edmund S. (1968), 'Money-wage dynamics and labor market equilibrium', *Journal of Political Economy*, July–August, **76**, pp. 687–711.

Picciotto, Robert (2000), 'Concluding remarks', in Osvaldo Feinstein and Robert Picciotto (eds), *Evaluation and Poverty Reduction: Proceedings from a World Bank Conference*, foreword by James D. Wolfensohn, Washington, DC: The World Bank.

Pinilla, Nelson (2006), 'La corte constitucional terminó arrebatando la función legislativa', *Ámbito Jurídico*, 19 June–2 July.

Popper, K. (1962), *Conjectures and Refutations: The Growth of Scientific Knowledge*, New York: Basic Books.

Popper, K. (1965), *The Logic of Scientific Discovery*, New York: Harper Torch books.

Posada, Carlos Esteban (1996), 'Por qué ha crecido el gasto público?', *Borradores de Economía*, No. 51, Banco de la República, Bogotá, Colombia.

Posada, Carlos Esteban and Martha A. Misas (1995), 'La tasa de interés en Colombia 1958–1992', *Borradores de Economía*, No. 26, Banco de la República, Bogotá, Colombia.

Posada Carbó, Eduardo (2001), 'Reflexiones sobre la cultura política Colombiana', Cátedra Corona No. 2, Universidad de los Andes.

Poterba, James M. and Jürgen von Hagen (1999), 'Introduction', in James M. Poterba and Jürgen von Hagen (eds), *Fiscal Institutions and Fiscal Performance*, Chicago and London: The University of Chicago Press.

Prados de la Escosura, L. (2005), 'Growth, inequality, and poverty in Latin America: historical evidence, controlled conjectures', *Economics, History and Institutions Working Paper*, wh 054105, Madrid: Universidad Carlos III, Departamento de Historia Económica e Instituciones.

Przeworski, Adam (1994), Comment on 'The impact of constitutions on economic performance', by Jon Elster, *Proceedings of the World Bank Annual Conference on Development Economics*, Washington, DC: The World Bank.

Przeworski, Adam and Fernando Limongi (1993), 'Political regimes and economic growth', *Journal of Economic Perspectives*, 7(3), 51–69.

Putnam, Robert D. (2000), 'Conclusion', in Robert D. Putnam (ed.), *Democracies in Flux: The Evolution of Social Capital in Contemporary Society*, New York: Oxford University Press.

Rabello de Castro, Paulo and Marcio Ronci (1992), 'Sesenta años de populismo en el Brasil', in Rudiger Dornbusch and Sebastián Edwards (eds), *Macroeconomía del Populismo en la América Latina*, Lecturas 75, El Trimestre Económico, México: Fondo de Cultura Económica.

Rajan, Raghuram (2006), 'Separate and unequal', *Finance and Development*, March, Washington, DC: International Monetary Fund, IMF.

Rajan, Raghuram and Luigi Zingales (2006), 'The persistence of underdevelopment: institutions, human capital, or constituencies?', *NBER Working Paper No. 12093*, Cambridge, MA: National Bureau of Economic Research, NBER.

Ramcharan, Rodney (2006), 'Regressions: why are economists obsessed with them?', *Finance and Development*, March, Washington, DC: International Monetary Fund, IMF.

Ramirez, Juan Mauricio (2006), *El Tiempo*, 30 June, Bogotá, Colombia.

Ravallion, Martin (2005), 'Inequality is bad for the poor', *Policy Research Working Paper No. 3677*, Washington, DC: The World Bank.

Rawls, John (1971), *A Theory of Justice*, Cambridge, MA: Harvard University Press.

Rawls, John (1993), *Political Liberalism*, New York: Columbia University Press.

Redrado, Martin (2006), 'A Latin American view of IMF governance', in Edwin M. Truman (ed.), *Reforming the IMF for the 21st Century*, Special Report 19, April, Washington, DC: Institute for International Economics.

Rentería, Carolina (2005), 'El presupuesto de 1970 y el presupuesto de 2005: evidencias de decisiones económicas, fiscales de los últimos 35 años', *Coyuntura Económica*, FEDESARROLLO, Il Semestre de 2005, Bogotá, Colombia.

Restrepo, Juan Camilo (1999), *Memoria de Hacienda 1998–1999*, Tomo 1, Ministerio de Hacienda, Bogotá, Colombia.

Restrepo, Juan Camilo (2000), *Itinerario de la Recuperación Económica*, Universidad Externado de Colombia, Bogotá, Colombia.

Restrepo, Juan Camilo (2003), *Hacienda Pública*, Universidad Externado de Colombia, Bogotá, Colombia.

Restrepo, Juan Camilo (2006), *Portafolio*, 27 June, Bogotá, Colombia.

Rodrik, Dani (1996), 'Why is there multilateral lending?', in Michael Bruno and Boris Pleskovic (eds), *Annual World Bank Conference on Development Economics 1995*, Washington, DC: The World Bank.

Rodrik, Dani (2003), 'Introduction', in Dani Rodrik (ed.), *In Search of Prosperity Analytic Narratives on Economic Growth*, Princeton, NJ: Princeton University Press.

Rodrik, Dani (2006), 'Goodbye Washington Consensus, hello Washington confusion? A Review of the World Bank's "Economic Growth in the 1990s: Learning from a Decade of Reform"', *Journal of Economic Literature*, **XLIV**, December, pp. 973–87.

Rodrik, Dani and Arvind Subramanian (2003), 'The primacy of institutions', *Finance & Development*, June, Washington, DC: International Monetary Fund, IMF.

Rogoff, Kenneth S. (1985), 'The optimal degree of commitment to an intermediate monetary target', *Quarterly Journal of Economics*, **100**(4), 1169–89.

Rogoff, Kenneth S. (2002), 'Moral hazard in IMF loans', *Finance and Development*, September, Washington, DC: International Monetary Fund, IMF.

Rogoff, Kenneth S. (2003), 'Disinflation: an unsung benefit of globalization?', *Finance and Development*, December, Washington, DC: International Monetary Fund, IMF.

Rogoff, Kenneth S. and A. Sibert (1988), 'Elections and macroeconomic policy cycles', *Review of Economic Studies*, **55**, 1–16.

Rose-Ackerman, Susan (1996), 'Altruism, nonprofits, and economic theory', *Journal of Economic Literature*, **XXXIV**(2), 701–28.

Rostow, W.W. (1960), *The Stages of Economic Growth: A Non-Communist Manifesto*, Cambridge: Cambridge University Press.

Roubini, Nouriel and Brad Setser (2004), *Bailouts or Bail-Ins? Responding to Financial Crises in Emerging Economies*, Washington, DC: Institute for International Economics.

Sachs, Jeffrey D. (2003), 'Institutions matter, but not for everthing: the role of geography and resource endowments in development shouldn't be underestimated', *Finance & Development*, June, Washington, DC: International Monetary Fund, IMF.

Sagasti, Francisco and Fernando Prada (2004), 'La banca multilateral de desarrollo en América Latina', in José Antonio Ocampo and Andras Uthoff (eds), *Gobernabilidad e Integración Financiera: Ámbito Global y Regional*, Santiago, Chile: Comisión Económica para América Latina y el Caribe, CEPAL.

Sahay, Ratna and Rishi Goyal (2006), 'Volatility and growth in Latin America: an episodic approach', *IMF Working Paper No. 06/287*, Washington, DC: International Monetary Fund, IMF.

Santiso, Javier (2006), *Latin America's Political Economy of the Possible: Beyond Good Revolutionaries and Free-Marketers*, Cambridge, MA and London: MIT Press.

Sarewitz, Daniel and Roger Pielke Jr (2002), 'Vulnerability and risk: some thoughts from a political and policy perspective', a discussion paper prepared for Columbia–Wharton/Penn Roundtable on 'Risk Management Strategies in an Uncertain World', New York, 12–13 April.

Sargent, Thomas (1986), *Rational Expectations and Inflation*, New York: Harper & Row.

Sargent, Thomas and Neil Wallace (1981), 'Some unpleasant monetarist arithmetic', *Federal Reserve Bank of Minneapolis Quarterly Review*, **5**(3), 1–17.

Sarmiento, Palacio Eduardo (1996), *Apertura y Cuento Económico: de la Desilusión al Nuevo Estado*, Bogotá, Colombia: Tercer Mundo Editores.

Sarmiento, Palacio Eduardo (1998), *Alternativas a Encrucijada Neoliberal*, Acádemia Colombiana de Ciencias Económicas, Bogotá, Colombia: Escuela Colombiana de Ingeniería.

Sarmiento, Palacio Eduardo (2005), *El Nuevo Paradigma de la Estabilidad, el Crecimiento y la Distribución del Ingreso*, Bogotá, Colombia: Editorial Norma.

Sarmiento, Palacio Eduardo (2007), 'Rienda suelta a la revaluación', *El Espectador*, 27 May–2 June, p. 3B.

Scartascini, Carlos (2006), 'The institutional determinants of political transactions', in forthcoming book by Ernesto Stein and Mariano Tommasi.

Schumpeter, Joseph A. (1954), 'The crisis of the tax state', *International Economic Papers*, **4**(7).

Schwartz, Anna J. (1993), 'Currency boards: their past, present, and possible future role', *Carnegie-Rochester Conference Series on Public Policy*, **39**, December, Amsterdam: North Holland.

Shah, Anwar (2005), *Fiscal Management: Public Sector Governance and Accountability Series*, Washington, DC: The World Bank.

Shleifer, Andrei (2002), 'The new comparative economics', *NBER Program Report*, Fall, Cambridge, MA: National Bureau of Economic Research, NBER.

Simon, Herbert A. (1957), *Models of Man, Social and Rational: Mathematical Essay on Rational Human Behavior in a Social Setting*, New York: John Wiley & Sons.

Simon, Herbert A. (1982), *Models of Bounded Rationality*, Cambridge, MA: MIT Press.

Singh, Anoop (2006), 'Macroeconomic volatility: the policy lessons from Latin America', *IMF Working Paper No. 06/166*, Washington, DC: International Monetary Fund, IMF.

Singh, Anoop and Martin Cerisola (2006), 'Sustaining, Latin America's resurgence: some historical perspectives', *IMF Working Paper No. 06/252*, Washington, DC: International Monetary Fund, IMF.

Singh, Anoop and Charles Collyns (2005), 'Latin America's resurgence', *Finance and Development*, December, International Monetary Fund, IMF.

Singh, Anoop, Agnés Belaisch, Charles Collyns, Paula De Masi, Reva Krieger, Guy Meredith and Robert Rennhack (2005), 'Executive summary', *Stabilization and Reform in Latin America: A Macroeconomic Perspective on the Experience Since the Early 1990s*, Occasional Paper No. 238, Washington, DC: International Monetary Fund, IMF.

Smith, Adam (1776), *The Wealth of Nations*, New York: The Modern Library.

Sokoloff, Kenneth L. and Stanley L. Engerman (2000), 'History lessons: institutions, factor endowments, and paths of development in the new world', *Journal of Economic Perspectives*, **14**(3), 217–32.

Solimano, Andrés (2000), 'Beyond unequal development: an overview', in Andrés Solimano, Eduardo Aninat and Nancy Birdsall (eds), *Distributive Justice & Economic Development: The Case of Chile and Developing Countries*, Ann Arbor: The University of Michigan Press.

Solow, Robert M. (1997), 'Is there a core of usable macroeconomics we should all believe in?', *American Economic Review*, **87**(2), 230–32.

Sourrouille, Jan Vital (2005), 'La posición de activo y pasivos externos de la República Argentina entre 1946 y 1948', *Serie de Estudios y Perspectivas No. 29*, CEPAL.

Spence, Michael (2002), 'Signaling in retrospect and the informational structure of markets', *American Economic Review*, **92**(3), 434–59.

Spiller, Pablo T. and Mariano Tommasi (2003), 'The institutional foundations of public policy: a transactions approach with application to Argentina', *Journal of Law, Economics and Organizations*, **19**(2).

Stallings, Barbara, Nancy Birdsall and Julie Clugage (2000), 'Growth and inequality: do regional patterns redeem Kuznets?', in Andrés Solimano, Eduardo Aninat and Nancy Birdsall (eds), *Distributive Justice & Economic Development: The Case of Chile and Developing Countries*, Ann Arbor, Michigan: The University of Michigan Press.

Stein, Ernesto, Talvi Ernesto and Alejandro Grisanti (1999), 'Institutional arrangements and fiscal performance: the Latin American experience', in James M. Poterba and Jürgen von Hagen (eds), *Fiscal Institutions and Fiscal Performance*, Chicago and London: The University of Chicago Press.

Stein, Ernesto, Mariano Tommasi, Eduardo Lora, Koldo Echebarria and Mark Payne (2005), *The Politics of Policies: Economic and Social Progress in Latin America 2006 Report*, Washington, DC: Inter-American Development Bank, IDB.

Stiglitz, Joseph E. (1997), 'The role of government in economic development', in Michael Bruno and Boris Pleskovic (eds), *Annual World Bank Conference on Development Economics 1996*, Washington, DC: World Bank.

Stiglitz, Joseph E. (1998), 'Distinguished lecture on economics in government', *Journal of Economic Perspectives*, **12**(2), 3–22.

Stiglitz, Joseph E. (2002a), 'Information and the change in the paradigm of economics', *American Economic Review*, **92**(3), 460–501.

Stiglitz, Joseph E. (2002b), 'Argentina, short-changed: why the nation that followed the rules fell to pieces', *Washington Post*, 12 May.

Sturzeneger, Federico (1992), 'Descripción de una experiencia populista: Argentina 1973–1976', in Rudiger Dornbusch and Sebastián Edwards (eds), *Macroeconomía del Populismo en la América Latina*, Fondo de Cultura Económica, México, Chicago and London: The University of Chicago Press.

Summers, Lawrence H. (1991), 'The scientific illusion in empirical macroeconomics', *Scandinavian Journal of Economics*, **93**(2).

Svensson, Lars E.O. (2003), 'What is wrong with Taylor rules? Using judgement in monetary policy through targeting rules', *Journal of Economic Literature*, **61**(2), 426–77.

Talvi, Ernesto (1997), 'Exchange rate-based stabilization with endogenous fiscal response', *Journal of Development Economics*, **54**(1).

Talvi, Ernesto (2003), 'Globalización financiera y desempeño macroeconómico en América Latina', *Argentina Crisis, Instituciones y Crecimiento*, Conferencias FIEL 2003, 40 Aniversario, Tomo 2, Buenos Aires, Argentina: Fundación de Investigaciones Económicas Latinoamericanas.

Tanzi, Vito (2000), 'Fiscal policy and income distribution', in Andrés Solimano, Eduardo Aninat and Nancy Birdsall (eds) (2000), *Distributive*

Justice & Economic Development: The Case of Chile and Developing Countries, Ann Arbor: The University of Michigan Press.

Taylor, John B. (1993), 'Discretion versus policy rules in practice', *Carnegie-Rochester Conference Series on Public Policy 39*, December, pp. 195–214.

Taylor, John B. (1997), 'A core of practical macroeconomics', *American Economic Review*, **87**(2), 233–5.

Taylor, John B. (1999), 'Monetary policy rules', *NBER Studies in Business Cycles*, Chicago and London: The University of Chicago Press.

Taylor, John B. (2000), 'Reassessing discretionary fiscal policy', *Journal of Economic Perspectives*, **14**(3), 21–36.

Taylor, John B. (2003), 'New policies for economic development', in Boris Pleskovic and Nicholas Stern (eds), *The New Reform Agenda*, Annual World Bank Conference on Development Economics, Washington, DC: The World Bank and Oxford University Press.

Taylor, John B. and Michael Woodford (1999), *Handbook of Macroeconomics*, Vol. 1C, Stanford University, CA and Princeton University, NJ: Elsevier.

Teijeiro, Mario O. (1996), 'La política fiscal durante la convertibilidad 1991–1995', June, Buenos Aires, Argentina: Centro de Estudios Públicos.

Teijeiro, Mario O. (2001), 'Una vez más, la política fiscal', Buenos Aires, Argentina: Centro de Estudios Públicos.

Teijeiro, Mario O. (2005), 'El péndulo Argentino', Buenos Aires, Argentina: Centro de Estudios Públicos.

Teijeiro, Mario O. (2006), 'Una reactivación sorprendente', Buenos Aires, Argentina: Centro de Estudios Públicos.

Tenembaum, Ernesto (2004), *Enemigos: Argentina y el FMI*, Buenos Aires, Argentina: Grupo Editorial Norma.

Tenjo, Fernando (2006), 'Temores infundados a que la junta haga su tarea', *Portafolio*, 10 July, Bogotá, Colombia.

Thaler, Richard (2000), 'From homo economicus to homo sapiens', *Journal of Economic Perspectives*, **14**(1), 133–41.

Tirole, Jean (2002), *Financial Crises, Liquidity, and the International Monetary System*, Princeton, NJ: Princeton University Press.

Titelman, Daniel (2004), 'La banca multilateral y el financiamiento del desarrollo en un contexto de volatilidad financiera', in José Antonio Ocampo and Andras Uthoff (eds), *Gobernabilidad e Integración Financiera: Ámbito Global y Regional*, Santiago, Chile: Comisión Económica para. América Latina y el Caribe, CEPAL.

Tommasi, Mariano (2002), 'Federalism in Argentina and the reforms of the 1990s', *Working Paper No. 147*, Stanford, California: Stanford Center for International Development.

Tommasi, Mariano (2005), 'The institutional foundations of public policy', Presidential Address to the Latin American and Caribbean Economic Association (LACEA), Paris, November, Universidad San Andrés, Buenos Aires, Argentina.

Truman, Edwin M. (2003), 'Inflation targeting in practice', in *Inflation Targeting in the World Economy*, Washington, DC: Institute for International Economics.

Truman, Edwin M. (2006a), 'Implication of structural changes in the global economy for its management', paper presented at the World Economic Forum – Reinventing Bretton Woods Committee Roundtable on Global Savings and Investment Patterns and the Changing Structure of the World Economy, Adelaide, Australia: Institute for International Economics.

Truman, Edwin M. (2006b), *Reforming the IMF for the 21st Century*, Special Report No. 19, edited by M. Truman, April, Washington, DC: Institute for International Economics.

Truman, Edwin M. (2006c), 'A strategy for IMF reform: policy analyses in international economics 77', Paper 0-88132-398-5, Washington, DC: Peterson Institute.

Tullock, G. (1967), 'The welfare costs of tariffs, monopolies and theft', *Western Economic Journal*, **5**, 224–32.

UNDP (2005), 'Inequality and human development', *Human Development Report 2005*, New York.

Uprimny, Rodrigo and Cesar A. Rodríguez (2005), 'Constitución y modelo económico en Colombia: hacia una discusión productiva entre economía y derecho', *Debates de Coyuntura Económica No. 62*, November, Bogotá, Colombia: Fundación para la Educación Superior y el Desarrollo, FEDESARROLLO, Konrad Adenauer Stiftung.

Uribe, José Dario (1994), 'Inflación y crecimiento económico en Colombia 1951–1992', *Borradores de Economía*, No. 1, Banco de la República, Bogotá, Colombia.

Uribe, José Dario (2000), 'Hacia un ajuste fiscal sostenible', *Debates de Coyuntura Económica: Ajuste Fiscal ¿Cuándo y Cómo? No. 42*, Fundación Social, June, Bogotá, Colombia: Fundación para la Educación Superior y el Desarrollo, FEDESARROLLO.

Uribe, José Dario and Hernando Vargas (2002), 'Financial reform, crisis and consolidation in Colombia', April, *Borradores de Economía*, No. 204, Banco de la República, Bogotá, Colombia.

Urrutia, Miguel (1984), *Los de Arriba y Los de Abajo: La Distribución del Ingreso en Colombia en Las Últimas Décadas*, Bogotá, Colombia: Fundación para La Educación Superior y el Desarrollo, FEDESAR-ROLLO, and Fondo Editorial CEREC.

Urrutia, Miguel (2004), 'Desbalance fiscal y deuda: ¿Qué hacer?, *Revista del Banco de la República*, **LXXVII**(919), May, Bogotá, Colombia.

Urrutia, Miguel (2006), 'Comments on country program evaluations', in Ajay Chhibber, R. Kyle Peters and Barbara Yale (eds), *Reform and Growth: Evaluating the World Bank Experience*, New Brunswick and London: Transaction Publishers.

Urrutia, Miguel and Albert Berry (1975), *Income Distribution in Colombia*, New Haven, CT: Yale University Press.

Urrutia, Miguel and Cristina Fernández (2003), 'Política monetaria expansiva en epocas de crisis: el caso Colombiano en el Siglo XX', *Revista del Banco de la República*, **LXXVI**(908), June, Bogotá, Colombia.

Váldes, Alberto (1999), 'Poverty and income distribution in a high-growth economy: Chile, 1987–95', in Guillermo Perry and Danny M. Leipziger (eds), *Chile: Recent Policy Lessons and Emerging Challenges*, Washington, DC: The World Bank.

Valdés, Juan Gabriel (1995), *Pinochet's Economists: The Chicago School in Chile*, Cambridge University Press.

Valenzuela, Arturo (2005), 'Putting Latin America back on the map', *Finance and Development*, December, Washington, DC: International Monetary Fund, IMF.

Valenzuela D., Luis Carlos (2003), 'Por una función de bienestar', *Revista Dinero*, 19 September, Bogotá, Colombia.

Valenzuela D., Luis Carlos and Alejandro Arregocés C. (2005), 'La constitución: concepción ética del bienestar', *Debates de Coyuntura Económica: Modelo Económico y Constitución*, No. 62, November, Bogotá, Colombia: Fundación para la Educación Superior y el Desarrollo, FEDESARROLLO.

Vane, Howard and Chris Mulhearn (2006), 'Interview with Robert Mundell', *Journal of Economic Perspectives*, **20**(4), 89–110.

Vargas, Hernando (1994), 'A qué juegan el gobierno y el banco central independiente?', *Borradores de Economia*, No. 9, Banco de la República, Bogotá, Colombia.

Vargas, Hernando (2006), 'Política cambiaria: hechos recientes en Colombia', Conferencia en la Universidad de los Andes, Bogotà, Colombia.

Vargas, Hernando (2007), 'The transmission mechanism of monetary policy in Colombia: major changes and current features', *Borradores de Economía*, No. 431, Banco de la República, Bogotá, Colombia.

Vargas, Hernando and José Dario Uribe (2002), 'Financial reform, crisis and consolidation in Colombia', Preparatory Workshop for the Madrid Seminar of the Euro-System and Latin American Central Banks, 21–22 March.

Velasco, Andrés (1997), 'When are fixed exchange rates really fixed', *Journal of Development Economics*, **54**(1).

Velasco, Andrés (1999), 'A model of endogenous fiscal deficits and delayed fiscal reforms', in James M. Poterba and Jürgen von Hagen (eds), *Fiscal Institutions and Fiscal Performance*, National Bureau of Economic Research, NBER, Chicago and London: The University of Chicago Press.

Velasco, Andrés (2001), 'Argentina's bankruptcy foretold', *Time*, Latin American edition, 23 July.

Velasco, Andrés (2006), 'Foreword', in Javier Santiso, *Latin America's Political Economy of the Possible*, Cambridge, MA: MIT Press.

Velez, Carlos Eduardo (1997), 'Eficiencia, equidad y reestructuración sectorial del gasto público social', *Borradores de Economía*, No. 80, Banco de la República, Bogotá, Colombia.

Velez, Carlos Eduardo (2004), 'Pobreza en Colombia: avances, retrocesos y nuevos retos', *Coyuntura Social, No. 30*, June, Bogotá, Colombia: Fundación para la Educación Superior y el Desarrollo, FEDESARROLLO.

Velez, Carlos Eduardo, R.P. de Barros and F. Ferreira (2004), 'Why is Brazil such an unequal society?', in *Inequality and Economic Development in Brazil*, Washington, DC: The World Bank.

Viale, Riccardo (1997), 'From neoclassical to cognitive economics: the epistemological constraints of feasibility and realism', in Riccardo Viale (ed.), *Cognitive Economics*, Quaderni Lascomes Series, 1/1997, Torino: La Rosa Editrice.

Villar, Gómez Leonardo (2001), 'Reflexiones para una evaluación de la política monetaria', *Revista del Banco de la República*, September, Bogotá, Colombia.

Villar, Gómez Leonardo (2003), 'Análisis', *Portafolio*, 19 December, Bogotá, Colombia.

Villar, Gómez Leonardo (2004), 'Inflación y finanzas públicas', *Borradores de Economía*, No. 291, Banco de la República, Bogotá, Colombia.

Villar, Gómez Leonardo (2006), 'Comments on Alberto Alesina and Guido Tabellini, "Why is Fiscal Policy Often Procyclical?" ', National Bureau of Economic Research NBER and FEDESARROLLO Inter-American Seminar on Economics (IASE), Bogotá, Colombia.

Villegas, Ramírez Fabio (2004), 'Situación y perspectivas de las finanzas públicas en Colombia', *Carta Financiera No. 126*, February, Bogotá, Colombia Asociación Nacional de Instituciones Financieras, ANIF.

von Neumann, John and Oskar Morgenstern (1944), *Theory of Games and Economic Behavior*, Princeton, NJ: Princeton University Press.

Wallace, Laura (2004), 'Freedom as progress', interviews, 'Box 1', *Finance and Development*, September, International Monetary Fund, IMF.

Webb, Richard (1991), 'Prologue', in Carlos E. Paredes and Jeffrey D. Sachs (eds), *Peru's Path to Recovery: A Plan for Economic Stabilization and Growth*, Washington, DC: The Brookings Institution.

Webb, Steven (2003), 'Argentina: hardening the provincial budget constraint', in Jonathan A. Rodden, Gunnar S. Eskeland and Jennie Litvack (eds), *Fiscal Decentralization and the Challenge of Hard Budget Constraints*, Cambridge, MA and London: MIT Press.

Weingast, Barry R. (1995), 'The economic role of political institutions: market-preserving federalism and economic development', *Journal of Law, Economics and Organization*, **11**(1), 1–31.

Weingast, Barry R. (2005), 'The constitutional dilemma of economic liberty', *Journal of Economic Perspectives*, **19**(3), 89–108.

Weingast, B., K. Shepsle and C. Johnsen (1981), 'The political economy of benefits and costs: a neoclassical approach to redistributive politics', *Journal of Political Economy*, **CXXXIX**, 642–64.

Wicksell, Knut (1896), *Finanztheoretische Untersuchungen*, Jena: Gustav Fisher.

Wiesner, Eduardo (1984), 'Discussion', *The International Monetary System: Forty Years After Bretton Woods*, Sponsored by: Federal Reserve Bank of Boston, Proceedings of a Conference Held at Bretton Woods, New Hampshire, May.

Wiesner, Eduardo (1985), 'Latin American debt: lessons and pending issues', *American Economic Review*, **75**(2).

Wiesner, Eduardo (1988), 'Latin America's policy response to the debt crisis: learning from adversity', in Martin Feldstein (ed.), *International Economic Cooperation*, Chicago: The University of Chicago Press.

Wiesner, Eduardo (1992), *Colombia: Descentralización y Federalismo Fiscal: Informe Final de la Misión para la Descentralización*, Bogotá, Colombia, Presidencia de la República, Departamento Nacional de Planeación, DNP.

Wiesner, Eduardo (1995), *La Descentralización, el Gasto Social y la Gobernabilidad en Colombia*, Bogotá, Colombia: Departamento Nacional de Planeación, DNP, Asociación Nacional de Instituciones Financieras, ANIF.

Wiesner, Eduardo (1997), *La Efectividad de las Políticas Públicas en Colombia: Un Análisis Neoinstitucional*, Bogotá, Colombia: Departamento Nacional de Planeación, DNP.

Wiesner, Eduardo (1998), 'Introduction', in Robert Picciotto and Eduardo Wiesner (eds), *Evaluation and Development: The Institutional Dimension*, New Brunswick and London: Transaction Publishers.

Wiesner, Eduardo (1999), 'Un aprendizaje difícil', *Revista Dinero*, March, Bogotá, Colombia.

Wiesner, Eduardo (2003a), 'The role of incentives and evaluations in enhancing development effectiveness', *Colombian Economic Journal*, **2**(1), Mauricio Pérez Salazar (ed.), Bogotá, Colombia: Universidad Externado de Colombia.

Wiesner, Eduardo (2003b), 'Decentralization y equidad en América Latina: enlaces institucionales y de política', *Archivos de Economía*, Documento No. 227, June, Bogotá, Colombia: Departamento Nacional de Planeación, DNP.

Wiesner, Eduardo (2003c), 'Politics, aid and development evaluation', in Patrick G. Grasso, Sulaiman S. Wasty and Rachel V. Weaving (eds), *World Bank Operations Evaluation Department: The First 30 Years*, Washington, DC: The World Bank.

Wiesner, Eduardo (2004a), 'Concept paper for the enhancement of country program evaluations, CPEs', Report to the Office of Evaluation and Oversight (OVE), Inter-American Development Bank.

Wiesner, Eduardo (2004b), 'El origen político del déficit fiscal en Colombia: el contexto institucional 20 años después', *Archivos de Economía*, Documento No. 250, Bogotá, Colombia: Departamento Nacional de Planeación, DNP.

Wiesner, Eduardo (2004c), 'The Resource-Restriction-Condition (RRC) for evaluation effectiveness', in George Keith Pitman, Osvaldo N. Feinstein and Gregory K. Ingram (eds), *Evaluating Development Effectiveness*, Washington, DC: World Bank Series on Evaluation and Development.

Wiesner, Eduardo (2007), 'The developmental effectiveness of multilateral institutions under "Collective Action" Restrictions (CARs)', forthcoming.

Williamson, Jeffrey G. (1991), *Inequality, Poverty and History*, Cambridge, MA: Basil Blackwell.

Williamson, John (2000), *Exchange Rate Regimes for Emerging Markets: Reviving the Intermediate Option*, Washington, DC: Institute for International Economics.

Williamson, John (2003), 'Visión general: una agenda para relanzar el crecimiento y las reformas', in Pedro-Pablo Kuczynski and John Williamson (eds), *Después del Consenso de Washington, Relanzando el Crecimiento y las Reformas en América Latina*, Lima, Perú: Fondo Editorial, Universidad Peruana de Ciencias Aplicadas (UPC).

Williamson, John (2004), 'The Washington Consensus as policy prescription for development', Institute for International Economics. A lecture in the series 'Practitioners of Development' delivered at the World Bank on 13 January.

Williamson, John and Stephan Haggard (1994), 'The political conditions for economic reform', in John Williamson (ed.), *The Political Economy of Economic Reform*, Washington, DC: Institute for International Economics.

Williamson, Oliver E. (1996), *The Mechanisms of Governance*, New York: Oxford University Press.

Williamson, Oliver E. and Scott E. Masten (1999), *The Economics of Transaction Costs*, Cheltenham, UK and Northampton, MA, USA: Edward Elgar Publishing.

Wolf, Martin (2005), 'Argentina's debt deal leaves it holding a weak hand,' *Financial Times*, 9 March.

Woodford, Michael (1995), 'Price-level determinancy without control of a monetary aggregate', *Carnegie-Rochester Conference Series on Public Policy*, **43**, December, 1–46.

World Bank (2000a), 'Argentina Country Assistance Evaluation', *Report No. 20719*, 10 July, Washington, DC: Operations Evaluation Department, OED.

World Bank (2000b), 'Annex No. 4: poverty profile and trend', *Report No. 20160-BR*, Country Assistance Strategy of the World Bank Group for the Federative Republic of Brazil, 6 March.

World Bank (2000c), 'Poor people in a rich country: a poverty report for Argentina', Volume I, *Report No. 19992-AR*.

World Bank (2004a), 'Country partnership strategy for the Republic of Costa Rica', *Report No. 28570*, April, Central Bank of Costa Rica.

World Bank (2004b), 'Developments in capital markets', in *Whither Latin American Capital Markets?*, regional study led by Augusto de la Torre and Sergio Schmukler, October, Office of the Chief Economist Latin America and the Caribbean Region.

World Bank (2004c), *Inequality and Economic Development in Brazil*, Washington, DC: The World Bank.

World Bank (2005), *World Development Report 2006 Equity and Development*, The World Bank and Oxford University Press.

World Bank and Inter-American Development Bank (IDB) (2005), 'Costa Rica: country financial accountability assessment', 30 June.

World Bank (2006a), 'Country Assistance Strategy for the Argentine Republic 2006–2008', *Report No. 34015 AR*, Document of World Bank, 4 May.

World Bank (2006b), *Equity and Development*, World Development Report 2006, Washington, DC: The World Bank and Oxford University Press.

World Bank Operations Evaluation Department (OED) (1996), 'Argentina: country assistance review', *Report No. 15844*, Washington, DC.

World Bank Operations Evaluation Department (OED) (2004), 'Brazil: forging a strategic partnership for results', Washington, DC: The World Bank.

Zagha, Roberto, Gobind Nankani and Indermit Gill (2006), 'Rethinking growth', *Finance & Development*, March, Washington, DC: International Monetary Fund, IMF.

Zettelmeyer, Jeromin (2006), 'Growth and reforms in Latin America: a survey of facts and arguments', *IMF Working Paper No. 06/210*, September, Washington, DC: International Monetary Fund, IMF.

Zuleta, Hernando (1995), 'Impuesto inflacionario y señoreaje', *Borradores de Economía*, No. 38, Banco de la República, Bogotá, Colombia.

Zuleta, Jaramillo Luis Alberto (1999), *Introducción a la Política Económica*, Universidad Externado de Colombia, Bogotá, Colombia.

Name index

Acemoglu, D. 3, 7, 14–15, 17, 18, 22, 52, 59, 61, 64, 65, 70, 77, 138, 195
Akerlof, G.A. 22, 60
Alchian, A.A. 89
Alesina, A. 7, 9, 10, 14, 17, 21, 22, 24, 57, 85–6, 87, 88, 139, 142, 158, 159, 166, 171, 190, 191, 192–3, 195, 205, 208, 218
Anderson, L.R. 61
Angeletos, G.-M. 166, 190, 192–3, 205, 208, 218
Aninat, E. 30, 155
Arbelaez, M.A. 195
Arias, A.F. 169, 193
Arriazu, R. 115
Arrow, K.J. 22, 23
Artana, D. 116
Attanasio, O. 78, 144, 196
Aumann, R. 64
Avella, M. 194

Baig, T. 124, 135
Barber, W. 155
Bardhan, P. 22
Barnard, C. 89
Barros, R. 129
Basco, E. 116
Baumol 18, 89
Belaunde, Fernando (President) 211
Bénabou, R. 61
Berg, A. 82, 119
Bergsten, F. 35, 58
Bernanke, B.S. 19, 84, 186
Berry, A. 60, 90, 165, 207
Besley, T. 154
Bird, R. 56, 190, 194
Birdsall, N. 5, 14, 18–19, 20, 47, 60
Blanchard, O.J. 82–3
Blinder, A.S. 191
Bloom, A. 135
Blustein, P. 100, 116, 117

Bogdanski, J. 126
Botero, R. 180, 186, 191, 195
Brennan, G. 60
Bruno, M. 65
Buchanan, J. 43, 60, 117, 154
Burnside, C. 57, 90

Caballero, R. 23, 154, 155
Cabrera, M. 58, 194
Cáceres, A. 211
Calvo, G. 20, 54, 59, 62, 90, 108, 117, 155
Cárdenas, E. 19
Cárdenas, M. 19, 157, 161, 162, 166, 169, 178, 184, 191
Cardemil, L. 200
Cardozo, Fernando (President) 106
Carrasquilla, A. 157, 158–9, 181, 192, 193
Carstens, A. 20, 146, 151, 205
Casas, K. 198, 206
Castelar, A. 120, 127, 130
Castellanos, D. 188
Castro, J. 161, 187, 195
Cavallo, Domingo (Minister of Finance, Argentina) 100
Cepeda, M.J. 190
Céspedes, L.F. 150, 152, 154, 155
Chang, R. 155, 176
Chari, V.V. 56, 88, 89
Chhibber, A. 23, 57
Claessens, S. 217
Clavijo, S. 182, 191, 192, 194, 195
Clements, B. 36, 53, 91, 168, 194
Cline, W.R. 125
Coase, R. 23, 61, 66
Coate, S. 154
Coeymans, J.E. 141
Cole, H.L. 6
Collyns, C. 152
Conway, P. 90
Cooper, R. 19

Subject index

Titles of publications are in *italics*.